THE CAMBRIDGE COMPANION TO
REFORMED THEOLOGY

This *Companion* offers an introduction to Reformed theology, one of the most historically important, ecumenically active, and currently generative traditions of doctrinal inquiry, by way of reflecting on its origins, its development, and its significance. Part I, Theological Topics, indicates the distinct array of doctrinal concerns which gives coherence over time to the identity of this tradition in all its diversity. Part II, Theological Figures, explores the life and work of a small number of theologians who not only have worked within this tradition but also have constructively shaped and inspired it in vital ways. The final part, Theological Contexts, considers the ways in which the resultant Reformed sensibilities in theology have had a marked impact both on theological and ecclesiastical landscapes in different places and on the wider societal landscapes of history. The result is a fascinating and compelling guide to this dynamic and vibrant theological tradition.

Paul T. Nimmo holds the Chair in Systematic Theology at the University of Aberdeen. He received a Templeton Award for Theological Promise for his book *Being in Action* in 2009, and is an editor of the *International Journal of Systematic Theology*. He has been a Fellow of the Center for Barth Studies since 2009, and has served on the AAR Reformed Theology and History Group Steering Committee and as Treasurer of the Society of the Study of Theology. He delivered the Kerr Lectures in Glasgow in 2008.

David A. S. Fergusson is Professor of Divinity and Principal of New College at the University of Edinburgh. He has delivered the Bampton Lectures in Oxford (2001), the Gifford Lectures in Glasgow (2008), and the Warfield Lectures in Princeton (2009). He was elected a Fellow of the Royal Society of Edinburgh in 2004 and a Fellow of the British Academy in 2013. His publications include several monographs and edited collections, including *Faith and Its Critics* (2009) and *Creation* (2014).

CAMBRIDGE COMPANIONS TO RELIGION
This is a series of companions to major topics and key figures in theology and religious studies. Each volume contains specially commissioned chapters by international scholars, which provide an accessible and stimulating introduction to the subject for new readers and nonspecialists.

THE CAMBRIDGE COMPANION TO

REFORMED THEOLOGY

Edited by

Paul T. Nimmo
University of Aberdeen

David A. S. Fergusson
University of Edinburgh

CAMBRIDGE
UNIVERSITY PRESS

CAMBRIDGE
UNIVERSITY PRESS

32 Avenue of the Americas, New York NY 10013-2473, USA

Cambridge University Press is part of the University of Cambridge.

It furthers the University's mission by disseminating knowledge in the pursuit of education, learning, and research at the highest international levels of excellence.

www.cambridge.org
Information on this title: www.cambridge.org/9781107690547

© Cambridge University Press 2016

First published 2016

Printed in the United States of America by Sheridan Books, Inc

A catalog record for this publication is available from the British Library.

Library of Congress Cataloging in Publication Data
Names: Nimmo, Paul T. (Paul Thomson), editor. | Fergusson, David A. S., editor.
Title: The Cambridge companion to Reformed theology / edited by
Paul T. Nimmo, David A. S. Fergusson.
Description: New York : Cambridge University Press, 2016. |
Series: Cambridge companions to religion |
Includes bibliographical references and index.
Identifiers: LCCN 2015040743| ISBN 9781107027220 (hardback) |
ISBN 9781107690547 (paperback)
Subjects: LCSH: Reformed Church – Theology.
Classification: LCC BX9406.C36 2016 | DDC 230/.42–dc23
LC record available at http://lccn.loc.gov/2015040743

ISBN 978-1-107-02722-0 Hardback
ISBN 978-1-107-69054-7 Paperback

Contents

Part III *Theological contexts*

Contributors

Michael Allen is Associate Professor of Systematic and Historical Theology at Reformed Theological Seminary in Orlando, Florida.

Michael Beintker is Professor Emeritus of Systematic Theology and was Director of the Seminar for Reformed Theology at the Westfälische Wilhelms-Universität, Münster.

J. Todd Billings is Gordon H. Girod Research Professor of Reformed Theology at Western Theological Seminary in Holland, Michigan.

James D. Bratt is Professor of History at Calvin College, Grand Rapids, Michigan.

Eberhard Busch is Emeritus Professor in Reformed Theology at the Georg-August-Universität Göttingen.

Alexander Chow is Chancellor's Fellow in World Christianity at the University of Edinburgh.

Oliver D. Crisp is Professor of Systematic Theology in the School of Theology, Fuller Theological Seminary, Pasadena, California.

David A. S. Fergusson is Professor of Divinity and Principal of New College at the University of Edinburgh.

Darrell L. Guder is Henry Winters Luce Professor of Missional and Ecumenical Theology Emeritus at Princeton Theological Seminary.

Susan Hardman Moore is Professor of Early Modern Religion at the University of Edinburgh.

Kevin W. Hector is Associate Professor of Theology and of the Philosophy of Religions at the University of Chicago Divinity School.

Bruce L. McCormack is Charles Hodge Professor of Systematic Theology at Princeton Theological Seminary.

Paul T. Nimmo is Professor in Systematic Theology at the University of Aberdeen.

Peter Opitz is Professor of Church History and Historical Theology and Director of the Institute for Swiss Reformation Studies at the University of Zürich.

Isabel Apawo Phiri is Associate General Secretary for Public Witness and Diakonia of the World Council of Churches, Geneva, and Honorary Professor of African Theology at the University of KwaZulu Natal.

Rinse H. Reeling Brouwer is the Miskotte/Breukelman Professor at the Protestant Theological University, Amsterdam and Groningen.

Cynthia L. Rigby is the W. C. Brown Professor of Theology at Austin Presbyterian Theological Seminary in Austin, Texas.

Yasuhiro Sekikawa is Professor of Historical Theology at Tokyo Union Theological Seminary.

Geoff Thompson is Co-ordinator of Studies in Systematic Theology at Pilgrim Theological College, in the University of Divinity, Melbourne.

Dolf (R. T.) te Velde is Assistant Professor of Systematic Theology at the Theological University of Kampen.

Sung Bihn Yim is Professor and Former Dean of the Presbyterian University and Theological Seminary in Seoul.

Randall C. Zachman is Professor of Reformation Studies at the University of Notre Dame.

Acknowledgements

The Editors would like to express their gratitude to Michael Bräutigam for his translation work and to David Robinson for his editorial labours. They would also like to thank their editors at Cambridge University Press, Kate Brett, Laura Morris, Alexandra Poreda, and Isabella Vitti, and their copy editor, Theresa Kornak.

Paul Nimmo would like to express his sincere appreciation for the ongoing collegiality and the profound friendship of Jason Fout, Tom Greggs, Stephen Manders, Mark Russell, Don Wood, Simeon Zahl, and Phil Ziegler. He would also like to acknowledge his enduring gratitude to those who have taught him of the Reformed tradition, in particular to his dear friend Ernest Marvin. Finally, he would like to acknowledge his loving indebtedness to his family, who continue to inspire and sustain him, and above all to Jill, Samuel, Daniel, and Rebekah.

David Fergusson wishes to acknowledge his gratitude to those congregations and ministers who have supported him over many years, especially at Holburn West Church in Aberdeen and Greenbank Church in Edinburgh. They have taught him more about the Reformed tradition than they may realise. And to Margot, Mark and Calum, he would like to express his appreciation for their constant support and cheerful companionship.

1 Introduction

PAUL T. NIMMO AND DAVID A. S. FERGUSSON

This collection of chapters provides a broad orientation to the theology of the Reformed tradition – to its core doctrines and its significant figures, and to its historical development in diverse contexts. The motivation for such a volume at the present time is threefold. First, there is the desire to indicate some of the ways in which the Reformed tradition of theological thinking emerged and developed to articulate an identifiably distinct array of doctrinal concerns within a series of diverse contexts. Second, there is the desire to explore some of the ways in which the resultant Reformed sensibilities in theology had a significant impact not only on the theological landscape in particular but also on various societal landscapes at large. And third, there is the desire to suggest that theological thinking from within the Reformed tradition continues to have much in its generative and constructive modes to offer the contemporary ecumenical enterprise of systematic theology.

Yet the term 'Reformed theology' itself is not one that is amenable to easy or quick definition. While Roman Catholic theology is regulated by magisterial teaching and papal authority, and while Lutheran theology is delineated by the *Book of Concord*, theology in the Reformed churches has always – and by no means capriciously – been a more diverse affair. Certainly, an important series of Reformed confessional and catechetical documents, many written in the sixteenth century (though with others produced in more recent times), articulate a variety of clear and careful theological positions spanning a broad range of theological loci. Yet without ever losing contact with these foundational documents, the Reformed theological tradition has developed at different times and in different places to the extent that there have emerged positions significantly removed from those advanced by the first generations of magisterial Reformers.

Against this background, perhaps it may be questioned whether the Reformed tradition has any theological coherence at all – whether it is simply too diverse to have any discernible centre(s) of gravity in terms of method deployed, form invoked, or content posited. Such a concern is exacerbated in light of two consistent (if not always realised) impulses of the tradition of the Reformed churches. The first is a foundational attentiveness to the witness of Scripture, which – precisely in its commonality across Christian traditions – can struggle to identify any particular uniqueness of the Reformed. The second, not unrelated to the first, is a foundational openness to the witness of other churches, which – precisely in its hospitality to other views – again risks rendering the particularity of the Reformed tradition rather aporetic. Yet precisely these difficulties should offer impetus – and encouragement – to those both within and outwith the Reformed theological tradition seeking to identify its characteristics.

In the first place, it is important to recognise the historical dimension of the meaning of the term 'Reformed'. In its original sixteenth-century use, the term simply referred to the churches and doctrines of the Reformation in general, as having departed in whatever way from the existing practices and beliefs of the Roman Catholic Church. But as the different factions of the Protestant movement began to identify themselves as distinct from each other, the term took on a rather more technical meaning. In time, it came to refer to the theology and practice held broadly in common by a particular series of churches which claimed to be 'reformed according to the Word of God' (*die nach Gottes Wort reformierten Kirchen*). This ecclesiastical movement had its roots in some major cities of the Swiss Confederation, such as Zürich, Basel and Bern, but rapidly expanded to the cities of southern Germany, to Geneva and Strasbourg, and beyond to the west, north and east.

This Reformed group of churches came in time to be distinguished ever more clearly not only from the Roman Catholic Church but also from both the Lutheran churches and the more radical movements of the Reformation. Individual places were often closely identified with particular Reformers – for example, Huldrych Zwingli in Zürich and John Calvin in Geneva. Yet the documents which crystallised the theology of this early period, and which form the starting-point for all later trajectories of Reformed thought, were generally ecclesial in nature, particular to and subscribed by the whole church in a given location. Sixteenth-century texts such as the the Scots Confession (1560), the Belgic Confession (1561), the Heidelberg Catechism (1563), and the Second Helvetic Confession (1566) were thus primarily local documents, albeit some had a profound impact on the wider tradition. In the same way, later documents such as the Canons of Dort (1618–1619), the Westminster

Confession (1647), and the Barmen Declaration (1934) had both local and wider impact.

At the same time, such documents do not in themselves define Reformed theology. First, given that they serve the church in one location, the confessional texts make no claim to being universally binding; indeed, they often explicitly recognise their fallibility and their openness to correction in light of Scripture. Second, the documents themselves are regularly open to different interpretations; and furthermore, the texts do not always materially concur – there are tensions and even contradictions at different points. And then there are the wider issues: many Reformed churches no longer require subscription to the letter of their historic standards of faith; the documents themselves could never realistically claim to be doctrinally comprehensive; and – perhaps most significantly – further developments in systematic theology have sometimes challenged and even overtaken original confessional positions. It is the nature of any living tradition to change, develop, and evolve.

In the second place, then, it is important to recognise the theological dimension to the meaning of the term 'Reformed' – if, for the reasons noted earlier, the idea of a confessional uniformity is unpersuasive. In the absence of any single confessional standard or any diachronic doctrinal consistency in the churches, the very concept of Reformed theology appears to be under threat of evacuation. At this juncture, it may be helpful as a point of orientation to bring to mind the familiar clarion calls of the Reformation: *sola scriptura, sola fide, sola gratia, solus Christus,* and *soli Deo gloria.* These calls offer an alternative way of identifying a common shape of theological commitment and doctrinal formulation that might serve to recognise the continuity and commensurability of very different expressions of Reformed theology. Yet precisely in their comprehensiveness of instinct, they could also be said to be shared by many other expressions of Christian faith – particularly other Protestant traditions such as Lutheranism.

A further way of identifying the particularity of the Reformed tradition is to speak of five-point Calvinism, famously encapsulated in the formulation TULIP (Total depravity, Unconditional election, Limited atonement, Irresistible grace, Perseverance of the saints). Such a determinant certainly encompasses a wide swathe of what would be considered Reformed theology. But to rest here risks three oversights. The first is to identify the Reformed tradition with the legacy of Calvin alone, as if no other thinker contributed to the formation of the tradition and its theology. The term 'Reformed' needs to be recognised as being more inclusive than simply 'Calvinist'. The second is to assume that the legacy of Calvin is uncontroversial and uncontested, a view which a series of interpretative controversies has rendered untenable. And third – in line with the idea of using confessions as markers noted earlier – it cannot be assumed that all Reformed thinkers would assent to this particular characterisation of their theology. Indeed, several theologians in the tradition have explicitly denied that the Canons of Dort provide an authoritative development of Calvin's theology. So while a formulation such as TULIP has some merit, it fails to account adequately either for the diversity of the Reformed tradition or for the theologies advanced within it. If the five *solas* provide too capacious a definition of 'Reformed', it seems that five-point Calvinism is too narrow.

Yet another way of attempting to characterise the term 'Reformed' is in terms of a distinct set of intellectual habits – these might be described as respectful but critical of tradition, open to fresh insight, and both practical and evangelical in orientation. Doubtless, there is much in this depiction of Reformed theology and plenty of historical material to illustrate the value of such dispositions; these are worthy of continued attention. But it is not easy to account for a distinctive set of habits independently of the normative theological commitments which have traditionally fostered and sustained them. Convictions about God, Scripture, the Christian life, and the world have all been closely allied to the way in which Reformed theologians traditionally understood their task as doctors of the church. While these habits could persist amidst significant doctrinal modifications, it is not clear that they can formally identify a discrete approach without some continuity of material concerns and principles.

The way in which Reformed theology is characterised in this volume is thus rather different. At its core is the idea that the Reformed tradition sets forth a particular agenda of theological discourse in a remarkably symphonic way. If there cannot be said to be univocity across all its expressions, there can at least be said to be material and thematic resonances across its diverse texts at a most profound level. Even in the absence of a single authoritative text or body of doctrine, there are sufficient common emphases and family resemblances to validate the notion of a discrete tradition. The originating documents of the sixteenth century are thus more the starting-point of a trajectory – or series of trajectories – than a set of timeless criteria, albeit a starting point that takes its foundations from Scripture and its bearings from apostolic tradition and patristic theology. They evidence an identifiable set of theological instincts, of doctrinal impulses – a certain Christian sensibility. This particular pattern of thinking carries forward in time; but as it does so it finds new instantiations and expressions evolving in new contexts. And this is true not only in form: on occasion such development can also lead to revision, even correction, of the content of previous views. Not only the manner but also the matter of this theology can change.

The practical context and concerns of the Reformed churches also contribute to these theological variations on common themes. From the outset, the regular preaching of the Word of God was accompanied by a commitment to adult Christian education, often in the form of catechising and sustained study of the Bible in the vernacular. Such a commitment correspondingly gave rise to a strong impulse towards literacy, and the consequent devotion of time and resources towards parish education in the broadest sense. Such a practical setting bred a suspicion of unduly speculative patterns of thought that could not readily be communicated to wider audiences. Most of the theologians studied in this volume were committed to the task of preaching and could readily move from lectern to pulpit, sometimes with striking effect.

In addition, the strong emphasis on social transformation in the Reformed churches generated a context in which ethics and politics were often dominant concerns. The close partnership of church and state in Geneva and Zürich may have been inflected in different ways in different places, especially after the spread of the Reformed churches to the New World. But the commitment both to the unity of Scripture and to a programme of individual and social sanctification ensured that systematic theology, practical theology, and ethics were often closely intertwined. Later divisions in the theological syllabus should not occlude the centrality of this holistic view in the Reformed tradition. A social vision was never far from the concerns of Reformed theology, even as that vision was adjusted to diverse circumstances.

It is the task of the first section of this book, 'Theological Themes', to articulate against the backdrop of certain doctrinal loci some of the most significant of these instincts and impulses that first shaped the tradition. To do this is to explore what makes a theology 'Reformed' and thus to set forth the sensibility – one might even say, the spirit – which remains broadly constant across all those expressions of faith and all those trajectories of development which sit within the Reformed tradition. This section therefore explores the core loci in respect of which the distinctiveness of Reformed theology comes to unique expression: the doctrine of Scripture, the place of confessions, the doctrine of election, Christology, the doctrine of the sacraments, and the Christian life. These chapters consider how this doctrinal particularity emerged in the sixteenth century, analyse the theological developments in each locus within the Reformed tradition, and reflect constructively on the doctrine in contemporary systematic theology.

The second section of the volume, 'Theological Figures', turns to some of the most significant theologians in the emergence and development of Reformed theology. There are five figures whose work in the tradition is engaged here: Huldrych Zwingli, John Calvin, Jonathan Edwards, Friedrich Schleiermacher, and Karl Barth – the constraints of space sadly exclude the possibility of considering further worthy figures. Each chapter considers one of these individuals, focussing particularly on the way in which they contributed to the discipline of Reformed theology and on the way in which they instantiate its core doctrinal sensibilities. In each case, the aim of the chapter is to offer an account of the relationship between the theologian and the Reformed tradition, to present a consideration of the specific emphases and trajectories within Reformed theology which result from their work, and to provide an evaluation of the contribution that each one has made to Reformed theology.

In the final section of the volume, 'Theological Contexts', the different contexts – historical and geographical – within which Reformed theology has been undertaken are examined. The initial chapters offer an exposition and analysis of two genuinely trans-national movements of the seventeenth century which had a significant impact on the shape and influence of Reformed theology – puritanism and scholasticism. Thereafter, a series of chapters explore the very diverse geographical contexts within which Reformed theology has been influential in the period from the eighteenth century to the present day. Though space precludes being fully comprehensive, these chapters explore some of the key developments which have occurred in Reformed theology in these diverse locations, the relevance of these developments for Reformed theology and the Reformed churches, and the present and future prospects of Reformed theology in these contexts and beyond.

By means of this structure, the volume aims to provide – as the title suggests – a genuine companion to explorations in Reformed theology. It seeks to represent something of the scope and breadth of the theology undertaken in the Reformed tradition across time and across borders, delineating some of its most significant contours and some of its most prominent writers. But it also seeks to capture something of the vibrancy and excitement which are hallmarks of the best theological work in any tradition, to indicate and to evidence the generative and constructive contributions which Reformed theology, in all its rich history and proud diversity, continues to make to ecclesial and ecumenical dialogues today. From the beginning the Reformed tradition has revealed strong impulses towards church unity, and today its contribution needs to be located in this broader ecumenical context. If the Reformed church is truly *semper reformanda* (always to be reformed), then so too its theology sits under the same mandate. For theological work undertaken in the Reformed tradition, as this volume attests, this command is not a challenge to be feared but an opportunity to be seized in each and every generation.

Part I

Theological topics

2 Scripture

J. TODD BILLINGS

For both its advocates and its critics, particular convictions and practices about the Bible as Holy Scripture are central to the Reformed tradition. This is often described with a series of watchwords: *sola scriptura*; Scripture as clear, self-interpreting, and self-authenticating; the inner witness of the Holy Spirit. These phrases and slogans are frequently detached from their larger doctrinal context to fit into modern, de-catholicised projects which either advocate or criticize a Reformed approach to Scripture. These caricatures have also resulted in a series of (contradictory) critiques: that a Reformed view of Scripture involves a rationalistic foundationalism, or that it leads to fideism; that it confuses the biblical text with God, or that it leads to individual subjectivism; that it is hermeneutically naïve about the ease of the process of biblical interpretation, or that it is overly "scholastic" in interpretation, making scriptural interpretation a scholarly task rather than one in which the Bible is formative for the Christian life.

The primary task of this chapter is to attend to the overall theological shape of a classical Reformed doctrine of Scripture, and to the broadly catholic commitments it shares with other premodern Christian theologies. In light of this, our own late modern assumptions and biases can be exposed, and we can be in a place to assess and retrieve from the earlier tradition in light of contemporary challenges. This chapter briefly characterizes key features of a Reformed doctrine of Scripture in a way that is attentive to the common misunderstandings of the doctrine. It then briefly considers the challenges of modernity and late modernity, and the contemporary promise of a Reformed theology of Scripture.

SCRIPTURE AS A *LOCUS* OF DOCTRINE

From its own standpoint, classical Reformed theology is first and foremost scripturally derived theology. For both the Reformers and later Reformed orthodoxy, the material content of theology is derived first

and foremost from biblical exegesis, not through deducing one doctrine from another. Reformed theology did not start with an idea, such
as "God's sovereignty" or "predestination," and build a system based
upon that central doctrine. Rather, each point (or *locus*) of doctrine was
grounded upon scriptural exegesis and ultimately stood or fell on that
ground. Classical Reformed theology had a place for tradition, and for
the use of philosophy and its analytic distinctions. But both of these are
to be used in service of scriptural interpretation – an act in which the
triune God addresses his people in and through Scripture.

For much of the history of the church catholic, a doctrine of Scripture
was presupposed rather than directly expounded as a *locus* of sacred
doctrine. But from the earliest generation of the Reformed tradition, its
theologians and confessions have not only *used* Scripture in particular
ways, but they have also *confessed* the way in which Scripture fits into
a particular vision of God's redemptive activity in Christ through the
Holy Spirit.

While early Reformed Christians did not seek to confess a "new
doctrine" with their theology of Scripture, their teachings *about*
Scripture and *use* of Scripture had both commonality with other traditions of the day and areas of distinctiveness. With Roman Catholics,
early Reformed theologians and confessions affirmed the divine
inspiration of Scripture, which makes it wholly reliable as a source
of Christian doctrine. But the Reformed insisted on the finality of
Scripture's authority in relation to the fallibility of the church in a way
that contrasted with their Roman Catholic counterparts. With early
Anabaptist groups of the Radical Reformation, the early Reformed tradition advocated a rediscovery of Scripture in the vernacular language
and encouraged the lay practice of Bible reading. But in contrast to the
traditions of the Radical Reformation, the early Reformed movement
gave a secondary yet important place to the early ecumenical creeds,
and Reformed scholars immersed themselves in the writings of patristic and medieval theologians as they sought to give biblical commentary. The closest kin to the early Reformed movement was the Lutheran
movement. Indeed, in locations such as the German Palatinate during
parts of the sixteenth century, the commonalities of certain strands
of early Lutheran and Reformed doctrine were coherently expressed in
the Heidelberg Catechism of 1563. With Lutherans, the early Reformed
movement shared convictions about the divine origin of Scripture,
and about the important yet subordinate role of ecumenical creeds
and pre-Reformation biblical commentators, as well as convictions
about the way in which God acts through the ministry of preaching

and the sacraments as central marks of the true church. Indeed, while there were disputes between early Lutheran and Reformed theologians about the interpretation of Scripture at key points (on the sacraments and Christology), there were not open disputes about the nature and authority of Scripture. While distinctive points of emphasis emerged over time, overall the classical Reformed and Lutheran traditions share a broad continuity of confession and practice with respect to the nature and authority of Scripture.

THE NATURE OF SCRIPTURE AS THE WORD OF GOD

We believe that the Word contained in these books has proceeded from God, and receives its authority from him alone, and not from men.

– French Confession of Faith (1559), article 5[1]

For the classical Reformed tradition, Scripture is not "the church's book," in the sense that the church authorizes and owns the book as a religious community. It is the Word and address of God, carrying the delegated authority of God himself through the Spirit. While Reformed theologians distinguish between the "essential," eternal Word of God made flesh in Jesus Christ, and Scripture as a form of divine revelation, the two were not divided. It is the triune God who exercises authority and makes himself known through his Word in Scripture. Thus, this is no "bare," coercive authority exercised from without, but the authority of the ascended Jesus, the Word of the Father, speaking by the Holy Spirit's power. As such, God's Word generates a community of hearers of the Word: the community of the church whose central marks are God's actions through the preaching and sacramental sign-act holding forth God's promise in Jesus Christ as received through Holy Scripture. The church is thus a "creature of the Word" – dependent on God's Word in and work through Scripture in its very life-blood. For Scripture is the Word of God through which the Spirit forms disciples of Christ, nourishes them as the Father's adopted children, enables them, and leads them to a life of love of God and neighbor.

As such, the Reformed belief that Scripture is the written Word of God was not just a theoretical doctrine to be affirmed by an educated

---

[1] Translated from *The Creeds of Christendom*, 6th ed., edited by Philip Schaff (Grand Rapids, MI: Baker, 1931), 362.

few, but also a belief expressed in practices involving a multifaceted immersion in the language and imagery of Scripture in nearly all aspects of life. Reformed theologians embraced the use of the literary and rhetorical tools of Renaissance humanism to give a close reading of biblical texts. But this did not make the reading of Scripture an exclusively "intellectual" endeavor. As one social historian notes about Geneva during the days of Calvin and a generation after his death, "the language and message of the Bible was nearly omnipresent in Geneva's religious life as it was proclaimed in sermons, recited in catechism, sung in the Psalter, studied in the *Congregation*, discussed in the marketplace, and read devotionally in households."[2] The same could be said for many other emerging Reformed communities. Indeed, even as the intellectual elements of doctrinal theology became increasingly sophisticated in Reformed scholasticism, Scripture was still utilized in worship, in devotion, and in broadly catechetical modes as well. Scripture is first and foremost the Word of God – thus the church finds its life in its ongoing nourishment by God's Word received in preaching, the sacraments, song, study, home Bible reading, and prayer.

When the French Confession says "the Word contained in these books has proceeded from God," does this mean that the human agency in the writing of biblical books is bypassed? It does not. John Calvin, whose theology was a key source for the French Confession, elaborates on the divine authorship of Scripture this way: Scripture "has flowed to us from the very mouth of God by the ministry of men."[3] God has authored Scripture, but through the creaturely means of human beings. For the first generations of Reformed theology, there was very little discussion and debate about exactly *how* this original inspiration took place. The mode of Scripture's divine inspiration was not an issue of Roman Catholic–Protestant, or intra-Protestant dispute in the Reformation era. Early Reformed theologians affirmed the divine authorship of Scripture by means of the Spirit's inspiration of human writers, but without elaborate theories. Calvin was not atypical in utilizing an analogy of dictation ("in a certain manner (*quodammodo*) dictating the words"[4]), but in a

---

[2] Scott M. Manetsch, *Calvin's Company of Pastors: Pastoral Care and the Emerging Reformed Church* (Oxford: Oxford University Press, 2013), 305.

[3] John Calvin, *Institutes of the Christian Religion*, edited by John T. McNeill, translated by Ford Lewis Battles (Library of Christian Classics; 2 vols.; Philadelphia: Westminster, 1960), I.vii.4.

[4] Ibid., IV.viii.8.

way that affirms that the particular authors of Scripture bring their own human styles and perceptions to bear.[5]

If Scripture is the holy written Word of God mediated by the Spirit through human beings, how does this creaturely language communicate God's Word? When the authors of Scripture speak about the hand or arm of God, or the "repentance" of God (e.g., Genesis 6:6–7 and 1 Samuel 15:11), does this creaturely language apply literally to God? The Reformed insisted that the Bible's "anthropomorphic" descriptions are not to be taken literally, but as analogies given as a precious gift of love to humans. In this, the Reformed tradition drew upon writers of the early church (such as John Chrysostom) and medieval theologians to differentiate between the way in which God fully knows himself and the way in which human beings come to know God through Scripture. Because Scripture is mediated through human beings, it does not give us a God's-eye view of God. Instead, reflecting God's extraordinary love toward weak, finite human beings, God accommodates himself to human capacity, utilizing human analogies in divine revelation. Thus, in the words of Calvin:

> For who even of slight intelligence does not understand that, as nurses commonly do with infants, God is wont in a measure to 'lisp' in speaking to us? Thus such forms of speaking do not so much express clearly what God is like as accommodate the knowledge of him to our slight capacity. To do this he must descend far beneath his loftiness.[6]

Through the notion of accommodation, Calvin affirms that God is the One who fully knows God, and the Spirit graciously utilizes human analogies in his self-disclosure to communicate God's Word to human beings. God remains incomprehensible, even as he is also truly made known through Scripture.

One of Calvin's students, Franciscus Junius, drew upon medieval catholic distinctions to provide further developments of this notion which clarifies the role of Scripture in God's plan of redemption. First, he distinguishes between archetypal knowledge of God (God's knowledge of himself) and ectypal knowledge (a mediated, accommodated, human knowledge of God). God truly makes himself known through

---

5 Richard Muller, *Post-Reformation Reformed Dogmatics: The Rise and Development of Reformed Orthodoxy, ca. 1520 to ca. 1725* (4 vols.; Grand Rapids, MI: Baker, 2003), vol. 2, *Holy Scripture*, 237.

6 Calvin, *Institutes*, I.xiii.1.

Scripture, but only in a way that gives ectypal knowledge of God, appropriate for creaturely understanding. Moreover, there are three forms of ectypal knowledge of God. The highest is the human knowledge that Jesus Christ has of God in the hypostatic union. The second highest is a knowledge of God afforded to the redeemed at the beatific vision, the final face-to-face vision of God. But our current theology is a third form of human knowledge, lower than the first two: we genuinely come to know God through his divine revelation in Scripture, but we are currently on a pilgrimage as ones who see through a glass darkly (1 Cor. 13:12). This knowledge of God is fully adequate for its purpose of bringing us into saving fellowship with God and showing the way to live as disciples of Christ. But "it is imperfect when compared with the theology of vision for which we hope."[7] In light of these distinctions, Scripture as a form of God's accommodation is both sufficient and appropriate for its redemptive purpose. Yet, the transcendence and mystery of God are maintained in a way that points to our pilgrim status as followers of Jesus who are awaiting a final, higher form of knowledge and communion with God.

Later theologians of Reformed scholasticism utilized similar distinctions to help them articulate a high place for Scripture as the Word of God that is also written and divinely accommodated in its character. The Spirit employs human writing as an instrument for this lavish gift of divine communication. In all of this, the biblical text is not equated with the being of God, and a distinction is maintained between God's written Word in Scripture and the eternal Word as the second person of the Trinity.

While the distinctions of Junius were not incorporated into the Reformed confessions, the teleological way in which Reformed confessions speak about the knowledge of God revealed through Scripture parallels Junius's emphasis: Scripture reliably shows us the benevolent promises of God, fulfilled in Jesus Christ, and the way for Christians to live. "The principle intent of all canonical Scripture is that God wishes to be good to mankind, and that He has declared that benevolence through Jesus Christ, His Son."[8] Indeed, this is the context in which a Reformation doctrine of the "clarity" of Scripture is confessed: not that

[7] Junius, *De vera theologia*, translated from Willem J. Van Asselt, "The Fundamental Meaning of Theology: Archetypal and Ectypal Theology in Seventeenth-Century Reformed Thought," *Westminster Theological Journal* 64 (2003): 319–335 (330).

[8] *First Helvetic Confession* (1536), article 5, in *Reformed Confessions of the 16th and 17th Centuries in English Translation*, vol. 1, edited by James T. Dennison, Jr. (Grand Rapids, MI: Reformation Heritage, 2008), 344.

Scripture is always easy to interpret or understand, but that it is sufficiently clear to communicate this essential knowledge of God required
for disciples of Christ on their pilgrimage of faith. In the words of the
Westminster Confession: "All things in Scripture are not alike plain in
themselves, nor alike clear unto all; yet those things which are necessary to be known, believed, and observed, for salvation, are so clearly
propounded and opened in some place of Scripture or other, that not
only the learned, but the unlearned, in a due use of the ordinary means,
may attain unto a sufficient understanding of them."[9]

THE SOURCES OF REVELATION: IN CREATION AND IN SCRIPTURE

Reformed confessions as well as early Reformed theologians (such as
Calvin, Bullinger, Vermigli, and Musculus) give a central place to God's
special revelation in Christ, made known through the written Word of
God. Yet, they do not reject the notion of a genuine yet imperfect natural
knowledge of God. While Calvin, for example, can affirm that "all thinking about God, apart from Christ, is a bottomless abyss which utterly
swallows up all our senses,"[10] he sees no incompatibility between this
and affirming that even apart from special revelation, people have a
knowledge – however corrupted – of God the Creator, and "within the
human mind, and indeed by natural instinct, an awareness of divinity."[11] Moreover, Calvin speaks of the working of the conscience, which
(imperfectly) reflects an "internal law" from God, which is "engraved,
upon the hearts of all, in a sense asserts the very same things that are to
be learned from the two Tables [the Ten Commandments]."[12]

However, for the classical Reformed tradition, the natural knowledge of God was not an independent "foundation" upon which to build a
revealed Christian theology. A natural knowledge of God was affirmed,
first and foremost, because Scripture itself affirms it, particularly in
Romans 1:20–21: "Ever since the creation of the world his eternal power
and divine nature, invisible though they are, have been understood and

---

[9] *Westminster Confession of Faith* (1647), chapter I.7, in *The Confession of Faith
and the Larger and Shorter Catechisms* (Glasgow: Free Presbyterian Publications,
1973), 23.

[10] From Calvin's commentary on 1 Peter 1:20, translated by Ford Lewis Battles in "God
was accommodating himself to Human Capacity," in *Readings in Calvin's Theology*,
edited by Donald K. McKim (Grand Rapids, MI: Baker, 1984), 42.

[11] Calvin, *Institutes*, I.iii.1.

[12] Ibid., II.viii.1.

seen through the things he has made. So they are without excuse; for though they knew God, they did not honor him as God or give thanks to him, but they became futile in their thinking, and their senseless minds were darkened" (NRSV). Repeatedly, the Reformed tradition affirmed that all people have some knowledge of God the Creator and of God's requirements of them (the Law), with the soteriological emphasis that they are "without excuse" for not serving God. Human beings are responsible, but sinful – they have been given the seeds of religion, but are idolaters. The knowledge of God in creation drives sinful humans to the knowledge of God the Redeemer available through Scripture – a knowledge that is essential for humans to overcome their idolatry before God.

While this soteriological function of the knowledge of God in creation is crucial, it is not the exclusive function of natural knowledge of God. Classical Reformed theologians could maintain this emphasis while upholding a modest version of catholic natural law tradition in their social and political thought. On the one hand, it is only through the lens or "spectacles" of Scripture that one can have a proper view of God as Creator, and of the content of the Law of God. Yet, on the other hand, some who are without the Scriptures (pagan philosophers, scientists) can still be used by God as instruments of nonsalvific truth, by their careful attention to God's beautiful book of creation. In all of this, Scripture remains the final norm for discerning which claims of natural theology are authentic and which are not. While natural knowledge of God is a gracious gift – to lead sinners to special revelation, and to be used in an ad hoc fashion in expositing special revelation – it is insufficient as a foundation for Christian theology.

THE SUFFICIENCY OF SCRIPTURE AND THE ROLE OF TRADITION

Early Reformed theologians had no significant disputes with Roman Catholics of the day on the nature of Scripture as God's authoritative, divinely inspired Word, and they drew on earlier catholic theologies in their development of a theology of God's revelation in creation and Scripture, as well as the nature of divine accommodation in Scripture. But the sufficiency of Scripture became a subject of dispute between Reformed and Roman Catholic theologians, and remains so to this day.

Those on the Reformed side, together with Lutherans, confessed Scripture as completely sufficient for its divinely ordained purpose: "sola scriptura," as this principle came to be known in the post-Reformation era. This slogan is misunderstood today by many both within and outside of the Reformed tradition. It did not mean that the ideal readers of Scriptures read it "alone" – apart from community, or "alone" – apart from the church's history of interpretation or doctrine. In the Reformation and post-Reformation era, this confession of the sufficiency of Scripture went hand in hand with a reception of Scripture in a communal context. It also meant that intertestamental books that Roman Catholics considered to be Deuterocanonical were to be evaluated in light of the Old and New Testaments. As the Belgic Confession states, "The church may certainly read these books and learn from them as far as they agree with the canonical books."[13]

In construing Scripture's authority in this way, *sola scriptura* did not mean bypassing ecclesiology, so that a "book" was the only authority: for the Reformed, scriptural authority was mediated through ministers, who exercised a delegated, subordinate authority as servants of God's Word. With the proliferation of confessions, catechisms, and sermons in Reformed communities, it would have been inconceivable to view the interpretative ideal either as bringing a "blank slate" to Scripture, or focusing simply on what the biblical text "means to me" subjectively. Instead, the Reformed insisted that Scripture alone is the final authority – indeed, that all of the church's confession and preaching find its true ground in Scripture, such that it can judge the confession itself. For example, in its concluding section, the First Confession of Basel states: "we submit our confession to the judgment of Sacred Scripture: and promise that if we are instructed in better things from the Scriptures as preached, we always intend to obey God and His most holy Word with great thanksgiving."[14] Those confessing here thus recognize themselves to be fallible interpreters of Scripture – Scripture stands above them as the final authority even over this very confession. Thus, they express their willingness gladly to relent on any part of the confession that can be shown to be out of accord with Scripture. Sometimes this principle is described by the Reformed tradition as the "self-interpreting" character of Scripture: in the words of the Westminster Confession, although "all things in Scripture are not alike plain in themselves," nevertheless "the infallible rule of interpretation of Scripture is the Scripture itself."[15] A characteristic Roman

---

[13] *Belgic Confession* (1561), article 6, translated in *Our Faith: Ecumenical Creed, Reformed Confessions, and Other Resources* (Grand Rapids, MI: Faith Alive, 2013), 29.

[14] *First Confession of Basel* (1534), chapter XII, in *Reformed Confessions*, 295–296.

[15] *Westminster Confession of Faith* (1647), chapter I.IX.

Catholic criticism of the Reformed is that they lack a church office to resolve theological disputes that could lead to ecclesial fragmentation. However, from a Reformed standpoint, locating the authority for resolving theological disputes in a church office would be an act of unfaithfulness, refusing to submit to the finality of God's Word through the Holy Spirit in Scripture: "The Supreme Judge, by which all controversies of religion are to be determined, and all decrees of councils, opinions of ancient writers, doctrines of men, and private spirits, are to be examined, and in whose sentence we are to rest, can be no other but the Holy Spirit speaking in the Scripture."[16]

While the Reformed insist that Scripture alone is the final theological authority, ecumenical creeds (such as the Nicene and Athanasian creeds), the Church Fathers, and some medieval theologians were frequently approached as theological authorities by Reformed theologians in the sixteenth and seventeenth centuries. In the material in the First Helvetic Confession on scriptural interpretation, the "ancient fathers" are to be received "as interpreters of the Scripture," and "we honor them as chosen instruments of God."[17] Clearly, the early Reformed tradition did not seek to interpret the "Bible alone" in the sense of being apart from or always opposed to catholic tradition. Yet, even these "chosen instruments of God" are valued *because* they give faithful interpretations of Scripture. Indeed, during the two centuries following the Reformation, Reformed theologians were heavily involved (with Roman Catholics and some Lutherans) in producing and refining editions of the patristic writings. The Reformed openly admitted that the Church Fathers were not a reliable final authority: at points they disagree with each other, and in other places they are either mistaken or unclear in their witness to scriptural truth. Nevertheless, patristic writings still had a normative place in scriptural interpretation, even if they were not the *final* norm, like Scripture itself.

Yet, how exactly is Scripture to be distinguished from tradition? Did not the church itself decide what biblical books are part of the canon, thus blurring any sharp distinctions between the authority of Scripture and the authority of tradition? In a way characteristic of the early Reformed tradition, Calvin argues that it is "a most pernicious error" to say that "Scripture has only so much weight as is conceded to it by the consent of the church."[18] This error reverses the proper ordering, since the church itself is a product of God's powerful Word

---

[16] Ibid., chapter I.X.

[17] *First Helvetic Confession* (1536), article III, in *Reformed Confessions*, 344.

[18] Calvin, *Institutes*, I.vii.1.

through Scripture. Rather than look to the church or to proofs outside of Scripture itself to show the veracity of Scripture, we should look to God: "The highest proof of Scripture derives in general from the fact that God in person speaks in it."[19]

In this context, Reformed theologians and confessions give a key place to the illuminating power of the Spirit in receiving Scripture. In the words of the Belgic Confession, "we believe without a doubt all things contained in them [the canonical books of the Bible] – not so much because the church receives and approves them as such but above all because the Holy Spirit testifies in our hearts that they are from God, and also because they prove themselves to be from God."[20] Thus, the sufficiency of Scripture is grounded explicitly in the work of God rather than human beings. In this characteristic affirmation, the Reformed insist that if the triune God is to exercise his Lordship over the church through Scripture, the church cannot recognize an authority above God the Lord as the final arbiter in confirming the divinity of Scripture.

This means that the doctrine of the Spirit's illumination of Scripture plays an especially important role in the Reformed tradition – for it is the Spirit, not the church itself, that provides the ultimate ground for Scripture as the Word of God. On this point, the Reformed tradition sought to articulate a middle ground between Tridentine Roman Catholicism and certain Radical Reformation/Anabaptist accounts of the sixteenth century. In contrast to a Tridentine affirmation that Scripture and tradition are parallel sources of divine revelation – with parity in authority – the Reformed affirmed the self-authenticating character of Scripture through the Spirit's internal witness. But in contrast to some in the Radical Reformation who disconnected the Spirit's ongoing Word from the written words of Scripture, the Reformed insisted that the Spirit bears witness to the Word of Scripture. Thus, the Reformed do not move from an external standard (tradition) to a purely internal one (the Spirit's working in one's heart). Rather, the Spirit's internal testimony is to the (external) Word of Scripture itself – God himself speaks by the Spirit in the written words of Scripture. In this way, the classical Reformed tradition held Word and Spirit in a very close relation. In the words of Calvin: "the Holy Spirit so inheres in His truth, which He expresses in Scripture, that only when its proper reverence and dignity are given to the Word does the Holy Spirit show forth His power."[21]

---

[19] Ibid., I.vii.4.
[20] *Belgic Confession* (1561), article 5, in *Our Faith*, 28.
[21] Calvin, *Institutes*, I.ix.3.

BIBLICAL COMMENTARY AND THE CHALLENGE
OF THE ENLIGHTENMENT

Biblical exegesis continued to take varied forms in the context of post-Reformation Reformed communities: devotion and homily, academic biblical exegesis and doctrinal clarification and debate. Biblical exegesis continued to provide the material for doctrinal theology as a collection of common places (*loci communes*). Through the sixteenth and seventeenth centuries, the genre of biblical commentaries grew in linguistic, textual, and rhetorical sophistication. But the basic approach continued to be a Reformed variation of a broader catholic approach toward Scripture: the unity of the biblical canon was assumed, finding its culmination in Jesus Christ, and the Trinitarian dynamic was affirmed – that the Spirit works through Scripture to conform a people adopted by the Father to the image of Jesus Christ. Reformed orthodoxy also insisted on the sufficiency and finality of God's Word in Scripture, but in a way that continued to give an important yet subordinate role to early ecumenical creeds, patristic and medieval commentators, and an ad hoc use of philosophical tools. In the eighteenth and nineteenth centuries, movements of "Enlightenment" would call into question these catholic assumptions of biblical interpretation. Characteristic Reformed affirmations about Scripture were challenged as well. Even when key notions such as *sola scriptura* or the natural knowledge of the Creator were drawn upon, they were often used in ways that contradicted the way in which they were used in the earlier Reformed tradition.

While these Enlightenment challenges were varied and complex, two areas were particularly significant for a Reformed theology of Scripture.

Reason and natural theology

As suggested in the preceding text, in the classical Reformed tradition, natural knowledge of God was not a philosophical foundation for theology, and reason was used as a servant to the exposition of divine revelation in Scripture. But under the influence of Enlightenment voices, a notion of "natural knowledge of God" became an autonomous foundation for theology and a criterion for truth in biblical exegesis. For example, in *The Education of the Human Race*, Gotthold Lessing affirms that the Bible is revelatory of nothing that could not be discovered by human reason on its own. Thus, the universal ethical and metaphysical precepts that can be derived from human reason should decide in advance what can be "revelatory" in biblical interpretation. In the process, the historical and narrative dimensions of divine revelation are strongly downplayed, and the Christological and Trinitarian affirmations of catholic biblical exegesis are denied: the "accidental truths of history can never become the proof for necessary truths of reason."[22] The truths of reason must be demonstrable and universal, and the claim that the God of Israel has been made known in the life and person of Jesus, the Son of God, cannot be verified by reason alone.

The literal sense and the unity of the canon

Classical Reformed theologians often criticized their Roman Catholic counterparts for an overly "allegorical" reading of Scripture and championed a return to the "literal" or "historical" sense. Yet, this was not a complete rejection of the earlier catholic practice of discerning various levels of meaning in Scripture, but an attempt to root those levels clearly in the literal sense. Indeed, as Richard Muller points out, for Calvin the literal sense "held a message concerning what Christians ought to believe, what Christians ought to do, and what Christians ought to hope for."[23] Accordingly, a "literal" interpretation of the Old Testament did not mean interpreting it *apart* from Christ. The Psalms of David were not just about David, or ancient Israel. They were about David *and* Christ – the true King in whom the Psalms find their fulfilment. In this way, Reformed biblical exegesis continued the catholic practice of assuming that the biblical canon is unified – by one divine author who speaks through human beings in a wide variety of times, places, and genres in a way that gives unified testimony to Jesus Christ as the Son of the Father by the Spirit's power.

The rise of a historical-critical method that distanced itself from other theological disciplines both challenged the unity of the canon and redefined the quest for the "historical" sense. Historical critics did not position themselves among Scripture's "ideal readers" who interpret and live out the text within a community of faith. Instead, they read as members of the Enlightenment university who sought to give historical reconstructions to explain the origin, authorship, and textual formation of the Bible as a collection of ancient texts. The interest in questions of authorship, textual-criticism, and historical origins was

---

22 Gotthold Lessing, "On the Proof of the Spirit and of Power," in *Lessing's Theological Writings*, translated by Henry Chadwick (Stanford, CA: Stanford University Press, 1956), 53.

23 Richard A. Muller, "Biblical Interpretation in the Era of the Reformation: The View from the Middle Ages," in *Biblical Interpretation in Era of the Reformation*, edited by Richard A. Muller and John L. Thompson (Grand Rapids, MI: Eerdmans, 1996), 11.

not new. But the assumption that this should be a purely historical, atheological science was new. With this immanent notion of "history" in place, traditional Christological and Trinitarian assumptions regarding the task of biblical exegesis were denied, as was the traditional affirmation of canonical unity – that the Scriptures as a whole find their unity and fulfilment in the person of Christ, thus leading toward saving fellowship with God in Christ, and love of God and neighbor.

LATE MODERNITY AND A REFORMED DOCTRINE OF SCRIPTURE

Through the course of the last two centuries, Reformed theologians have given a variety of responses to the challenges of Enlightenment approaches to biblical interpretation. At times, conservative Reformed theologians have responded to the naturalistic assumptions described previously by reasserting the role of the doctrine of inspiration. They rightly argued that in the older Reformed and catholic theologies, the Spirit-inspired Scripture as completely reliable and without defect. Yet, at times, they set up the doctrine of inspiration as a theological foundation *apart* from the larger Trinitarian and soteriological context of the earlier Reformed tradition: namely, that Scripture is God's wholly reliable Word not mainly for the purpose of providing general knowledge (about science, psychology, etc.), but for bringing about saving fellowship with the triune God in an ectypal, accommodated mode appropriate to creatures. In addition, in modern scholarly and popular circles, the Reformed slogan of *"sola scriptura"* was often used to oppose the Bible to the tradition of the church in general, a move that held particular currency in Enlightenment-oriented cultures that valued the new and "scientific" over that which was derived from church tradition.

Theologians such as Herman Bavinck and Karl Barth, in differing ways, sought to respond to the rationalistic assumptions of Enlightenment theologians by drawing deeply upon earlier Reformed thinkers. In his *Reformed Dogmatics*, Bavinck was significant in responding to both mechanistic and rationalistic theories of inspiration with an "organic" approach that refused to oppose divine and human agency: "the Holy Spirit, in the inscripturation of the word of God, did not spurn anything human to serve as an organ of the divine."[24]

---

[24] Herman Bavinck, *Reformed Dogmatics*, 4 vols., edited by John Bolt, translated by John Vriend (Grand Rapids, MI: BakerAcademic, 2003–2008), vol. IV, 271–585., vol. I, 442.

Bavinck also provided a rich retrieval of patristic and Reformed sources to exposit the accommodated, and yet fully sufficient knowledge of the mysterious triune God made known in Jesus Christ through Scripture. In his *Epistle to the Romans*, Barth gave a clarion call for theology to return to a theocentric mode of biblical interpretation, and his monumental *Church Dogmatics* expounded a thoroughgoing Trinitarian and Christocentric theology of revelation. As he did this, Barth sought to retrieve key elements of a Reformed theology of Scripture from classical sources.

At points, Barth's developments moved away from the earlier Reformed tradition on Scripture, particularly in the way in which he describes Scripture as "becoming" revelation, rather than enduring and existing as an ectypal mode of revelation. Barth did this by building upon, yet also modifying, earlier Reformed teaching about the three forms of the Word of God: Jesus Christ, Scripture, and proclamation. In the economy of salvation, Scripture and proclamation are properly grounded in Jesus Christ – by the Spirit they bear witness to the Word as instruments of revelation. But for Barth, the content of revelation per se is definitely constituted by the Word made flesh. "Revelation in fact does not differ from the person of Jesus Christ nor from the reconciliation accomplished in him."[25] Thus, Barth affirms that Scripture and proclamation both *"are* God's word" and "that they continually *become* God's word" in the church (emphasis added).[26] Barth emphasizes both a unity in the three forms of God's Word – Scripture and proclamation give witness to one Word, made flesh in Christ – and the differentiation of the forms in a way that shows their interdependent connection; as he does this, he presents a framework that has both commonality and contrasts with the "pilgrim theology" of earlier Reformed theology described previously. In addition, in response to the autonomous place that natural theology had come to occupy in modernity, Barth rejected natural theology – both in its modernist and classical forms. Nevertheless, Barth's theology has had a profound influence in leading a wide range of recent theologians to recover the importance of a Trinitarian and Christocentric theology of biblical interpretation. Moreover, although scholarship has often neglected this, Barth sought to restore biblical exegesis to a central place in the theological task of twentieth-century theology. In the twenty-first century, two of the most significant expositors of contemporary Reformed theologies

---

[25] Karl Barth, *Church Dogmatics*, 4 vols. in 13 parts, edited by G. W. Bromiley and T. F. Torrance (Edinburgh: T&T Clark, 1956–1975), vol. I/1, 119.

[26] Ibid., I/1, 118.

of Scripture – John Webster and Kevin Vanhoozer – draw deeply upon Barth, even as they move through and beyond him at key points.

In the twenty-first century, some scholars in biblical studies continue the Enlightenment practice of conceiving of their project in exclusively historical-critical terms, while others claim that there is a wide range of critical "tools" to be used in an ad hoc fashion toward a particular end. One movement, the Theological Interpretation of Scripture, takes the latter approach in a way that restores the catholic assumptions about Scripture that were lost by many Enlightenment exegetes: that Scripture should be approached within a Trinitarian framework, and that Scripture is a multivalent but unified narrative, finding its culmination in Jesus Christ. This varied movement seeks to combine textual and critical tools with key catholic assumptions about the unity of the biblical canon, and a fresh appropriation of exegetical dialogue partners from Christian history as well as various contemporary cultural contexts. In addition, key advocates have given a theological appropriation of speech-act theory, such as Nicholas Wolterstorff. He has explored how God performs different kinds of actions through speaking. God's Word is not abstract information, but a powerful, identity-forming action.

In today's late modern context, the development of a Reformed theology of Scripture involves both the critical retrieval of pre-Enlightenment, catholic theologies and practices related to Scripture, and a holistic development of characteristic Reformed motifs: *sola scriptura*, with its confidence in God's powerful speech through Scripture as the Word that both gives life to the church, and stands above even the church's acts of interpretation; the centrality of Christ's lordship over the church through the Spirit in the preached and sacramental Word; the centrality of biblical exegesis for theology – and for the practices of singing, memorizing, studying, and being shaped by Scripture in the process of growing into Christ's image by the Spirit. Amidst the consumerism and self-help of late modernity, with readers convinced of the inherent validity of their own experience apart from the working of the triune God, Reformed convictions about the power of God's written Word through Scripture are both compelling and generative for the church's ongoing life.

Further reading

Barth, Karl. *Church Dogmatics*. 4 vols. in 13 parts. Edited by G. W. Bromiley and T. F. Torrance. Edinburgh: T&T Clark, 1956–1975, vol. I/1.

Bavinck, Herman. *Reformed Dogmatics.* 4 vols. Edited by John Bolt. Translated by John Vriend. Grand Rapids, MI: BakerAcademic, 2003–2008, vols. III and IV.

Calvin, John. *Institutes of the Christian Religion.* 2 vols. Edited by John T. McNeill. Translated by Ford Lewis Battles. Philadelphia: Westminster, 1960.

Muller, Richard. *Post-Reformation Reformed Dogmatics: The Rise and Development of Reformed Orthodoxy, ca. 1520 to ca. 1725.* 4 vols. Grand Rapids, MI: Baker, 2003, vol. II.

Vanhoozer, Kevin J. *The Drama of Doctrine: A Canonical-Linguistic Approach to Christian Theology.* Louisville, KY: Westminster John Knox, 2005.

Webster, John B. *Holy Scripture: A Dogmatic Sketch.* Cambridge: Cambridge University Press, 2003.

Wolterstorff, Nicholas. *Divine Discourse: Philosophical Reflections on the Claim that God Speaks.* Cambridge: Cambridge University Press, 1995.

3 Confessions

MICHAEL ALLEN

While the Reformed Scripture principle has garnered wide prestige through the centuries, one cannot say the same for its confessional principle. Yet any attentive study of early Reformed theology must reckon with the fact that while biblical commentaries and doctrinal and polemical treatises abounded, among the most noteworthy and burgeoning theological genres was the confessional symbol. At the same time, we can see that the Reformed churches also developed a theology of Christian confession that was premised on understanding the church and its action in light of the Gospel itself. Perhaps there is some irony that a movement that qualified the authority of the confessional statement also showed the greatest gusto in producing, practicing, and discussing it. The practice, however, puts the lie to any sense that the Scripture principle denigrates the genuine exercise of ecclesiastical authority and points us instead toward reading Reformed ecclesiology and prolegomena in a vein understood along the lines of a Reformed catholicity rather than a thoroughgoing individualism or iconoclasm. To understand this, we need not only to survey the contents of Reformed confessions but also to address their underlying confessional principle. This chapter addresses the confessional principle in Reformed theology (a theology for confessing) as well as the common features of that confessional theology (the theology of the confessions).

THEOLOGY FOR CONFESSING: THE CONFESSIONAL PRINCIPLE

Reformed theology cannot do without confession. The ancients may have spoken of the law of prayer being the law of faith (*lex orandi, lex credendi*); with respect to the Reformed churches, we could press still further to say the law of confessing is the law of faith (*lex confitendi, lex credendi*). The Reformed movement inherited a soteriology and ecclesiology from Augustine, yet it sought to explicate both more fully under the judgment of the Gospel economy. In the area of ecclesiology, this further radicalization of Augustine's emphases meant a focus on the way in which God's authority was exercised through Scripture, church, and confession. To understand the Reformed theology for confessing, we must attend to each of these topics in their respective place in the economy of God's works.

"The holy, Christian Church, whose only Head is Christ, is born of the Word of God, abides in the same, and does not listen to the voice of a stranger."[1] These words, the first of the Ten Theses of Berne, the 1528 confession of that congregation, articulated the Reformed Scripture principle. The Scripture principle reshaped thinking about churchly confession and discipline. Ecclesiastical councils and confessions would henceforth have to demonstrate their derivation from biblical teaching, for they had no separate or autonomous standing on their own. Only the Word of God is self-attesting (*autopistia*) according to the Reformed confessional and dogmatic tradition. Confessions exercise valid authority in as much as they are attested to by God's self-attesting Word.[2]

The Reformed churches employ the distinction of magisterial and ministerial authority to clarify the economy of theological authority in the church's life. Whereas Christ alone is Lord (*magister*) of the church, he and his Word have sole magisterial authority. Yet Christ, like so many lords in political spheres, works typically through means, involving subordinates in his task of exercising rule and dominion. These auxiliaries serve a ministerial capacity rather than an executive function, and their authority, while real, is derivative and subordinate to that of their Lord. Heinrich Bullinger's assessment of authority makes use of this distinction: "Canonical truth teaches us that Christ himself holds and exercises absolute or full power in the Church, and that he has given ministerial power to the Church, which executes it for the most part by ministers, and religiously executes it according to the rule of God's Word."[3] Again the Ten Theses of Berne in 1528 prove instructive: "The Church of Christ makes no laws or commandments without God's Word. Hence all human traditions, which are called ecclesiastical

[1] *The Ten Theses of Berne* (1528), thesis 1, in *Reformed Confessions of the Sixteenth Century*, edited by Arthur Cochrane (Louisville, KY: Westminster John Knox, 2003), 49.

[2] *Westminster Confession of Faith* (1647), chapter I.5, in *The Confession of Faith and the Larger and Shorter Catechisms* (Glasgow: Free Presbyterian Publications, 1973), 21–22.

[3] Heinrich Bullinger, "Of the Holy Catholic Church," in *Zwingli and Bullinger*, edited by G. W. Bromiley (Library of Christian Classics; Louisville, KY: Westminster John Knox, 2006), 324.

commandments, are binding upon us only in so far as they are based on and commanded by God's Word."⁴ Indeed the Geneva Confession of 1536 speaks similarly: "To these [ministers of the Word] we accord no other power or authority but to conduct, rule, and govern the people of God committed to them by the same Word, in which they have power to command, defend, promise, and warn, and without which they neither can nor ought to attempt anything."⁵

These limits to confessional authority, however, do not minimize the importance or function of such ecclesiastical statements, as if biblical authority requires the nullification of all other authorities. John Calvin stated that, "if any discussion arises over doctrine, that the best and surest remedy is for a synod of true bishops to be convened, where the doctrine at issue may be examined."⁶ Calvin's comments here belie the frequent depiction of the Reformation as a movement away from ecclesiastical authority toward individual rationalism, whether in the celebratory mood of Alexis de Tocqueville or the more recent lamentations of Brad Gregory.⁷ The Reformed churches functioned in a markedly different way than the congregations of the Radical Reformation, refusing to pit scriptural authority over against the need for genuine ecclesiastical discipline and advocating instead, as an instrument of that rule, the need for ecclesial confessions to serve as arbiters of biblical truth.⁸ The Reformed churches also approached confessing differently than the Lutherans, inasmuch as Reformed confessions were localized and none approached the universal authority held by the *Book of Concord* and its constituent parts in the Lutheran tradition.

The role of confessions in the life of the church is not merely political or social, as one among many efforts at groupthink or as a prudent,

⁴ *The Ten Theses of Berne* (1528), thesis 2, in *Reformed Confessions of the Sixteenth Century*, 49.

⁵ *The Geneva Confession* (1536), chapter 20, in *Reformed Confessions of the Sixteenth Century*, 125–126.

⁶ John Calvin, *Institutes of the Christian Religion*, edited by John T. McNeill, translated by Ford Lewis Battles (Library of Christian Classics; 2 vols.; Philadelphia: Westminster, 1960), IV.ix.13.

⁷ *contra* Alexis de Tocqueville, "On the Philosophical Method of the Americans," in *Democracy in America*, translated by Arthur Goldhammer (New York: The Library of America, 2004), 485; Brad S. Gregory, *The Unintended Reformation: How a Religious Revolution Secularized Society* (Cambridge, MA: Belknap Press of Harvard University Press, 2012).

⁸ *contra* Gregory, *The Unintended Reformation*, 95; see the analysis of Karl Holl, "Luther und die Schwärmer," in *Gesammelte Aufsätze zur Kirchengeschichte*, Band I (Tübingen: Mohr-Siebeck, 1923), 420–467; Mark U. Edwards, *Luther and the False Brethren* (Stanford, CA: Stanford University Press, 1975).

natural attempt to benefit from the work of many hands.[9] Again, the Reformed churches have reflected on the nature of confessions by locating them within the economy of grace administered by Christ through his Spirit. Specifically theological reasons are given for prizing the proclamations of church confessions: "[T]he Church is the pillar and ground of truth because being established upon the foundation of the prophets and apostles, Christ himself, which is the everlasting truth of God and the Church's only strength, by the fellowship which it has with him it is granted to be with him the pillar and foundation of the truth."[10] Bullinger here observes the distinction between natural and gracious authority. Whereas Christ is authoritative by nature, in and of himself, "it is granted" to the church graciously to function as an authority: a "pillar and foundation of the truth." The idiom employed here is not merely causal, however, as if Christ commissions the church at a distance; rather, the language is covenantal: "by the fellowship which it has with him." Union with Christ brings the church not only into his benefits but also into his commission. For this reason the Heidelberg Catechism attests to the way in which his threefold office is shared in by the church.[11] And, centuries later, Karl Barth will expand Calvin's double grace (*duplex gratia*) in his doctrine of reconciliation to speak also of a third element of salvation in Christ: sharing in his vocation or mission.[12] Whether construed broadly as the individual Christian's vocation to witness to Christ or more narrowly on the congregation's calling to share in the anointing of Christ and the ministry of his proclamation, the Christian confession participates by grace in that of the Christ himself.

Christian confession is not only united to Christ but is also empowered by the power of the Holy Spirit. The illumination of the Spirit enables the church to hear and to see the radiant and life-giving Word of God. As Huldrych Zwingli put it, God's Word can be understood due to the "light and Spirit of God, illuminating and inspiring the words in such a way that the light of the divine content is seen in his own light, as it says in Psalm 35 (A.V. 36): 'For with thee, Lord, is the well of

---

[9] Note, however, that the confessions do regularly address the nature and role of the civil magistrate, beginning with Huldrych Zwingli's *Sixty-Seven Articles* (1523), articles XXXV–XLIII, for which see *Reformed Confessions of the Sixteenth Century*, 40–41.

[10] Bullinger, "Of the Holy Catholic Church," 316.

[11] *Heidelberg Catechism* (1563), questions 31–32, in *Reformed Confessions of the Sixteenth Century*, 310.

[12] Karl Barth, *Church Dogmatics*, 4 vols. in 13 parts, edited by G. W. Bromiley and T. F. Torrance (Edinburgh: T&T Clark, 1956–1975), vol. IV/3, especially §§71–72.

light, and in thy light shall we see light'.... God reveals himself by his own Spirit, and we cannot learn of him without his Spirit."[13] This spiritual illumination not only effects understanding of the scriptural Word, but does so by energizing an effectual ecclesial authority. The Pastoral Epistles are regularly cited by Reformed theologians in this regard: "By the Holy Spirit who dwells within us, guard the good deposit entrusted to you" (2 Tim. 1:14). The Spirit applies the objective Word of Christ to the church's common mind, in this case enabling and empowering vital pastoral protection of the "good deposit" or Christian confession of faith.

The nature of confessions has been located by Reformed theology in the economy of the Gospel. They serve as auxiliaries – spiritual yet subordinate – to point the congregation to the Word of God. They function ministerially, then, on behalf of that magisterial Messiah who is alone Lord of the church. In so doing they are called to an expository task: to show that their judgments derive from the testimony of the prophets and apostles. They bind in as much as they echo and extend those scriptural words of life. Yet these qualifications characterize and in no way nullify the vital place of confessions within the life of the Christian community. By the Word of Christ and the illumination of the Spirit, they do serve as authorized witnesses to guide the church's own witness and worship.

THEOLOGY OF THE CONFESSIONS: THE CONFESSIONAL CONSENSUS

The classical Reformed churches offered fresh reflection on the nature and function of Christian confessions by locating them within the divine economy of grace. We do well now to consider their material content: What did they confess? How did they confess it? We shall consider some key themes to see where the catholic consensus was maintained and where reform was pronounced according to God's Word.

Holy Scripture and divine revelation
The most notable feature of Reformed confessions remains their very first feature. Unlike previous ecclesiastical pronouncements, early Reformed confessions such as the Ten Theses of Berne begin with methodological

---

[13] Huldrych Zwingli, "On the Clarity and Certainty of the Word of God," in *Zwingli and Bullinger*, 78, 82.

claims about Holy Scripture. Later national confessions – such as the French Confession (1559), the Belgic Confession (1561), and eventually the Westminster Confession of Faith (1647) – would also begin with attention to bibliology. In so doing, of course, the confessions are not making pre-theological statements about intellectual method. They are offering prolegomena, but only as derived from the economy of grace and expressed in the voice of a confession or profession of faith. The prolegomenal statements of the Reformed confessions regarding Holy Scripture (and, at least in the case of the French and Belgic Confessions, regarding general revelation as well) are themselves theological claims expressed on the basis of biblical teaching affirmed in faith, rather than some purportedly objective claims accessed by reason alone.

A distinction might be observed between the approach of classical Reformed confessions regarding divine self-revelation and the approach found in perhaps the most famous of twentieth-century confessions, the Theological Declaration of Barmen (1934). Over against the Nazi claim that National Socialism represented divine revelation, Barmen confessed that "Jesus Christ, as he is attested for us in Holy Scripture, is the one Word of God which we have to hear and which we have to trust and obey in life and in death."[14] Written almost entirely by Karl Barth, this confession represents a stern rebuke to the idea of general revelation. It is worth noting, of course, that classical Reformed confessions regularly affirmed general revelation, nowhere opposed it, and sometimes assumed it. Barth (in)famously debated with Emil Brunner about the presence of natural theology in the writings of Calvin; whatever the merits of their constructive arguments, it is clear that Brunner was right about Calvin, and that the case could be furthered to note that the Reformed tradition more broadly had consistently affirmed the place of natural theology or general revelation. For example, both the French Confession and Belgic Confession give explicit mention to natural revelation in between their opening confession regarding Scripture and their affirmation of the triune character of God.

Catholic orthodoxy on God and Christ

By and large, Reformed confessions have seen fit to speak with economy regarding the doctrine of the Trinity and the doctrine of the incarnation. Many early confessions do not deal with the doctrine

---

[14] *Theological Declaration of Barmen* (1934), article 1, in *Reformed Confessions of the Sixteenth Century*, 332.

of God at all, inasmuch as they were more polemically bounded (for example, the Sixty-Seven Articles, the Ten Theses of Berne, or the Tetrapolitan Confession). Later confessions would explicitly affirm what had been previously confessed by Nicaea and Chalcedon, as in the case of the French Confession, Belgic Confession, and Thirty-Nine Articles (1563). Eventually the Westminster Confession of Faith (1647) would include a lengthy confession of the divine attributes, drawing on classical catholic theism, as well as the doctrine of the triunity of the Godhead.[15] As noted by a host of anecdotal observations along the way, Reformed theologians had no desire to modify catholic teaching on the doctrine of God.

Herman Bavinck would later perceive something that he called "Calvinism," but that we might more actually describe as the classical Reformed confessional tradition (including not only Calvinian but also other tributaries and streams). Concerning this, Bavinck writes: "The root principle of this Calvinism is the confession of God's absolute sovereignty. Not one special attribute of God, for instance His love or justice, His holiness or equity, but God Himself as such in the unity of all His attributes and perfection of His entire Being is the point of departure for the thinking and acting of the Calvinist." Indeed Bavinck went so far as to say that "from this root principle everything that is specifically Reformed may be derived and explained."[16] The doctrine of God is not itself unique, but the thoroughgoing application of the doctrine of God is distinctive. Bavinck traced its influence into the distinction between Creator and creature, the singular authority of the Bible, the sole sufficiency of Christ, the power of grace, the distinction of Christ's two natures, the distinction of external and internal calling, the distinction between the sacramental sign and the thing signified, as well as host of other issues.

Reformed Christology developed the Nicene and Chalcedonian tradition in two notable ways. First, an emphasis on Christ's fulfillment of particular Old Testament offices was highlighted. Reformed confessions

---

[15] *Westminster Confession of Faith* (1647), chapter II, in *The Confession of Faith*, 24–27.

[16] Herman Bavinck, "The Future of Calvinism," *The Presbyterian and Reformed Review* 5, no. 17 (January 1894), 3–4. Bavinck does not mean by "root principle" a "central dogma" from which all other theological claims may be deduced logically (as in the claims of others such as A. Schweizer, F. C. Baur, and W. Gass, and as critiqued historiographically by the likes of Richard A. Muller), for he identifies this "root principle" with the sum total of divine attributes rather than one divine action or characteristic.

and catechisms spoke regularly of the threefold office (*munus triplex*) of the Messiah. The Heidelberg Catechism (1563) illustrates this approach:

Q. 31. *Why is he called CHRIST, that is, the ANOINTED ONE?*

A. Because he is ordained by God the Father and anointed with the Holy Spirit to be *our chief Prophet and Teacher*, fully revealing to us the secret purpose and will of God concerning our redemption; to be *our only High Priest*, having redeemed us by the one sacrifice of his body and ever interceding for us with the Father; and to be *our eternal King*, governing us by his Word and Spirit, and defending and sustaining us in the redemption he has won for us.[17]

The catechism suggests that the messianic identity of the incarnate Son must be determinative for our understanding of his work. His life, death, and resurrection must be viewed through the lens of messianic categories drawn from Israel's Scriptures. This emphasis on the threefold office, and its attendant insistence to read Christ in light of the tutorial found in God's promises to Israel, became a mainstay in later Reformed confessional writings.

A second Christological development was an insistence that the human nature of the incarnate Son be treated with full integrity as perfectly human. In other words, there was opposition to any divinizing of that nature that might morph it into something other than authentic creaturely existence; indeed, the Reformed were the first to insist that the Son was Mediator according to both natures (not just his human nature). This general approach to Christology manifested itself in controversies regarding the presence of the Son in the Lord's supper, wherein Reformed confessions insisted that the human Jesus could not be present in more than one place at any given moment (for single local presence was viewed as essential to human existence) over against the doctrine of ubiquity (or what we might call simultaneous, multiple local presences) which shaped the Lutheran doctrine of consubstantiation. Yet this approach to Christ's humanity had wider application than eucharistic controversy. It affected the doctrine of the atonement, in reference to which Calvin famously affirmed that "from the time he took on the form of a servant, he began to pay the price of liberation in order to redeem us."[18] With regard to both of these Christological developments – the threefold office and the humanity of Christ – the Reformed

---

[17] *Heidelberg Catechism* (1563), question 31, in *Reformed Confessions of the Sixteenth Century*, 310.
[18] Calvin, *Institutes*, II.xvi.5.

confessions were prompting an appreciation of the historical nature of God's economy. Whether in the patient preparation for the Messiah's work in the ministry of kings, priests, and prophets of old, or in the lifelong work of atonement offered by the incarnate Son, the Reformed confessions sought to emphasize the pace of God's promises and their realization.

Covenant

In a matter not unrelated to these historical developments regarding Reformed Christology, the doctrine of the covenant attained higher prestige in the Reformed tradition than it had ever possessed henceforth. Its importance owed much to two major factors. First, the terminology of covenant was emphasized as a result of the return to primary sources inspired by the humanist movement and, by extension, as a result of the biblical frequency of discussing covenants throughout the course of the Scriptures. This careful textual study prompted affirmation that communion with God takes various forms dependent on historical location. Second, the terminology of covenant was employed as a rubric under which the connections between the Old and New Testaments might be explored, particularly in ecclesiastical debate with the Roman Catholic Church and the Anabaptist movement. Whereas Reformed churches viewed Rome as failing to note the newness of our current covenantal reality, they simultaneously viewed the Anabaptists as threatening a complete separation of the New from the Old.

The doctrine of the covenant attained its fullest expression in the Westminster Standards, wherein the so-called "federal theology" finally found confessional attestation. This movement toward organizing the communion of God and humanity into various covenantal administrations had begun in the mid-sixteenth century (initially in the work of Bullinger). And it developed before too long into the form of federal theology wherein all human interaction with God was distinguished into two paradigmatic covenants, that administration most frequently referred to as the "covenant of works" and that known commonly as the "covenant of grace." While this bicovenantal hermeneutic was developed by the 1560s in the work of Caspar Olevian and others, Westminster was the first occasion wherein it became a structuring principle of a Reformed confession.[19]

---

[19] See *Westminster Confession of Faith* (1647), chapter VII, in *The Confession of Faith*, 41–45.

The Christian life and the order of salvation

Reformed confessions of the sixteenth and seventeenth centuries greatly expanded the attention given to the Christian life. They typically did so under the banner of what is now termed the "order of salvation" (*ordo salutis*), the scope and sequence of acts and events wherein the work of Christ's redemption accomplished in the Gospel history of salvation (*historia salutis*) would be applied to particular men and women. Reform had been caused in the early sixteenth century largely because of lay anxiety about their standing before God. Lay participation in holy communion, for example, had flagged greatly in the late medieval period because of unease regarding fitness for reception of the elements. Luther and other Reformers sought to bolster the nature of Christian faith by returning to the laity genuine assurance of salvation in Jesus Christ.

The first emphasis of confessional theology was the distinction between justification and sanctification. Both benefits were given in union with Christ, but this "double grace" (*duplex gratia*, a term introduced by Calvin with great effect and wide influence) was truly twofold: Christ brought forgiveness before God, and he renewed the members of his body after the image of God. This distinction stood over against the Roman Catholic approach, wherein renewal in virtue related to one's standing before God as a material ground and basis for justification. By affirming a logical distinction and order – justification and sanctification enjoyed at the same time temporally, but always in a logical sequence whereby justification precedes sanctification – the confessions furthered a newfound assurance that one could know God's fatherly favor as a son or daughter adopted in Christ.

Justification was confessed to occur in Christ alone and to be received by faith alone. Key distinctions were intended in each statement. First, justification's basis was wholly in Christ, not in the believer's own self or doing. It was the bearing of the curse and the obeying of the Law (both accomplished in Jesus' own life and death) that provided the material basis for one's standing before the Almighty Judge. Causal language drawn from the Aristotelian tradition was often employed to note the way in which the action of both Christ and the Christian action relates to justification. While Christ was the material cause, the Christian's faith was nonetheless an instrumental cause, whereby the man or woman is united to Christ by faith. Again, a distinction is intended. Reformed confessions argue that the apostle Paul juxtaposes the way of faith with the law of works: while Paul was focused primarily on specifically Jewish forms of Torah observance, the Reformed theologians of the sixteenth century followed Luther, Zwingli, and others in seeing that Paul's juxtaposition would surely rule out any other human actions (if obedience of the best sort – in observance of divinely rendered commands – was not acceptable before the bar of divine justice). The claim that justification was "by faith alone" (*sola fide*) attested the unique role played by Christian faith, then, as the instrumental cause whereby the Christian was bound to and participated in Christ's person and work.

The distinction between justification and sanctification, and the insistence that justification was wholly on the basis of Christ's work alone and received only by faith, were not intended in any way to undercut or lessen the gravity and reach of Christian moral transformation. The doctrine of sanctification was another facet of the Gospel, whereby God not only offered pardon from sin but also removed the power of indwelling sin throughout the life of the Christian. Early Reformed confessions made a strong point of arguing that sanctification involved the grace-empowered fulfillment of God's Law, and that mere "human traditions" were not binding upon either ordained pastors or the laity. Indeed, this term becomes a technical term for the confessions and the early Reformed dogmatic tradition: "human traditions" are those unfortunate ecclesiastical developments which purport to carry churchly authority yet lack biblical warrant.[20] For example, Zwingli's Sixty-Seven Articles of 1523 says that "in the Gospel we learn that human doctrines and traditions are of no avail to salvation"; the First Helvetic Confession of 1536 says that "we regard all other human doctrines and articles which lead us away from God and true faith as vain and ineffectual"; and the Geneva Confession of 1536 says that "all laws and regulations made binding on conscience which oblige the faithful to things not commanded by God, or establish another service of God than that which he demands" are human traditions and "perverse doctrines of Satan."[21]

In so doing these confessions opposed the way in which late medieval piety had supplemented biblical teaching with many religious traditions that were frequently viewed as essential to the Christian life. Developing an emphasis that had begun with Martin Luther's 1521 treatise *The Freedom of a Christian*, the Reformed tradition would go still

---

[20] "Human traditions" are juxtaposed with "divine traditions" in this technical terminology (see *The Tetrapolitan Confession* (1530), chapter 14, in *Reformed Confessions of the Sixteenth Century*, 71–72).

[21] *Zwingli's Sixty-Seven Articles* (1523), article 17, in *Reformed Confessions of the Sixteenth Century*, 37; *The First Helvetic Confession* (1536), chapter 4, in *Reformed Confessions of the Sixteenth Century*, 101; and *The Geneva Confession* (1536), chapter 17, in *Reformed Confessions of the Sixteenth Century*, 124.

further and note that the church could not bind consciences unless moral or liturgical directives were taught in Holy Scripture. The Westminster Confession of Faith codifies this concern for liberty of conscience in its twentieth chapter, "Of Christian Liberty, and Liberty of Conscience."[22] Yet this liberty from human devices was in no way a warrant for antinomianism, as Westminster and the other Reformed confessions insisted that God's moral law continued to bind the conscience.[23] The confessions insisted that holiness was to be defined by God alone, through the auxiliaries of his prophetic and apostolic Scriptures, but that it continued to be given and demanded by him, even of those who are justified in Christ Jesus.

Predestination eventually rose to the surface as a confessional issue. While it was affirmed earlier in most confessions and catechisms, it was because of the Arminian crisis of the early seventeenth century that the Reformed churches felt compelled to testify clearly to their Augustinian approach to the doctrine of election. While "Freedom of Choice" was addressed as early as the First Helvetic Confession of 1536,[24] divine sovereignty and divine predestination/election were only objects of discrete reference later, as in the 1559 French Confession of Faith (articles VIII and XII, respectively).[25] Even in the earliest confessions of divine predestination, this election was defined as occurring apart from works and unto redemption in Jesus Christ by faith. Typically confessions have employed different language to speak of predestination and reprobation (which is certainly attested, but often with the language of "leaving the rest" or of "permission"), suggesting that the way in which God wills redemption is not identical to the manner in which God determines the eternal penal judgment of the reprobate.[26]

The followers of Jacobus Arminius (1560–1609), led most notably by Simon Episcopius (1583–1643), raised a host of objections to this

---

[22] *Westminster Confession of Faith* (1647), chapter XX, in *The Confession of Faith*, 84–89.

[23] Ibid., chapter XIX.5–7, in *The Confession of Faith*, 82–84.

[24] *First Helvetic Confession* (1536), chapter 10, in *Reformed Confessions of the Sixteenth Century*, 102–103.

[25] *French Confession of Faith* (1559), articles VIII and XII, in *Reformed Confessions of the Sixteenth Century*, 147 and 148.

[26] For example, see *French Confession of Faith* (1559), article XII in *Reformed Confessions of the Sixteenth Century*, 148: "God ... calleth those whom he hath chosen ... leaving the rest in this same corruption and condemnation." Later, the *Westminster Confession of Faith* (1647), chapter V.4, qualifies the language of permission by noting that God's action in this regard cannot be construed as "not by a bare permission," that is, in the same way as a creature would permit something (in *The Confession of Faith*, 35–36).

confessional teaching in the early seventeenth century that began to run under the name of "Remonstrant" theology. The National Synod of Dordrecht (Dort) (1618–1619) was convened in the Netherlands and gathered an international fraternity of Reformed theologians to offer response through its Canons. The Synod not only opposed the Remonstrants but also responded by adopting the Three Forms of Unity as confessional standards of its theological position: not only the Belgic Confession and the Heidelberg Catechism but also the newly penned Canons of Dort. The work of the Synod of Dort not only drew upon an international collaboration of delegates from the European continent and the British Isles, but also led to international consensus thereafter, as its approach to matters such as original sin, divine predestination, effectual calling, and assurance of salvation would be shared by later confessional texts such as the Westminster Standards and the Helvetic Consensus Formula (the latter adopted in Swiss cities between 1675 and 1678). Some debate continued regarding how specific Reformed churches should be in regarding the extent of the atonement: while no church favored the Arminian viewpoint (of a purely universal extent), debate remained as to whether or not the "hypothetical universalism" of Moses Amyraut, John Cameron, and others should be allowed within the pale of Reformed orthodoxy. Churches rallied behind the teaching that the atoning work of Christ had both infinite value and limited application to the elect; debate nonetheless swirled around whether one should say that in some way it had universal extent.

Church, worship, and sacraments

The Reformed confessions address ecclesiastical and liturgical matters head on; indeed, one might say that basic to the entire Reformation movement of the sixteenth century was a concern to reform worship practices and their underlying church structures along more biblical lines. The ancient cry *lex orandi, lex credendi* ("the law of prayer is the law of faith") surely applies in this time frame, as Protestant theology developed in wide scope and great detail, always tethered tightly to lived expressions of worship and forms of devotional piety.

Confessional affirmations explicitly address the nature of the church. Going beyond the supposedly apostolic identification of "the holy, catholic church, the communion of saints" as the locus of God's work and the later Nicene description of that church as "one, holy, catholic, and apostolic," the Reformed confessions also speak of two key distinctions. First, the church has both a visible and an invisible reality: its spiritual composition only imperfectly but nonetheless really finds expression in the concrete and historical community of the people of God. Second, the church is located amidst true and false churches, that is, various communions either were or were not genuine expressions of the invisible church's valid historical expression. Confessions went still further, noting that churches could be "more or less pure" in this age where even the beloved children of God are still marked by sin.

Attention to the nature of the church leads to consideration of the shape of that church's worship. Reformed confessions espouse what is called the "regulative principle" of worship, whereby worship is meant to be ruled or regulated by God's scriptural exhortations. Churches must include biblical elements in their worship, and they may not include either activities precluded by the biblical writings or matters left unaddressed by the scriptural authors. This hermeneutical approach to worship was shaped by a number of biblical passages that suggest that God cares not only about the subjective manner of worship, but also about the objective form of worship (for example, the judgment of Nadab and Abihu in Leviticus 10; the second commandment in Exodus 20).

Central to Reformed worship, then, would be the reading and preaching of God's Word. Many Reformed confessions noted that the preaching of the Word of God was itself the Word of God, a genuine means of grace. Accompanying the spoken Word would be the visible Word of God – the sacraments – administered according to the institution of Christ. As the Heidelberg Catechism would define sacraments, "They are visible holy signs and seals, instituted by God, so that by our use of them, he might make us understand the promise of the Gospel better and seal it. This promise of the Gospel is that because of Christ's one sacrifice finished on the cross, he will grant us by grace forgiveness of sins and eternal life."[27] And only those practices instituted by Christ himself would be continued as sacraments for the whole church: to Rome's seven, the Reformed posited only two sacraments.

Baptism, whether of adult converts or of the children of believers, was meant to serve as an initiating rite that symbolized and sealed persons as members of Christ. The Lord's supper or holy communion

---

[27] *Heidelberg Catechism* (1563), question 66, in *Reformed Confessions of the Sixteenth Century*, 316. Note that the language "make us understand ... and seal" is especially refined, drawn from Melanchthon's *Loci Communes* (1521), Zacharias Ursinus's *Catechismus Minor*, Heinrich Bullinger's *Catechismus*, and Calvin's *Genevan Catechism* (1545) – as observed by Lyle D. Bierma, *The Doctrine of the Sacraments in the Heidelberg Catechism: Melanchthonian, Calvinist, or Zwinglian?* (Studies in Reformed Theology and History NS 4; Princeton, NJ: Princeton Theological Seminary, 1999), 11–12.

was practiced as an ongoing sacrament wherein believers commune or fellowship spiritually with the incarnate Son and, by extension, with one another in the remembrance of his passion. The Reformed confessions were consistently fixed upon an approach to the sacrament that referenced some notion of Christ's spiritual presence, either "symbolic parallelism" or "symbolic instrumentalism" as described by historian Brian Gerrish.[28] While confessions varied somewhat in expressing this communion and the symbolic functionality of the Lord's presence, all were committed to expressing both facets of the sacrament, as a sign and a seal of God's favor.

In summary, then, Reformed confessions in the sixteenth and seventeenth centuries were envisioned as serving a fundamental role as an authority subservient to God's scriptural Word and formative of God's ecclesial community. To that end, they focused on practical applications of dogmatic issues, in particular regarding the use of Holy Scripture, the worship and sacraments of the church, and the Christian life. While they were plentiful in number and diverse in expression, they both then and still now represent a largely cohesive vision of catholic orthodoxy that is reformed according to certain scriptural principles regarding God and his relations to his creation. Of course, Reformed confessing continues, and with it various debates arise: whether to continue to employ sixteenth- or seventeenth-century symbols (either the Three Forms of Unity or the Westminster Standards) or to compose new accredited statements of faith; what precisely is involved judicially in such statements (old or new) binding churches and their officers; and how such confessional statements and their judicial function (however construed) may be related to the actual practice of ministry. These ongoing, and frequently feisty, debates only further manifest the centrality of confession in the Reformed tradition.

Further reading

Allen, Michael. "Confessions and Authority." In *Reformed Theology*. Doing Theology. London: T&T Clark, 2010: 133–155.

Bucer, Martin. "*De Regno Christi*." In *Melanchthon and Bucer*. Edited by Wilhelm Pauck. Library of Christian Classics. Louisville, KY: Westminster John Knox, 2006: 175–225.

[28] Brian Gerrish, "Sign and Reality: The Lord's Supper in the Reformed Confessions," in *The Old Protestantism and the New* (Chicago: University of Chicago Press, 1982), 118–130.

Cochrane, Arthur C. (ed.). *Reformed Confessions of the Sixteenth Century.* Louisville, KY: Westminster John Knox, 2003.

Dennison, James T. Jr. (ed.). *Reformed Confessions of the Sixteenth and Seventeenth Centuries in English Translation.* 4 vols.; Grand Rapids, MI: Reformation Heritage Books, 2008–2014.

McCormack, Bruce L. "The End of Reformed Theology? The Voice of Karl Barth in the Doctrinal Chaos of the Present." In *Reformed Theology: Identity and Ecumenicity.* Edited by Wallace Alston and Michael Welker. Grand Rapids, MI: Eerdmans, 2003: 46–64.

Muller, Richard A. "Reformed Confessions and Catechisms." In *The Dictionary of Historical Theology.* Edited by Trevor Hart. Grand Rapids, MI: Eerdmans, 2000: 466–485.

Rohls, Jan. *Reformed Confessions: From Zurich to Barmen.* Translated by John F. Hoffmeyer. Columbia Series in Reformed Theology. Louisville, KY: Westminster John Knox, 1998.

Vischer, Lukas (ed.). *Reformed Witness Today: A Collection of Confessions and Statements of Faith Issued By Reformed Churches.* Veröffentlichung/ Evangelische Arbeitsstelle Oekumene Schweiz; Nr. L. Bern: Evangelische Arbeitsstelle Oekumene Schweiz, 1982.

Webster, John. "Confession and Confessions." In *Nicene Christianity: The Future for a New Ecumenism.* Edited by Christopher R. Seitz. Grand Rapids, MI: Brazos, 2001: 119–132.

4 Election

RINSE H. REELING BROUWER

Within the whole of catholic Christianity the stress upon the topic of election in Reformed theology represents something of a minority emphasis. Nevertheless it is not heretical, because it can be seen as a new interpretation of major assertions on the part of Augustine in the last decades of his theological development. And, at least in the western church, it was never seen to be appropriate explicitly to distance oneself from this Church Father.

In his radical re-reading of the apostle Paul during his struggle with Pelagius and his adherents (397–429), Augustine advanced a number of significant arguments: that faith is not a capability of ourselves, but completely a divine gift ('what do you have that you did not receive?', 1 Cor. 4:7); that the cause of our will and ability to do good can only be found in God ('For it is God who works in you to will and to act according to his good pleasure', Phil. 2:13); and finally that predestination involves the divine preparation of the gift of grace for the elect, not because they believed but in order that they will believe (Rom. 9). During the reign of the Carolingians the monk Gottschalk went as far as to teach a double predestination, that is to say, to teach that there was a divine decision also in respect of the condemned – an issue on which Augustine had been silent. Initially Gottschalk was spontaneously condemned by his archbishop (848). In the debates following, however, it quickly became clear that it would not be so easy for the church to distance itself from its Augustinian heritage.

In the fourteenth century the magister and Augustinian hermit Gregory of Rimini (†1358), who as a representative of the *via moderna* was less interested in the divine essence than in the will of the personal God, recognized the danger that the voluntarism of the age could lead to a new Pelagianism. Before him Thomas Bradwardine, archbishop of Canterbury (†1349), had given similar warning, but that time from the point of view of the *via antiqua*. In his commentary on several distinctions in the first and second books of the *Libri Sententiarum* by

Peter Lombard (on the attributes of God, and on sin and grace respectively), Gregory carefully traced and revived the Augustinian argument together with its implications.[1] This respected scholar can be shown to have had an influence on Martin Luther (especially on the Leipzig Disputation with Eck of 1519), although explicit proof of a similar influence on John Calvin has so far not been forthcoming. We now turn to some of Calvin's major texts on the topic.

JOHN CALVIN ON ELECTION AND PREDESTINATION

The *Institutes* (1539 and 1559)

Taking refuge in Strasbourg after being forced to leave Geneva, Calvin found the opportunity to edit a second edition of his earlier great catechism, the *Institutes of the Christian Religion*. Under the influence of conversations with Martin Bucer, the Reformer of the city, and of his lectures on Paul's Epistle to the Romans, Calvin treated the doctrine of predestination separately in this new edition (it had been an aspect of the *credo ecclesiam* in the explanation of the Creed in the first edition of 1536).

At the beginning of the seventh chapter of this second edition of 1539, the author looks back at the first six chapters of the work as a *summa doctrinae*, as setting forth the essence of doctrine.[2] In several additional chapters Calvin now proposes to highlight different aspects of that doctrine. The chapters 'Similarity and Difference between the Old and the New Testament' (chapter 7) and 'Predestination and Providence of God' (chapter 8) are interconnected. From the beginning of the world there has been one doctrine by which God saves people and invites them into his covenant (chapter 7). Unfortunately experience tells us that not all people hear the preaching of the covenant of life, and not all who hear its call respond to it. This happens because God gives salvation only to the elect (chapter 8).

The order predestination, then providence is remarkable. In the Aristotelian-scholastic tradition predestination was seen as a part of providence: the more general care of God for the world becomes particularised in God's care for the elect. But Calvin reverses this reasoning. He first focuses his attention on God's goodwill for his people, and only

---

[1] Heiko A. Oberman, *The Dawn of the Reformation. Essays in Late Medieval and Early Reformational Thought* (Grand Rapids, MI: Eerdmans, 1992), 8–12.

[2] Frans H. Breukelman, *The Structure of Sacred Doctrine in Calvin's Theology*, edited by Rinse H. Reeling Brouwer and translated by Martin Kessler (Grand Rapids, MI: William B. Eerdmans, 2010), 118.

after that explains how this people will experience the general care of God for the world. For Huldrych Zwingli providence as the main aspect of the doctrine of God had a central place in his theology, perhaps as important as the place of grace in that of Luther. Although Calvin never denies its importance, it is at the same time a doctrine of secondary rank, for its general point of view must be seen in light of the particularity and primacy of election.

In the final edition of the *Institutes of the Christian Religion* (1559), the shape of the whole of the work underwent a major revision. The order of the Apostle's Creed was now the guiding principle. In this connection the previous chapter on 'Predestination and Providence' was taken apart. Providence became the conclusion of Book I on God the Creator, whereby its origin in the particular care of God became less apparent. Predestination then became a topic towards the end of Book III, on the Holy Spirit.[3] After describing the life of the Christian as a life of faith, that is, as a life of repentance, self-denial and bearing the cross, Calvin also depicts it as a life in which a godless person is justified by grace and therefore lives a life of freedom and boldness, having access to the divine heart through prayer: it is a life anchored in eternity as the life of the eternally elect under the rule of free grace, in the expectation of the Last Judgement and in the hope of eternal life. Therefore, predestination provides the highest eschatological ground for the person who receives the Gospel of grace.

In the actual text on the topic we do not find many additions to the text of 1539. The loss of the connection with the chapter on the covenant (a doctrine that is now located in the second Book) causes some lack of clarity. For how can one speak of the election of a people, primarily the people of Israel, when election as well as rejection are both thought of as divine decisions regarding individuals within the people? This question does not appear to have been resolved.

Writings in the context of the Bolsec affair of 1551

In the *Institutes*, Calvin stresses the double decision of God: the destiny of those rejected cannot be found outside the eternal will of God. In Geneva it was Jérôme Bolsec, who, having established himself as a physician there, had the imprudence to visit a *congrégation* (a public Bible-reading) and to accuse Calvin of making God the author of sin

---

[3] John Calvin, *Institutes of the Christian Religion*, edited by John T. McNeill and translated by Ford Lewis Battles (Library of Christian Classics; 2 vols.; Philadelphia: Westminster, 1960), III.xxi–xxiv.

through this doctrine of double predestination. Because of the close co-operation (in spite of their tensions) between the civil authorities and the ministers, Bolsec was arrested and condemned. In that context, however, Calvin felt obliged to answer Bolsec's accusations on multiple levels, the level of scholarly debate and the level of parish sorrows. On the first level he now finally wrote the continuation of his answer to the attacks on Reformation doctrine by Albert Pighius of Kampen, a skilled scholastic theologian who had enjoyed connections in the circles of several popes until he passed away in 1542. Pighius had chosen two fields of debate in Reformation theology, which were in effect two sides of the same coin: the teaching on the bondage of the will and the doctrine of grace. Calvin had responded on the first point in 1543, and now he published the sequel on the second point under the title *Concerning the Eternal Predestination*. The connection of the two points is significant. When in the anthropological field the will is not able to honour God as God, it is important on the theological level to stress that this is possible only thanks to the gracious will of God, in that God proves his love to his people by the gift of grace and by the gift of faith, through which they are able to receive grace. The human subject who is tempted by the devil and by doubt receives relief when the preaching of justification is heard, but now, moreover, and 'higher' than that, the human subject also appears to be saved in the divine heart of the father. That, for Calvin, is the essence of what he means by eternal election. It is remarkable to note in passing that the combination of predestination and the denial of free will can also be found in the Renaissance philosophy of Lorenzo Valla. But there it serves a rigid, neo-Stoic, deterministic system. Calvin does not distance himself from Valla, but differs importantly from him in stressing the divine freedom within the eternal counsel: the mercy of God is undeserved, and the fact that God does not give this mercy to all people serves as a comparison (!) to illustrate this undeservedness.[4] Unfortunately in Calvin there is a tendency to confuse this mere comparison with the *res* (matter) of the merciful divine freedom itself.

In the parish of Geneva Calvin also resisted the attacks of Bolsec in a pastoral context, in the *congrégation* of 18 December, 1551. The main emphasis in his presentation is the invitation to those who believe to be grateful. When they become introspective and reflect upon the divine grace towards them granted in Christ their head as in a mirror, they will acknowledge that they have been saved from damnation even though they too are descendants of the fallen Adam. Indeed in the following years the

---

[4] Ibid., III.xxi.1.

emphasis in Calvin's preaching on election comes to lie increasingly on consolation. These were years of growing tensions in France between the Huguenots and the authorities who were connected to the old church. In this connection Heiko Oberman speaks of a new experience that encouraged the doctrine – the political context of exile: 'The Calvinist doctrine of predestination is the mighty bulwark of the Christian faithful against the fear that they will be unable to hold out against the pressure of persecution. Election is the Gospel's encouragement to those who have faith, not a message of doom for those who lack it.'[5]

THE LOCATION OF PREDESTINATION AFTER THE DOCTRINE OF GOD IN REFORMED ORTHODOXY

The Reformed tradition is multi-centred, and hence the way Reformed doctrine was shaped is also far from uniform. Nevertheless, at the end of the sixteenth century a certain codification in the scholarly systematic *Compendia, Syntagmae, Institutiones* and so on can be found. Thus one can observe that not in all yet in most of such works the locus of predestination finds its place just after the doctrine of God. In the older literature (e.g., Brian Armstrong) one sometimes comes across the criticism that this would be a dangerous deviation from the conviction of Calvin. Now it is certainly true, as we saw previously, that Calvin never placed election in this context and that his final placement of it was in the context of the appropriation of the work of Christ in the Spirit. It is also true that the development of a doctrine of God in Calvin was intentionally defective: repeatedly he warns against any idle reflection on the mysteries of the counsel of God. But one can also say that being silent on a topic has its own danger, for what happens with questions that remain unanswered? Later Reformed orthodoxy had the courage not to let such hesitations have the last word. But then one must ask: What statements did it dare make in this dangerous field?

The doctrine of God was often followed by a locus on the decrees of God, and amongst these decrees predestination had an important place. Johannes Wollebius, the Basel theologian who wrote his popular *Compendium* at the beginning of the seventeenth century, provides the following definition: 'Immanent or internally directed are those works which occur within God's essence; to these belong the divine decrees.'[6]

---

[5]   Heiko A. Oberman, *The Two Reformations: The Journey from the Last Days to the New World* (New Haven: Yale University Press, 2003), 114.

[6]   Johannes Wollebius, *Compendium Theologiae Christianae* (Amsterdam, 1655), III, §2.

Because of the divine simplicity, however, there exists only one decree of God, namely 'an internal action of the divine will, by which He from eternity has in complete freedom determined which things would happen within the realm of time'.[7] One can become somewhat annoyed with this metaphor of a decree, which can easily be associated with dictatorial rule – indeed, Calvin on his part tried to avoid this metaphor. But one can also admire how this kind of reasoning (already present in some later medieval scholastics) intervenes in the reign of classical metaphysics. For speaking in this way God is sketched not as an absolutely simple and immovable highest Being, but as a living God, who precisely in his essence is moved by the inner grounds within himself for the sake of his relationship to the world in time outside of himself.

Now the doctrine of God consists of two main parts, which in the Ramistic didactical arrangement of many teachers of that time should be read as a parallel approach to the same entity: the triune God and God in his essence and attributes. Many Reformed scholars declared that God as the author of the decree of predestination should be conceived of as the undivided Trinity as a whole, whereas each of the three Persons has a particular role in initiating the divine act of discernment in humanity. Karl Barth found this pattern to be present already in Polanus (1609),[8] but Richard Muller has proven that it is found in many doctrinal works around 1600.[9] In other words, Christ is not only the mirror in which the eternal will of God may be recognised by the faithful. He is also the Subject of that divine will himself.

But is Christ also the first and prototype of the elect? This statement was much more difficult to maintain for these Reformed orthodox theologians. Of course they wanted to affirm election before the foundation of the world 'in him', as Eph. 1:4 intends. But there was a difficulty. Certainly Christ as Mediator in his two natures was the foundation of salvation, but his work of satisfaction should be seen as a means to fulfil a presupposition of the accomplishment of the decree: through this work, he acquired the elect who would glorify God as vessels of mercy (Rom. 9:23). But in this way his work only realizes a subordinate purpose, and it is inadmissible to invert the

---

[7] Wollebius, *Compendium*, III, §3.

[8] Karl Barth, *Church Dogmatics*, 4 vols. in 13 parts, edited by G. W. Bromiley and T. F. Torrance (Edinburgh: T&T Clark, 1956–1975), vol. II/2, 119.

[9] Richard A. Muller, *Christ and the Decree: Christology and Predestination in Reformed Theology from Calvin to Perkins* (Grand Rapids, MI: Baker Academic, 2008), 159.

main and subsidiary purposes of the divine decree. We find Reformed orthodox theologians from different generations –, such as Wollebius[10] and Francis Turretin[11] – arguing in exactly this way. Therefore one cannot say that in their systems predestination is a deductive principle. Rather, it was in a certain sense a separate truth, admittedly connected to central Christian doctrine, yet with its own value and with its own problematic nature.

CURRENTS, DISPUTES AND CONFESSIONAL DIFFERENCES IN THE SEVENTEENTH CENTURY

The Arminians and the Synod of Dort

Jacobus Arminius, professor in Leiden, was well-educated in Reformed theology. However, questions arose in his mind that were comparable to those of Bolsec or the earlier Dutch humanist Coornhert. According to the remarkable nineteenth-century analysis of H. Fr. Kohlbrugge, Arminius' objection was against the Reformation doctrine of justification: he considered the *sola gratia* to undermine the responsibility of the human being as the receiver of the Word of God. Arminius then succeeded in transposing the same objection to the field of the Calvinist double decree. But there it became clear that his main interest – as expressed, for example, in his statement in the States of Holland in 1608 – was to show that faith and obedience were human merits that had to be honoured by God Eternal. One might say: the fear of God as the author of sin had led him to a fear of God as the author of grace too. And thus the proper divine decision in the end had to follow the human situation, even though the former was made beforehand thanks to God's precognition of it.

The international Reformed Synod of Dordrecht (Dort) in 1618–1619, nine years after the death of Arminius himself, denounced the theses of his followers in an inductive way. The Synod stressed the character of faith as a gift of God (I.5), with its origin in a divine decree with two sides (I.6), defined as a decree of predestination for election as well as for

---

[10] Wollebius, *Compendium*, IV, §2.9.

[11] Francis Turretin, *Institutes of Elenctic Theology*, edited by James T. Dennison, Jr. and translated by George Musgrave Giger (Philipsburg, NJ: Presbyterian and Reformed Publishing Company, 1992), Fourth Topic, 'The Decrees of God in General and Predestination in Particular', question 10: 'Is Christ the cause and foundation of election? We deny', in vol. 1, 350–355.

rejection (I.7).[12] Thus the teaching of Calvin, albeit with some nuance, became dominant in the Reformed world in a confessional form.

The process leading up to the Synod had deeply shocked the whole of society in the young Republic of the United Netherlands. Initially the ruling class, immersed in the tradition of Erasmus and Coornhert, tried to protect the Arminians and to silence any public debate either through legal means or by force. In the end, by way of a coup d'état by Maurice of Nassau, the head of the army, the convocation of the Synod was enforced. For the image of Reformed orthodoxy as a conversation partner in public debate all over Europe, the outcome appeared not to be very helpful.

The Lutheran position

Many Lutherans had the feeling that their doctrine was condemned by the Synod of Dort as well. That is debatable but at the same time understandable. The Lutheran theologians of the seventeenth century had distanced themselves from the Luther of the dispute with Erasmus and had tried to steer a middle course between the absolutism of Calvin's Geneva and the new Pelagianism of the Arminians. To achieve this they made the following distinction. In the first place there is the universal benevolence of God towards the fallen human race. In this general will God has shown his intention in Christ that all people be saved. However, subsequently there is the special divine will, in which God takes into account the actual behaviour of each human being that God in his precognition has already foreseen, and determines that only the person who accepts the salvation offered and remains in it will be saved. Predestination – as well as rejection – is a result of this second, special divine will. It is not completely honest, nor is it completely surprising, that strict Reformed theologians discovered in such a doctrine little more than a vague compromise.

In the Leuenberg Concord of 1973, a series of (initially European) Lutheran and Reformed Churches revoked the main disagreements of former centuries, including those concerning predestination, in articles 24–26.[13] With Calvin the text of article 25 acknowledges: 'It is the experience of faith that the message of salvation is not accepted by all;

---

[12] *The Canons of Dort* (1618–19), in *The Three Forms of Unity* (Reformed Church in the United States, 2012).

[13] *Leuenberg Concord* (1973), articles 24–26, in *Konkordie Reformatorischer Kirchen in Europa*, edited by Michael Bunker and Martin Friedrich (Leipzig: Evangelische Verlagsanstalt, 2013).

yet faith respects the mystery of the action of God.' The next sentence reads: '[faith] bears witness at one and the same time to the seriousness of human decision and to the reality of God's universal purpose of salvation'.[14] This suggests that the orthodox confessors of Dort on the one hand, and the Arminian heretics on the other, erroneously made God and humanity into opponents. In addition the Lutheran category of the 'universal divine benevolence' is adopted. The last sentence sounds rather resolute: 'The witness of the scriptures to Christ forbids us from supposing that God has uttered an eternal decree condemning for all time specific individuals or a whole people.'[15] In addition, article 18 – on the Lord's supper – also denies any division into two classes of people (that is, the elect and the rejected) in an actualistic way, by declaring: 'Faith receives the Lord's Supper for salvation, unfaith for judgement.'[16] Reformed churches which had granted a confessional status to the first Canon of Dort in effect revoked that acknowledgement by signing the Leuenberg Concord. However, not even this Concord necessarily implies that the theological problems behind the debates of past ages have been resolved.

The Amyraut controversy

At the Huguenot Academy of Saumur several lines of thought were developed that created some commotion in the Reformed world. Because of a treatise that he had written on predestination, the scholar Moses Amyraut was nearly condemned at a trial in Alençon in 1637, but in the end he was acquitted.[17] Amyraut saw himself as a pupil of Calvin, one of the fathers of French Protestantism, in spite of the fact that the Reformed orthodox claimed Calvin for their own position. He particularly appealed to Calvin in his distinction between two wills of God, which he extended into a distinction between two covenants. On the one hand there is the universal sacrifice of Christ, which is universal in intention and scope, because God willed the salvation of all humanity, and this will was based on a hypothetical covenant. On the other hand there is the will of God to select a few people, and that will is based on an absolute covenant. However, in our experience the two covenants never meet, because of the hidden character of the absolute covenant; indeed,

---

[14] Ibid., article 25.

[15] Ibid., article 25.

[16] Ibid., article 18, in *Konkordie Reformatorischer Kirchen in Europa*.

[17] Brian G. Armstrong, *Calvinism and the Amyraut Heresy: Protestantism and Humanism in Seventeenth-Century France* (Madison: The University of Wisconsin Press, 1969), 88.

this absolute decree is so very mysterious that it is best simply to keep preaching the Gospel to all people. Thus whereas in Calvin the tensions in this teaching are always evident, Amyraut softens these with his view of a progression of the divine rule over time, connected with his view of the succession of the dominance of the different persons of the Trinity in history. A universal call goes out to all people based on the work of the Son, and only during the reign of the Spirit does it become clear who really belongs to Christ. In spite of his claim to be a pupil of Calvin, a new spirit from a new age can be seen here in Amyraut – the tendency to historicize.

Supra- and infralapsarianism

Who is the object of predestination?[18] Is it the human being not yet created or at least not yet fallen? This position is defended by those who ascend beyond the scope of the Fall (*supra lapsum*). Or is it the human being as fallen, but also as redeemed through Christ, either believing or unbelieving? This is defended by those who descend within the scope of the Fall (*infra lapsum*). The dispute over this question between Reformed theologians was seen as not fundamental and thus not disruptive to the unity of the church. Although Gomarus, the main opponent of Arminius, held to the supralapsarian view, the majority at the Synod of Dort did not follow him in this respect. Nevertheless, the Synod permitted the variant opinion. The strength of the infralapsarian view was based on the fact that it attended to the drama of history (the Fall of Adam and its consequences) and that it avoided a deductive reflection that took its starting point in eternity. In retrospect, however, its Achilles' heel is the presupposition of the historicity of the Fall. Of course the supralapsarians in the seventeenth century shared the same presupposition, but their approach was not dependent on it. Moreover, it is entirely conceivable to situate the drama of God's involvement with humanity at the heart of the eternal Trinitarian life, as the supralapsarians did.

Federal theology: Johannes Cocceius

From the beginning the topic of the covenant(s) of God with his people was important in Reformed tradition. It was especially developed in Zürich, Heidelberg, and among the puritans (notably in the Westminster Confession and Catechisms). Among the many theological proposals on this topic, that of Johannes Cocceius (1648, 1662) was particularly

---

[18] Cf. Turretin, *Institutes of Elenctic Theology*, Fourth Topic, question 9, in vol. 1, 341–350.

impressive. In the whole of his exegetical and systematic effort, and independently using the concepts of earlier thinkers, he presented a comprehensive overview that was Trinitarian in disposition. In paradise God offered his friendship to Adam and bound him with a contract. After Adam broke that contract, God the Father entered into an eternal pact or 'counsel of peace' (Zech. 6:13) with Christ as the second Adam: in that pact the Son promised to fulfil the obligations which the first man had failed to achieve. On his part the Father gave the elect to the Son as a reward. This was sealed by an eternal Testament in which the Father described the result of the inner Trinitarian transaction. Lastly, the Holy Spirit would work in the elect by bringing about regeneration, whereby they would become heirs of the divine treaty.

Initially Karl Barth was of the opinion that Coccejus identified the intra-Trinitarian 'counsel of peace' with the absolute decree of Reformed orthodoxy.[19] However, Willem van Asselt has proven that this is not correct.[20] For Coccejus predestination precedes the *pactum*. Thus in the treaty the Father gives the elect who were already known beforehand to the Son. The decision about the elect is therefore presupposed when the Son asks for those who are promised to him, and the Son is electing only as he executes his task of salvation. In this way the innovative federal theology of Coccejus does not undermine the decisions of Dort, and in his work the double decree remains the background of the dynamics of the history of the covenants.

Reformed pietism

We have seen how Amyraut held on to the idea of the public will of God – that all people should be saved – but tried to keep silent about the hidden will to elect only some. The tension caused by the doctrine of the two divine wills was thus softened as much as possible. In the pietistic circles of the Reformed world one can observe the opposite movement, namely an intensifying of this kind of tension. In theology, according to Turretin, a distinction is made between the divine will of decree, that is, the will of good purpose or the hidden will on the one hand, and the divine will of precept, that is, the signified and revealed will on the other.[21] We hear the Gospel and receive the precept to believe, but we do not really know what God has decided in his hidden decree, whether or not we belong to

---

[19] Barth, *Church Dogmatics*, vol. II/2, 114; in vol. IV/1, 63 he expresses himself more cautiously.

[20] Willem J. van Asselt, *The Federal Theology of Johannes Coccejus (1603–1669)* (Leiden/Boston/Köln: Brill, 2001), 216.

[21] Turretin, *Institutes of Elenctic Theology*, Third Part, question 15, in vol. 1, 220–232.

the people he has elected. In the movement of the 'second Reformation' this dichotomy caused an infinite process of self-examination, doubt and uncertainty. In the fifth of the Canons of Dort wise and consolatory remarks were made to address the issue, but these did not take away the doctrinal grounds for doubting. Besides the psychological problems of such lack of assurance, there is also an enormous sociological impact. In a narrow view of the church where the Augustinian view of the *corpus mixtum* on earth, in which the elect and the wicked must live together, is seen as too tolerant towards unbelief, only predestined members can be taken up in the constitution of a church. But because nobody knows who the predestined members actually are, a real edification of the community can be very problematic.

ON CALVINISM AND SPINOZISM: SOME DEVELOPMENTS RELATED TO THE NINETEENTH CENTURY

In his *Short Treatise* (around 1661) Benedictus Spinoza speaks of the predestination of God or nature in a completely deterministic sense (I.6): in God there is an omni-causality, and every qualification of good or sin is only an effect of human imagination.[22] Actually this way of thinking is not part of the Reformed tradition, but an heir to the humanistic-Stoic thought of someone such as Lorenzo Valla. Nevertheless, by the end of the seventeenth century followers of Spinoza could be found in the Reformed church in the Netherlands. And in the nineteenth century some theologians, such as J. H. Scholten, defended a combination of Calvinistic and Spinozistic thinking to argue for the agreement between Reformed teaching and modern physical science.[23] It was along this line of thinking that predestination could be conceived as one of the most important central dogmas or *Zentraldogmen* of Reformed doctrine, as was asserted by Alexander Schweizer of Zürich (who was a follower of Friedrich Schleiermacher and the great example for Scholten). This view showed a tendency toward supralapsarianism, stressing human dependency on a sovereign being and defending one great plan for the world by this being in its all-embracing love. Within such a presupposition, the historicity of the Fall was unnecessary. And the corollary of an original 'state of righteousness' was seen at best as a primitive and unripe evolutionary state of humanity (Scholten) and at worst as inaccessible for human religious

---

[22] Benedict Spinoza, *Short Treatise on God, Man and His Well-Being*, translated and edited by Abraham Wolf (London: Adam and Charles Black, 1910).

[23] For example, J. H. Scholten, *The Doctrine of the Reformed Church*, 2 vols. (Leiden: 1848 and 1850).

experience (Schleiermacher). Meanwhile the present inequality between those who believe and those who do not believe would, at the end of this process of growth, albeit after death, be abolished. In such a historicizing perspective, exemplified by the work of Friedrich Schleiermacher on the one hand, 'it is not possible that all living persons are ever accepted equally in the kingdom of God founded by Christ', because the church originates in one historical point and spreads out gradually;[24] but on the other hand, the unification of the divine being with human nature in the person of the Redeemer implies that the continuation of life after death is not reserved only for those who believe.[25]

THE SUM OF THE GOSPEL: KARL BARTH ON ELECTION

After a profound conversation with the Reformed doctrine of election, Karl Barth published his far-reaching revision of it in 1942 as a proposal for the whole ecumenical community. In light of the earlier observations in this chapter, we will now try to offer a concise summary of the outcome of his powerful thinking.

In line with the method developed earlier in his *Church Dogmatics*, Barth refuses to think in terms of the dichotomy between a *hidden* and a *revealed* will of God. The veiling of God can be found only in the unveiling of his Word and by his Spirit: there is no hidden God behind the God who has made himself known in his revelation. And revelation to humanity is more than simply divine accommodation, because it belongs to the essence of the triune God that God wishes to become human and in communication with his creation. For classical theology such a conceptual figure was hardly thinkable. It thus belongs to the modernity of the theological thinking of Barth. But on the topic of election it causes the disappearance of many traditional dilemmas and tensions. In Barth's view there is no hidden will of God that does not point to the mystery of his revealed will.

Barth does not base the doctrine primarily on a *fact of experience*,[26] as Calvin did, nor upon a *deductive and necessary line of thought*, as Valla or Zwingli did. He finds his starting point in 'the sum of the Gospel because of all words that can be said or heard this is the best: that God elects man; that God is for man too the One who loves in freedom'.[27]

---

[24] Friedrich Schleiermacher, *The Christian Faith* (1830/1831), translated and edited by H. R. Mackintosh and J. S. Stewart (Edinburgh: T. & T. Clark, 1999), §117.

[25] Schleiermacher, *The Christian Faith* (1830/1831), §117.4.

[26] Barth, *Church Dogmatics*, vol. II/2, 38.

[27] Ibid., vol. II/2, 3.

Therewith Barth situates the topic of election in the *doctrine of God*. Yet the concept of a deciding and discerning God fundamentally alters traditional ontology. For the *subject of election* is not a hidden God, nor simply the undivided Trinitarian God (as Polanus and others rightly said), but it is concretely Christ as the electing God. It is not that we are electing him, but that he is electing us (John 15:16), and Christ is the subject from the very beginning, from before the foundation of the world. The *object of election* is neither the human being as fallen (the infralapsarian position), nor the human being not yet created in a general sense (although this supralapsarian position makes some sense!), but concretely the person of Jesus Christ, who was in the beginning with God (John 1:1). In him (Eph. 1:4) all people are elected. Here the pastoral advice about Christ as the mirror of election finds its deepest ground.

Moreover, predestination in the eternal counsel of God is the presupposition of the covenant of God and humanity as it takes place in history. The operation that Cocceius did not want to perform in the end (although Barth thought he did), is realized here after all: the eternal decree of predestination is identified with the 'counsel of peace'. Similarly, in contrast with the teaching of Wollebius, Turretin and others, Christ as the foundation of salvation is at the very same time also the foundation of election. Consequently predestination does not have to be seen as part of providence, but, as Calvin proposed in the *Institutes* of 1539, the general idea of providence must be seen from the point of view of the particular mystery of predestination. In this way the doctrine of providence will appear in no other light than that of the covenant of grace, as founded in divine election.[28]

The eternal decision of God is certainly a double decision (in spite of Leuenberg, one has to say). But there are no two classes of human being. On the contrary: 'in Jesus Christ God in his free grace determines Himself for sinful man and sinful man for Himself. He therefore takes upon Himself the rejection of man with all its consequences, and elects man to participate in His own glory.'[29] The church should not be seen only as the context in which some individuals will appear to be elected; rather, in Christ there is such a reality as 'the Election of the Community'.[30] Israel and the church of Jew and heathen together

[28] Ibid., vol. III/3.
[29] Ibid., vol. II/2, 94.
[30] Ibid., vol. II/2, 195.

mirror both the shadow of rejection as well as the promise of election. Therefore the claim that the essence of the doctrine of predestination is the thesis that God has foreordained some to blessedness and others to damnation must be revised as follows: the main goal of election must be seen in the witness to the mercy and justice of God.[31] The political context for this thesis is a new one: not the reformation of the cities (1538), nor the exile of the refugees (1555), nor the ruling church (1619), but the Christian minority with a ministry of witness.

In this way, there remains a connection between the message of election and the calling of humanity. 'Then He shall say to them on his left hand: depart from me, ye cursed, into everlasting fire, prepared for the devil and his angels' (Matt. 25:41). The fire is not prepared for us – we should not be there! But then we must believe and behave as Christ desires and commands. And so doctrinal reflection, not only with Barth, but also essentially, always ends up in 'the open situation of proclamation'.[32]

CONCLUSION

We said at the beginning of this chapter that the Reformed emphasis on the topic of election is not heretical. Reformed theology regarding this issue vindicates the heritage of radical Augustinianism: the consciousness that the gift of our faith is rooted in the inner heart and counsel of God. And therewith it is, or was, ready to accept the dark side of this confession, if need be even divine double predestination. However, through the proposals of the school of Schleiermacher, and the more challenging thought of Barth, this heritage is being challenged. Could it be that, rereading the Scriptures and rethinking the doctrine, in some respects – such as the traditional answers to the questions of the subject and the object of election, the lack of Christological thinking through of the double divine decision, the modality of the relationship between universality and particularity in theology – there can also be seen to be something heretical in the Augustinian heritage? This conversation cannot be neglected. Orthodox Calvinists and others have an obligation to continue asking each other questions and investigating together.

---

[31] Ibid., vol. II/2, 309.
[32] Ibid., vol. II/2, 476.

Further reading

Armstrong, Brian G. *Calvinism and the Amyraut Heresy: Protestantism and Humanism in Seventeenth-Century France.* Madison: The University of Wisconsin Press, 1969.

Asselt, Willem J. van. *The Federal Theology of Johannes Coccejus (1603–1669).* Leiden/Boston/Köln: Brill, 2001.

Barth, Karl. *Church Dogmatics.* 4 vols. in 13 parts. Edited by G. W. Bromiley and T. F. Torrance. Edinburgh: T&T Clark, 1956–1975, vol. II/2: 1–194.

Breukelman, Frans H. *The Structure of Sacred Doctrine in Calvin's Theology.* Edited by Rinse H. Reeling Brouwer. Translated by Martin Kessler. Grand Rapids, MI: William B. Eerdmans, 2010.

Calvin, John. *Concerning the Eternal Predestination of God.* Translated by J. K. S. Reid. Louisville, KY: Westminster John Knox, 1997.

Muller, Richard A. *Christ and the Decree: Christology and Predestination in Reformed Theology from Calvin to Perkins.* Grand Rapids, MI: Baker Academic, 2008.

Oberman, Heiko A. *The Dawn of the Reformation: Essays in Late Medieval and Early Reformational Thought.* Grand Rapids, MI: Eerdmans, 1992.

The Two Reformations: The Journey from the Last Days to the New World. New Haven, CT: Yale University Press, 2003.

Turretin, Francis. *Institutes of Elenctic Theology.* Edited by James T. Dennison, Jr. Translated by George Musgrave Giger. Philipsburg, NJ: Presbyterian and Reformed Publishing Company, 1992), vol. 1: 311–430.

5 Christology

BRUCE L. McCORMACK

TWO NATURES UNIMPAIRED: THE DISTINCTIVE
EMPHASES OF REFORMED CHRISTOLOGY

Reformed Christology was born in a situation of conflict, leading to sharp polemic. The starting point of the conflict lay in the question: What is the nature of Christ's presence in the Lord's supper? Are the body and blood of the crucified and risen Christ so united with the elements of bread and wine that he is made to be present locally and physically? Or is the "sacramental union" *spiritual* in nature, that is, effected by the Holy Spirit in such a way that the ontological distinction between the two things being united – body and blood on the one side, bread and wine on the other – is strictly maintained precisely in their union? The first was the answer given by the Lutheran churches, the second by the Reformed churches. A second set of questions followed immediately on this one. Is the presence of the crucified and risen Christ in the sacrament unique, such that participation in the bread and wine is made to be *the* God-given means by which Christians participate in Christ himself? Or is the faith that receives the gifts of God's grace in the observance of the sacrament a faith that is active always and everywhere in the Christian life, such that the "feeding by faith" that occurs in the Lord's supper is not unique but is more rightly conceived as a visible representation of an ongoing "feeding" that takes place in a more or less continuous fashion in Christian life? Here again, the Lutheran churches gave the first answer, the Reformed churches the second.

Clearly much was at stake in the decisions being made here that had an enormous practical value where worship and Christian life were concerned. Bearing that in mind may, perhaps, help a bit in keeping that which follows from seeming abstract and uninteresting. For the debate over sacramental presence very quickly resolved itself into a debate over the metaphysics of Christ's person. Both sides understood themselves as faithful to the church's dogma as formulated by the bishops at

Chalcedon in 451. Both sides affirmed that Jesus Christ was "of one sub-stance" (*homoousios*) with the Father as regards his divinity and "of one substance" (*homoousios*) with us as regards his humanity. Both sides affirmed that two distinct natures (divine and human) "subsist" in one person, thus upholding both the unity of the God–human and the dif-ferentiation of his natures. The divisive question had to do with the relation of the natures to the "person of the union" and to each other. The Lutherans held more consistently to the originating significance of Chalcedon, in accordance with which the "person of the union" was identified with the preexistent Logos (or eternal Son of God), a move that made the human nature the instrument (and even the object) of his redemptive activity in the world. The Reformed had a divided mind when it came to the identity of the "person of the union." They too wanted to affirm the Chalcedonian identification of the "person" with the Logos and to insist that the human nature "subsists" (or has its existence made concretely real "in") the person of the Logos. And so, when striving to uphold the unity of the person of the union, they too identified the person of the union with the preexistent Logos. But as we shall now see, arguments over the "communication of attributes" would, at significant turning points in the debate, lead the Reformed to identify the "person" with the "whole Christ" (i.e., the God–human in his divine human unity). That inconsistency was nothing new, as we shall see. But given the polemical situation, it is undeniable that the Reformed finally found their center of gravity not so much in the origi-nating significance of Chalcedon as they did in the history of its effects.

The treatment of Reformed Christology that follows is divided into two movements: one corresponding to the person of Christ, the second to the work of Christ (in accordance with the customary divi-sion employed by virtually all Protestant theologians in the sixteenth and seventeenth centuries). This is followed by a section that treats some important modifications of classical Reformed Christology that occurred in the modern period.

THE PERSON OF CHRIST

The doctrine of the "person" of Christ constituted an attempt to describe, as faithfully as possible, the ontological constitution of the Mediator. Among the questions dealt with by the Reformed under this heading were the conception of Jesus in the womb of the Virgin by the Holy Spirit; the "assumption" of the human "nature" by the Logos in the moment of conception – an act in which that nature (taken from the "substance" of the Virgin) is made to be a concretely existing human individual through being granted a share in the Logos' personal "subsistence" (or "hypostasis"); and the problem of the "communication of attributes." It is the last-named topic that is of central importance for our purposes here, as it is in that area of reflection that the distinctive emphases of Reformed Christology emerge. But the decisions made there also impact what is said under the first two headings, so we would do well to pause, however briefly.

Where the details of the teaching on conception and assumption are concerned, Johannes Wollebius provides a nice summary. First, "Whereas in ordinary generation the time required for formation of the body is forty days, the body of Christ was absolutely completed in a moment."[1] And, second, what is then born of the Virgin is a man – "not the birth of the nature but of the person,"[2] as Wollebius puts it. Not surprisingly, the assumed definition of the "person" reflects the vacillation spoken of earlier. When speaking of the act of assumption, the "person" (or agent performing the act) is the Logos.[3] When speaking in the context of the "communication of attributes," however, Wollebius speaks of a "divinely human person"[4] in whom the properties essential to each nature are maintained in their original integrity.

The great strength of the second definition of the "person" (i.e., the whole Christ) lies in the fact that it enables Wollebius to soften the tendency toward an instrumentalization of the man Jesus that had been the great temptation of Chalcedonianism in its more original form. Wollebius can speak, for example, of "infirmities" of both body and soul in Jesus with a forthrightness that mitigates in advance the standard nineteenth-century criticisms of Chalcedon. Infirmities of the body include the experience of physical pain, of want (either of food or drink), of loss, of fatigue, and so on. Infirmities of the soul include "sadness, fear, ignorance, etc."[5] To be sure, Wollebius also affirms that where the human passions of Jesus were concerned, he "suffered no lack of

---

[1]   Johannes Wollebius, *Compendium Theologiae Christianae*, XVI, 2, iii, in *Reformed Dogmatics: Seventeenth-Century Reformed Theology through the Writings of Wollebius, Voetius, and Turretin*, edited and translated by John W. Beardslee (Grand Rapids, MI: Baker Book House, 1977), 89–90. First published in Latin in 1626 in the immediate aftermath of the Synod of Dordrecht, Wollebius' *Compendium* provides a useful guide to the Reformed orthodoxy of the seventeenth century at a relatively early stage of its development.

[2]   Ibid., XVI, 5, ii, 94.

[3]   Ibid., XVI, 4, i, 91.

[4]   Ibid., XVI, 4, proposition, 91.

[5]   Ibid., XVI, 3, iii, 90.

control" – thus suggesting an "impassibility" somehow fitted to human being. Still, the stress laid on the infirmities of Jesus is remarkable.

We come then to the knotty problem of the "communication of attributes." Perhaps the best place to begin is with a definition of the word "nature." To speak of a "nature" is to speak of a catalogue of essential properties that make a thing to be what it is – the "what-ness" of a thing, in other words. In the case of the God–human, to raise the question of a "communication" is to ask: *To whom* should the attributes of the "natures" be ascribed? Whose attributes are these? The answer to this question suggested by Chalcedon itself was the Logos. The equation of the "person of the union" with the preexistent Logos ought to have meant that the attributes of both natures are rightly ascribed (or "communicated") to him. But there is a major obstacle standing in the way of the completion of this thought. The problem has to do with the presupposition that simplicity and impassibility are proper to the divine "nature" and, therefore, to the Logos as a concrete hypostatization of that "nature." To ascribe human attributes (and the experiences they make possible; see the just discussed infirmities!) to the Logos would either mean that the Logos had undergone change or that the grounds for such a "communication" were somehow proper to the Logos as such, which would make an ongoing affirmation of simplicity and impassibility questionable. It was because of this problem that theologians began, by the eighth century at the latest, to think of the "person" to whom such attributes were "communicated" as the "whole Christ" (divine and human) rather than the Logos as such. What was being said, in effect, was that human attributes are rightly ascribed to the God–human *according to his human nature only* and divine attributes to the God–human *according to his divine nature only*. The net result was that the attributes of both natures were preserved in their original integrity.

A classic example of this tendency is to be found in the eighth-century theologian, John of Damascus. In the context of treating the problem of the "communication" in chapters 3 and 4 of his great work *De fide orthodoxa*, the thesis is advanced that "Christ" is a "composite person"[6] made up of "different things which remain the same."[7] And so, "we confess one Person of the Son of God incarnate in two natures that remain perfect, and we declare that the Person of his divinity and of his

---

[6] John of Damascus, "An Exact Exposition of the Orthodox Faith," in *Saint John of Damascus: Writings*, translated by Frederic H. Chase, Jr. (Washington, DC: Catholic University Press, 1958), 274–277. The phrase is used five times in those four pages.

[7] Ibid., 272.

humanity is the same and confess that the two natures are preserved intact in him after the union. We do not set each nature apart by itself, but hold them to be united to each other in one composite Person."[8] Again and again, John says of the natures subsequent to their union that each has "its essential difference maintained intact."[9]

The "communication" is then handled in the following way. After stoutly maintaining that the properties of the human are wrongly applied to the divine nature and that the properties of the divine nature are wrongly applied to the human nature, John says that "we" (meaning the "orthodox") do indeed apply the properties of both to the person. But notice now how he is defining the "person":

> In the case of the person, however, whether we name it from both of the parts or from one of them, we attribute the properties of both the natures to it. And thus, Christ – which name covers both together – is called both God and man, created and uncreated, passible and impassible. And whenever He is named Son of God and God from one of the parts, He receives the properties of the coexistent nature, of the flesh, that is to say, and can be called passible God and crucified Lord of Glory – not as being God, but insofar as the same one is also man.[10]

That the person can be named from one of the parts or from both is due to the fact that the "person" is being considered as composite, as the whole Christ in both natures. And so, when Paul says in 1 Cor. 2:8 that the Lord of glory was crucified, John understands him to be speaking of the whole Christ in terms of one of his "parts" (the divinity) and ascribing to the whole Christ what is in fact proper to the other part, namely, suffering. It the God–human (the whole Christ) who suffers but he does so as *human* and, therefore, humanly. The purpose of this figure of speech – referring to the whole by reference to that part in relation to which the ascription would, in fact, be improper – is to underscore the unity of the person, the fact that what we have before us is *one* composite person. The figure of speech is meant to convey something real; that suffering is rightly (realistically) ascribed to the composite person.

Eight centuries later, John Calvin set forth an understanding of the "communication" which agreed in all of its details (if not in its nomenclature) with the one we have just seen in John. True, he does not use the

---

[8] Ibid., 273–274.
[9] Ibid., 274.
[10] Ibid., 276.

term "composite person." But the conceptuality denoted by the term is clearly present when he writes, "For we affirm his divinity so joined and united with his humanity that each retains its distinctive nature unimpaired, and yet these two natures constitute one Christ."[11] Clearly, the one Christ is the compound of the two natures taken together. Calvin writes, "it was necessary for the Son of God to become for us 'Immanuel, that is, God with us' [Isa. 7:14, Matt. 1:23], and in such a way that his divinity and our human nature might by mutual connection grow together".[12] And so, when he comes to the problem of the communication, we are not surprised to find that his solution is the same as John's. Referring specifically to passages like 1 Cor. 2:8, Acts 20:28 and 1 Jn 1:1, Calvin writes, "Surely God does not have blood, does not suffer, cannot be touched with human hands. But since Christ, who was true God and also true man, was crucified and shed his blood for us, the things he carried out in his human nature are transferred improperly, although not without reason, to his divinity."[13] And what was the reason for this improper reference? Calvin answers: "because the selfsame one was both God and man, for the sake of the union he gave to the one what belonged to the other."[14] The reason that the whole is named by one of its parts – and, indeed, by the wrong part where the attribute in question is concerned – is to draw the reader's attention to the unity of the whole. Clearly, Calvin's solution is John's – which leads to a couple of historically significant questions.

Why did Calvin choose to lay greater emphasis upon the "two natures unimpaired" than upon the unity of the person? And why did he prefer to define the "person" in terms of both natures rather than in terms of the singularity of the Logos? The answers, of course, are contextual. It was noted earlier that the Lutherans had retained the original Chalcedonian identification of the "person" with the Logos. Their interest – given the requirements of their eucharistic theology – was to understand how the human nature of Christ might obtain a share in the divine attributes of omnipotence, omniscience, and – most importantly where the question of the real presence is concerned – omnipresence. To participate in the divine omnipresence would, so the theory went, explain how it could be that the body and blood of Christ were "present"

---

[11] John Calvin, *Institutes of the Christian Religion*, edited by John T. McNeill and translated by Ford Lewis Battles (Library of Christian Classics; 2 vols.; Philadelphia: Westminster, 1960), II.xiv.1, 482.

[12] Ibid., II.xii.1, 464.

[13] Ibid., II.xiv.2, 484.

[14] Ibid., II.xiv.2, 484.

in, with, and under the sacramental elements of bread and wine in more than one simultaneously occurring eucharistic celebration. But, of course, if the goal was, at the same time, to uphold the *uniqueness* of the sacramental presence, then the ascription to the human nature of a share in divine ubiquity would prove too much. A way had to be found to limit the effects of the basic move without undermining it. The basic move was to affirm the "communication" of divine attributes to the human nature as a consequence of the hypostatic union, a move that meant, in principle, that the human nature ought to have obtained a share in the divine attribute of omnipresence as soon as the union was complete – in the conception, in other words. The way forward would lie through an act of will. The Logos gives to his human nature a share in the attribute of omnipresence when and where he wills.[15] The way had been cleared for the emergence of what later came to be called (after the Christ-hymn in Phil. 2:6–11) the two "states" theory.[16] When, finally, this step was taken, Lutheran Christology and Lutheran eucharistic theology would be rendered fully coherent. The full effects of the union and the communication it makes possible were realized only in the state of exaltation – or so the theory went.

Calvin's unhappiness with the Lutheran Christology, however, had nothing to do with an alleged incoherence. It had to do with the more basic move, the idea of a communication of divine attributes to the human nature. For Calvin, a body that can be in more than one place at the same time was not a real body; it was a "phantasm."[17] And so, he sought to take the ground out from beneath the Lutheran understanding of the "communication" by insisting that the "communication" was to the whole Christ, not from one nature to another. In fact, there was no direct *perichoresis* of the natures, no penetration of the human nature by the Logos acting upon it – an idea that would have made possible the Lutheran "genus of majesty."[18] That is why Calvin insisted on "two natures unimpaired" in their original integrity subsequent to their union. And that is why he was drawn to the idea of a "communication" to the whole Christ (divine and human) – because such a communication allowed him to maintain that divine attributes are rightly ascribed to the God–human with respect to his divinity alone.

---

[15] *Solid Declaration*, article VIII, 64, in *The Book of Concord*, edited by Robert Kolb and Timothy Wengert (Minneapolis, MN: Fortress Press, 2000), 628.

[16] Ibid., article VII, 25–27, in *The Book of Concord*, 620–621.

[17] Calvin, *Institutes*, IV.xvii.17, 1380.

[18] Martin Chemnitz, *The Two Natures in Christ*, translated by J. A. O. Preus (Saint Louis, MO: Concordia Publishing House, 1971), 241–246 and 287–311.

In later Reformed theology, Calvin's account of the "communication" (or one quite like it) was taken for granted, its results summarized and extended in some important ways. To reject the thought of an interpenetration of natures laid upon the later Reformed the need to explain the extraordinary capacities and activities of the human Jesus. This was accomplished in the main by means of an appeal to pneumatology. And so, for example, Wollebius held that the extraordinary knowledge possessed by Jesus of "heavenly affairs" was a gift of the Holy Spirit. Moreover, the knowledge "infused" by the Spirit, though surpassing that even of angels, was still to be distinguished from the eternal omniscience possessed by the Logos as God.[19] Such a claim reflected the view that the gifts of Christ by virtue of which he excelled his fellow humans were bestowed upon him by the Holy Spirit and were not to be thought of as the consequence of a participation in divine attributes. Such gifts were, therefore, finite, created, fitted to the "capacity of the recipient" as Francis Turretin would later put it.[20]

Directly connected to this claim was another. If it was the case that the human Jesus had no share in the divine omnipresence, it followed that the Logos (who left nothing proper to deity behind in becoming human) continued to fill heaven and earth during the days of his earthly sojourn but also, at the same time, to be circumscribed locally by the body that he had assumed.[21] Here again, such a view was hardly new. We can find it, for example, in John of Damascus and it was wrongly characterized by Lutheran polemic as a *novum* in the history of theology (under the heading of the *extra Calvinisticum*).[22] Here again, the net result of this line of thought was to reinforce the emphasis on an undiminished and unchanged humanity of Christ in the hypostatic union.

THE WORK OF CHRIST

Credit for devising the concept of a threefold office of the Mediator (*munus triplex*) as an organizing principle for discussing the work of Christ in all of its dimensions belongs to John Calvin, though he did not make the expansive use of it that later Reformed theology would. In

[19] Wollebius, *Compendium*, XVI.4.xii, xiv, 93.
[20] Francis Turretin, *Institutes of Elenctic Theology*, edited by James T. Dennison, Jr. and translated by George Musgrave Giger (Philipsburg, NJ: Presbyterian and Reformed Publishing Company, 1992), vol. 2, 321.
[21] Wollebius, *Compendium*, XVI.4.vii, 92.
[22] John of Damascus, "An Exact Exposition of the Orthodox Faith," 282.

fact, having introduced the claim that Christ's work is at once prophetic, kingly, and priestly in Book II, chapter 15 of the fifth and definitive revision of his *Institutes* (1559), Calvin immediately reverted in chapter 16 to an earlier method of arrangement along the lines laid down by the Apostle's Creed. And other schemes would continue to suggest themselves. Wollebius, for example, made the two states of humiliation and exaltation to be the overarching principle of organization and ordered the threefold office to it. Still, the idea of a threefold office did eventually become central to the Reformed presentation of the work of Christ.

More significant than questions of organization, however, was the content assigned to each aspect of this threefold office. Calvin understood the prophetic aspect of the mediatorial office to consist in the fact that Christ was a "herald and witness" of the Gospel enacted in his person, thus bringing an end to all prophecy.[23] But having so defined this aspect, he allowed it quickly to fall from view to concentrate his attention on the priestly function. Noting that the Christ "began to pay the price of liberation" as soon as he took on the "form of a servant" (i.e., in the assumption of human flesh), Calvin nevertheless held that the accomplishment of our salvation is treated by Scripture as "peculiar and proper to Christ's death."[24] And so, he says that it is for this reason that "the so-called 'Apostle's Creed' passes at once in the best order from the birth of Christ to his death and resurrection, wherein the whole of perfect salvation consists."[25]

What then is the purpose of that perfect obedience that characterized the life of Jesus Christ in this world? For Calvin, Christ's sinlessness does not contribute directly to the salvation achieved but is rather to be understood as the necessary precondition of that perfect sacrifice in which the priest and the "victim" are one and the same – that is, the priest offers himself as a spotless offering to the Father in the place of those he has been sent to redeem.[26]

Notwithstanding Calvin's use of cultic imagery in establishing the need for a sinless offering, however, the central theme in his understanding of the saving significance of Christ's death is that of a judicial sentence – the satisfaction of a just penalty due to sin. In fact, the very form that his death took – namely, through a trial leading to crucifixion – was

---

[23] Calvin, *Institutes*, II.xvi.2, 496.
[24] Ibid., II.xvi.5, 507.
[25] Ibid., II.xvi.5, 508.
[26] Ibid., II.xv.6, 501–502.

designed by God to teach us that in death, Christ was satisfying the just sentence of God. Calvin writes:

> If he had been murdered by thieves or slain in an insurrection by a raging mob, in such a death there would have been no evidence of satisfaction. But when he was arraigned before the judgment seat as a criminal, accused and pressed with testimony, and condemned by the mouth of a judge to die – we know by these proofs that he took the role of a guilty man and evildoer.[27]

How was Christ made liable to divine judgment in death? By means of "imputation."[28] Calvin explains: "This is our acquittal: the guilt that held us liable for punishment has been transferred to the head of the Son of God [Is.53:13]."[29] Clearly, this is a penal substitution theory; of that, there should be no doubt. The fact that Calvin understood the work of Christ to have other dimensions (the prophetic and the kingly) that are not captured by his judicial interpretation of Christ's death must not prevent us from acknowledging this.

Calvin was well aware of the chief criticism that might be brought against such a judicial theory – that it seems to involve a "contradiction" because it makes it seem that the Father has been moved from anger to mercy by the offering made by his Son. Calvin puts his finger very neatly on the reason such a conception is deeply problematic: "For how could he have given in his only-begotten Son a singular pledge of his love to us if he had not already embraced us with his free favor?"[30] If God were not eternally disposed to be merciful to us, God would not have sent his Son into this world in the first place. So the "wrath of God" is not the ultimate horizon against which the saving death of Christ is to be interpreted. And yet, the outpouring of divine wrath is clearly attested in Scripture. What, then? Calvin's answer is that talk of divine wrath in Scripture has, to some extent at least, been "accommodated to our capacity."[31] We would not be stirred to awe and gratitude for God's mercy were we not first instructed "by fear of God's wrath and by dread of eternal death".[32] Ultimately, however, Calvin's explanation for why God's wrath and his merciful love do not contradict one another

---

[27] Ibid., II.xvi.5, 509.
[28] Ibid., II.xvi.6, 510.
[29] Ibid., II.xvi.5, 509–510.
[30] Ibid., II.xvi.2, 504.
[31] Ibid., II.xvi.2, 504.
[32] Ibid., II.xvi.2, 505.

is one he draws from Augustine. Calvin writes: "Thus in a marvelous and divine way he loved us even when he hated us. For he hated us for what we were that he had not made; yet because our wickedness had not entirely consumed his handiwork, he knew how, at the same time, to hate in each one of us what we had made, and to love what he had made."[33] And because this is so, God's love precedes and grounds the exercise of his just judgment in the cross.

Remarkable in Calvin is his exposition of the theme of Christ's "descent into hell". The satisfaction of God's just penalty, Calvin holds, necessitated not only a bodily death but also a spiritual one that entailed battle with "the armies of hell" and "the dread of everlasting death." To be sure, Calvin did not think that the order of the Creed – "crucified, dead and buried" and only then "He descended into hell" – provided any reason to think that the "descent" occurred after Christ's death. The order has to do rather with a distinction between that which was externally visible and that which was spiritual and, therefore, hidden to view. But both the bodily and the spiritual sufferings are ascribed to the Passion itself. Still, Calvin recognized that if penal substitution was to be complete, not to mention coherent, there needed to be an equivalence between the penalty owed to human sinfulness and the penalty paid (i.e., between the eschatological judgment of God and the death of Christ). That he was not completely successful in explaining this equivalence also has to be granted. For Calvin could not acknowledge a real abandonment of Christ by the Father, a real dereliction. And yet, he came close to it when he said "surely no more terrible abyss can be conceived than to feel yourself forsaken and estranged from God; and when you call upon him, not to be heard. It is as if God himself had plotted your ruin.... Christ was so downcast as to be compelled to cry out in deep anguish: 'My God, my God, why hast thou forsaken me?' [Ps. 22:1; Mt. 27:46]."[34] So the experience of the divine silence was real enough, but an abandonment by the Father is not something Calvin could envision. Calvin acknowledged, "we do not suggest that God was ever inimical or angry toward him. How could he be angry toward his beloved Son, 'in whom His heart reposed' [cf.Matt.3:17]? How could Christ by his intercession appease the Father towards others, if he were himself hateful to God?"[35]

---

[33] Ibid., II.xvi.4, 507.
[34] Ibid., II.xvi.11, 516–517.
[35] Ibid., II.xvi.11, 517.

The kingly aspect of the mediatorial office came to the fore for Calvin in the resurrection and ascension of Christ. The rule of Christ over the church (through the instrumental activity of the Holy Spirit) consists in his provision of those spiritual gifts needed to enable the individual to triumph over sin in this life and in the protection of the church from her enemies.[36] In his session at the right hand of God, Christ intercedes with the Father on behalf of his people, thus giving to the kingly work of Christ a priestly aspect.

The threefold office of Christ quickly became a standard feature of Reformed soteriology. In the seventeenth century, as Reformed theology gave birth (at least in one of its strands) to covenant theology, the definitions given to the three aspects of the mediatorial office underwent some change – partly through formalization and partly through the often baleful consequences of having been wed to the notion of a "covenant of works." The history of the emergence of covenant theology has been well-told and cannot be rehearsed here.[37] The decisive point to be made here is that the so-called covenant of works was thought to have been with Adam (as the "federal" head of the human race) prior to the Fall. In this first covenant, eternal life was promised to Adam and his posterity on the condition of his "perfect and personal obedience."[38] This Adam failed to do, thereby bringing eternal death on himself and his posterity. The covenant of works was thus a *conditional* covenant. It was succeeded by a covenant of grace that was intended to be wholly unconditional. But the shadow cast by the covenant of works also fell even on the Christology of the covenant theologians, thus introducing an element of conditionality into the accomplishment of reconciliation and redemption.

Where Calvin conceived of "satisfaction" strictly in terms of a gracious offering, covenant theologians now conceived of it as having two parts: the satisfaction of the Law in Christ's perfect obedience and the satisfaction of the penalty of death. In that the latter was undertaken, the guilt accruing to sin was atoned. In that the former was accomplished, eternal life was merited for us. To be sure, Calvin had already introduced the concept of merit into his discussion of the saving significance of Christ's work.[39] But in his hands, the concept of merit is fitted

---

[36] Ibid., II.xvi.4, 5, 498–501; cf. II.xvi.16, 525.
[37] See Gottlob Schrenk, *Gottesreich und Bund im älteren Protestantismus, vornehmlich bei Johannes Coccejus*, 2nd ed. (Giessen/Basel: Brunnen Verlag, 1985); D. A. Weir, *The Origins of the Federal Theology in Sixteenth-Century Reformation Thought* (Oxford: Clarendon Press, 1990).
[38] *Westminster Confession of Faith* (1647), chapter VII.2.
[39] Calvin, *Institutes* II.xvii.1–6, 528–534.

more consistently into an overarching horizon of unconditional grace. He had no covenant of works.

The covenant of works also impacted treatment of the prophetic office, which was now understood to include a legal as well as an evangelical aspect. The *prophetia legalis* consisted in setting forth "the true righteousness which the law requires."[40] Slowly but surely, fulfilment of the Law was no longer simply seen as a precondition to carrying out the kind of salvific work Christ accomplished but was being made central to its accomplishment. To just that degree, the graciousness of God's saving work was being qualified.

MODERN DEVELOPMENTS

In the modern period, theologians in general (and not just the Reformed) did away with the classically Protestant distinction of the person and work of Christ. This was done in two ways. Either one subsumed the work of Christ into an account of his person or one subsumed the person of Christ into an account of his work. The first of these strategies was pursued by Friedrich Schleiermacher, the second by Karl Barth. These differences aside, both these theologians sought to uphold the theological values that had sought expression in Chalcedon but neither rested content with its categories. And both made the threefold office basic to their respective presentations of the work of Christ.

In Schleiermacher's Christology, the being of God in Christ was interpreted along the lines of a union of divine "causality" with the consciousness of the man Jesus. In Jesus alone was there to be found that "living receptivity" to the divine causality that made it possible for him to completely dominate or control the sensible stimuli which came to him from without.[41] In this way, "living receptivity" to divine influence gave rise in Jesus to a relation of pure activity in relation to all that came to him from the world around him. That this is indeed a doctrine of "incarnation" is made clear where it is realized that Jesus Christ was, on the plane of human existence, the perfect replication of the pure activity that God is.[42] As God relates to the world, so too does

---

[40] Heinrich Heppe, *Reformed Dogmatics* (Grand Rapids, MI: Baker Book House reprint, 1978), 454.

[41] Friedrich Schleiermacher, *The Christian Faith* (1830/1831), edited and translated by H. R. Mackintosh and J. S. Stewart (Edinburgh: T. & T. Clark, 1999), §94.2, 387.

[42] Kevin Hector, "Actualism and Incarnation: The High Christology of Friedrich Schleiermacher," *IJST* 8 (2006), 311–312.

Jesus – making him to be qualitatively different from his fellow humans (and not merely quantitatively).

It should be clear from the foregoing that Schleiemacher was on traditional ground in at least two respects. First, he affirmed a certain kind of divine and human "impassibility." The fact that Jesus' God-consciousness is undisturbed by external forces and conditions means that his passions were ordered by his God-consciousness so as to remain undisturbed even when suffering physically. Suffering, therefore, was not denied by Schleiermacher. But suffering never gave rise in Christ to misery because his experience of it was controlled by his God-consciousness.[43] Schleiermacher refers to this condition – and the sinlessness to which it gives rise – as Christ's "unclouded blessedness."[44] In this, too, Christ was understood to be like God insofar as an affectivity that is strictly nonreactive in nature was not denied by him. Second, Schleiemacher gave powerful expression to the tendency of the Church Fathers to "instrumentalize" the human Jesus. In fact, Schleiermacher goes so far as to say that "the existence of God in the Redeemer is posited as the innermost fundamental power within Him, from which every activity proceeds and which holds every element together; everything human (in Him) forms only the organism for this fundamental power."[45] If one were to seek to find a "modern" version of Athanasius, one need look no further than Schleiermacher. That this did not result, in his case, in diminishment of Christ's full humanity (as it did with the ancients) had to do with the fact that he made Christ's humanity to be the concrete realization of true humanity – a point to which we will return.

The being of God in Christ is thus active in relation to those around him. His unclouded blessedness is a "person-forming divine influence."[46] In that those near to him were attracted to it, they in turn experienced an elevation in the potency of their God-consciousness and, with that, a newly created capacity to control sensible stimuli so that they do not become the occasion for sin.

In that Christ assumes believers into fellowship with his unclouded blessedness, he also reconciles them to God. The need for reconciliation arises, according to Schleiermacher, from the sense that the suffering and misery we endure is deserved and, therefore, received by us as

---

[43] Schleiermacher, *The Christian Faith*, §101.2, 432.
[44] Ibid., §101.1, 431.
[45] Ibid., §96.3, 397.
[46] Ibid., §100.2, 427.

divine punishment. Where, however, the connection between sin and evil is dissolved, we no longer understand ourselves to be deserving of punishment.[47] We are set free to respond to God in faith and love and so be reconciled to him.

Schleiermacher's theory of redemption is closely related to ancient "divinisation" soteriologies. Redemption is something that takes place internally, in the person of Christ. But there are also significant differences. Schleiermacher's theory is teleologically ordered. For him, Christ's work becomes reconciling in that it has its redeeming effect on others. Some might well wonder whether such a theory is not too "subjective" – whether, in fact, the work of Christ is somehow incomplete until it has its effect in others. To this, it must be responded that nothing further need be done by Christ or even by the Holy Spirit to make his work effective. It is effective in being performed. The power unleashed by Jesus' perfectly potent God-consciousness is adequate in itself to explain all of its effects. It should be added, where the theme of reconciliation is concerned, that Christ needed no reconciliation for himself. It is only the sinner who needs to be reconciled. And so, given the nature of redemptive work of Christ as conceived by Schleiermacher, reconciliation would have to happen in us.

And finally, as already mentioned, Schleiermacher makes extensive use of the threefold office in unpacking his understanding of Christ's work. That each aspect of the office undergoes considerable revision is not to be denied. The prophetic aspect is transformed by being grounded in the *self*-proclamation of Christ. Teaching, prophesying, the working of miracles – all are seen as externalizations of Christ's person.[48] Here too, the complete integration of the person and work of Christ comes to the fore.

The priestly aspect is seen to include (quite traditionally) Christ's perfect fulfilment of the Law (the active obedience), his atoning death (the passive obedience), and his intercession with the Father on behalf of believers.[49] But here too, modifications in the received understanding prove necessary. If obedience to the Law were taken to imply "a distinction and severance between a higher will which commands and an imperfect will which is subordinate to it,"[50] it could not be true of Christ. On the contrary, Christ's will is so completely at one with his Father's will that the two can scarcely be distinguished. He does not

---

[47] Ibid., §101.2, 432.
[48] Ibid., §§103.2, 103.3, 443, 446.
[49] Ibid., §104.thesis, 451.
[50] Ibid., §104.3, 455–456.

then obey as if there were a command extrinsic to him but obeys as the perfect expression of God's being in him. Moreover, his obedience does not need to be "imputed" to us, as the power at work in him is also (now) at work in us as well, making us to be the objects of God's good pleasure.[51] In a similar way, what is redemptive in the sufferings of Christ is that he freely gives himself over to them when it becomes clear that they are unavoidable. Thus, it is not his physical sufferings as such which redeem (and, ultimately, reconcile) but his response to them. This also means, however, that God does not punish our sins in Christ's death; nor is his forgiveness a reward given to Christ for having suffered our punishment – which is then distributed to others. Forgiveness is the experience of those who, having been regenerated by Christ's redemptive power, turn away from sin.

The kingly aspect too is conditioned by the fact that Christ's redemptive power issues forth from his innermost self. What Christ does to govern the church and to provide it with all the assistance it needs for its well-being in the world is already complete in him; nothing further need be added. It is therefore not the case that the kingly aspect only begins to be fulfilled when Christ is raised from the dead. It is being carried out in Christ's historical existence.[52]

Is this Christology "Reformed"? It is that – and more. It is "Reformed" insofar as the qualitative distinction between the divine and human is preserved precisely in the realm of Christology. True: Christ's humanity is "instrumentalized" on this account. But, for Schleiermacher, what it means to be human is defined by Christ's humanity, not our own. Ours is to be judged by his, not his by ours. True: Schleiermacher has done away with penal substitution in its received sense. But he did not do away with the thought of penal desert altogether. Instead, he found a creative way to show how the punishment we deserved was turned away by the work of Christ that takes place in us. And at each step along the way, he managed to remain within hailing distance of the prophet–priest–king schema so beloved of the old Reformed.

There is no locus on the "person" of Christ in the later Karl Barth's Christology. What takes its place is a narration of the *history* of the God–human in his divine–human unity – first from the standpoint of the humiliation of God in that history, then from the standpoint of the exaltation of the human in the same history and finally from the standpoint of the true witness to the nature of both God and the human. In

---

[51] Ibid., §104.3, 455.
[52] Ibid., §105.1, 467.

this way, the "person" of Christ has been subsumed into his "work" and metaphysics has been completely supplanted by the narrated history of Jesus of Nazareth. In taking this step, Barth had radicalized the protest against natural theology already registered by Schleiermacher. But he had also taken something from the great Berliner: hypostatic union was replaced by an ongoing hypostatic uniting, so as to turn the Chalcedonian "natures" into a history.

What were Barth's innovations over against the Reformed tradition where Christology is concerned? First, the great surprise is that he should have treated the "humiliation" of God in the incarnation not simply in terms of that concealment of his identity which results from taking on human flesh but in making himself to be the subject of human suffering, death, and perdition. That the human is exalted in the same history, that his obedience should result in the creation of true humanity, is not so surprising. Like Schleiermacher, but with greater consistency, Barth grounds what it means to be human Christologically. The surprise, though, is to be found in the self-humiliation of God; the understanding that humility and obedience are *proper* to God's eternal being and not something added to him that leaves his being unaffected. Barth writes:

> It is only the pride of man, making a god in its own image, that will not hear of a determination of the divine essence in Jesus Christ. The presupposition of all earlier Christology has suffered from this pride ... This presupposition was a Greek conception of God, according to which God is far too exalted for ... His incarnation, and therefore the reconciliation of the world and Himself, to mean anything at all for Himself, or in any way to affect His Godhead.[53]

The impassible, utterly simple God celebrated by the older Reformed orthodoxy (and not just the ancients) was a God who, in Barth's view, was "dead of sheer majesty."[54] The true God is a passible God, the God made known in a work of reconciliation that finds its most complete expression in the cry of dereliction. Barth explains: "The meaning of the incarnation is plainly revealed in the question of Jesus on the cross: 'My God, my God, why hast thou forsaken me?' (Mk.15:34)."[55] God subjects himself to the human experience of death in God-abandonment. He takes that human experience into himself and makes it his own so that

---

[53] Karl Barth, *Church Dogmatics*, 4 vols. in 13 parts, edited by G. W. Bromiley and T. F. Torrance (Edinburgh: T&T Clark, 1956–1975), vol. IV/2, 84–85.

[54] Ibid., vol. IV/2, 85.

[55] Ibid., vol. IV/1, 185.

his just judgment on human sinfulness is made to fall upon him. Clearly, every last vestige of an instrumentalization of the human Jesus has been swept away on this account.

Second, the meaning of the cross is not simply that guilt is atoned (though that too happens). Even more fundamentally, however, *the being of sin and of the sinner as such* is put to death and destroyed. Barth writes:

> That is what happened when Jesus Christ, who willed to make Himself the bearer and representative of sin, caused sin to be taken and killed on the cross in his own person (as that of the one great sinner). And in that way, not by suffering our punishment as such, but in the deliverance of sinful man and sin itself to destruction, which He accomplished when He suffered our punishment, He has on the other side blocked the source of our destruction.[56]

Barth stands here in close proximity to the traditional Reformed teaching on penal substitution, but he has radicalized it. "Punishment" is not an act performed by God (or his proxies) upon an innocent human being. It is an act which belongs to God's self-humiliation. And the punishment in question is not physical per se (torture and execution); it is the complete absorption of that eternal death that is the destruction of the sinner.

Third, Barth understands the work of Christ to be effective for us *in being performed*. What is achieved in Jesus Christ is the *reality* of reconciliation and redemption and not merely its possibility – a possibility to be realized in individuals in their own time and place at the point at which the Holy Spirit awakens them to faith and obedience. For Barth, the work of Christ is already effective for all human beings before they are made to be aware of it. And this can be so because the concrete realization of reconciliation and redemption in Jesus Christ is an eschatological event. As such, it stands behind us in the form of a promise and before us as our final end.

CONCLUSION

Reformed Christology, like all doctrinal constructions (however authoritative they may be in the churches) is inherently reformable. To be sure, its originating formulation with its emphasis on "two natures unimpaired" subsequent to their union and its insistence that the gifts given

---

[56] Ibid., vol. IV/1, 254.

to Jesus that exalted him above his fellows were created gifts established a trajectory of meaning and a set of values that would need to be upheld in any Reformed Christology. But it was never intended to preclude further development. And even today, it remains – precisely in its character as a *witness* to the witness of Holy Scripture itself to Jesus Christ – a provisional achievement, subject to further revision. In this chapter, we examined two significant attempts to revise the received Christology. But neither Schleiermacher nor Barth has the final word. We cannot, of course, know what the future holds. But this much we do know: any putatively Reformed Christology of the future will show itself to be such by upholding (as Schleiermacher and Barth tried to do) the values resident in that originating trajectory of witness.

Further reading

Edmondson, Stephen. *Calvin's Christology*. Cambridge: Cambridge University Press, 2004.

Hector, Kevin W. "Actualism and Incarnation: The High Christology of Friedrich Schleiermacher." *International Journal of Systematic Theology* 8.3 (2006): 307–322.

Klappert, Bertold. *Die Auferweckung des Gekreuzigten*, 3rd ed. Neukirchen-Vluyn: Neukirchener Verlag, 1981.

McCormack, Bruce L. "Divine Impassibility or Simply Divine Constancy? Implications of Karl Barth's Later Christology for Debates over Impassibility." In *Divine Impassibility and the Mystery of Human Suffering*. Edited by James F. Keating and Thomas Joseph White, O.P. Grand Rapids, MI: Eerdmans, 2009: 150–186.

  For Us and Our Salvation: Incarnation and Atonement in the Reformed Tradition. Studies in Reformed Theology and History. Princeton, NJ: Princeton Theological Seminary, 1993.

  "Union with Christ in Calvin's Theology: Grounds for a Divinization Theory?" In *Tributes to John Calvin: A Celebration of His Quincentenary*. Edited by David W. Hall. Phillipsburg, NJ: Presbyterian and Reformed Publishing Company, 2010: 504–529.

Opitz, Peter. *Heinrich Bulllinger als Theologie: eine Studie zu den "Dekaden*. Zürich: TVZ, 2004.

Willis, E. David. *Calvin's Catholic Christology: The Function of the so-called Extra Calvinisticum in Calvin's Theology*. Leiden: Brill, 1966.

6 Sacraments

PAUL T. NIMMO

The theology and practice of the sacraments stand central to the events of the Reformation in general and to the distinct identity of the Reformed tradition in particular. Polemic disputes concerning the validity of the sacramental economy of the mediaeval western church were an essential dimension of the former, while no less polemic disputes concerning what should replace that economy had a significant impact upon the latter. Even within the Reformed tradition, there emerged and persist diverse views on the theology of the sacraments. This chapter explores the emergence of specifically Reformed understandings of the sacraments, and the way in which these understandings have been communicated and developed in the tradition to the present day.

EARLY REFORMED VIEWS

A feature common to the writers and churches of the Reformation was a rejection of many features of the mediaeval sacramental system of the western church. Early Protestants were united in denying that there were seven sacraments, positing instead the existence of just the two, dominically commanded sacraments of baptism and eucharist. They also joined in denying that grace was automatically conferred to participants in the sacrament simply by virtue of the rite being performed, emphasising instead the necessity of the Word preached and faith present in the valid administration of the sacraments.

In terms of baptism, early Protestants viewed the sacrament as of import for the whole of life, and thus broadly rejected the sacrament of penance. In terms of the eucharist, early Protestants were additionally agreed in denying the character of the eucharist as propitiatory sacrifice, in rejecting the doctrine of transubstantiation and the adoration of the elements and in insisting upon communion in both kinds and in public worship. Within these delimitations, however, an array of Protestant views developed and flourished. The single most significant division arose between Reformed and Lutheran approaches to the presence of Christ in the eucharist, a division manifest in the failure of Martin Luther and Huldrych Zwingli to reach agreement on the subject in the Marburg Colloquy of 1529. For Luther and the Lutherans, the body and blood of Christ are truly and essentially present in the eucharist, being distributed and received with the eucharistic elements. For Zwingli and the Reformed, however, the body and blood of Christ remain truly and naturally ascended in heaven in the eucharist, and are therefore not locally present with the eucharistic elements.

Yet for all the early Reformed came clearly to distinguish their sacramental theology from that of the early Lutheran tradition, there emerged precisely within the Reformed tradition a variety of approaches to the sacraments. One way to explore this diversity is to attend to the work of three of the tradition's prominent early representatives – Zwingli, Heinrich Bullinger and John Calvin – whose views were paradigmatic for later Reformed sacramental theology.

Huldrych Zwingli

Zwingli developed what might be considered the first Reformed position in sacramental theology. In his late writings, Zwingli writes that a sacrament is merely 'a sign of a sacred thing, i.e., of grace that has been given'.[1] The overall outworking of this definition is to give his sacramental theology something of a memorial emphasis, with the focus upon participants recalling grace already offered and bestowed. Indeed, in his earlier writings, Zwingli offered a sacramental theology that was almost exclusively memorialist in orientation.[2] Yet in his mature work, far from rejecting or downplaying the importance of the sacraments, he posits their manifold virtue: they are sacred and venerable things, instituted and received by Christ himself; they testify to historical facts and represent high things, taking the place of that which they signify and positing an analogy to the things signified; and they augment faith and serve as an oath of allegiance.[3] Indeed, for Zwingli, the sacraments are a divine gift in the administration of which God is active, and they have a correspondingly profound role to play in the liturgical performance of the church. And although he considers the sacraments to be 'so far from

---

[1]   Huldrych Zwingli, 'An Account of the Faith', in *On Providence and Other Essays*, edited by William John Hinke (Eugene, OR: Wipf & Stock, 1999), 48.
[2]   See Huldrych Zwingli, 'On Baptism' and 'On the Lord's Supper', in *Zwingli and Bullinger*, edited by G. W. Bromiley (Library of Christian Classics; Louisville, KY: Westminster John Knox, 2006).
[3]   Huldrych Zwingli, 'An Exposition of the Faith', in *Zwingli and Bullinger*, 262–265.

conferring grace that they do not even convey or dispense it',[4] this view stems not primarily from a humanist rationalism against sacramental realism or a neo-Platonic dualism of inward and outward, but rather directly from his insistence on the unique efficacy of the cross and the divine freedom of the Spirit, both grounded in his exegesis of Scripture.

Zwingli's mature view of baptism thus denies that baptism is a means of grace or necessary for salvation, either of which would bind the activity of Christ and the freedom of the Spirit to human ceremony. There is instead posited – and argued on the grounds of exegesis of Scripture – a clear distinction between Christ's baptism with the Spirit and ecclesial baptism with water. Positively, Zwingli emphasises that (water) baptism is primarily a sign of God's covenant of grace attesting the salvific divine act of election, and secondarily the church's obedient public response in faith to this covenant. The identification of this covenant with the covenant inaugurated with Adam and confirmed with Abraham provides Zwingli with his principal argument against the Anabaptist rejection of infant baptism: 'the promise of God precedes, [such] that He regards our infants, no less than those of the Hebrews, as belonging to the Church'.[5]

In respect of the eucharist, Zwingli again denies the instrumental or salvific efficacy of the sacrament. Once again, there is a clear distinction – here between the internal spiritual participation in the body and blood of Christ, and the external material participation in the sacramental bread and wine. The former is not tied to the sacrament in any way, being equivalent for Zwingli 'to trusting with heart and soul upon the mercy and goodness of God thought Christ'.[6] To partake of the body and blood of Christ sacramentally thus means to partake of the eucharistic signs in just this assurance of unbroken faith in the promises of God – and thus to do inwardly what is attested outwardly. Despite this distinction, and his insistence that the physical body of Christ is ascended to heaven, Zwingli in his later work affirms explicitly that in the eucharist the body of Christ truly has a spiritual and sacramental presence.[7] Indeed, the particular value of the materiality of the sacrament is to direct and discipline the physical senses, and thereby to aid the mind in its spiritual contemplation of Christ who is made present by the Spirit and represented by the elements. The eucharist for Zwingli also possesses a strong corporate dimension, in terms of providing an occasion for and

4 Zwingli, 'An Account of the Faith', 46.
5 Ibid., 47.
6 Zwingli, 'An Exposition of the Faith', 258.
7 Ibid., 258–259.

witness to not only the public thanksgiving and faithful celebration of the church, but also its ethical commitment to reconciliation.

Heinrich Bullinger

Bullinger's sacramental theology has strong affinities with that of Zwingli, but evidences a more theocentric focus. In his *Decades*, Bullinger writes that the sacraments are given in light of human weakness, 'to be witnesses and seals of the preaching of the gospel, to exercise and try faith, and ... to represent and set before our eyes the deep mysteries of God'.[8] There is a clear distinction made by Bullinger between the external visible signs of the sacraments and the internal invisible reality that underlies them; yet the two sides are 'coupled together in a faithful contemplation', joined together 'in likeness and signification'.[9] Thus the sacraments are testimonies of God's grace and seals of God's promises: they neither contain nor convey grace. In celebrating the sacraments, the church offers a visible testimony of its unity with Christ and the unity of its members, and is called once again to renew its faith and obedience. The sacraments are thus effective only for participants who are members of the covenant.

Bullinger defines baptism as a 'holy action ... whereby the Lord Himself represents and seals unto us our purifying or cleansing, gathers us into one body, and puts the baptized in mind of their duty'.[10] First, then, the sacrament of baptism testifies to the regeneration and forgiveness that God by the Spirit alone effects. Second, baptism seals the union of the one undergoing baptism not only with Christ but also with the body of Christ, a union that is founded upon the promise of God and communicated by the Spirit. And finally, the sacrament serves as a public confession of the Christian faith and as a clear exhortation to the Christian's conscience. The justification for infant baptism is once again that 'the young babes and infants of the faithful are in the number or reckoning of God's people, and partakers of the promise'.[11] The forgiveness and adoption of infants is not effected in baptism, but is rather sealed and confirmed in baptism by the mercy and grace of God, who counts infants within the covenant.

In parallel fashion, the eucharist is defined by Bullinger as 'the holy action ... wherein the Lord ... certifies unto us his promise and

---

[8] Henry Bullinger, *The Decades*, 5 vols., edited by Thomas Harding and translated by H. I. (Eugene: Wipf & Stock, 2009–2010), vol. V, sermon 6, 234.

[9] Ibid., V.6, 279.

[10] Ibid., V.8, 352 (translation modernised).

[11] Ibid., V.8, 382.

communion, and shows unto us his gifts, ... gathers [us] into one body visibly, ... and admonishes us of our duty'.[12] In the celebration of this sacrament, then, God renews God's promise to the faithful, and the faithful renew the communion they have received in Christ. Such renewal is not unique to the sacrament: there is a 'spiritual, divine, and quickening presence of our Lord Christ, both in the supper and also out of the supper'.[13] But in both cases, this presence is not by way of signs which lack life, but by way of the Spirit who gives life. Hence although Bullinger agrees that God performs what God promises, the means of communion with Christ in the sacraments is solely faith; the eucharist is but the seal and confirmation of an existing membership of the covenant, keeping the death of Christ and its benefits in the minds of the faithful. Finally, for Bullinger, the eucharist makes the communion of believers with Christ and with each other visible, and there is a public confession of Christian faith and a common exhortation to good works.

John Calvin

The sacramental theology of Calvin bears many resemblances to that of Bullinger, but ascribes rather more mediatorial significance to the sacraments. Writing in the *Institutes*, Calvin posits that a sacrament is 'a testimony of divine grace toward us, confirmed by an outward sign, with mutual attestation of our piety toward him'.[14] Such a testimony is an example of divine accommodation to human weakness, and serves to represent, confirm and seal the promise of grace; to offer instruction and assurance to the recipient; and to establish, sustain and increase their faith. Though the efficacy of a sacrament is void without the instruction of the Word and the power of the Spirit, Calvin does not hesitate to speak of the sacraments as instruments employed by God, such that they not only attest but also effect that which they represent. Indeed, at certain points in his work Calvin is even more explicit that the sacraments were a 'means of grace'.[15] Yet though the sacraments in the *Institutes* are said to have the same function as the Word – to 'offer and set forth Christ to

---

[12] Ibid., V.9, 403 (translation modernised).

[13] Ibid., V.9, 452.

[14] John Calvin, *Institutes of the Christian Religion*, edited by John T. McNeill and translated by Ford Lewis Battles (Library of Christian Classics; 2 vols.; Philadelphia: Westminster, 1960), IV.xiv.1.

[15] See, for example, John Calvin, 'Exposition of the Heads of Agreement', in *Tracts and Letters*, vol. 2, edited and translated by Henry Beveridge (Edinburgh: Banner of Truth, 2009), 227, where the sacraments are described as 'means and instruments of [God's] secret grace'.

us, and in him the treasures of heavenly grace'[16] – nevertheless Calvin avers that the sacraments confer nothing more or different than the Word received in faith, and cautions that their efficacy is confined to the elect. For Calvin, the church confesses publicly its faith and obedience by its participation in the sacraments.

Christian baptism, according to Calvin, serves to set forth the promises of God. First, it offers a token and proof of the forgiveness of sins through Christ, according knowledge and assurance of salvation; second, it renders and demonstrates the recipient a participant in the death and resurrection of Christ; and third, it testifies to the union of the believer with Christ and the sharing of the former in the latter's blessings. Indeed, Calvin writes, 'all the gifts of God proffered in baptism are found in Christ alone'.[17] Baptism does not release the recipient from original sin; however, it does offer assurance that the condemnation of original sin has been removed, and additionally serves as a token of public confession that is received in faith. Christian children, as members of the covenant, are also to be baptised: baptism replaces circumcision as the sign of the covenant, attests Christ's command to allow the children to come to him, and testifies that God's promise of mercy extends to children. Children are baptised 'into future repentance and faith', for 'the seed of both lies hidden within them by the secret working of the Spirit'.[18]

The eucharist, for Calvin, is 'a spiritual banquet, wherein Christ attests himself to be the life-giving bread, upon which our souls feed unto true and blessed immortality'.[19] The sacrament thus seals and confirms the promise that the soul of the participant is fed by the body and blood of Christ just as the bread and wine sustain the physical life. This eucharistic communion with the body and blood of Christ takes place as 'Christ offers and sets forth the reality there signified to all who sit at that spiritual banquet'.[20] The physical body of Christ remains in heaven, but by the mysterious power of the Spirit the souls of the elect are lifted up to heaven to feed on his body, and so to become one with him and to partake of his benefits. The 'flesh of Christ', Calvin writes, 'is like a rich and inexhaustible fountain that pours into us the life springing forth from the Godhead into itself'.[21] Hence, for Calvin, 'In his Sacred

---

[16] Calvin, *Institutes*, IV.xiv.17.
[17] Ibid., IV.xv.6.
[18] Ibid., IV.xvi.20.
[19] Ibid., IV.xvii.1.
[20] Ibid., IV.xvii.10.
[21] Ibid., IV.xvii.9.

Supper [Christ] bids me take, eat, and drink his body and blood under the symbols of bread and wine.'[22] The eucharistic elements are thus intermediaries, truly setting forth the reality behind the signs: under their symbols, the elect feed truly upon Christ, confess their faith and are exhorted to good works of reconciliation.

Common and uncommon ground

With the help of the preceding exploration, a number of features common to the sacramental theologies of the emerging Reformed tradition can be recognised. For the Reformed, the sacraments do not add anything materially to the content of the Word, and hence there is no unique grace pertaining to their celebration. Correspondingly, there is a strong emphasis on the divine institution of the sacraments as a didactic aid serving to accommodate human weakness and insecurity and to lift the mind and the soul to the promises of God. The sacraments serve as divinely instituted markers of the covenant of God, as signs and seals of the promises of God to the elect, and their eligibility is limited to those with faith or in the context of faith. This limitation relates to the Reformed insistence on a clear distinction between the physical elements used and the spiritual realities signified. The sacraments are also seen to offer a public attestation of covenant membership, and to serve as a strong exhortation to the covenant people to respond to God's promise in ongoing faith and obedience.

In their approach to baptism, the Reformed thus warmly embrace infant baptism as a sign of the covenant, drawing on the continuity of the old and the new covenants to recognise infants as members of the covenant. However, the Reformed reject emergency baptism as unnecessary, thus according higher significance to the covenant promise of God than to the sacramental efficacy of baptism. As for the eucharist, the Reformed insist upon the post-ascension presence of the body of Christ in heaven and on the clear distinction of his divine and human natures, such that no local or corporeal presence of the body of Christ is possible in the sacrament; only a spiritual or sacramental – though no less real – presence is possible. As a corollary, the Spirit plays a pivotal role in the Reformed understanding of the sacrament, uniting the covenant faithful with and in the body of Christ while denying the unworthy or unfaithful any communication at all with the body of Christ. In the celebration of both sacraments, the only appropriate setting is the public service of worship and the only appropriate officiant is the lawfully

[22] Ibid., IV.xvii.32.

ordained minister. Church discipline often featured prominently in ascertaining which of the faithful could participate.

At the same time as recognising these broad contours of a Reformed view of the sacraments, however, it is also readily apparent that the three Reformers explored earlier exhibit rather different tendencies in their particular formulations. Zwingli's main emphasis is on the human activity in the sacraments, responding to the divine promise and witnessing to the church's obedience. Even in his mature theology, where the initiative of God and the presence of Christ are affirmed more decisively, there is a clear separation of internal and external, and the balance of the material remains on the ethical dimension of the sacraments. Bullinger's approach is rather more even-handed in its weighting, emphasising first the institution and initiative of God in the sacraments and then the action and witness of the church. With his language of 'seal' and 'testimony', he posits a conception of the sacraments where the earthly sacramental activity provides an analogy of the invisible spiritual activity, without conceiving the relationship between the two activities in terms of means or instrumentality. Calvin, while acknowledging fully the didactic and ethical importance of the sacraments, writes of the sacraments as instruments or even means of grace, which effect what they signify. The result is a greater willingness to speak about God acting through or under or by the sacraments and thus a sometime explicit causal connection between the external and the internal.

The Reformed confessions and catechisms

Though the material exposition in the preceding text has concerned itself primarily with the theological views of three of the most significant voices in the early Reformed tradition, it has always been the case within the tradition that such individual voices are far less significant than the ecclesial statements which underpin the faith of the Reformed churches. In turning to the confessions and catechisms of the early Reformed churches, however, one is immediately struck by the way in which the theological contents of these documents broadly tend to align with one or other of the three trajectories delineated earlier. On one level, this can hardly surprise, given that some of these documents were authored by the figures themselves, or at least by their close allies. On another level, it reflects the fact that within the spectrum of theological terrain delimited by the Reformed, only so many theological trajectories are possible. In what follows, a series of examples will be used to evidence these alignments, with a particular focus on the extent to which the sacraments are conceived as instruments or means of grace.[23]

The church documents which directly follow Zwingli are the least numerous in number. The Zürich Confession of 1545, one example, posits of the eucharist that 'the memorial of the sacrificed body and shed blood [of Christ] for the forgiveness of sins is [its] principal centre and end'.[24] The purpose of the eucharist is thus to be a memorial of what Christ has done, 'serving our stupidity, showing clearly that Christ gives Himself completely to be ours and is one with us, giving significant assistance, provocation, and nourishment to faith'.[25]

More numerous are those documents which seem to align more with Bullinger. The Heidelberg Catechism of 1563, for example, describes the sacraments as 'visible, holy signs and seals' for God 'the better [to] intimate and seal the promise of the gospel'.[26] On baptism, it posits that 'by this divine pledge and sign he wishes to assure us that we are just as truly washed from our sins spiritually as our bodies are washed with water physically'.[27] And on the eucharist, it states that 'we come to share in his true body and blood by the working of the Holy Spirit as truly as we receive with our own mouth these holy signs in remembrance of him'.[28] There is little sense of instrumentality here, but in contrast – and in line with Bullinger – there is a pronounced parallelism of external and internal which results in a view primarily testimonial and didactic in nature. The same is true, perhaps predictably, of Bullinger's own composition, the Second Helvetic Confession of 1566. This text declares not only that the sacraments keep in mind the benefits of God but that by them, God 'seals his promises, and represents outwardly those things which he himself provides to us inwardly'.[29] Analogous statements follow on the parallel of outward and inward in the two sacraments.[30]

In the French Confession of 1559, to the writing of which Calvin contributed, a rather different note is sounded. Here, the sacraments

[23] Cf. B. A. Gerrish, famously, in 'Sign and Reality: The Lord's Supper in the Reformed Confessions', in *The Old Protestantism and the New: Essays on the Reformation Heritage* (Edinburgh: T&T Clark, 1982), 118–130.

[24] *Zürich Confession* (1545), in *Reformierte Bekenntnisschriften* (hereafter RB), six volumes to date (Neukirchen: Neukirchener, 2002–), 1/2, 457.

[25] Ibid., in RB 1/2, 463.

[26] *Heidelberg Catechism* (1563), in RB 2/2, 191 – A. 66.

[27] Ibid., 193 – A. 73.

[28] Ibid., 195 – A. 79.

[29] *Second Helvetic Confession* (1566), in RB 2/2, 323, §19.

[30] Ibid., 328, §20, and 330, §21.

are described as 'outward signs through which God operates by his Spirit, in order that he does not signify anything to us in vain'.[31] This note of instrumentality is consistent with the treatments of baptism and eucharist, which suggest more than a simple parallelism of internal and external: in baptism, 'we are grafted into the body of Christ in order to be washed and cleaned by his blood and then renewed unto holy life by his Spirit', while 'we conjoin with the [eucharistic] signs the true possession and enjoyment of that which is presented to us there'.[32] Similar instrumental language marks the Belgic Confession of 1561, whose composition owes much to the French Confession. Here, it is stated that the sacraments are '[a] symbol and visible signs of the interior and invisible matter, by which God works in us by the power of his Spirit'.[33] Such language is highly reminiscent of Calvin, though it is of note that both of these confessions avoid following Calvin's descriptions of the human body of Christ in itself being essentially life-giving.

Highly significant in respect of the last two explorations is the text of the Consensus of Zürich of 1549, a statement on the sacraments in general and the eucharist in particular which was agreed by Bullinger and Calvin. There is evidence that, in their desire to reach unity, both thinkers had to compromise: for example, Bullinger explicitly agrees to the description of the sacraments as 'implements' and 'aids', while Calvin implicitly agrees to the omission of the descriptors 'instruments' and 'means of grace'.[34] Throughout the document, any claim which inclines towards Calvin's position is immediately qualified or succeeded by a claim more reflecting Bullinger's position. The resultant compromise may have been politically expedient and successful, but theologically it remains ambiguous.

LATER REFORMED VIEWS

The post-Reformation Reformed tradition continued to adhere to the broad contours of sacramental theology outlined earlier without demurral, departure, or controversy. However, within those rather capacious bounds, a diverse range of positions developed and flourished, falling into a familiar series of patterns.

---

[31] *French Confession* (1559), in RB 2/1, 27, article XXXIV.
[32] Ibid., 27, article XXXV, and 28, article XXXVII.
[33] *Belgic Confession* (1561), in RB 2/1, 339, article XXIII.
[34] *Consensus of Zürich* (1549), in RB 1/2, 485, articles 13 and 14.

Reformed orthodoxy

In the movement of Reformed orthodoxy in the seventeenth century, the view of Zwingli broadly continued to recede from view; however, during this period the differing influences of Bullinger and Calvin remain clearly in evidence. In apparent line with the former, for example, Amandus Polanus writes that the sacraments 'save us, certainly not as efficient causes or as instruments for the conferral of grace and salvation ... but as signs and seals to believers for the attestation of grace and salvation, which are conferred by God alone'.[35] Meanwhile, in apparent line with the latter, for example, Francis Turretin avers that 'God uses [the sacraments] as organs and instruments for offering and conferring grace upon us in their own way.'[36] Examples of both tendencies might be multiplied, while the Westminster Confession evidences both approaches: on baptism, its language is instrumental – 'by the right use of this ordinance, the grace promised is not only offered, but really exhibited, and conferred, by the Holy Ghost';[37] on the eucharist, it evidences a parallel – 'Worthy receivers, outwardly partaking of the visible elements, ... do then also, inwardly by faith, ... receive and feed upon, Christ crucified, and all benefits of His death'.[38]

Such currents of similarity and difference continued broadly unchanged through the eighteenth century, and the complex interplay of theological scholasticism, Enlightenment rationalism, and evangelical pietism perpetuated the broad spectrum of positions within the sacramental theology of the Reformed tradition. In an age marked by growing metaphysical scepticism, however, the bodily absence of Christ in the eucharist and – as a corollary, the moral duty and importance of the eucharist – were both increasingly emphasised.

Friedrich Schleiermacher

The work of Friedrich Schleiermacher in the early nineteenth century contributed two rather fresh notes to the Reformed theology of the sacraments. First, Schleiermacher questions the validity of the (non-biblical) concept of 'sacraments' as a genus containing the species of baptism and

---

[35] Amandus Polanus, *Syntagma theologiae christianae* (Hanau: Wechel, 1615), VI.LI, 492.

[36] Francis Turretin, *Institutes of Elenctic Theology*, edited by James T. Dennison, Jr. and translated by George Musgrave Giger, 3 vol. (Philipsburg, NJ: Presbyterian and Reformed Publishing Company, 1992), vol. 3, 347.

[37] *Westminster Confession of Faith* (1647), chapter XXVIII.6, in *The Confession of Faith and the Larger and Shorter Catechisms* (Glasgow: Free Presbyterian Publications, 1973), 116.

[38] Ibid., chapter XXIX.7, in *The Confession of Faith*, 119.

eucharist. While Zwingli raised (and dropped) the same query centuries before, Schleiermacher relegates the concept of 'sacrament' to an appendix, concluding that 'if the term is still to be used, nothing more is left to us than to mark it in a purely arbitrary way and without any further consideration for its original sense as a communal description for both these institutions'.[39] Second, spurred by the desire to strengthen the Prussian union of Lutheran and Reformed churches, Schleiermacher presents his theology of the eucharist in irenic fashion, akin to the sporadic early Protestant attempts to pursue dialogue and unity. Though aware of the different eucharistic views of the two churches, he comments on 'how little it is suited to justifying a separation of the church community'.[40]

Baptism, Schleiermacher observes, is an act of the church in which it receives the individual into its community and the medium of the justifying divine activity, by which the individual is taken up into communion of life with Christ. This would suggest a highly instrumental view of baptism, yet Schleiermacher acknowledges that such is in truth an ideal picture. The reality is that the external event of baptism in the church and the internal event of regeneration by the Spirit may not coincide at all. Nevertheless, internal and external are not to be severed: if the Spirit works first, there exists an 'imperative demand' to have baptism follow immediately, and if baptism occurs first, this is legitimated only when it is believed that the 'regeneration of the one received [in baptism] will follow from the influences of the community'.[41] This latter view undergirds Schleiermacher's defence of infant baptism, though he notes: 'at the time of the Reformation, one could very reasonably have abandoned infant baptism ... and we could do this even now without thereby seceding from the community in that period'.[42]

The eucharist, Schleiermacher writes, has at its heart the strengthening and uniting of two communions – the communion of Christ with the believer, and the communion of the believer with the church. Once again, there is in view a material activity of the church and a spiritual activity of Christ; once again, the issue is how to relate them. Eschewing the 'empirical' views of sacramentarians and the 'magical' views of Roman Catholics, Schleiermacher affirms a Protestant middle path, offering careful presentations and astute criticisms of the

---

[39] Friedrich D. E. Schleiermacher, *The Christian Faith*, 2nd ed. (1830/1831), translated by H. R. Mackintosh and J. S. Stewart (Edinburgh: T & T Clark, 1928), §143.1, 659 (translation revised).

[40] Schleiermacher, *The Christian Faith*, §142.3, 657 (translation revised).

[41] Ibid., §136.3, 623 (translation revised).

[42] Ibid., §138.1, 637 (translation revised).

sacramental theologies of Zwingli, Luther, and Calvin. However, he considers that not one of these is able to explain fully the relationships involved in the eucharist. Instead, he optimistically concludes that 'it is to be expected that, on the basis of the continued unprejudiced work of the interpreters, a still further [conception] will develop, which will not be shipwrecked on all these cliffs'.[43] Schleiermacher, then, has little by way of a position of his own to advance here.

Mercersburg controversy

Shortly after the time of Schleiermacher, a major sacramental controversy arose within Reformed theology in the United States. On the one side were the Mercersburg theologians, notably John Nevin, a minister Reformed in instinct yet influenced by German Idealism. The vision of sacramental theology Nevin offers was one that he believed to be true to Calvin, but to stand in marked contrast to the dominant contemporary view which he considered more rationalist, more subjective and indebted to Zwingli. Nevin emphasises Calvin's idea that in the eucharist the participant is united by the power of the Spirit to the whole person of Christ – divine and human. Nevin writes: '[t]he participation is not simply in His Spirit but in his flesh also and blood ... not figurative merely and moral, but real, *substantial* and *essential*'.[44] The result is that the sacrament exerts 'a peculiar, and altogether extraordinary power ... to the benefit of the believer'.[45] On the other side were the Princeton theologians, represented by Charles Hodge, who rejected both the eucharistic doctrine that Nevin advanced and the interpretation of Calvin that grounded it. Hodge notes that to write of the eucharist as having a peculiar power – over and against the Word – is not a move which Calvin makes. And Hodge argues that the true Reformed doctrine 'offers a complete estoppel of the claim ... that our union with Christ involves a participation of his human body, nature or life'.[46] Though Hodge does agree with Calvin (and Nevin) that the eucharist is a means of grace, then, his resistance to Calvin's teaching that the humanity of Christ is essentially offered in the Supper is more in line with the view

---

[43] Ibid., §140.4, 650–651 (translation revised).

[44] John W. Nevin, 'The Mystical Presence', in *The Mystical Presence and The Doctrine of the Reformed Church on the Lord's Supper*, edited by Linden J. DeBie (Mercersburg Theology Study Series; Eugene, OR: Wipf & Stock, 2012), 48.

[45] Ibid., 104.

[46] Charles Hodge, 'Doctrine of the Reformed Church', review of John W. Nevin, 'The Mystical Presence', quoted in Nevin, 'The Doctrine of the Reformed Church on the Lord's Supper', in *The Mystical Presence*, 236.

of Bullinger or Zwingli. Again, divisions in the tradition of sacramental theology seem to fall along historical lines.

Karl Barth

In the twentieth century, the work of Barth underwent a notable evolution in respect of its understanding of the sacraments. Commenting on this change in his sacramental theology, Barth writes: 'here ... I have learned to consider a respectfully careful "demythologising" as advisable'.[47] At its root, his sacramental 'demythologisation' rejects the idea that baptism or the eucharist is a 'sacrament' or a 'mystery'. Instead, it endorses the view that there is only one sacrament or mystery – Jesus Christ – and that the 'sacraments' of the church simply respond to that mystery. For this reason, Barth treats baptism (and planned to treat the eucharist) within the ethical part-volume of his doctrine of reconciliation.

Baptism, Barth posits, is a matter of 'a basic human Yes to God's grace and revelation, but not of a sacrament, not of a means of grace and revelation'.[48] A corollary of this position is that the clear distinction that Barth posits between the two basic elements which found the Christian life – between baptism with the Spirit and baptism with water. Barth writes '[o]n the one side it is completely about the activity of God turned towards the human being; on the other side, it is completely about the activity of the human being turned towards God that is enabled and evoked by it'.[49] There is thus a clear distinction of internal and external that is basic to Barth's view of baptism and that has much in common with the teaching of Bullinger. The internal is the divine Word and command, given in God's gift of new life; the external is the human response to this gift by way of undergoing baptism in corresponding freedom and obedience. The liberty and responsibility involved leads to Barth famously rejecting infant baptism.

Though Barth did not survive to write his mature treatment of the eucharist, he indicated that its shape could be deduced from his doctrine of baptism. On that basis, it would seem that Barth would deny that the Lord's Supper was a sacrament, understood as a means of grace or revelation, and that he would posit a distinction between the divine feeding of the Christian with the body and blood of Christ and the human response of eating the bread and wine of the Supper. In this way,

---

[47] Karl Barth, *Church Dogmatics*, 4 vols. in 13 parts, edited by G. W. Bromiley and T. F. Torrance (Edinburgh: T&T Clark, 1956–1975), vol. IV/2, xi (translation revised).

[48] Ibid., vol. IV/4, 118 (translation revised).

[49] Ibid., vol. IV/4, 41 (translation revised).

Barth would once again align with Bullinger. In responding to the divine act of reconciliation through the body and blood of Christ, Barth writes, 'Our human work has to acknowledge the work of God, to bear witness to it, to confess it, to respond to it, to honour, praise and glorify it.'[50] The obedient response to the command to celebrate the eucharist would thus be humble and modest work: the sacramental presence of Christ is not at its discretion, for the movement of Christ is something that can be sought only in prayer.

Recent trends

In the latter half of the twentieth century, the Reformed churches have played a significant role in bilateral and multilateral ecumenical dialogues, and there have been notable shifts in sacramental practice in many Reformed churches.

First, in respect of ecumenical dialogue, one significant landmark has been the Leuenberg Concord between many Lutheran and Reformed churches in 1973, establishing a mutual recognition of ministries and sacraments. The Concord itself states that '[i]n preaching, Baptism and the Lord's Supper, Jesus Christ is present through the Holy Spirit',[51] though it does not specify the mode of personal presence further. The statements on the individual sacraments are similarly open to interpretation. The Concord posits that 'In Baptism Jesus Christ receives irrevocably human beings ... into his fellowship of salvation, that they might become new creatures.'[52] In the Lord's Supper, the Concord states, 'the risen Jesus Christ imparts himself in his body and blood, given up for all, through his word of promise with bread and wine',[53] and 'We cannot separate communion with Jesus Christ in his body and blood from the act of eating and drinking'.[54] In both cases, the mode of the presence of Christ and the instrumentality of the elements are felicitously ill-defined, being explicitly considered of secondary importance, and the text is thus generally susceptible of interpretation in modes consonant with Calvin and Bullinger (and Luther). With the statement indicating a lack of separability of spiritual and sacramental feeding, however, it may be that the Concord goes beyond what some traditional Reformed theologians could accept.

---

[50] Ibid., vol. IV/4, 72 (translation revised).
[51] *Leuenberg Concord* (1973), article 13, at http://www.leuenberg.net/sites/default/files/media/PDF/publications/konkordie-en.pdf (accessed 1 March, 2015).
[52] Ibid., article 14.
[53] Ibid., articles 15 and 18.
[54] Ibid., article 19.

A further major landmark in Reformed involvement with the ecumenical process was the signing by many Reformed churches of the World Council of Churches statement on 'Baptism, Eucharist, and Ministry' in 1982. This was a major achievement, reflecting a significant degree of convergence between the major Christian confessions on matters sacramental without pretending a realised consensus. While the core ecumenical difficulties over the eucharist – the understanding of its sacrificial dimension and the nature of Christ's eucharistic presence – remain explicitly unresolved, the contribution of Reformed theology to the document's agreed emphases on the memorial dimension of the eucharist and the Spirit's agency in the eucharist should not be overlooked.[55]

Efforts to render the Reformed understanding of the eucharist ecumenically fruitful – notably in conversation with Roman Catholic and Eastern Orthodox teaching – have naturally focussed on the teaching of Calvin and those who followed him doctrinally. This is an obvious strategy insofar as there can arise in this trajectory vivid eucharistic discourse concerning the presence and communion of the body and blood of Christ. Such a trajectory is visible in the work of a series of recent Reformed theologians who have sought to foster conversation with other communions, including Alasdair Heron and George Hunsinger.[56]

Second, in respect of Reformed practice, there have been two perceptible developments in sacramental activity in Reformed churches. A first shift has been that in many Reformed congregations, the frequency of eucharistic celebration has increased, with monthly rather than quarterly or biannual celebrations now a regular norm. It has always been a source of irony that some of the pioneers of the Reformed tradition such as Calvin advocated a weekly eucharist, but that this view found normative acceptance only in other traditions. This situation is now slowly changing. A second shift has been the growing tendency in some Reformed denominations for parents to prefer infant dedication over infant baptism, allowing children to decide on baptism in later years. This trend finds theological support in the work of Barth, as noted previously, and of Jürgen Moltmann, who also discerned little exegetical or

---

[55] *Baptism, Eucharist and Ministry* (1982), in *Baptism, Eucharist and Ministry: The Agreed Text* (Geneva: WCC Publications, 1982), Eucharist sections II.B.5–13 and II.C.14–18 respectively.
[56] See, for example, Alasdair Heron, *Table and Tradition: Towards an Ecumenical Understanding of the Eucharist* (Edinburgh: Handsel Press, 1983), and George Hunsinger, *The Eucharist and Ecumenism: Let Us Keep the Feast* (Cambridge: Cambridge University Press, 2008).

doctrinal support for infant baptism.[57] Many denominations now offer the choice of baptism or blessing for infants. In both these respects, as in many others, the Reformed churches continue to reform.

CONCLUSION

The Reformed tradition does not possess one sacramental theology; rather, within certain circumscribed bounds, the tradition evidences a diverse array of sacramental theologies. For all this diversity, such variety – particularly in terms of eucharistic theology – has seldom been church-dividing, and precisely this ability to navigate differences within a common confessional discourse has resonances with recent ecumenical discussion. At the same time, it would be troubling if in the understandable desire for ecumenical consensus the full range of Reformed sacramental theologies was eclipsed. On one level, such a manoeuvre would be historically unrepresentative and theologically limiting by dint of its suppressing insights with good scriptural foundation and important theological justification. But on another level, it might damage the possibility of the Reformed tradition to reach out to churches that are currently ill-served by contemporary ecumenism – particularly free churches, Pentecostal churches, and emerging churches. Over and above its foundational and evolving content, in its very multivocity the Reformed sacramental tradition may have much to offer.

Further reading

Gerrish, B. A. *Grace and Gratitude: The Eucharistic Theology of John Calvin.* Minneapolis, MN: Fortress, 1993.

Heron, Alasdair. *Table and Tradition: Towards an Ecumenical Understanding of the Eucharist.* Edinburgh: Handsel Press, 1983.

Riggs, John W. *Baptism in the Reformed Tradition: An Historical and Practical Theology.* Louisville, KY: Westminster John Knox, 2002.

   The Lord's Supper in the Reformed Tradition: An Essay on the Mystical True Presence. Louisville, KY: Westminster John Knox, 2015.

Rorem, Paul. *Calvin and Bullinger on the Lord's Supper.* Nottingham: Grove Books, 1989.

Wright, David F. *Infant Baptism in Historical Perspective: Collected Studies.* Studies in Christian History and Thought. London: Paternoster, 2007.

---

[57] Jürgen Moltmann, *The Church in the Power of the Spirit*, translated by Margaret Kohl (London: SCM Press, 1992), 240–242.

7 The Christian life

CYNTHIA L. RIGBY

Reformed theologies teach that all lives are lived before the sovereign God. What distinguishes "The Christian Life" is perception of this fact – Christians live, day-by-day, with some awareness of the character of their existence. Reformed communities have, historically, attended to fostering accurate perception in both themselves and others. This is because, as John Calvin puts it, without knowledge of their election God's children can neither enjoy God's "benefits"[1] nor embrace the particular vocations to which they are called. To live the Christian life, Reformed theologians teach, is actively to inspire and nurture this perception, so the people of God might be positioned to receive God's good gifts gratefully and to take their respective places obediently in the "theatre of God's glory."[2]

The challenge is that sin and finitude skew the vision even of those who are eager to perceive rightly. Living the Christian life requires that the children of God repent of sin, acknowledge their forgiveness, and remember they are clothed with the righteousness of Christ before the God who has claimed them. When necessary, it may also entail being disciplined by other Christian believers to whom they are accountable. Abraham Kuyper explains, along these lines, that church discipline is necessary for "purifying" the church.[3]

Finitude can impede perception, but in a different way than does sin. Calvin asserts that the elect are, in and of themselves, too "bleary-eyed"[4] to see clearly either who God is or who they are in

---

[1] See John Calvin, *Institutes of the Christian Religion*, edited by John T. McNeill and translated by Ford Lewis Battles (Library of Christian Classics; 2 vols.; Philadelphia: Westminster, 1960), throughout but especially III.xx.

[2] See, for example, Calvin's Commentary on Psalm 104:31, quoted in William J. Bouwsma, *John Calvin: A Sixteenth-Century Portrait* (New York: Oxford University Press, 1988), 135.

[3] See James D. Bratt (ed.), *Abraham Kuyper: A Centennial Reader* (Grand Rapids, MI: Eerdmans, 1998), 194.

[4] Calvin, *Institutes*, I.vi.1.

relationship to God. Given this, Reformed Christians reassure one another with the "good news" that salvation rests not with humanity's capacity to reach God, but with God's determination to meet human beings. Calvin taught, along these lines, that God "accommodates" Godself to us, "lisping" to us as a nanny might speak to a small child.[5] And this accommodating God is not only "the Lord who is Servant," according to Barth, but also "the Servant who is Lord." Jesus Christ humbles himself to be with us and then exalts us along with him, raising us to new life.[6] "Our hearts are lifted up," the Reformed often say in the communion liturgy, celebrating believers' participation in the very life of the triune God.

Historically, Reformed Christian believers commonly reflect on how Christian life is formed, maintained, and lived out in the context both of self-identified Christian communities and of the secular world. The first part of this chapter considers, then, how Reformed theologians describe Christian life in the context of what Calvin and others have called "the visible church" – the church comprising those who confess Jesus as Lord and who participate in the worshipping community.[7] How have Reformed theological resources understood the role of prayer, Bible study, confession, obedience to the Law, worship, sacraments, and service in Christian life? How does attention to such spiritual practices assist God's children in remembering their union with Christ?[8] How and why do Christians shape an "ordered life" together, as members of the community of faith? How might Christian believers of the twenty-first century learn from earlier Reformed understandings of the biblical mandate to "submit to one another out of reverence for Christ" [Eph. 5:21] as a strategy for living life in the Christian community? And how are contemporary theologians understanding differently the submission required for life together, amending older understandings in the spirit of the Reformed commitment to ever being reformed "according to the Word of God"?[9]

---

5 Ibid., I.xiii.1.

6 Karl Barth, *Church Dogmatics*, 4 vols. in 13 parts, edited by G. W. Bromiley and T. F. Torrance (Edinburgh: T&T Clark, 1956–1975), vols. IV/1 and IV/2.

7 Calvin makes the distinction between the church visible and the church invisible in *Institutes*, IV.i.7.

8 For an insightful discussion of how Calvin understands "union with Christ" to make possible our "communion with the incomprehensible God," see chapter 3 of Todd Billings' *Union with Christ: Reframing Theology and Ministry for the Church* (Grand Rapids, MI: Baker Academic, 2011).

9 This idea is commonly conveyed in the Latin, *"Ecclesia reformata semper reformanda secundum verbum Dei."*

The second part reflects on Reformed understandings of the Christian life in the context of the "church invisible"[10] – the church in the world, the places where believers recognize the Holy Spirit in evidence outside the visible church, in the work of those who do not identify themselves as "Christian." How have Reformed theologies reflected on what Christian life should look like in the "public square"? What is the place of evangelism – the importance and shape of witness in the context of cultural discourse and debate? Here, a second controversial matter is considered, namely: According to Reformed understandings, is there any sense in which faithful Christian living can advance the coming of the Kingdom of God?

CHRISTIAN LIFE AND THE VISIBLE CHURCH

God's decision and our agency

We have noted that Reformed understandings of what it means to live the Christian life begin with the acknowledgment that faithfulness is accomplished not by the application of creaturely wherewithal, but solely by way of God's power at work in the life of a believer. A logical question emerges at this point, one that is raised almost universally but addressed in a variety of ways by different Reformed theologians. It is this: If God is the sole agent of salvation, how is it that human beings are not rendered passive in the dynamic? Reformed theologians work very hard at explaining how human beings exercise real agency in events that are accomplished solely by God. Calvin, for example, is appalled at the charge that his doctrine of predestination is understood to be deterministic, taking on his critics with the argument that, though the sovereign God can use evil human actions to accomplish good, it is nonetheless the case that human beings are exercising their free will when doing harm.[11] Jonathan Edwards argues that works of love are the "grand evidence" faith, and is consequently accused of believing that charity is in some way required for salvation. He insists, however, that he in no way wavers from the doctrine of justification by faith alone, but rather believes (with the writer of James) that faith will inevitably "issue in practice."[12] Barth holds that, in and through the person of the One who

---

[10] Calvin, *Institutes*, IV.i.7.

[11] Ibid., I.xvii.5.

[12] Conrad Cherry, *The Theology of Jonathan Edwards: A Reappraisal* (Bloomington: Indiana University Press, 1990), 133–134, citing from Jonathan Edwards, *Works of Jonathan Edwards* II, edited by Perry Miller (New Haven, CT: Yale University Press, 1957), 441.

is "fully human and fully divine," we can see how human beings can be "genuine subjects" in the event of salvation without compromising the sovereignty of God.[13] All three of these theologians are examples of Reformed thinkers who understand Christian life to be a gift that is given entirely by God but also fully and freely shaped by the gifted ones who, in Christ, have been made partners in the work of God in the world.

Embracing this idea that God and human beings are "double agents," Reformed theologies exhort human beings to be good stewards of their Christian lives, taking responsibility for nurturing their own faith and the faith of others in their charge. An image that colorfully illustrates this is that of Calvin, sitting with the consistory in Geneva, interviewing men and women about the content and regularity of their faith practices. "Were you in church this past Sunday? Did you understand the sermon? Can you say the Lord's Prayer?" – these are some of the basic questions people were asked about spiritual behaviors they were expected to cultivate.[14] While the work of the consistory is interpreted by some as being overly meddlesome, it seems the interviews required by the consistory were devised less for the purpose of controlling people and more as a way of encouraging them to learn the practices that would enable them to deepen in their perception of their relationship with God.

Gratitude, humility, and freedom

Recognizing that the favor God extends to us is pure gift, Reformed theologians insist that Christian life be marked by *gratitude*. Brian Gerrish notes that there is an inextricable connection, in Christian life, between "gratitude" and "grace."[15] Donald McKim advises his students to "breathe in grace" and to "breathe out gratitude."[16] The idea is that when the children of God perceive that they have been claimed, by the grace of God, "before the foundation of the world" (Eph. 1:4), and when they accept that God is "completing this good work in us until the day of Jesus Christ" (Phil. 1:6), they will be filled with gratitude, empowered to act. The spiritual disciplines and works of love that follow will be

---

[13] Barth, *Church Dogmatics*, vol. IV/2, 10.

[14] Remarkably, we have transcripts of some of these interviews. See *Registers of the Consistory of Geneva in the Time of Calvin*, vol. 1, 1542–1544, edited by Isabella Watt and Robert Kingdon(Grand Rapids, MI: Eerdmans, 2002). It is not clear how often John Calvin was actually in attendance, or how many questions he asked.

[15] Brian Gerrish, *Grace and Gratitude: The Eucharistic Theology of John Calvin* (Eugene, OR: Wipf & Stock, 2002).

[16] Donald McKim, "Grace and Gratitude," in *Gathering Voices: Conversations from TheThoughtfulChristian.com*. At http://blog.thethoughtfulchristian.com/2011/12/grace-and-gratitude.html (accessed February 20, 2015).

funded by appreciation and determination to enjoy ever more fully this gift of overflowing, superabundant life and promise.

Recognizing that the favor God extends is accomplished in no way due to some superior worthiness, the life of a Christian believer is grounded in *humility*. Reformed theologians unfailingly teach that the "elect" are saved by grace alone, "so that no one may boast" (Eph. 2:9). But Reformed theologians often emphasize that this humility issues not from a perfunctory recognition a person has received a gift he or she has not earned. Rather, the humility that, ideally, characterizes Christian life ensues when individuals embrace the transforming reality that they have been undone and remade by a grace that lays claim to them even though they are – in and of themselves – entirely unsuitable. Barth speaks, in relation to this phenomenon, of experiencing "startled humility" – a joyous humility Christians feel when they perceive they are fully included in God's salvific work by virtue of their union with Christ. Barth identifies "startled humility" to be at play in Philippians 2:13: "Work out your salvation with fear and trembling." Barth comments that what Paul means, here, is that "fear and trembling is what it takes! In the reality of the kingdom of Christ, everyone who there puts their future salvation into practice is placed in a position of humility. They are put there by remembering the grace in which they participate in Jesus Christ."[17] Barth's read, again, is not that it is a sense of unworthiness that here humbles the Christian believer. Rather, what humbles the Christian to the core is the surprising news that he or she has been made wholly worthy in Christ and can therefore discern what God wills and do things that help.

Recognizing that the favor God extends to us is irrevocable, the life of a Christian believer is characterized by *freedom*. Calvin asserts that the freedoms of the Christian are three: they are free from the Law to obey it, they are free from things that do not matter (*adiaphora*), and they are free to use God's gifts for God's purposes.[18] As those who are already seen by God, in Christ, as completely righteous, Christians have no compulsion to keep the Law in the hope they can accrue favor with God. Free of that pressure, they keep the Law because it helps them to be, in actuality, the righteous people they believe they already are in Christ. Reformed theologians have commonly identified this as "the third use of the Law." If the first use of the Law is to unveil our sin and direct us to Christ, and the second use of the Law is the "civil" use that preserves God's children in the context of the world at large,

---

[17] Karl Barth, *Epistle to the Philippians* (Nashville: Westminster John Knox, 2002), 73.
[18] Calvin, *Institutes*, III.xix.

the "third use of the Law" is, as Calvin puts it, to "urge Christians on in well-doing."[19] As Serene Jones points out, the Law helps Christians imagine what it is that God desires not only for them, but also for the world.[20] Paul Lehmann holds that the Decalogue helps people of faith live out their conviction that human beings are created and are being redeemed for promoting life (keeping the Sabbath, not killing or stealing), for honoring covenant relationships (worshipping God alone, not committing adultery, respecting parents), and for being honest with one another (not lying). Free from having to worry about what does not matter (such as, for example, debates about dietary restrictions), human beings have the time and energy to invest in enjoying the blessings of this world. In contrast to asceticism, Reformed traditions following the Law generally encourage family life and friendships, appreciation of science and culture, and enjoyment of food and drink.[21]

Faith practices in Christian life

Reformed traditions, remembering God's steadfast claim on each of God's children, emphasize that each one should appreciate and nurture a direct relationship with God. This idea is supported by the Reformation teaching known as "the priesthood of all believers" – the idea that all Christian believers are "priests" in the sense that they need no other Mediator between themselves and God than Jesus Christ himself (1 Tim. 2:5). Faith practices should, then, be consistent with the Reformed conviction that salvation lies "in Christ alone" (*solus Christus*) "by grace alone" (*sola gratia*) "through faith alone" (*sola fide*) for the glory of God alone (*soli deo gloria*). Christians are also expected to acknowledge brothers and sisters in Christ as fellow priests who similarly enjoy unmediated fellowship with God. Together they gather to worship, trusting God to be present wherever the Word is proclaimed and the sacraments rightly administered. Together they claim the Good News that God is with them in ministry to the community both inside and outside the walls of the church.

Calvin understands prayer to be the "chief exercise of faith" through which we receive all God's benefits. Believers are invited to pray about anything and everything, always honestly, without pretention, and with

---

[19] Calvin discusses the three uses of the Law in *Institutes*, II.vii.12–13.

[20] See Serene Jones, "Glorious Creation, Beautiful Law," in *Feminist and Womanist Essays in Reformed Dogmatics* (Nashville: Westminster John Knox, 2006), 19–39.

[21] See Paul Lehmann, *The Decalogue and a Human Future: The Meaning of the Commandments for Making and Keeping Human Life Human* (Grand Rapids, MI: Eerdmans, 1994).

a sense of need. In prayer we are assured of our justification in Christ, reclaiming "firm and certain knowledge of God's benevolence to us."[22] In prayer we are also well positioned for the Holy Spirit to engage in the work of sanctification.

Reformed Christian communities have two sacraments: baptism and the Lord's supper: "Bath" and "Table." The sacraments help Christians maintain a perception of who they are before God by using ordinary means to convey extraordinary realities. Believers can see, feel, touch, smell, and taste. They have multiple avenues for deepening in their perception of who they are before God because a number of senses are in play. Reformed theologian David Willis taught that Calvin would have used, in baptisms, very cold, running water. And Calvin would have served the elect huge chunks of bread at the Lord's Table, Willis went on to explain – pieces that would have required multiple bites to chew and swallow.[23] To use water cold and fresh as the water pumped from the depths of a well and bread reminiscent of a fresh loaf centered on the family dinner table is to remember that God habitually enters into ordinary things and makes them extraordinary. It is to remember, also, that God has entered into our ordinary existence and lifted us up to participation in God. And so Christians remember their baptisms, and feast at the Table, week after week. It helps them live their lives with the perception that they belong to God, and that God is feeding them, in this world, along the way.

Christian believers are encouraged to read and study Scripture for themselves, in the context of Christian community. The approach should not be, according to Barth, that Christians go to the Bible for answers to their questions, but that they allow the Bible to question them.[24] To allow oneself to be reoriented by the teachings of Scripture is, from a Reformed perspective, to be open to the Spirit's work of transformation.

As those who are habitually engaged in discerning the Word of God through studying Scripture and through prayer, Christians are invited to shape and adjust church traditions in accordance with God's will for each particular time and place. Theology is also subject to being changed by the witness of Scripture. Calvin explains, in the opening

---

[22] This is the beginning of Calvin's definition of faith, found in *Institutes*, III.ii.7.

[23] Rev. Dr. E. David Willis was the author's teacher at Princeton Theological Seminary 1986–1989. The comments reported were witnessed by the author, who was Willis' student.

[24] See Karl Barth, "The Strange New World Within the Bible," in *Word of God and Word of Man* (Gloucester, MA: Peter Smith, 1978), 28–50.

pages of his *Institutes*, that the purpose of his theology is to prepare his readers better to read the Scriptures, "in order that they may be able both to have easy access to it and to advance in it without stumbling."[25] Once they are able to read the Scriptures on their own, however, Calvin invites them to make any improvements to his theology.

Christian life, understood as a grateful, humble appropriation of the gracious work God has done in us, can look many different ways. There is no one formula, no one program. But this does not mean that any way of living will do, in terms of deepening our perception. As has been suggested in the preceding paragraphs, Christians attending to the shape of their lives will be centered in Christ and attentive to the Spirit. They will study Scripture and engage in prayer. They will, in various ways, worship with others and share their faith with the world.

As those centered in Christ and attentive to the Spirit, Christian believers live their lives in an ongoing process of sorting out what is worthwhile to think about and invest in. Reformed traditions teach that this work of discernment is engaged not only by our hearts, but also by our intellect – the Holy Spirit makes use of both. Christians are free to exercise discipline in relation to their thoughts, focusing on, as Paul instructed the Philippian church, "whatever is true, whatever is honorable, whatever is just, whatever is pure, and whatever is pleasing" (Phil. 4:8). The final criterion for making assessments such as how to order priorities, how and with whom to spend time, or what form of entertainment to pursue, is Jesus Christ himself. Focusing on how he lived and on those whom he calls his disciples helps guard Christians against pursuing idols that can only drain their perception of God. Christ models for his followers, for example, what a life of habitual prayer looks like, and how important it is to share food and conversation around the table with those we love. The example of Christ's life reminds Christians – and all people – that when the pursuit of wealth or status so drives our schedules that we think it necessary to forego such fundamental blessings, we have forgotten who we really are as those created and loved by God.

From the perspective of Reformed traditions, Christian believers are welcome to bring to their study of Scripture and to their times of prayer a full array of tools, emotions, and experiences. Commentaries, knowledge of Greek and Hebrew, lessons learned in Sunday school class, insights gleaned from an article in *The New Yorker* – all are fair game if they help the reader learn, explore, discern, and be transformed by the

---

[25] See "Prefatory Letter to King Francis" in the frontmatter of Calvin, *Institutes*.

living Word of God as the Spirit conveys it through Scripture. Great joy and great grief, praise and lament, thanking and berating – any and all human emotions may be included in our prayers, and one is not inherently more faithful than another. What is always faithful is to be honest and transparent before God.

Both the practice of Bible reading and the practice of prayer, as they are present in Christian life, can take either individual or communal form. It is important, especially in relation to Bible study, that individual interpretations are checked against the interpretations of others. This is because it is possible for any individual Christian believer inadvertently to understand the Bible to be saying something that actually contradicts the message of the Gospel as a whole. The confessions of the church serve, in part, to help biblical interpreters reflect on particular interpretations of particular texts in the context of what the church has, historically, understood to be most important. Devotional materials, published by Reformed constituencies, have also proven to be helpful for supporting Christians engaged in biblical interpretation and in deepening perceptions of what it means to live life before God. *The Golden Booklet of the True Christian Life* by John Calvin, for example, has been offering reassurance for more than four centuries.[26] *The Footsteps of the Master*, published in 1877 by Harriet Beecher Stowe, has also been very well received and faithfully studied.[27] One reviewer commended it for its inspirational focus on the life events of Christ, noting that Mrs. Beecher successfully avoided "dogma."[28]

Praying communally as well as individually reminds Christians that even the prayers Christians offer in their "prayer closets" are not isolated from the prayers of the Great Cloud of Witnesses. Reformed theologies insist that, when Christians pray, they join in the ongoing singing of the celestial chorus of saints who intercede for one another and whose diverse voices blend in harmony to the glory of God.

If Christian life is lived before God, and Christian practices aim to help believers deepen in their perception of God's love for them, worship is the context where Christians expect this perception to be most fully actualized. What Christians believe they are doing, when they

---

[26] John Calvin, *The Golden Booklet of the True Christian Life* (Grand Rapids, MI: Baker Books, 2007).

[27] Harriet Beecher Stowe, *The Footsteps of the Master* (CreateSpace Independent Publishing Platform, 2014).

[28] See review (April 7, 1877) in "Spectator Archive" at http://archive.spectator.co.uk/article/7th-july-1877/24/footsteps-of-the-master-by-harriet-beecher-stowe-s (accessed March 10, 2015).

participate in a worship service, is joining in the ongoing, celestial, adoration of God. A Reformed order of worship begins by giving praise to the God who is sovereign. It then moves quickly to confession of sin and assurance of pardon. The humble, grateful, forgiven people of God are then ready to listen for the living Word of God through the reading of Scripture and the sermon. Through hearing, they are changed. They are reoriented and challenged. Barth likes to speak of the Word unmaking and remaking us again in an event of constructive "crisis." As new and wobbly-kneed creations, then, Christians who have heard the Word proclaimed visit the Font and the Table to be reassured of God's claim on them and nourished by Christ's radical presence. Their hearts are, there, "lifted up" in the fullness of gratitude and praise. Finally, strengthened worshipers are sent forth in the name of the triune God to share what they have received, to love and serve the Lord.

The Reformed self-understanding holds that worship is more than an important element of Christian life, though it is certainly that. It is also a microcosm of life before God, a distillation of the elements that are to frame our existence. Christians begin their days, as they begin their worship, with acknowledging who God is (praise) and are immediately awed and humbled by the reality of God's claim on us. And so they confess their sins as they face the slate of their daily responsibilities, emptying themselves before the Christ who emptied himself and became obedient unto death on the cross (Phil. 2). Assured of forgiveness, they are lifted up in the life of the resurrected One, prepared to discern the Word that is offered in encounters with others, in the work they have been given, in their personal devotions, and in their reading of the newspaper. Undone and remade by God's ongoing self-disclosure, Christians find reassurance and comfort around all the tables (both metaphorical and literal) at which they gratefully break bread, sharing life together. And then they clear the dishes and get on with it, moving out and serving this world God so loves with "energy, intelligence, imagination, and love."[29]

A radical claim of Reformed traditions is that what Christians glimpse in worship and try to live out, day by day, is the "real reality" in which they – and all of God's children – actually participate. This contrasts to the common but mistaken notion that periodic worship serves as a sort of "fix" that enables believers to survive another week in the so-called "real world."

---

[29] These words are used in the ordination vows taken by teaching elders in the Presbyterian Church (USA).

Here at the start of the twenty-first century, there is considerable pressure to try to live the Christian life apart from life in community. In the United States and Europe, the increase in numbers of those who identify as the "religiously non-affiliated" or "spiritual, but not religious," and the possibility of "attending" church not in body, but as an avatar over the Internet, all prompt the question: Why go to church at all? While a Reformed response to this question might be crafted in any number of ways, two of its pivotal doctrinal emphases should certainly come into play. First, the doctrine of the incarnation underscores the beauty and importance of bodies. As the Word became flesh to be with fellow creatures in tangible ways related to the concrete experiences of our lives – sharing meals with us, comforting us, journeying with us, healing us – so believers have the privilege of being with and for each other, as bodies that feed each other, comfort each other, journey together, and heal each other. Second, the doctrine of the Trinity calls Christians to recognize the communal character of their identity. Human beings are made in the image of God who is not only one, but also three. Just as important to humanity's identity as the fact of our autonomy and particularities, then, is our relationship to and participation in the lives of one another. Even as Father, Son and Spirit share life together, so human beings are created to share life not only with God, but also with those around them.

Shared life offers mutual support. It offers a context in which the people of God can develop their gifts – as teachers, preachers, encouragers, exhorters, and evangelists. Paul explains, along these lines, that each person is (analogously speaking) a member of the one body. Just as hands have need of eyes, and eyes have need of ears, so members of the body of Christ each have need of each other. And so all, together, are one (1 Cor. 12). Reformed traditions therefore emphasize that each person in Christian community nurtures their own particular gifts and encourages the identification and development of the gifts of others. Each has a related and particular vocation or calling. Insofar as each is faithful to his or her own vocation, he or she glorifies God and serves the community. No vocation is superior to any other.

Shared life offers mutual support, but it also makes for conflicts that need be negotiated. Christian life in community requires, therefore, that believers attend to how they order their interactions, and how they hold each other to account when agreed-upon orderings are neglected or violated. Reformed traditions, working to honor the communal nature of our existence, have often tried to find ways of including all church members in the processes of developing guiding principles and disciplines.

A controversial issue: submission and the body of Christ

A word that has fallen for good reason into ill repute, but that none-theless names a posture that seems essential for Christian life in community, is "submission." To submit is to yield to another, even if one disagrees with or does not understand their perspective. It is exemplified in Jesus' interaction with the Father, particularly in his acceptance of going to the cross, as he struggles in the Garden of Gethsemane just before Judas betrays him (Lk. 22:42). Paul encourages members of various church communities to "submit to one another" even as Christ submitted to us (Phil. 2, Eph. 5, Col. 3). Certainly, submission is an efficient strategy for maintaining the rhythms of communal life in the wake of conflict. At the extreme, it might even guard against schism, ensuring the very unity of the church.

But a problem comes when someone is coerced into submitting, rather than yielding voluntarily to another who is trusted. Most notably, concerns have been raised about the more specific, Pauline instruction that "wives submit to their husbands" (Eph. 5:22). Historically, this is an instruction that has been used to keep women from developing and exercising their gifts in those areas in which men want to be dominant. Even talk of "mutual submission" has been known to devolve quickly, in the Reformed theological literature, into discussion of how men submit to their "superordinate" role and women submit to their "subordinate" role.[30] Such submission is not actually mutual. Many have therefore moved away from the language of "submission" altogether since it is so laden with oppressive tonalities.[31]

The question is: Can life together in Christian community be formed and maintained without some version of submission? If not, how might it be possible to "submit to one another" (Eph. 5:21) without oppressing anyone in the dynamic? These are questions it will be prudent for Christian believers to consider as they reflect on how to go about shaping ecclesial life into the future, particularly insofar as they believe corporate life in Christ should be characterized by unity.

---

[30] See, for example, Barth, *Church Dogmatics*, vol. III/4, §54.

[31] The term "submission" appears only once in the anthology *Feminist and Womanist Essays in Reformed Dogmatics*, edited by Amy Plantinga Pauw and Serene Jones (Nashville: Westminster John Knox, 2006). It appears not at all in Johanna von Wijk-Bos, *Reformed and Feminist* (Louisville, KY: Westminster, 1991).

CHRISTIAN LIFE AND THE INVISIBLE CHURCH

Reformed theological traditions generally recognize Christian life as lived in relation to the invisible church, as well as the church visible. The notion of the "invisible church," as Calvin names it, follows from the conviction that only the sovereign God determines who is elect. Reformed traditions, then, resist the idea that the church is exhausted by those who self-identify as Christian believers. Calvin thinks that because only the sovereign God knows for sure who is elect and who is not, professing Christians should treat everyone as though they are elect. Schleiermacher, two centuries later, holds that all people are "absolutely dependent" on God. As different as these Reformed thinkers are in so many ways, they are both driven by the desire to help human beings deepen in their perception that they are the claimed, beloved, children of God.

Christian life, then, is not to be only inwardly focused, whether on individual spiritual journeys or on life, together, as a community of confessing believers. Christian life is also to have an outward focus, characterized by those who do perceive God's loving claim offering words of hope, comfort, and challenge to the world. "We should get the simple truth straight, dear friends," Barth preached at the Basel prison on Ascension Day, 1956: "We are in the world not to comfort ourselves, but to comfort others."[32] Reformed traditions teach that this outward focus might take various forms, depending on the gifts individual members of the community bring to bear. Some will find ways to teach in a public forum, perhaps giving theologically inclined lectures or writing for a local newspaper. Others will be good at telling the story of their own spiritual journey to colleagues in the office or to interested seat partners they have met on a plane. Still others will reach out by offering meals to the hungry, friendship to the lonely, or rides to the physically challenged. Finally, some will be very intentional about engaging the politics surrounding well-being, lobbying for new policies and laws that are more consistent with the biblical mandate to "do justice." Reformed communities honor the fact that every person claimed by God has a particular vocation. A major contribution of the Reformers, consistent with their teaching about the priesthood of all believers, is the idea that one can honor God every bit as much doing a menial job as doing a privileged one, if that is one's calling.

---

[32] Karl Barth, "Ascension Day Sermon" (1956), in *Deliverance to the Captives*, translated by Marguerite Wieser (London: SCM, 1961), 48.

Christian believers are to embrace their vocations not only in the context of the visible church, but also in the world God so loves. The world is God's good gift, and Christians, in freedom, should enjoy it. Calvin emphasizes this in a sermon where he insists that "there is not a single blade of grass, there is not a color in this world, that is not intended to make us rejoice."[33] Those who identify with Reformed traditions come from a long line of forbears who go out of their way to promote the flourishing of life not only for themselves and their immediate communities, but also for all. John Calvin advocates for social reforms including the building of a closed sewer system in the city of Geneva. Abraham Kuyper is a Reformed pastor who founds and writes for a Christian newspaper, later holding a seat in the Dutch parliament. Simon Hosack is a Presbyterian minister who mentors future suffragette Elizabeth Cady Stanton, teaching her Latin and Greek, leaving her his library, and reassuring her that it was *not* "too bad she hadn't been born a boy." Karl Barth is a professor who refuses to pledge allegiance to Hitler and is subsequently removed from his teaching position. Allan Boesak is a Reformed theologian who fights apartheid in South Africa alongside Nelson Mandela.

One arena of social justice in which Reformed Christians have been especially prominent, historically, is public school education. Making it possible for everyone to get an education is important for the early Reformers for at least two reasons. First, the Reformers are passionately committed to people reading the Bible for themselves, and so they look for ways to help every person learn to read. Second, the Reformers held the sovereign God wants us to grow in our perception of who God is and who we are in relationship to God, believing all kinds of learning can make a contribution to this growth. In the strength of these convictions, Calvin establishes state-supported public schools in Geneva that all children are required to attend. John Knox, similarly, helps establish free schools for all children in Scotland.

More recently, William Placher suggests that Christians not only support education, but become themselves life-long learners. Marveling in the range of themes in the *Church Dogmatics*, Placher exults in Barth's view that "from a Christian perspective one can engage in conversation with anybody about anything – from Mozart to Nietzsche to Pure Land Buddhism."[34] The Christian life, from this

---

[33] Calvin's Sermon #10 on 1 Corinthians, quoted in William J. Bouwsma, *John Calvin: A Sixteenth-Century Portrait* (New York: Oxford University Press, 1988), 134–135.

[34] William C. Placher, *The Triune God: An Essay in Postliberal Theology* (Nashville: Westminster John Knox, 2007), 23.

perspective, is a life wide open to inquiry and growth. It is a life of "faith seeking understanding," as Anselm once put it. It is a life that engages all disciplines fearlessly and enthusiastically, seeking better to understand who God is and what God is up to. It is a life that keeps a close eye on what is going on in the world even as it engages in constructive self-reflection.

The primary purpose of study and learning in the Christian life is, for Reformed theologians, to gain in one's perception of God and God's presence in the world. Study, like prayer and worship, is to be celebrated for its own sake. But study also – like prayer and worship – prepares and positions Christian believers to discern the shape of God's Word as it comes to them new again every morning. "What is God up to in this world, in my community, in our church, in our lives?" it provokes them to ask. "And what am I called to do, in relation to what God is doing?"

Praying, worship, and study lead to service, Reformed traditions hold. Christians, before receiving the benediction, are charged to "go out into the world" and (for example) to "do justice, love kindness, and walk humbly with God" (Mic. 6:8). They are expected to bring what they have experienced in worship out the door of the sanctuary, looking for ways the reality of the Kingdom can be actualized in the world.

A controversial issue: do we advance the Kingdom of God?

The Reformed have sometimes been reticent to say that human beings contribute to the coming of God's Kingdom. The concern, on the one hand, is that to suggest Christians can either expedite or slow down the work of God by virtue of how they live their lives seems to compromise their conviction that God is sovereign, and that human beings are saved not by what they do, but by grace alone. The concern, on the other hand, is that to say how Christians live their lives has absolutely no bearing on when or how the Kingdom of God will come is to de-value the role of human agents, who are called in Scripture "heirs together with Christ" (Rom. 8:17) and who are invited to participate in "the ministry of reconciliation" (2 Cor. 5:18). Reformed Christian believers have a long history of wanting to take both of these concerns into account. For Calvin, it is motivating to remember our calling to be obedient to the One who is sovereign, trusting that God somehow uses all human actions for God's purposes without manipulating our free will. The Westminster Confession (1647), along these lines, emphasizes that the God who is the "first cause" often chooses to work by way of "secondary causes," including the exercise of human will.[35]

With the modern rise of optimism about humanity's capacity to accomplish and achieve, Reformed Christians of the nineteenth and early twentieth centuries continue working to articulate how it is that God's sovereignty welcomes and includes human agency with no compromise to either. The Presbyterian Church (USA), in the context of the Social Gospel movement so prominent in the United States, in 1908 adopts the "Great Ends of the Church," insisting that faithful Christian living contributes to the reign of God insofar as it "proclaims the Gospel," "nurtures the children of God," "maintains divine worship," "preserves the truth," "promotes social righteousness," and "exhibits the Kingdom of heaven to the world."[36] In the late nineteenth century, Dutch Reformed theologian Abraham Kuyper argues that there are various God-given "spheres" in which sovereignty is exercised, all of which are subsumed, of course, under the authority of the sovereign God who authorizes each sphere.[37] Christians exercise their power in the sphere of the church, to be sure, but might also be appointed by God to exert influence in the context of other spheres – in the sphere of government, for example, or in the sphere of education or art. Kuyper's successor, Herman Bavinck, similarly builds on Calvin's idea that the world is the theater of God's glory, recognizing human beings as actors in the play being performed. "Wherever God works by ... Word and Spirit in the hearts" of human beings, Bavinck thinks, there the "invisible church" should be acknowledged. There, confessing Christians should join in life and work even with those who do not explicitly confess Jesus as Lord.[38] To live the Christian life is, from Bavinck's perspective, to live with an openness to enjoying and participating in the redemptive work of God wherever and through whomever this work is taking place.

Reflecting further in this spirit, Reformed theologian Jürgen Moltmann imagines Christian life in relationship to "play." We generally think of play as "merely reproductive," he explains – a time to

---

[35] *Westminster Confession of Faith* (1647), chapter V.2, in *The Confession of Faith and the Larger and Shorter Catechisms* (Glasgow: Free Presbyterian Publications, 1973), 34.

[36] For more on the "Great Ends of the Church," see *The Great Ends of the Church Series* (6 vols.; Louisville, KY: Witherspoon Press, 2005–2010).

[37] Abraham Kuyper, *Lectures on Calvinism* (Grand Rapids, MI: Eerdmans, 1999).

[38] Herman Bavinck, "Calvin and Common Grace," in *Herman Bavinck: Selected Shorter Works*, edited by John Hendryx; originally published in *The Princeton Theological Review*, vol. 6, no. 3 (1909), 437–465.

"refuel" so we can again return productively to our work. But what if we thought of play as itself "productive," Moltmann asks – what if we thought of it, in a sense, as our most real and generative work? It might be, he suggests, that our play could then foster "an imagination productive of a more liberated world."[39]

Barth states, just as boldly, that "our work cannot be anything but play" when "done before the sovereign God."[40] He asserts that when Christians think there is "no other way" to live their lives except to be stressed out all the time, "they are always wrong." They have forgotten that God has taken responsibility not only for final outcomes, but even for sins and shortcomings along the way. They have lost sight of the fact that they live as creatures before the Creator God who has claimed them. To live with the perception that God is sovereign, Barth explains, is to live without anxiety, abiding through the Spirit in the One who invites us freely and fearlessly to create, knowing that the Kingdom will come even if, in the short term, we have little success with our efforts.

Moltmann notes that the word "play" can be easily misunderstood. To live "playfully" before the sovereign God does not mean, of course, that Christians should curb concerns about injustice, stave off righteous anger, or try to imagine they are somehow immune from the sufferings of the world. On the contrary, to be attuned to God's beautiful, creative work leads Christians, in their lives, to be even more disheartened by war, violence, pain, abuse, and tragedy. To be people of hope is, in a world still awaiting the completion of redemption, to be people who struggle to process disappointment and who actively reposition themselves, again and again, to be renewed and to move forward. This is why they worship, and exhort, and encourage, and intercede. This is why they repent of and correct the ways in which Calvinism was used to drive witch-hunts, and Kuyper's "sphere sovereignty" was used to justify apartheid. Christians actively claim the new world our sovereign One has promised, and so engage the work of play, ever again.

CONCLUSION

Reformed traditions have thought of Christian life not only as a gift God gives us, but also as a gift they offer back to God. In a sermon he preached in 1918 on Romans 12:1–2, Barth points out that Paul says we are to offer our *bodies* "as living sacrifices" – not our *souls*, but our *bodies*. What

---

[39] Jürgen Moltmann, *Theology of Play* (New York: Harper & Row, 1972), 12.
[40] Karl Barth, *Church Dogmatics*, vol. III/4, 553.

Paul is trying to convey, Barth says, is that we are to give our "whole selves" to God – not only that which is "spiritual" about us, but also our "private lives ... our family ... our business."⁴¹ For Reformed traditions, life before the sovereign God who has held nothing back from us is life that, in turn, holds nothing back from God. And the promise is that this sovereign God is ever in process of making "all things new," transforming those who offer all they have and are so that they, in turn, might resist conforming to the world and instead be vehicles of transformation in it. Comprised of these believers, the church is, similarly, "Reformed and always reforming, according to the Word of God." Life before God is dynamic and engaged, empowered by the Holy Spirit, centered in the person, work, and witness of Jesus Christ, and directed toward that day when all creation will perceive God's "glorious splendor" and be caught up in "wonderment."⁴²

Further reading

Barth, Karl. *Church Dogmatics*. 4 vols. in 13 parts. Edited by G. W. Bromiley and T. F. Torrance. Edinburgh: T&T Clark, 1956–1975.

Bavinck, Herman. "The Origin, Essence, and Purpose of Man." In *Herman Bavinck: Selected Shorter Works*. Edited by John Hendryx. Amazon Digital Services: Monergism Books, 2011.

Boulton, Matthew Myer. *Life in God: John Calvin, Practical Formation, and the Future of Protestant Theology*. Grand Rapids, MI: Eerdmans, 2011.

Calvin, John. *Institutes of the Christian Religion*. Edited by John T. McNeill. Translated by Ford Lewis Battles. Library of Christian Classics; 2 vols. Philadelphia: Westminster, 1960.

Horton, Michael. *Calvin on the Christian Life: Glorifying and Enjoying God Forever*. Wheaton: Crossway, 2014.

Johnson, David W. *Trust in God: The Christian Life and the* Book of Confessions. Louisville, KY: Geneva Press, 2013.

Lehmann, Paul. *The Decalogue and a Human Future: The Meaning of the Commandments for Making and Keeping Human Life Human*. Grand Rapids, MI: Eerdmans, 1994.

Moltmann, Jürgen. *Theology of Play*. New York: Harper & Row, 1972.

Pauw, Amy Plantinga and Serene Jones (eds.). *Feminist and Womanist Essays in Reformed Dogmatics*. Nashville: Westminster John Knox, 2006.

Placher, William C. *The Triune God: An Essay in Postliberal Theology*. Nashville: Westminster John Knox, 2007.

---

⁴¹ Karl Barth and William H. Willimon, *The Early Preaching of Karl Barth* (Nashville: Westminster John Knox, 2009), 52.

⁴² Calvin, *Institutes*, I.v.9.

Part II

Theological figures

8 Huldrych Zwingli

PETER OPITZ

Huldrych Zwingli is the father of Reformed Protestantism. Although that movement has been equated with and often restricted to "Calvinism," especially in the English-speaking world, Reformed Protestantism undeniably owes its fundamental design to this Zürich Reformer.

BECOMING A REFORMER

Ulrich Zwingli (who would later adopt the name "Huldrych," "rich in grace") was born on January 1, 1484, in Wildhaus, in eastern Switzerland. His father belonged to the rural elite and held political office as *Landammann*, the chief local magistrate. Exposed to local politics from an early age, Zwingli developed a particular interest in political concerns – a trait that would be very evident in the later life of the Swiss Reformer.

After grammar school, Zwingli was sent by his parents first to Bern and then to the University of Vienna. He subsequently attended the university in Basel, from 1502 to 1506, where, having completed his Master's examination, he studied theology for one semester. During these years of study, he received a scholastic education and became familiar with the philosophical tradition of the *via antiqua*. It is more than likely that Thomas Wyttenbach (ca. 1472–1526), who was professor in Basel and pastor in Biel, introduced Zwingli to the writings of Thomas Aquinas and Peter Lombard and to the commentaries on Lombard's *Sentences* by Duns Scotus.

After leaving Basel, Zwingli worked as a pastor in Glarus, in central Switzerland, for ten years and then, from 1516 to 1518, served as a preacher at the pilgrimage site of Einsiedeln. These years were marked by diligent private study. Zwingli's remarkable education included studying the Bible in its original languages, reading the Church Fathers, and pursuing an interest in classical antiquity and poetry. During these years, Zwingli also became increasingly aware of clerical and political abuses, which were a cause of injustice and a source of grievance within the Swiss Confederation. His criticism targeted ecclesial superficiality and commercialized religiosity in particular, and he pursued a political agenda that challenged mercenary service and the associated agreements that formed alliances between the Swiss states, on the one hand, and France and the pope, on the other – agreements that Zwingli denounced more and more emphatically. At the root of the Swiss Confederation's policy of hiring out mercenaries, the Reformer identified egoism, immorality, and corruption. Zwingli belonged to the circle of Swiss humanists and patriots who hoped for a renewal of the church through the revival of an ethically determined faith in Christ according to the teachings of the New Testament, which would in turn regenerate the Swiss political-Christian community.

According to Zwingli's own testimony, he began to preach "the Gospel" in 1516 and had already discerned his key reformatory convictions during his time in Glarus and Einsiedeln. From Erasmus he learned that the Bible alone must be both source and standard for Christianity (*sola scriptura*) and that to live a Christian faith is to listen to Christ's voice alone. From Thomas Wyttenbach he learned that Christ's death on the cross was a single and unrepeatable sacrifice for all human sin (*solus Christus*). The intellectual and existential assimilation of these insights and the elaboration of his particular theological stance, as the pioneer of Reformed Protestantism, was a process that occurred through continuous reading, reflection, and practical experience. Written evidence that Zwingli's ideas had grown beyond the boundaries of Erasmian humanism comes from the early 1520s, by which time Zwingli had taken on the position of *Leutpriester* (people's priest) at the Grossmünster in Zürich.

PROPHETIC PREACHER AND COUNSELOR IN AN URBAN REFORMATION

The Zwinglian Reformation can be termed an urban reformation, for its reform was sanctioned and implemented by the political authorities of the city of Zürich. Zwingli's role was advisory; he had no executive powers. Although for Zwingli the church could not be independent of the state, to term Zwingli's model reformed city a "theocracy" would be misleading; in the Reformer's eyes, divine and human (political) righteousness should never be confused.

Sixteenth-century Zürich was a city of about 5,000 residents, with an additional 55,000 people living in the surrounding countryside. The total area is comparable to that of today's Canton of Zürich. Zürich had joined the Swiss Confederation in 1351. Politically the town functioned by means of a complicated balance between various guilds. It was governed by small and large councils, led by two Bürgermeisters, who were in office alternately for half a year each. Although the political order was closer in character to patrician rule than to a democracy, the voice of the people was important, if not in the rural areas then at least in the city itself.

Although the bishop of Constance was the official spiritual overlord, the civil authorities in Zürich had taken on increasing responsibility not only for political affairs but also for clerical matters. The two areas were difficult to distinguish, in particular when it came to questions about jurisdiction; the staffing of clerical benefices; the supervision of religious foundations at the Grossmünster and the Fraumünster, the major churches in the city; and the administration of the property and income of the monasteries. A clear separation of religious and secular spheres was unknown.

Elected to his new office as *Leutpriester* on January 1, 1519, Zwingli began his ministry with the *lectio continua* (continuous reading) of the Gospel of Matthew, a demonstration of the *sola scriptura* principle. Zwingli saw himself as a prophetic interpreter of the divine Word, to which he attributed the power to change individuals and society. The fast-growing number of adherents among both the leading families and the guilds was a product of his ability to draw people in a climate marked by anticlericalism, calls for religious renewal, and the desire for greater political independence from ecclesiastical influences.

In spring 1522, when some of Zwingli's supporters broke with tradition by not keeping the Lenten fast, Zwingli immediately sprang to their public defense both orally and in writing. His text *Regarding the Choice and Freedom of Food* (April 1522) has often been termed the first programmatic tract he published as a Reformer.[1] In September 1522, Zwingli defended the principle of *sola scriptura* with a treatise entitled *The Clarity and Certainty of the Word of God*.[2] The practical issues surrounding Christian freedom in respect of laws imposed by ecclesiastical authorities and the emphasis placed on the power of the Word of God were not coincidentally the starting points of Zwingli's reformation.

In August 1522, at the urging of the bishop of Constance and developing the critical consequences of his principle of *sola scriptura*, Zwingli

---

[1]   Huldreich Zwingli, *Vom Erkiesen und Freiheit der Speisen*, in *Sämtliche Werke* (hereafter Z followed by volume number). Corpus Reformatorum 88–108. (Berlin / Leipzig /Zürich, 1905–2013), vol. I, 74–136.

[2]   Huldreich Zwingli, *Klarheit und Gewissheit des Wortes Gottes*, in Z I, 328–384.

published an extensive apology entitled *Apologeticus Archeteles*, in which he defended his principle of "Christ alone," as well as his attacks on human traditions and unscriptural practices.[3] A few months earlier, together with ten colleagues, he had written to the bishop demanding the right to preach the Gospel freely and an end to enforced clerical celibacy. Celibacy, they had written, was contrary to Scripture and the cause of public scandal, as many priests in the diocese of Constance lived with unofficial wives or had children. The regular payments these priests made to the bishop on account of their children born out of wedlock formed part of the diocese's income. Early in 1522 Zwingli himself started to live with a young widow, Anna Reinhard, whom he married publically in April 1524, one year after the first public marriage of a Zürich priest, in Witikon. The couple had seven children: Margaretha (born 1505), Agathe (born 1507), and Gerold (born 1509) were from Anna Reinhard's first marriage; together Zwingli and Anna had Regula (born 1524), Wilhelm (born 1526), Huldrych (born 1528), and Anna (born 1530).

As tensions grew, the bishop sought to intervene, and as the pope dragged his feet over the convocation of a much desired council, the Zürich city council called for a public disputation by the various parties. The idea of a public disputation had been inspired by the tradition of local councils held in the ancient church. About 600 people attended the event, which took place at the Zürich town hall on January 29, 1523, with Zwingli invited to give a public account of his teachings. The Bürgermeister of Zürich formulated the ground rules at the outset: only Scripture could be used to argue against Zwingli. The four-member episcopal delegation was not prepared for these rules of debate, and the decision in favor of Zwingli, who had formulated his teaching in sixty-seven theses, came quickly. That verdict was delivered by the political authorities, for as a Christian authority, the Zürich city council had taken charge of religious matters in their city. The outcome of the disputation would, in the longer term, prove to be the first step toward the establishment of a Protestant church in the city. The Zürich practice of public disputation grew to be a widely used method for introducing the Reformation in the Empire.

Shortly after the disputation, Zwingli published a detailed account of his sixty-seven theses, working them out in an extensive text, *Interpretation and Justification of the Theses*.[4] His Reformed understanding of the concepts of *solus Christus* and *sola scriptura* was the

---

[3] Huldreich Zwingli, *Apologeticus Archeteles*, in Z I, 249–327.
[4] Huldreich Zwingli, *Auslegung der Thesen*, in Z II, 1–457.

starting point for his line of reasoning. The second of his theses insisted that "The summary of the gospel is that our Lord Jesus Christ, true Son of God, has made known to us the will of his Heavenly Father and has redeemed us from death and reconciled us with God by his guiltlessness."[5] For Zwingli, Christ alone is "guide and leader" and "head of all believers, who are his body." As a positive consequence, "all who dwell in the head are members and children of God, and that is the church or communion of the saints, the bride of Christ, *Ecclesia catholica*" (theses 6–8). Zwingli also drew a critical consequence, however: "Hence we see in the clerical (so-called) ordinances, concerning their splendor, riches, classes, titles, laws, a cause of all foolishness, for they do not also agree with the head" (thesis 11).

These theological principles formed the foundation of Zwingli's stand on the ecclesial and political issues of his day. His criticism was directed at all claims to power in religious matters and focused on oppressive church laws that resulted in hypocrisy, the sale of indulgences, and other issues on which he deemed the position of the Roman Catholic Church deplorable. The Roman Catholic Church was proving unwilling to reform itself and as the church was not to be understood as existing "where some prelates get together, but rather, there, where one sticks to God's Word, and where one lives Christ,"[6] a political community like Zürich, led by a Christian authority, could form the true church.

In the aftermath of a number of acts of iconoclasm in the autumn of 1523, a second disputation, held in October 1523, debated the removal of images and the abolition of the mass. While the council hesitated, a diversity of practices continued and conflicts and further acts of provocation occurred. In June 1524 the council finally decided that all images that served or could serve as objects of religious adoration were to be removed from the churches and returned to their benefactors in a well-regulated matter. By the end of that year, churches had been "cleansed" of images and relics, and many religious traditions and customs such as feast days and processions had ceased. Katharina von Zimmern, abbess of the important abbey of Fraumunster, handed over the corporate property of the cloister to the council. As a result of the preaching of Zwingli and his colleagues, monks and nuns left their cloisters. Step by step, the monasteries were dissolved, although older nuns and monks were allowed to stay on. Zwingli even drafted a new

5 Ibid., 27; Huldrych Zwingli, *Writings*, 2 vols., edited and translated by E. J. Furcha and H. W. Pipkin (Allison Park, PA: Pickwick Publications, 1984), vol. 1, 14.
6 Huldreich Zwingli, Z III, 750.

evangelical liturgy for the monks of the monastery of Ruti that emphasized the reading of Scripture and its explication.[7] The idea of an order
of Christianity that was higher and more spiritual than that of the common people found no support in Scripture, however.

The property of the monasteries and their income were now
overseen by the city council and largely employed to assist the
poor and for educational purposes. The newly created *Almosenamt*
("Poor-and-Needy Relief") of January 1525, administered by four delegates from the council, also provided help for the needy. Begging was
no longer allowed. While the sick, the poor, and the elderly were to
be supported by the newly created relief funds, all who were in good
health were expected to work, including former monks, who were to
learn a trade. According to Zwingli, the ability to work is a mark of
human dignity, for humans are created in the image of God. Religious
reform led not only to the reform of the church and its institutions but
also to the reform of society – and in the long run encompassed also
the mentality of the people.

In May 1525, the episcopal jurisdiction over marriage was replaced
by the institution of the marriage court, in which the political authorities presided, with pastors as advisors. While adultery was punished
harshly, emphasis was placed on the free choice and consent of the couple, in contrast to forced and arranged marriages, and on the rights of
young women. The official, legal character of the relationship was to be
secured by means of a religious ceremony that included public prayer
for the couple. In cases of adultery, divorce was now an option, and, in
some instances, a year of marriage by way of trial was even envisaged.[8]
Marriage had been instituted by God for the good of men and women
and should be organized according to this principle.

The Word of God as revealed in Scripture was to be the sole guiding
principle, and therefore interpretation of the Bible was of vital importance. Zwingli emphasized that the Bible interprets itself, and that the
literal meaning of the Word is decisive, not an allegorical interpretation
as adopted by Roman Catholics and humanists. Zwingli was intensely
devoted to the Bible, but he was no naïve Biblicist. He always sought
an understanding of the original Hebrew and Greek texts that was as
exact as possible, and he developed hermeneutic rules for handling

---

[7]   Huldreich Zwingli, Z IV, 526–529.
[8]   E. Egli, *Aktensammlung zur Geschichte der Zürcher Reformation in den Jahren
      1519–1533* (Neudruck der Ausgabe Zürich 1879) (Nieuwkoop: B. de Graaf, 1973), 329.

biblical statements.[9] In so doing, Zwingli became a pioneer of Reformed exegesis.

The centrality of the Bible and its interpretation to the Zürich Reformation is clearly visible in the gatherings that would be institutionalized in the *Lectorium*, also known as the *Prophezei*. Beginning in 1525, the Bible was interpreted publically, five times a week, in the choir of the Grossmünster. Discussion of an Old Testament text followed the opening prayers. First, a Hebraist analyzed the text in the original Hebrew, then another scholar repeated that process using the Greek Septuagint, and finally, a pastor presented the results to the audience assembled in the nave of the church. In the Fraumünster, the New Testament was treated in a similar way. The *Prophezei* was a forerunner of the Zürich *Hohe Schule* (1532), a theological school intended for the education of Protestant pastors. The school successfully recruited renowned European scholars of Hebrew and exegetes like Konrad Pellikan, Theodore Bibliander, and Peter Martyr Vermigli. The Zürich *Hohe Schule* became a model for many other Protestant theological schools and academies, such as those in Bern (1535), Lausanne (1536), Strasbourg (1538), and Geneva (1559). One fruit of the *Prophezei* was the first complete translation of the Bible into German of the Reformation era. The Froschauer Bible was published in 1531 and reprinted in various forms innumerable times during the sixteenth century. A plethora of Bible commentaries were also the yield of subsequent years.

REFORMATION IN THE MIDST OF INTERNAL TENSION AND POLITICAL THREAT

The Zürich Reformation was not a peaceful process of self-renewal carried out by an acknowledged sovereign state. It took place in an atmosphere defined by internal tension and an increasingly hostile climate within the mainly Roman Catholic Swiss Confederation. The political developments that led finally, in October 1531, to the War of Kappel and Zwingli's death can be understood only against the background of complex political alliances, a sophisticated legal system involving a variety of agents, and the role of religion in sixteenth-century society and culture.

---

9 See Peter Opitz, "The Exegetical and Hermeneutical Work of John Oecolampadius, Huldrych Zwingli and John Calvin: II. Huldrych Zwingli," in *Hebrew Bible/Old Testament: The History of Its Interpretation*, vol. II, edited by Magne Saebø *From the Renaissance to the Enlightenment – B Reformation* (Göttingen: Vandenhoeck & Ruprecht, 2007), 413–428.

A brief sketch must suffice here: as the Reformation movement spread within the territories of the Swiss Confederation (by 1529 St. Gallen, Appenzell, Glarus, Graubunden, Bern, Basle, and Schaffhausen had joined the Reformation), the determination of the Roman Catholic states to eradicate the Reformation "heresy" grew. That hostility was bolstered by the condemnation of "Lutheranism" by the pope and the emperor at the Diet of Worms in April 1521. The situation was particularly fraught in the so-called Mandated Territories in which the population wanted to introduce the Reformation but were under the jurisdiction of a Roman Catholic *Landvogt* (bailiff) appointed by the confederates. As the Roman Catholic majority among the confederates was not willing to allow the Gospel to be preached freely in such territories – the right to preach freely was the central issue for Zwingli – and as, additionally, Roman Catholic states and even the Swiss Diet were not averse to beheading and burning Protestant government officials and preachers, war seemed imminent. In 1528/29 both parties sought out and established political alliances that they believed would protect their faith: the Protestants cities formed the "Christliches Burgrecht"; the Roman Catholics allied with Ferdinand, the Habsburg ruler of Austria, in a "Christliche Vereinigung." Over the course of what would prove to be the final two years of his life, Zwingli tried to secure the Protestant faith in Switzerland politically, but in the end he could see no alternative to a preemptive military attack. A good number of the Zürich pastors took up arms, for there was no longer a special class of "religious" persons freed from the responsibilities of regular citizens, which included the duty to aid in the defense of the city.

Internal conflicts were initially a result of the strong opposition to religious change that Zwingli faced during the early years of the Reformation. In the long run, however, groupings and individuals who sought more radical reform would provide the greater challenge. Parallels with the German Peasants' Revolt can be found in the demands made by the population of various areas for greater political autonomy and the plundering of monasteries. But Zwingli was no revolutionary. While he did propose material changes in policies involving loans and taxation in his desire to eliminate misuse and injustice, he at the same time rejected radical action that might endanger the economic system or risk the city council's support for the Reformation.

This led to Zwingli's stance toward the (heterogeneous) early "Anabaptist" movement that emerged in 1524, during a critical period of religious, social, and political transformation. Its first leaders came from among those closest to Zwingli and were essentially motivated by dissatisfaction with the manner and pace of the religious reforms after the Second Disputation, in October 1523. The first adult baptism took place on January 21, 1525: Konrad Grebel, son of a former member of the Zürich city council, baptized Joerg Blaurock, and Blaurock in turn baptized other friends gathered in a house in the center of Zürich. Within the week, thirty-five "brethren" had been baptized in Zollikon, near Zürich. The movement grew quickly, especially in rural areas where its concerns merged with political and social issues.

In Zwingli's eyes, in light of the highly charged political situation and the isolation of Reformed Zürich within the Swiss Confederation, the challenge of these radicals represented a danger to the Reformation movement as a whole. In addition, viewed through a theological lens, the attempt to separate visibly "true" believers from allegedly "false" Christians appeared to him to be an illegitimate human anticipation of God's sovereign judgment. The political authorities saw a perilous threat to a well-regulated political community under their leadership, as well as a challenge to the entire local *corpus Christianum*. Like every city in contemporary Europe, Zürich was conceivable only as a homogeneous social, political, and religious unit in which every member of the community had specific duties determined by his or her place in society, with the welfare of the community clearly above the right of the individual to dissent. By refusing to endorse infant baptism, participate in public church services, or swear a public oath, all actions that were integral to communal life, the Anabaptists were assailing the entire social order. Zwingli participated in a number of debates with Anabaptists and authored a series of works against the radical movement.

Initially the city council permitted Bible study groups to meet, but step by step, as the Anabaptist leaders defied various sanctions, the council tightened its measures and penalties. Some Anabaptists broke the promise to stop baptizing that had been the condition for their release from prison. In March 1526 a mandate that included the death penalty for notorious disobedience was issued. Felix Manz, who was convicted of repeated disobedience and of perjury, was condemned to death by drowning, a sentence carried out on January 5, 1527. Manz was the first of four Anabaptists whom we know to have been sentenced to death in Zürich during Zwingli's lifetime. Zürich's pursuit of minorities was minor when compared to the burning of Protestants in Roman Catholic states (and, at times, to the execution of Roman Catholics in Protestant states), with the imperial Diet at Speyer in 1529 threatening death to any adherent of Anabaptism. Felix Manz may have been, however, the first Anabaptist martyr.

As a result of the Anabaptist disputes, Zwingli put increasing emphasis on the unity of the Old and New Testaments. He vindicated child baptism by referring to the covenant of God with his people – a covenant of grace that embraced both Testaments.[10] Heinrich Bullinger, Zwingli's successor in Zürich, would greatly expand the concept of covenant, as also would Martin Bucer and, subsequently, John Calvin. Indeed, in the future the idea found its way into many areas of Protestant theology, albeit not without substantial modification.

Zwingli also grappled with social questions linked to the local peasant rebellions. His 1524 treatise *Who Gives Cause for Revolt* demonstrates a strong awareness of the issues involved and sharply condemns exploitation and opposes usury.[11] Moreover, he advocated a gradual return to the initial intention of tithing – to assist the poor. In a significant treatise entitled *Divine and Human Righteousness*,[12] he wrote of the essential difference between perfect divine righteousness, on the one hand, and external, always imperfect but necessary, secular justice, on the other. Temporal authority was not to be detached from the divine will, for it is the responsibility of Christian authorities to organize the political, social, and economic spheres, however imperfectly, in accordance with divine righteousness. It is the prophetic office of the church to remind the authorities of this divine justice dutifully and repeatedly. The reign of Christ cannot be restricted to the hearts of believers; it concerns the whole of society in all its facets.

Zwingli always emphasized, however, the difference between the invisible church and the visible church. The invisible church consists of the elect, illuminated by the Holy Spirit, but they are known only to God and therefore no one has the right to judge a neighbour's faith. The visible church is not defined by an ecclesiastical hierarchy, offices, or ritual acts such as preaching and the distribution of the sacraments; it is a community of people who profess Christ as their Lord and therefore listen to his Word and act accordingly.[13] Because of his clear distinction between the invisible church and the visible church, Zwingli the theologian could be much more tolerant of other forms of Christianity than most of his adversaries. In his critical attitude toward the Anabaptists, however, Zwingli was typical of his age.

---

[10] Huldreich Zwingli, *Antwort über Balthasar Hubmaiers Taufbüchlein*, in Z IV, 577–642.
[11] Huldreich Zwingli, *Wer Ursach gebe zur Aufruhr*, in Z III, 355–469.
[12] Huldreich Zwingli, *Die göttliche und menschliche Gerechtigkeit*, in Z II, 458–525.
[13] See Huldreich Zwingli, Z VI.5, 108.

THE LORD'S SUPPER – A CELEBRATION OF RECONCILIATION

Zwingli's image has been shaped primarily by his conflict with Luther over the Lord's Supper, with the Zürich Reformer often portrayed as having denied the real presence of Christ in the eucharist. To launch any discussion of Zwingli's doctrine of the eucharist with the Luther debate, however, is to risk overlooking his own teaching on the eucharist and failing to note how closely he sought to follow the biblical account of the Last Supper, celebrated in the context of the Old Testament tradition of the Passover. His teaching stemmed also from his allegiance to the principles of *solus Christus* and *sola fide*.

In *Interpretation and Justification of the Theses* (1523), Zwingli explicates his Christological rationale for rejecting the doctrine of a sacrificial mass in thesis 18: "That Christ who offered himself up once as a sacrifice, is a perpetual and valid payment for the sin of all believers; from this it follows that the mass is not a sacrifice, but a memorial of the sacrifice and a seal of the redemption which Christ has manifested to us."[14] As a result, the Lord's Supper is a celebration of a once-and-for-all and everlastingly valid act of reconciliation. Its celebration must be an act of faith, with simple trust in Jesus Christ, his deeds, and his being for humankind. The Lord's Supper is a real eucharist, a thankful, joyful meal of remembrance and confession. Zwingli's April 1525 work *Aktion und Brauch des Nachtmahls* ("The Action and Practice of the Lord's Supper") was an attempt to provide a liturgical blueprint for this theological idea.

Liturgically, the church acts; theologically, Christ alone acts, inviting his disciples to his table. Zwingli's liturgy features Christ's invitation, with Christ's words from John 6:47–63 to be read from the pulpit immediately before or while the elements of the eucharist are distributed. The *sursum corda* (lift up your hearts) from the traditional liturgy is located in Christ's description of himself as the true spiritual bread of life and in his invitation to come to him. Christ's intention is to give peace to the "weary and heavy-laden" (Matt. 11:28). The eating and drinking of the elements transpires in light of the promise of peace from Christ – the host at the meal. The church is invited to come to the table that Christ has prepared, just like the beggars in the parable of the banquet (Luke 14:15–24).

---

[14] Zwingli, *Auslegung der Thesen*, in Z II, 111, 27–32; Zwingli, *Writings*, vol. 1, 92.

In addition, the celebration of the eucharist illustrated the close connection in Zwingli's thought between the spiritual and the social in the lives of believers. While reconciliation in Christ was celebrated, the bread was to be passed around in a wide bowl in order that all individuals could break off a piece "with their own hand," a revolutionary act when compared not only to the late medieval mass but also to Luther's understanding of "the sacrament of the altar." In his justification of this practice, Zwingli pointed out that real cases of reconciliation between people sitting next to each other occurred. The collective memory of reconciliation in Christ within the imagery of a banquet could lead to reconciliation between beggars and sinners sitting at his table.

For Luther, unlike Zwingli, the real presence of Christ's body was experienced in the elements of the eucharist. In the monastic tradition, the adoration of the elements in the mass was a core element of Christian piety, and Luther, the former monk, increasingly emphasized the "bodily presence of Christ" – however mysterious – "among" the elements as necessary for the assurance of individual faith. The humanist Zwingli proved much more able to free himself from this traditional piety; he saw Luther's position as a step backward toward superstition. Zwingli's conviction that no physical element can serve to bring the believer into communion with Christ through the Holy Spirit would have been confirmed by his reading of authors influenced by neo-Platonism such as Augustine; his principal witness was, however, Christ himself, as attested in the Gospel of John.

During the Marburg Colloquy of 1529, organized by Philip of Hesse with the aim of uniting the Protestant movements, Zwingli and Luther were able to agree on all but one of the essential articles of faith – demonstrating just how close the Swiss and Wittenberg Reformations really were. Only the question of the Lord's Supper remained controversial. For Zwingli the difference in interpretation was not reason enough to break the ecclesial communion of the Protestant movement. It was Luther who declared the Swiss Reformers to be heretics.

Zwingli held Christ's presence in the eucharist to be real but spiritual. What can have more reality than the spirit of the risen Christ, which he promised his disciples would be present whenever they met in his name (Matt. 18:20; John 14:18)?[15] Communion with the risen Christ and all of his goodness is only possible through faith (*sola fide*), and Christ is present in his spirit when the congregation looks at him in faith, putting its trust in him alone. Indeed, faith is the result of the presence

---

[15]   See Huldreich Zwingli, *Fidei expositio*, in Z VI.5, 90, 14–93, 3.

of the Spirit of God. Bread and other earthly elements should not be considered simply a means for transporting God's presence. The elements are signs that point to Christ and his redemption, accomplished on the cross at Golgotha. In his later writings, Zwingli compared the elements with a ring that a husband leaves behind with his wife when he goes on a journey. The ring is not valuable because it is of the same substance as the body of the absent husband, but rather because it is a pledge and guarantee of his marital love and faithfulness.[16]

ZWINGLI'S THEOLOGICAL STARTING POINT

Is there a fundamental theological principle in Zwingli's thought that holds together the various aspects of his work and teaching? Zwingli's intention as a Reformer was not to add something new to Christian doctrine. For him, "reformation" meant going back to, and taking as seriously as possible, the basic truth of the Christian faith: that the triune God was revealed in Christ's act of reconciliation.

Redemption is in Christ alone, and Christ's spirit alone can bring human beings into communion with God, by planting faith in their hearts. This spiritual communion leads Christians to worship God "in spirit and in truth" (John 4:24), in particular by seeking to make church and society conform to the will of Christ, because, as images of God the Creator, humans are destined to work and be creative.

This understanding led Zwingli to make a radical distinction. In effect, he asks, should a person, or a nation, claiming to be Christian seek comfort in creaturely things like religious rituals and laws, personal acts of piety, human traditions, and political alliances or in God the Creator, who is singularly eternal, the source of all good who graciously reaches out to people in Christ? The distinction between idolatry and real piety, between false and true religion, was central to Zwingli's thought. That distinction encompassed Luther's position on justification by (religious) works and justification by faith alone, but it also reached far beyond the confessional. "True religion" meant placing complete trust in God the Creator alone and not in earthly things, from which the faithful must instead be rescued, church laws and all means of self-justification included.

> If we worship one God, we place all our confidence in one God only.... Therefore, we can presume to come to him. For what can he

---

[16] Ibid., 155–163.

deny us, if he even gave his only Son and has made him an eternal surety for the payment of our sins? He himself stands calling Matt. 11:28: 'Come unto me, all you that labor and are heavy laden, and I will give you rest.' Note how he calls us unto himself and does not point us to this one or that one of the advocates ... Therefore all persons ought to call on God earnestly that he may kindle his light more and more fully to illumine human hearts and draw them into the hope of the one God. For this is certain that whoever turns to a creature is an idolater.[17]

Zwingli had been brought up in the climate of the Swiss Confederation and was a people's priest; his concern transcended his personal salvation. He felt responsible for his nation, and he was convinced that the Gospel, concentrated in Christ's work of reconciliation and his call to enter into communion with God through faith alone, addressed the individual, the Christian community, and society as a whole. As a consequence, biblical themes such as covenant, church, community, and election formed the leading theological categories in his thought, categories that are also found in the later Reformed tradition.

THE LEGACY OF ZWINGLI AS PIONEER OF REFORMED THEOLOGY

It was never Zwingli's intention to create his own school of theology. In his writings he repeatedly called on the reader to test out his teachings against the Bible. History has largely associated Reformed Protestantism with the name Calvin, but no teaching of John Calvin had not already been addressed by Zwingli. Other Reformers – Johannes Oecolampadius in Basle, Martin Bucer and Wolfgang Capito in Strasbourg, Guillaume Farel and Pierre Viret in Geneva, Lausanne, and Neuchâtel – also owed a significant theological debt to Zwingli. Heinrich Bullinger, in particular, drew on Zwingli's teachings as he developed his own thought; Bullinger's name is also all too readily forgotten. The most widely used Reformed confession, the Second Helvetic Confession, was the work of Bullinger and bears many marks of Zwingli. And the most widely used Reformed catechism, the Heidelberg Catechism, was written with advice from Bullinger, and as a result it too reflects Zwingli's thought, in particular in its teaching on the eucharist. Once familiar with Zwingli's theology, one finds it not only everywhere within Reformed Protestantism but

---

[17] Huldreich Zwingli, Z II, 221, 16–27; 222, 3–6; Huldrych Zwingli, *Writings*, vol. 1, 174.

also among various denominations within the ecumenical movement, although they themselves may be unaware of their ties to the Zürich Reformation.

Further reading

An annual bibliography on Zwingli is published in *Zwingliana*. Zürich: Theologischer Verlag Zürich. www.zwingliverein.ch/zwingliana/

Cameron, E. *The European Reformation*. Oxford: Clarendon Press, 1991.

Egli, E. *Aktensammlung zur Geschichte der Zürcher Reformation in den Jahren 1519–1533*. Neudruck der Ausgabe Zürich 1879. Nieuwkoop: B. de Graaf, 1973.

Gäbler, U. *Huldrych Zwingli: His Life and Work*. Translated by Ruth Gritsch. Philadelphia: Fortress Press, 1987.

Gordon, B. *The Swiss Reformation*. Manchester and New York: Manchester University Press, 2002.

Locher, G. W. *Die Zwinglische Reformation im Rahmen der europäischen Kirchengeschichte*. Göttingen: Vandenhoeck und Ruprecht, 1979.

Opitz, Peter. *Ulrich Zwingli – Prophet, Ketzer, Pionier des Protestantismus*. Zürich: Theologischer Verlag Zürich, 2015.

Potter, G. R. *Zwingli*. Cambridge: Cambridge University Press, 1976.

Stephens, W. *The Theology of Huldrych Zwingli*, Oxford: Clarendon Press, 1986.

Voigtländer, J. *Ein Fest der Befreiung: Huldrych Zwinglis Abendmahlslehre*. Neukirchen-Vluyn: Neukirchener Verlag, 2013.

Zwingli, Huldreich. *Sämtliche Werke*. Corpus Reformatorum 88–108. Berlin/ Leipzig/Zürich, 1905–2013.

   Writings. 2 vols. Edited and translated by E. J. Furcha and H. W. Pipkin. Allison Park, PA: Pickwick Publications, 1984.

9 John Calvin

RANDALL C. ZACHMAN

John Calvin (1509–1564) was deeply committed to two restoration movements sweeping through Europe during his life: the recovery of classical and patristic literature, best exemplified by Guillaume Bude and Desiderius Erasmus, and the recovery of the Gospel in the midst of the Roman Catholic Church, best exemplified by Martin Luther and Philip Melanchthon.[1] Calvin used the skills and insights gained by the recovery of the liberal arts in his day to teach the Gospel and interpret the Scriptures with clarity and integrity. He therefore saw himself as one of the orthodox and evangelical teachers of the church, going back to Justin Martyr, Irenaeus, Chrysostom, and Augustine, and including in his own day Luther, Melanchthon, Martin Bucer, Thomas Cranmer, and Heinrich Bullinger. Calvin would therefore likely be both surprised and disappointed to see himself confined to the Reformed tradition, as he saw himself as a catholic theologian, and dedicated a great amount of energy to overcoming the division that separated Luther and the Wittenberg Reformers from Zwingli and the Reformers in Zürich.

THE LIFE OF CALVIN

Calvin was born in Noyon, France, and was initially educated in the home of Charles de Hangest, a local aristocrat, and then at the College de Montaigue at the University of Paris, which he first attended at the age of fourteen. While at Paris, Calvin had the opportunity of studying with one of the finest Latinists there, Mathurin Cordier, who was himself part of the recovery of classical Latin in the sixteenth century, and who first awakened in Calvin a love for good letters and refined Ciceronian Latin.[2]

---

[1] See Randall C. Zachman, *John Calvin as Teacher, Pastor, and Theologian: The Shape of His Writings and Thought* (Grand Rapids, MI: Baker Academic, 2005), chapter 1.

[2] John Calvin, Dedication to Comm. First Thessalonians, *Calvin's New Testament Commentaries*, edited by David W. Torrance and Thomas F. Torrance (Grand Rapids, MI Michigan: Eerdmans, 1959–72), vol. 8, 331, henceforth CNTC 8:331.

Calvin then pursued the study of law at the request of his father, first at Orleans, and then at Bourges, and attained his degree in law. While at Orleans, Calvin studied classical Greek with the German Hellenist Melchior Wolmar, who reinforced Calvin's love of classical arts and letters, and gave him "a good grounding in the rudiments of the language and that was of great help to me later on."[3] Indeed, so deeply committed was Calvin to the study of classical Latin and Greek literature that he may have ruined his health studying both law and literature during his time as a law student. Calvin continued to study the writings of classical authors for the rest of his life, especially Plato, whom he deemed to be the most sober and religious of the philosophers, as well as Cicero, Seneca, and Aristotle. Indeed, like Erasmus, Calvin thought that it was impossible to interpret Scripture properly without a thorough knowledge of classical literature.

After his father's death in 1531, Calvin directed the whole of his attention to the study of classical literature at the newly founded College of Royal Readers in Paris. There Calvin came under the influence of the two great philologists of his day, Guillaume Bude and Desiderius Erasmus. Calvin may have come across the work of Bude in his study of law.[4] Calvin also came to appreciate the labors of Erasmus in the recovery of Greek and Latin literature, especially in his critical editions of the classical authors and Church Fathers, and also in his collections in the Adagia (1508). Calvin learned from Bude and Erasmus the importance of establishing reliable critical editions, and of interpreting texts in light of their literary, linguistic, and cultural contexts, so that their genuine meaning would emerge from that context. He first applied this method to Seneca's treatise *De Clementia*, in a work published at his own expense in April of 1532. The work itself was an attempt to restore Seneca to his rightful place of honor in the world of the most learned, over against the critical comments of Quintialian about Seneca's inferior Latin style. However, under the influence of Luther, Calvin was soon to apply his skills in the interpretation of literature to a new objective – restoring the reading of Scripture to its rightful place in the church, especially for those who never before learned to read.

Calvin first appears to have come to an appreciation of the writings of Martin Luther in the years of 1533–1534, during which time he most likely experienced his "sudden conversion to teachableness" detailed

---

[3] Dedication to Comm. 2 Corinthians, CNTC 9:1.
[4] T. H. L. Parker, *Calvin's New Testament Commentaries*, 2nd ed. (Louisville, KY: Westminster John Knox, 1993), 187.

in his Preface to his Psalms Commentary.[5] In the only letter he wrote directly to Luther (a letter not actually delivered), Calvin addresses him as "the very excellent pastor of the Christian Church, my much respected father."[6] It is quite likely that Calvin viewed Luther as the one who brought him to faith in the Gospel, most likely through his own reading of Luther's 1520 treatises, *The Freedom of a Christian* and *The Babylonian Captivity of the Christian Church*.[7] Calvin had the highest praise for the role of Luther in restoring the church of his day, viewing him as an apostle raised up miraculously by God to free the church from the papacy.[8] Because of Luther's role in restoring the Gospel, Calvin was willing to acknowledge that the evangelical churches were in fact founded on his ministry, as the divine restoration of apostolic doctrine: "God raised up Luther and others, who held forth a torch to light us into the way of salvation, and on whose ministry our churches are founded and built."[9] Calvin was firmly convinced by Luther's claim that justification by faith alone apart from works was the turning-point of the controversy with Rome, and that such faith could be created and sustained only by the preaching of the Gospel of the free grace and mercy of God in Jesus Christ, through the power of the Holy Spirit. Calvin also agreed with Luther, over against Zwingli, that the sacraments are signs appended to the Gospel to aid and strengthen faith.[10] Calvin was willing to give Luther the pride of place in the restoration of the church in his day, but he was not willing to let Luther be the dominant individual in

---

[5] John Calvin, *Ioannis Calvini opera quae supersunt omnia*, edited by Wilhelm Baum, Edward Cunitz, and Eduard Reuss (Brunswick: A. Schwetschke and Son (M. Bruhn), 1863–1900), vol. 31, 21; henceforth CO 31:21; John Calvin, *Calvin: Commentaries*, translated by Joseph Haroutunian (Philadelphia: Westminster, 1958), 52; henceforth *Calvin: Commentaries*, 52. See B. A. Gerrish, "The Pathfinder: Calvin's Image of Martin Luther," in *The Old Protestantism and the New: Essays on the Reformation Heritage* (Edinburgh: T&T Clark, 1982), 27–48.

[6] CO 12:7; John Calvin, *The Letters of John Calvin*, translated by Jules Bonnet, IV vols. (New York, Burt Franklin, 1972), vol. I, 440; henceforth *Letters* I, 440.

[7] I say this because the last two sections of the 1536 *Institutes* directly echo these two treatises, whereas the first section directly echoes Luther's *Small Catechism*. See Alexandre Ganoczy, *The Young Calvin*, translated by David Foxgrover and Wade Provo (Philadelphia: Westminster, 1987), 137–145.

[8] CO 6:250; John Calvin, *The Bondage and Liberation of the Will*, translated by A. N. S. Lane (Grand Rapids, MI: Baker Books, 1996), 28.

[9] CO 6:459; John Calvin, *The Necessity of Reforming the Church* (1543), *Calvin: Theological Treatises*, translated by J. K. S. Reid (Philadelphia: Westminster, 1954), 185; henceforth *Calvin: Theological Treatises*, 185.

[10] For a detailed comparison of Luther and Calvin on the nature of faith, see Randall C. Zachman, *The Assurance of Faith: Conscience in the Theology of Martin Luther and John Calvin* (Minneapolis, MN: Fortress, 1993).

the newly restored church, and later in his career he intentionally demonstrated his independence from Luther.[11]

After his sudden conversion to teachableness, Calvin likely saw himself as a member of the evangelical Roman Catholic teachers who had gathered around Jacques Lefevre D'Estaples. As a result of the persecution of this community, Calvin was led first to internal exile within France, and then to exile in the city of Basel in the years 1535–1536. While he was in Basel, Calvin most likely first studied Hebrew under the tutelage of the great Christian Hebraist Sebastian Muenster.[12] Calvin also came into contact with the teaching and exegesis of the Swiss Reformers, especially Johannes Oecolampadius and Huldrych Zwingli. Oecolampadius had been the Reformer of Basel until his death in 1531, and was deeply admired by Calvin for the depth of his learning and for his skill as a biblical interpreter.[13] Calvin appreciated the way Oecolampadius recovered for the church of his day the symbolic thinking of the fathers, especially about the sacraments, over against the language of substance that had dominated the papacy after the Fourth Lateran Council. While in Basel, Calvin undoubtedly read Zwingli's *Commentary on True and False Religion* of 1525.[14] Calvin was persuaded by Zwingli's claim that the true body of Christ is in heaven, where it will remain until he comes again in glory. He was also persuaded by Zwingli's criticism of the Roman Catholic doctrine of *ex opere operato*, for that bound the efficacy of the sacraments too much to the ministry of the church, and not to the free mercy of God in Christ through the Holy Spirit. Calvin also seems to have been decisively influenced by Zwingli's description of God as the freely self-giving fountain of every good thing, both as Creator and as Redeemer. However, Calvin throughout his life was highly critical of the way Zwingli divorced the sacraments from the self-offering of Christ, making them empty signs. He was also critical of Zwingli's disorderly method of teaching, and of his exegesis, which wandered too far from the text.[15] Calvin throughout his life demonstrated more respect for Oecolampadius than for Zwingli, even though he insists that the memory of both Zwingli and Oecolampadius "ought to be held in honorable esteem by all the godly."[16]

[11] Calvin to Philip Melanchthon, 28 June 1545, CO 12:99; *Letters* I, 467.

[12] Max Engamarre, "*Johannes Calvinus trium linguarum peritus?* La Question de l'Hebreu", *Bibliotheque d'Humanisme et Renaissance* 58 (1996); Darryl Phillips, 'An Inquiry into the Extent of the Abilities of John Calvin as a Hebraist' (Oxford: Oxford University DPhil thesis, 1998).

[13] CO 11:36; *Letters* I, 188.

[14] Alexandre Ganoczy, *The Young Calvin*, 90–102, 151–158.

[15] Calvin to Viret, 19 May 1540, CO 11:36; *Letters* I, 188.

[16] Calvin to Melanchthon, 21 January 1545, CO 12:11; *Letters* I, 437–438.

We owe it to Guillaume Farel to have presented to Calvin the call of God to the public ministry of teaching and preaching the Gospel, when Farel summoned Calvin to help in the restoration of the church in Geneva, under the threat of God's wrath were he to refuse this call.[17] Calvin accepted this call, first as teacher of Scripture, then as pastor, in the newly restored church of Geneva, with absolutely no training either as a public teacher or as a pastor. Calvin's acceptance of these callings represented his first clear and public break with the Church of Rome. Calvin was therefore initiated into his public ministry both by Farel and by his colleague from the Pays-de-Vaud, Pierre Viret. Calvin always understood himself as first assisting, and then inheriting, the work of restoring the church first begun in Geneva by Farel and Viret.[18]

After the expulsion of Calvin and Farel from Geneva in 1538, Calvin thought he was no longer suited for the ministry. However, the great Strasbourg Reformer Martin Bucer refused to let Calvin go back into hiding, comparing him to Jonah in his desire to flee from his calling from God to be a teacher and pastor in the church.[19] Calvin came to Strasbourg deeply conscious of his failings as a pastor and teacher in the church. He therefore sought above all else to learn how to become a more effective teacher and pastor. Martin Bucer was above any other in his life the one from whom Calvin learned the most about the office of ministry, reflected in his description of Bucer as "that most distinguished minister of Christ."[20] Calvin especially learned from Bucer how rightly to order the polity and worship of the church, especially with the fourfold office of teacher, pastor, elder, and deacon, and how to order the community via discipline, which Calvin came to describe as the sinews of the body of Christ. Calvin also developed a deep appreciation for Bucer's skill as an interpreter of Scripture, demonstrating his great depth of learning and attention to context.[21] Bucer also convinced Calvin to get married, and Calvin chose for his wife the widow of a former Anabaptist, Idulette de Bure.

If Bucer was a decisive influence on Calvin's effectiveness as a pastor and interpreter of Scripture, Johann Sturm and Philip Melanchthon were equally influential in terms of Calvin's development as a teacher. Calvin was called to teach Scripture at Sturm's new Academy in Strasbourg, which not only refined his abilities as an interpreter of

---

[17] CO 31:23; *Calvin: Commentaries*, 53.
[18] Dedication to Titus, CNTC 10:347.
[19] CO 31:25; *Calvin: Commentaries*, 54.
[20] Ibid.
[21] Calvin to Heinrich Bullinger, March 12, 1539, *Letters* I, 114.

Scripture, beginning with the publication of the Romans commentary in 1539, but also gave him a vision of how to train and educate a new generation of pastors in the newly restored church. Calvin's deep appreciation for Sturm's work at the Academy of Strasbourg was to bear fruit twenty years later in the opening of the Geneva Academy in 1559, which had as its primary task the training of future pastors for ministry in Geneva and in France.[22] Calvin also used his time in Strasbourg to redesign the purpose and method of his *Institutes*, under the influence of Melanchthon's 1535 *Loci Communes*. The impact of Melanchthon on Calvin was reinforced by the personal meetings they had at the colloquies of Worms and Ratisbon, which Calvin attended as part of the Strasbourg contingent, leading to an epistolary friendship that would last until Melanchthon's death in 1560.[23]

If Bucer was to Calvin the most distinguished minister of Christ, Melanchthon was to him the "most illustrious light and distinguished teacher of the Church."[24] Calvin was especially impressed by the clear, orderly, and simple plan of teaching that Melanchthon followed in his major theological handbook, the *Loci Communes*.[25] Calvin sought from 1539 onwards to bring that same clarity to his own *Institutes*, being finally content with the clarity of the order of its topics in the 1559 edition.[26] Like Melanchthon, Calvin understood the office of the teacher to involve guiding future ministers of the church by setting forth the major topics to be sought in their reading of Scripture, so that they might teach this doctrine to their congregations.

Calvin also joined the efforts of Bucer and Melanchthon to unite the divided evangelicals, especially over the question of the Holy Supper of the Lord.[27] Calvin accepted as legitimate the Wittenberg Concord of 1536, signed by Luther, Melanchthon, and Bucer, to unite the churches

[22] Karin Maag, *Seminary or University? The Genevan Academy and Reformed Higher Education, 1560–1620* (Aldershot, UK: Ashgate, 1995).

[23] Timothy Wengert, "'We Will Feast Together in Heaven Forever': The Epistolary Friendship of John Calvin and Philip Melanchthon," in *Melanchthon in Europe*, edited by Karin Maag (Grand Rapids, MI: Baker Books, 1999), 19–44; and Zachman, *John Calvin as Teacher*, chapter 2.

[24] Calvin to Philip Melanchthon, December 13, 1558, CO 17:384–386; *Letters* III, 484.

[25] CO 6:229–30; *The Bondage and Liberation of the Will*, 3.

[26] For the influence of Melanchthon on Calvin's *Institutes*, see Richard A. Muller, *The Unaccommodated Calvin: Studies in the Foundation of a Theological Tradition* (New York: Oxford University Press, 2000).

[27] See Randall C. Zachman, "The Conciliating Theology of John Calvin," in *Conciliation and Confession: The Struggle for Unity in the Age of Reform, 1415–1648*, edited by Howard Louthan and Randall Zachman (Notre Dame, IN: University of Notre Dame Press, 2004), 89–105.

of Wittenberg and Strasbourg. It is also highly likely that he signed the 1540 Augsburg Confession, which included the terms of this concord in its article on the Lord's Supper, that is, that the body of Christ are both exhibited and presented in the bread and wine. Calvin was convinced (perhaps wrongly) that he and Melanchthon were of one mind concerning the Supper, and that it was therefore possible to reach a union between Wittenberg, Strasbourg, Geneva, and Zürich. For such an agreement to succeed, however, Calvin would need to bring Heinrich Bullinger and the pastors of Zürich from their adherence to Zwingli's position to one that reflected the Wittenberg Concord and the 1540 Augsburg Confession.[28]

Calvin had deep respect for Heinrich Bullinger as his senior pastor in the evangelical churches of the Swiss regions. Bullinger was renowned for his learning, both of Scripture and of the Church Fathers.[29] However, Calvin was aware that Geneva and Zürich were not of one mind regarding the meaning of the Holy Supper of the Lord. At the urging of Farel, Calvin went to Zürich (itself a sign of deference to the greater authority of the church there), to initiate talks designed to reach an agreement on the Supper, which finally came to fruition in the Zürich Consensus of 1549, published in 1551. This ecumenical achievement of Calvin, demonstrating an irenic side of his nature not often noted, was quickly brought under a cloud by the harsh attacks on it by the Lutherans, first by Westphal, and then by Heshusius. Both rejected Calvin's claim that the Zürich Consensus reflected the teaching of the Augsburg Confession. Calvin himself describes this period of his life as one of the most bitter, made all the more painful by the utter silence of Philip Melanchthon on the dispute, perhaps indicative of the latter's own problems with the Consensus.[30] However, Bullinger never wavered in his adherence to the consensus reached with Calvin, as is reflected in the Second Helvetic Confession, written by Bullinger as a statement of his faith in 1566, two years after the death of Calvin. We owe it to the Zürich Consensus, and its rejection by the Lutherans, that Calvin came to be seen as a Reformed theologian, and not as an adherent of the Augsburg Confession.

---

[28] One can see his interest in reaching such an agreement early during his stay in Strasbourg, when he wrote his *Short Treatise on the Holy Supper of Our Lord and Only Saviour Jesus Christ*, 1539, CO 5:429–460; *Calvin: Theological Treatises*, 140–166.

[29] Parker, *Calvin's New Testament Commentaries*, 72.

[30] CO 31:33; *Calvin: Commentaries*, 56–57.

Calvin's years in Geneva were marked by several controversies that came to shape the way history has remembered him. The physician Jérôme Bolsec claimed that Calvin's doctrine of predestination made God into an arbitrary tyrant. Once Bolsec was expelled from Geneva, he returned to the Roman Catholic Church and wrote the first (highly negative) biography of Calvin. Calvin is also remembered for his part in the burning of Michael Servetus, which tended to reinforce Bolsec's portrait of Calvin as an intolerant leader of the church in Geneva. Calvin was involved in a bitter struggle with the Geneva City Councils over the status of discipline and excommunication, which Calvin wanted to be independent of civic authority, in part so that civic leaders could also be disciplined. However, the bulk of Calvin's energy was devoted to preaching and lecturing on Scripture, and publishing commentaries on almost every book of the Bible, to help other pastors in their labors. Calvin's dedication to this task is shown by the way he asked to be carried to the lecture hall to give his lectures on Ezekiel, as his health was too poor for him to walk to the hall. Calvin died in 1564.

THE ORDER TO RIGHT TEACHING

Calvin devoted a great deal of attention to developing a clear, orderly, and persuasive manner of teaching. Calvin's method of teaching constitutes his greatest contribution to the subsequent Reformed tradition, in two distinct ways. First, Calvin developed a series of distinct but inseparable realities, which mutually confirm their truth. Second, Calvin developed a series of contrasting realities, in which the truth of one is illuminated by its contrast with the other.

Distinct but inseparable realities

In the *Institutes*, Calvin developed a distinctive method of teaching that seems to reflect the Definition of Chalcedon, in which two distinct realities are held inseparably together, in such a way that they confirm each other in the truth. The final edition of the *Institutes* reflects the importance of these distinct but inseparable realities. Calvin claims that all true wisdom consists of the knowledge of God and the knowledge of ourselves, "But, while joined by many bonds, which one precedes and brings forth the other is not easy to discern."[31] The knowledge of the benefits

---

[31] John Calvin, Inst. I.i.1, *Ioannis Calvini opera selecta*, edited by Peter Barth, Wilhelm Niesel, and Dora Scheuner (Munich: Chr. Kaiser, 1926–1952), vol. III, 31, lines 8–10; henceforth OS III.31.8-10; John Calvin, *Institutes of the Christian Religion*, edited by

we experience in ourselves leads us to seek the source of these benefits in God, out of a movement of genuine gratitude. The knowledge of our poverty leads us to seek the good things we lack in God out of a true and heartfelt humility. In both ways, God is known as the author and fountain of every good thing, whom we must thank for everything we have received, and from whom we must seek all that we lack.

Calvin then distinguishes between the knowledge of God the Creator and the knowledge of God the Redeemer. He writes: "First, as much in the fashioning of the universe as in the general teaching of Scripture the Lord shows himself to be simply the Creator. Then in the face of Christ [cf. II Cor. 4:6] he shows himself the Redeemer."[32] The former teaches us that God is the author and source of all the benefits of this life, which we still experience even in the state of sinfulness. The latter reveals God as the author and source of all good unto eternal life. God sets forth in Christ every good thing that sinners lack, to be sought especially in Christ risen and ascended. Moreover, Christ reconciles God and sinners in his death, thereby removing every evil from them. Thus God's work in redemption confirms the nature of God revealed in creation, that God is the author and source of every good thing, who created us to be united to God in eternal life.

God the Redeemer is revealed in Christ, but Christ himself is disclosed in two distinct yet inseparable ways, first in the Law revealed to Israel, and then in the Gospel proclaimed to all nations. The Law reveals Christ to Israel under earthly symbols and types, such as the promised land of Israel, sacrifices, the priesthood, and the Davidic kingship. The Gospel reveals the reality and antitype represented in the symbols and types of the Law, and so confirms its truth even as it brings the Law to its end and completion. However, even after the Gospel brings the time of the Law to an end, the truth of the Gospel is confirmed by comparing the types of the Law with the antitype revealed in Christ by the Gospel.[33] By moving from Law to Gospel, and from Gospel back to Law, the fountain of every good thing set forth by God in Christ is more fully revealed, and its truth more solidly confirmed.

Christ himself must be true God and true human if he is to fulfill his office as Mediator. However, the distinction between Christ's divinity and humanity is also essential to his work of mediation. Calvin was

---

John T. McNeill and translated by Ford Lewis Battles. Library of Christian Classics; 2 vols. (Philadelphia: Westminster, 1960), vol. 1, 35; henceforth (1:35).

[32] Inst. I.ii.1, OS III.34.21–25; (1:40).

[33] Inst. II.ix.1, OS III.398.11–14; (1:423).

especially concerned not to allow the divinity of Christ to override or threaten his humanity. Even though Christ is fully divine throughout his life, he also establishes the truth of his fellowship with us by growing in wisdom and knowledge, and by praying to God, thereby showing himself at times as fully human. Most importantly, Christ can only offer to God the obedience that freely reconciles God and sinners if he offers this obedience freely as a human being, and not by means of his divine power. To explain how this happens, Calvin borrows from Irenaeus the idea that the divinity of Christ increasingly conceals itself and remains at rest throughout his life, until it is completely concealed in his suffering and death. Calvin intensifies the human suffering of Christ in his death by endorsing the claim made in some versions of the Apostles' Creed that he descended into hell. Calvin takes this to mean that Christ suffered in himself the wrath of God directed toward condemned sinners, "in order that we might know not only that Christ's body was given as the price of our redemption, but that he paid a greater and more excellent price in suffering in his soul the terrible torments of a condemned and forsaken man."[34]

Once the divinity of Christ reveals itself in his resurrection, and especially in his ascension, Calvin is still at pains to maintain the distinction between Christ's divinity and humanity. The ascension of Christ into heaven and eternal life is the pledge that we also will inherit eternal life in and with him.[35] This is why the apostles see Jesus ascend into heaven, and why they are told that Jesus will return from heaven in the same way they saw him depart. The ascended Lord is the pledge of our own hope for eternal life, and any attempt to divinize his humanity undermines our hope. Once we are brought to the goal of our redemption, and are fully transformed into the image of God, we will see God face to face, and will no longer need the mediation of Christ's humanity to know God. This is how Calvin understands Paul's claim that the Son will hand the Kingdom back to the Father, so that God will be all in all: "But when as partakers in heavenly glory we shall see God as he is, Christ, having then discharged the office of Mediator, will cease to be the ambassador of his Father, and will be satisfied with that glory which he enjoyed before the creation of the world."[36]

Although Christ contains in himself every good thing sinners lack that can unite them to God, faith in Christ receives in particular two

[34] Inst. II.xvi.10, OS III.495.23–27; (1:516).
[35] Inst. II.xvi.16, OS III.503.22–24, 504.1-2; (1:524).
[36] Inst. II.xiv.3, OS III.462.11–14; (1:485).

distinct yet inseparable gifts: repentance and justification. These gifts reveal that the faithful cannot be forgiven without being renewed in the image of God, while also showing that throughout their lives, the faithful continually need the forgiveness of sins, as their renewal is never complete in this life. Calvin explains: "For when this topic is rightly understood it will better appear how man is justified by faith alone, and simple pardon; nevertheless actual holiness of life, so to speak, is not separated from free imputation of righteousness."[37] The goal of our adoption as children of God is our regeneration in the image of God, whereby we are united to God in eternal life, and may hope to see God face to face. Both the Ten Commandments and Christ himself represent the image of God that our lives should express, and the Law in its third use exhorts believers in this direction. However, the basis of our adoption is the forgiveness of sin, as our transformation in this life does not remove all sin from us. Calvin will therefore agree with the Roman Catholic theologians that faith is inseparable from regeneration, but will insist that regeneration is distinct but inseparable from justification and forgiveness, which we also need throughout this life. Calvin will also agree with the Lutherans that the basis of our adoption is the free forgiveness of sins in Christ, but will insist that God never forgives those whom God does not also renew, as both distinct graces are inseparably united in Christ.

Calvin also holds together the distinct forms of divine self-revelation in manifestation and proclamation.[38] God freely offers Christ to us not only in the preaching of the Gospel, but also in the visible sacraments of the church, even as Christ was revealed to Israel in the teaching of Moses and the sacraments of circumcision, Passover, and sacrifice. The Word of the Gospel is necessary to make these symbols "living images" that convey to us the reality that they represent, but the symbols themselves are also necessary to confirm the truth of the Word to us, as we are creatures of sense, and the Gospel offers us spiritual realities we cannot directly perceive with our senses. Calvin observes that "Since, however, this mystery of Christ's secret union with the devout is by nature incomprehensible, he shows its figure and image in visible signs best adapted to our small capacity. Indeed, by giving guarantees and tokens he makes it as certain for us as if we had seen it with our own eyes."[39] Hence the truth of what we hear in the Gospel is confirmed by what we

---

[37] Inst. III.iii.1, OS IV.55.11–15; (1:593).
[38] See Randall C. Zachman, *Image and Word in the Theology of John Calvin* (Notre Dame, IN: University of Notre Dame Press, 2006).
[39] Inst. IV.xvii.1, OS V.342.30–32, 343.1–2; (2:1361).

see in the sacraments, even as the Word that we hear confirms the truth that we see in the sacraments. Indeed, these distinct yet inseparable forms of revelation in proclamation and manifestation are found in the knowledge of God the Creator and God the Redeemer. God is revealed as the author and fountain of every good thing in the living images of God in the universe and in Christ, but these images can be known only if we open our ears to the Word while we view these images with our eyes.

Calvin's discussion of the sacraments themselves also reflects the same concern with distinct but inseparable realities. The symbol of the sacrament must be distinguished from the reality it represents, which is Christ himself with his benefits. However, this reality is inseparable from the symbol that exhibits it, so that when we see the symbol, we know that Christ is offering himself and all his benefits to us.[40] The bread and wine of the Holy Supper of the Lord are distinct from the body and blood of Christ, for the former are on earth and are eaten with the mouth while the latter are in heaven to be eaten spiritually. However, the faithful truly partake of the spiritual food of the body and blood of Christ when they eat and drink the symbols of body and blood in the bread and wine. Over against the Roman Catholic and Lutheran theologians, Calvin will distinguish eating the bread and wine from eating the body and blood of Christ. Over against Zwingli, Calvin will insist that God does not mock us with empty symbols, for when we are offered the symbols of Christ's body and blood, we are also offered the body and blood of Christ, even though that body and blood must not be sought in the bread and wine, but in heaven.[41]

Contrasting opposing realities

Over and above his way of confirming the truth by holding together two distinct but inseparable realities, Calvin also seeks to confirm the truth by contrasting two opposing realities. To distinguish the true worship of God from idolatry and superstition, Calvin cites the claim made by the prophets that the ungodly worship the work of their own hands, whereas the pious worship God, the Creator of heaven and earth. He writes: "But as Scripture, having regard for men's rude and stupid wit, customarily speaks in the manner of the common folk, where it would distinguish the true God from the false it particularly contrasts him with idols."[42] Calvin develops two different grounds for his rejection of human images

---

[40] Inst. IV.xvii.5, OS V.346.26–29; (2:1364–1365).
[41] Inst. IV.xvii.10, OS V.351.29–31; (2:1370).
[42] Inst. I.xi.1, OS III.88.17–19; (1:99–100).

in worship. The first is related to the inseparability of manifestation and proclamation. As God has already made Godself somewhat visible in the "living images" of Christ, baptism, and the Holy Supper, the godly should reject the "dead images" that are formed according to the human imagination. Only living images truly offer the reality they represent, whereas dead images at best only represent an absent reality.[43]

The second basis of Calvin's rejection of images rests on his insistence that the Creator is essentially invisible, and cannot be represented in any visible way. Calvin roots this claim in the statement made in Deuteronomy that on Sinai the Israelites only heard the voice of the Lord, but saw no form: "We see how openly God speaks against all images, that we may know that all who seek visible forms of God depart from him."[44] This second basis of the rejection of images is in significant tension with the first, and may account for our lack of appreciation for the way Calvin unites manifestation and proclamation. As a consequence of these thoroughgoing criticisms of idolatry, Calvin sought to rid worship spaces of any images made by human beings, including crosses, crucifixes, statues, paintings, frescos, and stained glass. Over against Gregory the Great's claim that such images are "the books of the unlearned," Calvin cites Jeremiah and Isaiah to say that such images are the "teachers of falsehood." He explains: "Since there is one true God whom the Jews were wont to worship, visible figures are wickedly and falsely fashioned to represent God; and all who seek the knowledge of God from these are miserably deluded."[45] Rather than teaching the godly falsehood by having them look at images produced by the human imagination, the church should teach the godly how to read Scripture for themselves, for Scripture is truly the book of the unlearned.

Calvin also contrasts the providential care God shows toward the godly with the way God treats their enemies who oppress them, observing that "the principal purpose of Biblical history is to teach that the Lord watches over the ways of the saints with such great diligence that they do not even stumble over a stone [cf. Ps. 91:12]."[46] Calvin became increasingly concerned with God's care of the godly, whom he identified as members of the evangelical communities emerging from the Church of Rome. Calvin thought that God's providential care for them should be manifestly different than the way God governed their enemies, and that this should be clear to the eyes of all. He writes: "I speak not only

---

[43] Inst. I.xi.13, OS III.102.18–25; (1:113–114).
[44] Inst. I.xi.2, OS III.89.8–13; (1:100–101).
[45] Inst. I.xi.5, OS III.93.26–30; (1:105).
[46] Inst. I.xvii.6, OS III.209.30–33; (1:218).

concerning mankind; but, because God has chosen the church to be his dwelling place, there can be no doubt that he shows by singular proofs his fatherly care in ruling it."[47] Hence it bothered him a great deal that the Church of Rome did not fall in his day, but rather seemed to increase in power, prestige, and wealth. He expected the members of the evangelical communities to be persecuted at first, but thought that God's love for them should be visibly manifested in the way God cares for them over against those who oppose them, even as God's favor towards David became manifest after Saul persecuted him. Calvin therefore devotes a great deal of attention to counseling the godly on how to discern God's care for them even though they appear to be left to the power of their enemies, especially in France. If they turn their eyes from the confusing appearance of things to God, who governs all in heaven, they will be able to acquire the patience needed to wait until God acts to distinguish them from the ungodly. Calvin concludes: "So we must infer that, while the disturbances of the world deprive us of judgment, God out of the pure light of his justice and wisdom tempers and directs these very movements in the best-conceived order to a right end."[48]

Calvin wants the godly to contrast their situation in Christ with what their lives would be like apart from Christ, for he thought that only in this way would they appreciate the astonishing mercy of God. In particular, he wants believers to consider the danger they were in under the wrath of God, to appreciate the mercy of God revealed in Christ, when Christ takes this wrath upon himself. We truly appreciate the mercy of God in Christ only when we feel in ourselves the wrath of God against sinners, and consider what our fate would be without Christ: "we are taught by Scripture to perceive that apart from Christ, God is, so to speak, hostile to us, and his hand is armed for our destruction; to embrace his benevolence and fatherly love in Christ alone."[49] Calvin's way of contrasting life in Christ to life outside of Christ will lead him state that God is our hostile enemy apart from Christ, and needs to be reconciled to us. Calvin claims that Christ reconciles God to us by offering a sacrifice that appeases God's wrath and renders God propitious toward us: "He offered as a sacrifice the flesh he received from us, that he might wipe out our guilt by his act of expiation and appease the Father's righteous wrath."[50] Calvin knows that Christ came to die for us because God already loves us, but he was convinced that we

[47] Inst. I.xvii.6, OS III.210.10–13; (1:219).
[48] Inst. I.xvii.1, OS III.203.6–9; (1:211).
[49] Inst. II.xvi.2, OS 484.11–18; (1:505).
[50] Inst. II.xii.3, OS III.440.17–18; (1:466–467).

would underestimate that love if we did not feel that God was hostile to us apart from Christ. Hence Calvin consistently teaches that God is our enemy apart from Christ, so that in Christ God is being reconciled to the world as much as God is reconciling the world to Godself. He observes that "In this ruin of mankind no one now experiences God either as Father or as Author of salvation, or favorable in any way, until Christ the Mediator comes forward to reconcile him to us."[51]

Similarly, we appreciate the gift of faith only when we compare ourselves to those who are not given faith. Faith itself is the free gift of God, revealed to our minds and sealed on our hearts by the Holy Spirit through the preaching of the Gospel. However, Calvin insists that the free gift of the Spirit to the elect must be held together insepa- rably with the refusal of that gift to the reprobate. We know the free mercy of God only by this contrast, that God freely gives to some what God freely denies to others: "We shall never be clearly persuaded, as we ought to be, that our salvation flows from the wellspring of God's free mercy until we come to know his eternal election, which illumines God's grace by this contrast: that he does not indiscriminately adopt all into the hope of salvation but gives to some what he denies to others."[52] Those who speak only of an election unto eternal life via the Gospel, as do Melanchthon and Bullinger, ignore the contrasting truth of divine rejection, and therefore do not fully appreciate the free mercy of God.

THE LEGACY OF CALVIN FOR REFORMED THEOLOGY

The strength of Calvin's contribution to the Reformed tradition is found in the way he holds distinct realities inseparably together. Over against the tendency to seek all knowledge of God in Christ, Calvin reminds us that we are to combine this knowledge with the self-revelation of God in creation, not only in Scripture, but also in experience and learned inves- tigation. Over against the tendency to eclipse God's relationship with Israel with the self-revelation of God in Christ, Calvin reminds us that the self-manifestation of God in Christ must be held together insepa- rably with the self-disclosure of God to Israel, in a way that carefully attends to the whole dynamic of Israel's long history with God. Calvin also reminds us that all knowledge of God leads to the greater knowledge of ourselves, while all knowledge of ourselves increases and confirms our knowledge of God. Calvin's doctrine of providence has reminded

---

[51] Inst. I.ii.1, OS III.34.15–17; (1:40).
[52] Inst. III.xxi.1, OS IV.369.10–14; (2:921).

the Reformed tradition to focus on God's continuing, intimate care both of all human life, and also of all creatures, reinforcing the attention he would have us direct to the self-disclosure of God in the universe. Finally, Calvin's focus on the eternal election of God has been a continual reminder of the freedom of God, reinforcing Calvin's concern that God's grace cannot be bound or controlled by any creature, even as God's love is freely offered to us in the Gospel by the Holy Spirit.[53]

Further reading

Calvin, John. *Institutes of the Christian Religion*. Edited by John T. McNeill. Translated by Ford Lewis Battles. Philadelphia: Westminster, 1960.

Ganoczy, Alexandre. *The Young Calvin*. Translated by David Foxgrover and Wade Provo. Philadelphia: Westminster, 1987.

Gerrish, Brian A. *Grace and Gratitude: The Eucharistic Theology of John Calvin*. Minneapolis, MN: Fortress, 1993.

Gordon, Bruce. *Calvin*. New Haven, CT; London: Yale University Press, 2009.

Muller, Richard A. *The Unaccommodated Calvin: Studies in the Foundation of a Theological Tradition*. New York: Oxford University Press, 2000.

Zachman, Randall C. *The Assurance of Faith: Conscience in the Theology of Martin Luther and John Calvin*. Minneapolis, MN: Fortress, 1993.

John Calvin as Teacher, Pastor, and Theologian: The Shape of his Writings and Thought. Grand Rapids, MI: Baker Academic, 2005.

Image and Word in the Theology of John Calvin. Notre Dame, IN: University of Notre Dame Press, 2006.

Reconsidering John Calvin. Cambridge: Cambridge University Press, 2012.

---

[53] See Randall C. Zachman, *Reconsidering John Calvin* (Cambridge: Cambridge University Press, 2012), especially chapter 6.

10   Jonathan Edwards

OLIVER D. CRISP

Jonathan Edwards (1703–1758) is often hailed as 'America's theologian'. However, he lived and died before the United States was formed, in the British colonies of New England, and considered himself an Englishman.[1] Consequently, it would be more accurate to speak of him as a British-colonial theologian than as an American. Edwards was born into a ministerial family of English and Welsh descent, and grew up under the austere and pious puritan discipline of his father, Timothy Edwards. He was educated in the classical and biblical languages in the home-school his father ran from his parsonage, and matriculated to what is now Yale College at the age of thirteen. There he took undergraduate and graduate degrees (A.B., A.M.), and, after a brief spell of pulpit supply and ill health, became a college tutor. From there he was called to become the assistant minister to his grandfather, Solomon Stoddard, a formidable and somewhat eccentric patriarch. Eventually Edwards become sole pastor of the congregation in Northampton, where he remained for the majority of his career. During this period he became associated with, and eventually recognized as a leader of, the series of revivals now known as the Great Awakening. One of his most influential works, *The Religious Affections*, was the final product of his reflection on these spiritual upheavals. However, Edwards was eventually

---

[1] For instance, in his *Some Thoughts Concerning the Revival* (1743), Edwards says, 'though it may be thought that I go out of my proper sphere to intermeddle in the affairs of the colleges, yet I will take the liberty of *an Englishman* (that speaks his mind freely concerning public affairs) and the liberty of a minister of Christ (who doubtless may speak his mind as freely about things that concern the kingdom of his Lord and Master) to give my opinion in some things with respect to those societies; the original and main design of which is to train up persons, and fit them for the work of the ministry'. YE4: 510, emphasis added. (Hereinafter, all references given parenthetically in the body of the text to the 26 letterpress volumes of the Yale Edition of *The Works of Jonathan Edwards* [New Haven, CT: Yale University Press, 1957–2008], cited by volume number, colon, and page reference or range, e.g. YE20: 50. See also www.edwards.yale.edu [accessed 1 June 2015], for the online edition of the Works.)

dismissed from his position at Northampton ostensibly because of a change in his views on who was qualified to take communion (a departure from the views of his grandfather). He relocated to what was then the frontier, in Stockbridge, MA, where he served as a missionary to the Mahicans and as pastor to the small group of Europeans settled there. During this period of political turmoil and relative isolation, Edwards composed some of his most important works, including *Freedom of the Will, Original Sin*, and *Two Dissertations*. His time in Stockbridge was cut short by a call to become the president of the College of New Jersey (now Princeton University). With reluctance he took up his new duties, knowing they would deflect him from his life's ambition of writing a massive work of systematic theology, which he never lived to complete. To set an example, and perhaps because of his love for natural philosophy and the 'new learning', Edwards was inoculated with a smallpox vaccination. Complications arising from this procedure led to his death, a matter of a few months after taking up his duties as president of the College. He is buried in the Nassau Cemetery in Princeton, not far from the graves of nineteenth-century luminaries such as Charles Hodge and Benjamin Warfield.

EDWARDS AND THE REFORMED TRADITION

Despite the fact that he lived at a time when New England was an intellectual backwater, Edwards is most certainly a Reformed theologian of the first rank, and the most influential theologian yet to appear on the American continent. Nevertheless, he was not a confessional theologian in the mold of Hodge, who famously remarked that no new doctrine had been taught at Princeton during his tenure. He was not concerned merely to transmit a tradition, or to reiterate certain confessional standards, though he was willing to abide by the doctrinal norms of the New England Congregationalism that formed him and the Westminster Confession towards the end of his life, leading up to his brief tenure as the president of the College of New Jersey.[2] He was a constructive theologian who did not appeal to tradition, but Scripture, and 'called no man father' – not even John Calvin. Thus, in the preface to his great work, *Freedom of the Will*, he wrote, 'I should not take it at all amiss, to be called a Calvinist, for distinction's sake: though I utterly disclaim a dependence on Calvin, or believing the doctrines which I hold, because

---

[2] Edwards, Letter 117 to Revd. John Erskine, Northampton, 15 July 1750, in YE16: 355.

he believed and taught them; and cannot justly be charged with believing in everything just as he taught' (YE1: 131).

This is not to deny that Edwards regarded himself as one who stood on the shoulders of those who had gone before him. His theological formation was in the puritan and continental post-Reformation traditions to which he regarded himself an heir. To the end of his life he delighted in Protestant scholastics such as Petrus van Mastricht and Francis Turretin, recommending them to his students. Yet he viewed these theologians, as he viewed all the intellectual material he came across and devoured, as grist to his own theological mill. He was not an imitator of others, though his work is in some respects a synthesis of ideas gleaned from reading the works of many different writers. His earliest biographer, Samuel Hopkins, reports that he always read with pen in hand, and traced out his thoughts on paper to their logical ends, even if it meant missing a meal to do so. His fingers were permanently stained with ink as a consequence.

Such observations are of more than passing biographical interest. Edwards' scholarly habits involved carefully working through the implications of a particular problem with which he was fixated on paper, adding corollaries and addenda, cross-referenced in a series of minute notebooks he kept throughout his career. These he then plundered in his published works, often lifting gobbets verbatim and copying them into the text of his treatises. Thus, his method lent itself to a certain semi-detachment from tradition and confessional encumbrance, and to greater freedom of expression and thought than some of his theological contemporaries. Although he did not set out to be a revisionist, his intellectual project could be characterized as an attempt to re-envision Reformed theology using aspects of early Enlightenment philosophy. Rather than regarding with suspicion all the literary products of the 'new philosophy' exemplified by thinkers such as the Cambridge Platonists, Isaac Newton, Nicholas Malebranche, John Locke, Lord Shaftesbury, David Hume, and Thomas Hobbes, Edwards thought of these authors as providing (amongst other things) new tools by means of which he could underpin Christian theology. As Amy Plantinga Pauw puts it, Edwards 'lacked, on the one hand, any pretension to metaphysical purity and, on the other, any illusions about a permanent alliance between Christian faith and a particular philosophical tradition'.[3] In other words, he was no

---

[3]   Amy Plantinga Pauw, 'The Future of Reformed Theology: Some Lessons from Jonathan Edwards', in *Towards the Future of Reformed Theology: Tasks, Topics, Traditions*, edited by David Willis and Michael Welker (Grand Rapids, MI: Eerdmans, 1999), 458.

Thomist. He did not think in terms of a perennial Christian philosophy. Instead, he sought to provide a new synthetic account of Christian theism that reflected the Reformed tradition that had formed him, drawing on early modern philosophy to do so. He was a kind of intellectual magpie, gathering up useful material wherever he found it and copying it into his notebooks, all the while guided by the assumption (reflecting the rational optimism of the age) that 'all truth is God's truth' wherever it may be found. Although he regarded some of the philosophical notions and doctrines espoused by his peers as pernicious (he had a particular aversion to Hobbesian materialism and to deism), he did not rubbish everything written by thinkers with whom he disagreed – quite the reverse. He was willing to plunder ideas from every quarter, even those that appeared to many to be inimical to Christian doctrine. 'I confess,' he writes at one point in *Freedom of The Will*, 'it happens I never read Mr. Hobbes. Let his opinion be what it will, we need not reject all truth which is demonstrated by clear evidence, merely because it was once held by some bad man' (YE1: 374). Such careful discrimination meant he was not prone to the genetic fallacy, which confuses the provenance of an idea with its truth value.

However, the process of philosophical eclecticism that characterized his habits of mind did lead him to make more significant adjustments to the Reformed doctrine he had received than some enamored only of his more practical or evangelical writings have presumed. It is to these developments in his major writings that we now turn.

DOCTRINAL DEVELOPMENTS

Edwards made significant contributions to the doctrines of divine and human freedom, original sin, the Trinity, personal eschatology, theological aesthetics, theological ethics, religious psychology, and hagiography. In the course of setting out his views on these topics, he embraced a number of counterintuitive philosophical claims as well. At the time of his death, Edwards had published two major treatises, *Freedom of the Will* (1754) and *Original Sin* (1758), a collection of sermons, several public lectures, the *Life of David Brainerd* (a missionary to the Native Americans), several works of critical reflection on the revivals of the Great Awakening that culminated in the publication of the *Religious Affections* (1746), and some controversial works defending his revised views on the qualifications for communion which precipitated his dismissal from the pastorate at Northampton, Massachusetts, where he was minister for much of his career. The *Two Dissertations*, on *God's*

End in Creation and *True Virtue* (often published and read separately, though they are two parts of one whole), remained unpublished at his death, though they were bound and ready to go to the printers. His fragmentary works on idealism and on the Trinity, and his voluminous notebooks, were unpublished and not in a state that indicate he would have permitted their publication. Yet they form an important part of modern interpretations of Edwards as a Reformed theologian. Much of this unpublished work should be treated with caution, however, for it is not always clear that Edwards would have endorsed without cavil the views he expressed privately. His theological method allowed for much that was metaphysically and theologically speculative, not all of which he was willing to commit himself to in public discourse. This is not to imply that Edwards was a sort of Reimarus-like figure, preaching in public doctrines he secretly revised or repudiated. Rather, it is to say that Edwards was very careful about what he published, and the fact that certain works remained in notebook form with no indication that he was ready to publish them should give any reader of Edwards pause for thought when it comes to assigning a place of prominence to such works in his corpus. For this reason, we shall consider his most important published works first, then his *Two Dissertations*, before offering some remarks on important themes from his unpublished works, especially on his doctrine of the Trinity, and on his idealism.

The work by which Edwards' name was remembered until quite recently was his monumental *Freedom of the Will*. It stands as one of the most comprehensive accounts of divine and human freedom in theological literature. In it, Edwards delineates an uncompromising vision according to which human freedom and divine freedom have to do with acting according to the strongest desire one has. This, of course, is consistent with determinism, the view that all things that obtain have a cause (or causes) which is (are) necessary and sufficient for the bringing about of the effect in question. Edwards believed that God is 'determined' to act in the way he does because of the nature he has. Yet, Edwards averred with respect to the Deity, 'Tis no disadvantage or dishonor to a being, necessarily to act in the most excellent and happy manner, from the necessary perfection of his own nature' (YE1: 377). Edwards also thought that God could not have failed to create because he is essentially self-diffusive. In later works such as *God's End in Creation* and his unpublished *Book of Controversies* he goes even further than this, concluding in a manner reminiscent of Leibniz that God must create this world because it is the best possible. According to Edwards, God must act as he does because of the sort of being he is, one whose nature is immutable, eternal, perfect, and (as he puts it) 'excellent'. Humans, on the other hand, are constrained by the desires they have. Utilizing a distinction also found in the theology of the French Saumur school of the seventeenth century between moral and natural ability and necessity, Edwards reasons that fallen human beings have no natural impediment to turning to God for redemption, and are thus culpable for not doing so. However, all fallen humans have a moral inability to turn to God of their own initiative, which is a certain and complete obstacle to penitence. There is no possibility that this moral inability might be overcome without interposing divine grace. This distinction was to have considerable impact on the subsequent New England theology that grew out of Edwards' work.

Edwards was implacably opposed to what he called 'Arminianism'. Whether this is identical to historic Arminianism, or a broader category covering various free-thinking philosophies that were the product of the early Enlightenment, he was clear that theological libertarianism was not merely unacceptable, but incoherent. A libertarian choice is not caused by anything, otherwise (so it is said) it is not truly free. The agent in question makes the choice from a state of moral equilibrium having no predisposition to one option over another. However this, reasons Edwards, is equivalent to choices obtaining on the basis of no cause whatsoever. Far from establishing human freedom and responsibility, such thinking undermines both freedom and responsibility by removing any reason for the human agent choosing one thing over another. Edwards' devastating critique of such human freedom not only influenced the New Divinity that followed him in the early American Republic, but also found admirers in nineteenth-century Scottish Presbyterian theology. Thomas Chalmers regarded it as irrefutable, and William Cunningham discussed it at length in the context of whether Christian theological anthropology implied philosophical necessity.

Recent historiographical work has argued that Reformed theology is not aboriginally deterministic and that Edwards' doctrine represented a significant step-change in the way Reformed theologians dealt with the twin concerns of human freedom and moral responsibility.[4] Whether

---

[4] See *Reformed Thought on Freedom: The Concept of Free Choice in Early Modern Reformed Theology*, edited by Willem van Asselt, J. Martin Bac and Roelf T. te Velde (Grand Rapids, MI: Baker Academic, 2010); and Richard A. Muller, 'Jonathan Edwards and the Absence of Free Choice: A Parting of the Ways in the Reformed Tradition', *Jonathan Edwards Studies* 1.1 (2011): 3–22. Edwards himself resisted calling his position deterministic without careful qualification. See Edwards, Letter 227 to John Erskine, dated 25 July 1757, in YE16: 705–718.

this is right, two things about Edwards' position on this nodal theological doctrine stand out as signal contributions to the discussion within and beyond the bounds of the Reformed tradition. The first is that Edwards provided the basis for a systematic Reformed species of theological determinism. This was grounded not in the scholastic distinctions of his immediate forebears, nor in the faculty psychology that accompanied it (dividing human persons into apparently semi-autonomous faculties of intellect, will and so on), but in the ideas of John Locke's philosophy of mind. This was a significant and important contribution, articulating a strong doctrine of divine predestination and meticulous providence in the vocabulary of early modern philosophy. Edwards was engaged in the age-old theological project of articulating Christian doctrine in the mode of contemporary thought. Second, his views about divine freedom or the lack thereof represent at best a minority report in the Christian tradition. This is an important example of how his theological method of tracing out the implications of particular views to their utmost end pressed him in a direction that placed him outside the theological mainstream of western catholicism, and, as a consequence, the Reformed community that had formed him.[5]

Another doctrine to which Reformed theology has made an important contribution is original sin. In his work of the same name, Edwards first set out a Reformed view, including a fascinating discussion of the primal sin of our first parents; the doctrine of original sin and guilt; and the double guilt associated with the ascription of original guilt to the sinner followed by the guilt associated with actual sin. He went on to espouse an interesting doctrine on the transmission of original sin that has been the subject of some recent discussion in the philosophical literature. In essence, Edwards reasons that sin is not transmitted from one individual to another down through the ages, for this would appear to be monumentally unjust: How can I be punished for a sin I did not commit? Instead, he argues that Adam and his progeny all share in original sin because all are parts of one metaphysical whole scattered throughout space and time. He remarks, 'there is no identity or oneness in the case' of objects existing across time, 'but what depends on the *arbitrary* constitution of the Creator; who by his wise sovereign establishment so unites these successive new effects, that he *treats them as one*, by communicating to them like properties, relations, and circumstances; and so, leads us to regard and treat them as one' (YE3: 403,

---

[5]   For further discussion, see Oliver D. Crisp, *Jonathan Edwards on God and Creation* (New York: Oxford University Press, 2012).

author's emphasis). In other words, Edwards denies that we are things that endure through time, being wholly present at each moment we exist. He thinks we have temporal parts just as we have physical parts. The part of me that existed yesterday is numerically different from the part that exists today. Yet both are parts of one whole that exist across time according to divine convention, which is what makes it true that the different temporal parts form one whole thing across time.

Applied to the thorny question of the transmission of original sin, this means that Adam and his offspring may be treated by God as temporal parts of one whole thing, that is, humanity, existing across time. In this case, God does not merely ascribe the sin of Adam to you or me, strictly speaking, for we are parts of the entity that includes Adam. Just as an oak tree may share in the disease of the acorn from which it grew, as a later stage in the life of the one organism, so human beings today may share in the sin of the progenitor of the race, as different stages or phases of the life of the one entity that is the fallen human race.

In his *Religious Affections*, Edwards set out to provide, amongst other things, a set of guidelines for distinguishing true from false affections, against the backdrop of increasing antipathy towards the reported emotional and spiritual excesses of the Great Awakening. His notion of an affection is not identical to that of an emotion, as the former has a cognitive as well as a conative component. For this reason, religious affections that are appropriately formed are quite different from emotional excesses, such as those that characterized the Great Awakening in its more exuberant moments. Such excess is not a reliable gauge of a real secret working of the Holy Spirit, which Edwards thinks of as a purely emotional and psychological response to various phenomena. True spiritual character is formed via the affections, not via the emotions.

Edwards' mature work on this matter came too late to influence the trajectory of the revivals, which had already passed into history. Nevertheless, they are a profound study of religious psychology in the Reformed tradition that has an affinity with the work of John Calvin and Friedrich Schleiermacher. Calvin's discussion of the internal instigation of the Holy Spirit and the *sensus divinitatis* (sense of the divine) in the opening book of his *Institutes*, as well as his profound study of faith in the third book of the same in many ways complement the Edwardsian account of the affections. Moreover, like Schleiermacher, Edwards was preoccupied with religious experience, affections, and consciousness, as a litmus test of encountering the divine, although how he thought about this in relation to the formation of doctrine was somewhat different from his German-speaking successor. Edwards' work is testimony to his intense concern with the internal working of the spiritual life, and with the saving work of the Holy Spirit in the order of salvation that marked his own spiritual journey (as can be seen in his *Resolutions* and his *Personal Narrative*). He combined the fervour of puritan spiritual writings with the doctrinal casuistry of the continental Reformed tradition. It is a work that has had a lasting influence, as can be seen in the discussion of it William James provides in his *The Varieties of Religious Experience*, as well as in the more recent philosophical work of William Alston and Alvin Plantinga.

Edwards' *Two Dissertations* have also been of enduring significance. *God's End in Creation* is a profound study of eschatology, in which Edwards advocates a version of the doctrine of theosis. He envisages heaven as a 'world of love' in *Charity and its Fruits*, a series of sermons on 1 Corinthians 13. In *God's End in Creation* he speculates that those enjoying this heavenly bliss are eternal viators, forever engaged on a journey into God that will never end. Becoming 'partakers of the divine nature' does not mean being 'godded with God'. Instead, rather like a mathematical asymptote, those saints in the divine presence are on an infinite trajectory towards God that will never yield complete union with the divine essence, though it will involve ever closer communion with the divine nature. 'If the happiness of the creature be considered as it will be, in the whole of the creature's eternal duration, with all the infinity of its progress, and infinite increase of nearness and union to God', says Edwards, 'in this view, the creature must be looked upon as united to God in an infinite strictness' (YE8: 534). However, 'there will never come the moment', Edwards observes, 'that now this infinitely valuable good has been actually bestowed' (YE8: 536). The reason is that we are forever finite beings in communion with an infinite God.

True Virtue, the second of his *Two Dissertations*, is famous for being a pithy treatise on virtue ethics, which is unusual in the Reformed tradition, and for having no biblical references whatsoever. It is a philosophical work; that much is undeniable. However, it appears more peculiar than it ought to when read apart from the first dissertation, *God's End in Creation*, which in many ways supplies the theological underpinning for the vision of the good life set forth in *True Virtue*. Edwards' language is clear, careful and nuanced. Readers must often re-read what he says about a topic, not because he is obscure or difficult, but because he is so careful in what he does say that he wastes not a single word in explaining the topic in hand. That is also the case with *True Virtue*, although it is perhaps the most difficult of Edwards' works to understand. This is mainly due to his use of technical terms that have other connotations in modern theology or that belong to eighteenth-century moral discourse, such as 'being', 'benevolence' and 'complacence'. It is also due to the close connection he sees between the good life, that is, that which is truly virtuous, and Beauty, which is a notion that functions somewhat like a transcendental in his thinking. In the opening paragraphs of the work, Edwards remarks that, 'True virtue most essentially consists in benevolence to Being in general. Or perhaps to speak more accurately, it is that consent, propensity and union of heart to Being in general, that is immediately exercised in a general good will' (YE8: 540). Using the love command of Christ as a sort of organizing principle, Edwards goes on to claim that true virtue involves love to being in general, identified with God, and love toward others, as instances of created being, reflecting the beauty and harmony of the Creator. The truly virtuous life is a life characterized by happiness, and by delight in the good, which is an aspect or dimension of the true and the beautiful. This makes sense if the good life is a life lived in and through the being of God that sustains all creatures and gives them life.

Earlier I remarked that Edwards did not live to complete a treatise on the Trinity that was publishable. That said, his doctrine of the Trinity has garnered a great deal of critical attention over the years, beginning in the nineteenth century when it was rumoured that he was a closet Arian, and continuing in contemporary accounts of his theology according to which his Trinitarianism profoundly shaped other aspects of his thought. For this reason, it seems appropriate to say *something* about this vexed issue in Edwardsian studies, not least because his position does represent an innovation in Reformed theology. The main sources for his doctrine of the Trinity have been gathered together in YE21. They comprise his *Discourse on the Trinity, On the Equality of the Persons of the Trinity*, and *Treatise on Grace*. There are quite different interpretations of Edwards' doctrine. It appears that like many in the Reformed tradition he adopted a basically Augustinian account of the divine persons and essence. However, in Edwards' case this judgment must be carefully qualified because he offers certain important – indeed, crucial – modifications to the Augustinian account.

Those influenced by an Augustinian approach to the doctrine of the Trinity tend to think of divine persons as individuated by the relations they bear to one another, and by nothing more. Edwards takes up this model, and adapts it in two important respects. First, he has a particular notion of excellency. This has an aesthetic and ontological aspect. It is a quality a thing possesses provided it exemplifies beauty, proportion

and a certain sort of aesthetic complexity (between parts and their relations to a whole). Edwards thinks God is the supreme example of excellency because 'one alone cannot be excellent'. He presumes that a truly
perfect being would be an excellent being. As God is a perfect being,
he must be excellent. So he cannot be without internal differentiation.
This differentiation is provided by the divine persons of the Godhead.
Alongside this doctrine of excellency, Edwards maintains that the only
real distinctions to be found in God are the divine persons. These divine
persons he identifies with God (the Father), the understanding of God
(the Son), and his will (the Holy Spirit), respectively. They exist perichoretically in such a way that the relation of mutual indwelling is itself
person-constituting. That is, the divine persons exist because they are
perichoretically related to one another. This is why Edwards can affirm
that there is only one understanding and one will in God shared between
the divine persons. He does not deny that there is a divine essence, however. This contains those attributes that are not person-constituting,
but which are part of the divine nature such as omnipotence and omniscience. This doctrine, which is only now being given the attention it
deserves, represents an important peroration on an Augustinian model
that is an original contribution to Reformed theology.[6]

Edwards' theological project was intimately related to his idealism,
although he never published a work on this. The view that all that exists
are divine and created minds and their ideas, matter being a sort of fic-
tion, was 'in the air' in the eighteenth century. Edwards' position is
rather like that of Bishop George Berkeley, although it appears that they
came to their views independently. His early philosophical notebooks,
written whilst he was still in college, demonstrate a clear dependence
on the Cambridge Platonists, although he moved beyond Henry More's
claim that God is space to the view (developed in his later works) that
the world is contained 'in' God. Utilizing neo-Platonic imagery, Edwards
argues in *God's End in Creation* and elsewhere that the Deity emanates
himself in the creation, which is like his shadow. He also holds to a
doctrine of continuous creation. Although he does not spell it out in
quite this way, it appears that Edwards' doctrine is that God creates
the world (emanates it), whereupon it immediately ceases to exist. He
then creates a second, facsimile world which is qualitatively identical
to the previous one, with incremental changes built into it. This action

---

[6] See Steven M. Studebaker and Robert W. Caldwell III, *The Trinitarian Theology of
Jonathan Edwards: Text, Context and Application* (Aldershot, UK: Ashgate, 2012)
and Kyle C. Strobel, *Jonathan Edwards's Theology: A Reinterpretation* (London: T&T
Clark, 2012) on the current views of Edwards' Trinitarian theology.

continues with the creation of numerically distinct but qualitatively near-identical world-stages that he segues together so as to produce what appears to be action across time. This four-dimensionalist picture of how God creates denies the doctrine of divine conservation, strictly speaking, as there is no world to uphold across time. When his idealism is factored into other central doctrines he espouses the resulting picture is rather exotic, to say the least. It would appear that Edwards held to a species of what we would now call panentheism, and a view of creation that makes the world like a series of momentary photographic stills run together into a motion picture and projected out from God like a movie on the silver screen. Although these themes are deeply indebted to his Augustinian heritage, they can hardly be described as part of the theological mainstream of the Reformed tradition.

THE EDWARDSIAN LEGACY FOR REFORMED THEOLOGY

Edwards' intellectual legacy was a mixed one. His immediate disciples, theologians and ministers in New England, such as Samuel Hopkins, Joseph Bellamy and Edwards' son and namesake, Jonathan Edwards Jr., were instrumental in transmitting his ideas to a whole new generation of ministers in New England. Through the 'New Divinity' that they propounded, the first truly indigenous movement of American theology grew and flourished over the next century, mainly on the eastern seaboard and some of the Midwestern cities of the continental United States. It became known as the New England Theology, although there were various perorations of this as the movement developed and diversified. The most important of these was the New Haven Theology associated with the Divinity School at Yale, the college at which Edwards himself had been educated. Nathaniel Taylor, the main proponent of this brand of New England Theology, was – like his theological master – both somewhat theologically eccentric and very much a constructive theologian who called no person master.

In the process of its maturation and differentiation the New England Theology also came to include thinkers whose writings were very much at odds with the stated views of Edwards himself. This has been something of a puzzle to historians interested in the movement. However, it is easier to understand if one recognizes that what Edwards transmitted to his theological heirs was a method of working through a theological problem for oneself with meticulous attention to detail and careful theological distinctions, but without much reliance on confessions and the tradition. Alongside this method, he bequeathed to his disciples a certain set of theological problems to which successive generations of New England theologians returned, often with very different solutions. He did not leave behind him a carefully worked-out system of doctrines to which his disciples adhered, or which represented the movement as a whole. That task was taken up by his disciple Samuel Hopkins in his *System of Doctrines* (1793). In this sense, the New England Theology reflected the theologically entrepreneurial attitude of its founder. This sensibility was also a good fit with the developing American republic of the nineteenth century. It meant that the New England Theologians concerned themselves with the sort of problems that had been characteristic of Edwards' published writings (e.g., human freedom in relation to divine sovereignty, original sin, religious affections, and so on), but without slavish emulation of Edwards' views. Consequently, some later theologians in the movement ended up espousing views on human freedom completely at odds with Edwards on the basis of a similar method of careful, rigorous argumentation and reflection.

As the movement developed and grew, it was kept together largely through personal networks and allegiances, just as had been the case with Edwards and his immediate disciples who had studied under him in preparation for ordination. This was both a strength and a weakness. It meant there was a strong set of loyalties in those schools in which Edwardsian teaching flourished (e.g. Andover, Yale Divinity School, Brown, Union College, Mount Holyoke and elsewhere). Yet it also meant that the movement suffered from having few doctrines on which all were agreed, and around which they could unite. Themes characterized much of the movement, for example, concern with free will and original sin; particular positions on those topics did not. This meant that those who held views almost the opposite of Edwards himself felt free to appeal to Edwards as their theological mentor not despite their disagreement but because he had paved the way for constructive reflection on these topics, delivering them a body of work that included doctrinal themes that informed the various perorations of the school. He was a model of good scholarship and serious divinity even if his particular views were not adopted by all those who claimed his allegiance.

The New England Theology disintegrated at the end of the nineteenth century and with it Edwards' influence as a constructive theological force came to a temporary close, until recently. The reasons for its demise are complex, but in part it was due to the increasing theological diversity of different branches of the movement, which had become a sort of centrifugal force that eventually led its leaders in different directions, away from the Edwardsian center. By contrast, the more confessional Princetonian theology of Hodge, Warfield, and latterly Gresham Machen and others, survived into the twentieth century at least in part because there was a dogmatic core around which its adherents could gather. Nevertheless, both the Princetonian and Edwardsian divinity were in decline at the close of the nineteenth century when the more optimistic outlook of thinkers such as Walter Rauschenbusch and his Social Gospel was much more in vogue.

The New England Theology was a force to be reckoned with for a century after Edwards's death. Today it is largely unknown outside the limited circle of those with a professional research interest in the movement. This is unfortunate. It means that the theological impact of Edwards' views is often overlooked. It also means that the way in which Edwards' ideas influenced those who adopted his methods has been largely forgotten. After a period in which interest in Edwards languished, the revival of his work since the late 1940s has led to his being an interlocutor for a new generation of theologians and church leaders. Once more Edwards is regarded as a theological force to be reckoned with. He is one of the most widely read major theologians today. Some recent interpreters maintain that this is largely because his theological interests give him an appeal across denominational and intellectual boundaries.[7] There is much to be said for this claim. Edwards was not just a theologian or a Christian intellectual. He was a minister and latterly, a missionary, someone professionally interested in the life of the church in New England, and (eventually, and briefly) a president of Princeton. His influence as a founding father of modern evangelicalism, and his spiritual and psychological writings (e.g., his sermons, his *Life of David Brainerd* – a major influence on the nineteenth-century missionary movement – and his *Religious Affections*) have remained in print since their initial publication. In this respect Edwards' reach, and the diversity of those interested in his writings, make him a theologian with whom many will continue to grapple, within and without the Reformed tradition that formed him.

Further reading

van Asselt, Willem, J. Martin Bac and Roelf T. te Velde (eds.). *Reformed Thought on Freedom: The Concept of Free Choice in Early Modern Reformed Theology.* Grand Rapids, MI: Baker Academic, 2010.

[7] See Michael McClymond and Gerald McDermott, *The Theology of Jonathan Edwards* (New York: Oxford University Press, 2012).

Crisp, Oliver D. *Jonathan Edwards on God and Creation*. New York: Oxford University Press, 2012.

Edwards, Jonathan. *The Works of Jonathan Edwards*, 26 vols. New Haven, CT: Yale University Press, 1957–2008. Also hosted at www.edwards.yale .edu (Accessed 1 June 2015).

McClymond, Michael C. and McDermott, Gerald R. *The Theology of Jonathan Edwards*. New York: Oxford University Press, 2012.

Muller, Richard A. 'Jonathan Edwards and the Absence of Free Choice: A Parting of the Ways in the Reformed Tradition'. *Jonathan Edwards Studies* 1.1 (2011): 3–22.

Plantinga Pauw, Amy. 'The Future of Reformed Theology: Some Lessons from Jonathan Edwards'. In *Towards the Future of Reformed Theology: Tasks, Topics, Traditions*. Edited by David Willis and Michael Welker. Grand Rapids, MI: Eerdmans, 1999: 456–469.

Strobel, Kyle C. *Jonathan Edwards's Theology: A Reinterpretation*. London: T&T Clark, 2012.

Studebaker, Steven M. and Caldwell III, Robert W. *The Trinitarian Theology of Jonathan Edwards: Text, Context and Application*. Aldershot, UK: Ashgate, 2012.

11 Friedrich Schleiermacher

KEVIN W. HECTOR

Friedrich Schleiermacher was born on November 21, 1768, into a family of Reformed pastors; his mother, Katharina-Maria, came from a line of Reformed ministers, and his father, Gottlieb, served as a chaplain to the Prussian army. In 1778, Gottlieb Schleiermacher's travels with the army brought him to Gnadenfrei and, in turn, to an encounter with the Moravian community; he there experienced a pietistic awakening and became an "inward" Moravian, while remaining a Reformed chaplain. In 1783, Friedrich Schleiermacher left home to attend a Moravian school, in Niesky, and became, for a time, a devoted Moravian. He never saw his parents again: his mother died a few months after he left, and his father died in 1794. Schleiermacher eventually took up the family business, serving as an assistant pastor in Landsberg from 1794 to 1796, and then as pastor of Berlin's Charité Hospital. In Berlin, he struck up a lifelong friendship with Henriette Herz and became a regular at her literary salons, which is where he became better acquainted with, and influenced by, Romantic thinkers such as Friedrich Schlegel. Schleiermacher apparently had this circle in mind when he penned his famous – and controversial – *On Religion: Speeches to Its Cultured Despisers*. After that, Schleiermacher served as pastor in Stolp (1802–1804), then as Professor at Halle (1804–1807), before returning to Berlin to pastor Trinity Church (1807–1810), and finally, from 1810 until his death in 1834, to hold a theology chair at the newly founded University of Berlin.

Schleiermacher was a person of many talents, as is evident in his standard-setting translations of Plato into German and his signal contributions to the emerging discipline of hermeneutics. First and foremost, however, Schleiermacher was devoted to the investigation and advancement of theology and, in particular, *Reformed* theology. It has not always been obvious to later thinkers, however, how Schleiermacher's lifework can be seen as a contribution to Reformed theology (as opposed, say, to liberal or modern theology). For the purposes of a companion dedicated to such theology, accordingly, it will be helpful to explain why Schleiermacher's theology can and should be understood as such.

There are at least two ways this might be done. One would be to consider Schleiermacher's extensive engagement, throughout his *Glaubenslehre*, with the Reformed confessions. There is reason to think that this is the approach that Schleiermacher himself would recommend: theology, he famously claimed, is "the discipline which systematizes the doctrine prevalent in a Christian church at a given time," and he understood such doctrines, in turn, as accounts of "that which, in the public proceedings of the church ... can be heard as a portrayal of its common piety."[1] Schleiermacher saw the Reformed confessions as just such a portrayal and, so, as that which his theology was to systematize. There is a decisive drawback to this approach, however, namely that by the time Schleiermacher's readers have arrived at his treatment of particular doctrines (and, thus, their connection with the Reformed confessions), they have usually already decided what he can and must say about them. More specifically, readers have customarily drawn strong conclusions from (their interpretation of) the introductory sections of the *Glaubenslehre*, and these conclusions have tended to dictate their interpretations of its later, doctrinal sections; given that these conclusions almost always make it hard to see how Schleiermacher could retain characteristically Reformed theological commitments, it is not surprising that so many readers have had trouble seeing Schleiermacher as a distinctively Reformed theologian. Apparently, then, Schleiermacher's engagement with the confessions arrives too late to help readers understand his theology as Reformed.

For that reason, an alternative approach recommends itself, namely, to exhibit Schleiermacher's entire *Glaubenslehre* – introductory sections included – as characteristically Reformed. Naturally, the *Glaubenslehre* can be so exhibited only if we have some idea of what characterizes Reformed theology as such; toward this end, it will be helpful to adopt, as a rough criterion, Alexander Schweizer's plausible contention that what distinguishes Reformed theology is its insistence on the absolute primacy of God and, in consequence, the absoluteness of creation's dependence on God, as well as of humanity's dependence

---

[1]   Friedrich D. E. Schleiermacher, *The Christian Faith* [often *Glaubenslehre*], 2nd ed. (1830/1831), translated by H. R. Mackintosh and J. S. Stewart (Edinburgh: T & T Clark, 1928), §19 Thesis; §15 Thesis; §19.3. Hereafter cited parenthetically, by paragraph and section number (I have revised the Mackintosh/Stewart translation in several places).

on God's grace.[2] We see such insistence most plainly, Schweizer argues, in traditional Reformed claims about divine sovereignty and predestination, but the more fundamental commitment to God's primacy permeates the entirety of Reformed theology. Assuming that this is indeed a plausible account of what distinguishes Reformed theology, it would follow that insofar as Schleiermacher emphasizes the absoluteness of God's primacy and of our dependence, his theology can be recognized as distinctively Reformed.

THE INTRODUCTION TO *THE CHRISTIAN FAITH*

For the reasons just mentioned, it is important to begin by considering the *Glaubenslehre*'s introductory sections, to exhibit them as compatible with, and indeed an expression of, characteristically Reformed theology.[3] The argument of these sections proceeds through roughly the following steps: Schleiermacher claims (a) that creaturely life is characterized by relative freedom and relative dependence; (b) that relative freedom and dependence hang together only insofar as both are absolutely dependent upon a transcendent Whence; (c) that freedom and dependence are at odds with one another, for humans, insofar as we do not integrate them into our consciousness of absolute dependence, as we then treat relative freedom and dependence as if *they* were absolute; and (d) that if a person were wholly to integrate freedom and dependence into his or her consciousness of absolute dependence, then he or she would no longer experience freedom and dependence as if they were at odds.

One of Schleiermacher's favorite argumentative strategies is to claim that various finite oppositions can be overcome only in relation to an absolute in which these opposites coincide; we see an instance of this strategy in the *Glaubenslehre*, which Schleiermacher frames in terms

---

2 On these claims, see Bruce L. McCormack, "The Sum of the Gospel: The Doctrine of Election in the Theologies of Alexander Schweizer and Karl Barth," in *The Future of Reformed Theology: Tasks, Topics, Traditions*, edited by David Willis and Michael Welker (Grand Rapids, MI: Eerdmans, 1999), 470–493.

3 These sections adapt and summarize arguments I have defended elsewhere: "Actualism and Incarnation: The High Christology of Friedrich Schleiermacher," *International Journal of Systematic Theology*, 8.3 (2006), 307–322; "The Mediation of Christ's Normative Spirit: A Constructive Reading of Schleiermacher's Pneumatology," *Modern Theology*, 24.1 (2008), 1–22; "Attunement and Explicitation: A Pragmatist Reading of Schleiermacher's 'Theology of Feeling,'" in *Schleiermacher, The Study of Religion, and the Future of Theology*, edited by Brent W. Sockness and Wilhelm Gräb (Berlin: Walter de Gruyter, 2010), 215–242; and *The Theological Project of Modernism: Faith and the Conditions of Mineness* (Oxford: Oxford University Press, 2015), chapter 3, "Harmonizing Dependence."

of his claim that creaturely freedom and dependence can be united only in relation to God. He builds up to this claim by arguing, first, that "in every moment of self-consciousness there are two elements, which we might call respectively a self-posited element (*ein Sichselbstsetzen*) and a non-self-posited element (*ein Sichselbstnichtsogesetzthaben*)," and that "the latter presupposes for every moment of self-consciousness another factor besides the I, a factor which is the source of the particular determination, and without which the self-consciousness would not be precisely what it is" (§4.1). The idea is straightforward enough: every moment of one's life, Schleiermacher argues, is determined partly by oneself and partly by that which is other than oneself; Schleiermacher terms these, respectively, the *spontaneous* (*selbsttätig*) and *receptive* (*empfänglich*) elements of one's experience, which correspond, in self-consciousness, with a feeling of freedom and a feeling of dependence (§4.1).

Schleiermacher then argues that receptivity and spontaneity characterize not only one's own experience of the world, but also the world itself. To substantiate this point, he begins by considering an idealized example in which one's spontaneity and receptivity are related to a single object; in such a case, he claims, one's spontaneity would correspond precisely with the object's receptivity, and one's receptivity would correspond with its spontaneity. Schleiermacher characterizes such relationships as "reciprocal," and claims that all worldly relationships exemplify such reciprocity, as every spontaneous action affects something else, and every being-affected is due to some spontaneous act, in an organic network of mutual interrelationship. The entire realm of such reciprocity just is the "world," which Schleiermacher thus understands as a sort of organism or as a hanging-together of all finite entities, in which each is receptive to the spontaneity of all, and all receptive to the spontaneity of each (§4.2; §34.1).

From these claims about the world and one's place in it, Schleiermacher draws two decisive conclusions. The first, more obvious conclusion is that nothing in the world is absolutely free. Schleiermacher offers two reasons for this conclusion. The first is that an action is free, on Schleiermacher's account, only if something is affected by it, yet the very presence of such a thing implies receptivity on the side of the actor, not least inasmuch as the thing's existence is not itself due to one's freedom (§4.3). The second reason is that one's own existence, including one's freedom, is not itself due to one's freedom – even if I could presently act altogether freely, my very being could not itself be a product of that freedom, because my birth, for instance, was not something I brought about freely, nor was my being supplied with the physical and educational resources necessary to my eventual "coming of age" as a free person. Schleiermacher argues, therefore, that "not only is every distinct movement bound up with the state of our stimulated receptivity at the moment, but, further, the totality of our free inward movements, considered as a unity, cannot be represented as a feeling of absolute freedom, because our whole existence does not present itself to our consciousness as having proceeded from our own spontaneous activity." On the strength of these arguments, Schleiermacher concludes that "in any temporal existence, a feeling of absolute freedom can have no place" (§4.3).

This brings us to Schleiermacher's second conclusion, namely, that we, along with everything else in the world, are absolutely dependent, and that our relative freedom makes us immediately conscious of this fact. Schleiermacher argues, toward this end, that "the self-consciousness which accompanies all our activity ... and negatives absolute freedom, is itself precisely a consciousness of absolute dependence, for it is the consciousness that the whole of our spontaneous activity comes from a source outside of us in just the same sense in which anything towards which we should have a feeling of absolute freedom must have proceeded entirely from ourselves" (§4.3). On its face, this argument might seem to entail that one is absolutely dependent on the *world*, as one's birth, sustenance, and so on are apparently due to worldly factors, just as the objects to which one's freedom is directed are altogether worldly. Schleiermacher counters, however, that one's consciousness of absolute dependence finds its terminus neither in any worldly entity nor in the world itself, because (a) everything in the world is likewise caught up in a reciprocal relationship of spontaneity and reciprocity, and so is not the spontaneous source of its own spontaneity, and (b) the world itself is constituted by the entire network of such reciprocal relationships, and is therefore partly dependent on one's freedom; as such, it cannot be the terminus of one's absolute dependence (§32.2). Schleiermacher argues, accordingly, that everything in the world is absolutely dependent, and that humans are immediately conscious of this fact.

Schleiermacher thus understands the world, and our place in it, in terms of the relative opposition between freedom and dependence, and claims that this opposition is transcended, and so recognizable *as* relative, in light of that which absolutely transcends both. To elaborate this point, we must first register a terminological shift: given his view of the world and one's place in it, Schleiermacher gathers the entire realm of relative freedom and dependence into the category of "sensible life," and terms one's awareness of this realm "sensible self-consciousness" (§4.2; 5.1). Likewise, given his claims about the entire world's absolute dependence on that which transcends it, Schleiermacher contends that one's awareness of such dependence lies at the root of the concept "God," such that one's consciousness of absolute dependence can equally be termed one's "God-consciousness" (§4.4). Hence, when Schleiermacher hereafter discusses "God-consciousness," he is referring to one's consciousness of absolute dependence, and when he discusses "sensible self-consciousness," he is referring to one's consciousness of relative freedom and dependence – that is, one's consciousness of the reciprocal relationships by which the world, and one's place in it, is constituted.

With that terminology on board, we can now say more about how Schleiermacher understands the relationship between God-consciousness and the sensible-consciousness. There are in fact two ways in which they can relate, depending on the extent to which the latter is integrated into the former: if the sensible-consciousness is integrated into the God-consciousness, then one will experience one's life as a unified whole; if not, then one will experience freedom and dependence as at odds with one another, and one's life, therefore, as pervaded by oppositions. Schleiermacher argues, accordingly, that the freedom and dependence characteristic of sensible life need not stand in opposition to one another, and that they will not so stand insofar as one unites each in one's consciousness of absolute dependence. Schleiermacher thus contrasts "the sensible self-consciousness, which rests entirely upon the antithesis [between freedom and dependence]," with "the feeling of absolute dependence, in which the antithesis again disappears and the subject unites and identifies itself with everything which was set over against it" (§5.1). The more one is conscious of one's absolute dependence, therefore, the less one's freedom will seem to be at odds with one's dependence – or so Schleiermacher claims. As he sees it, then,

> ... once the higher grade of feeling [i.e., the feeling of absolute dependence] comes to preponderate over the lower [the sensible], so that in the immediate self-consciousness the sensible determination asserts itself rather as an opportunity for the appearance of absolute dependence than as containing the antithesis, which is therefore transferred to the realm of mere perception, then this fact, that the antithesis has almost disappeared again from the higher grade of life, indisputably means that the latter has attained its richest content of feeling. (§5.4)

Every moment of one's sensible consciousness can thereby be taken up into one's God-consciousness, and can in this way be experienced as hanging together.

Thus far, then, Schleiermacher has claimed that the entire realm of sensible life, including one's relationship to nature and other persons, can be included in one's God-consciousness, and that the God-consciousness can therefore integrate all of one's freedom and dependence vis-à-vis the world. Schleiermacher also thinks that God-consciousness is a necessary condition of such integration, which becomes clear when he considers what happens when persons become insufficiently attuned to the God-consciousness and, therefore, "lack the facility (*Leichtigkeit*) for introducing the God-consciousness into the course of our actual lives and retaining it there." In that case, one experiences "an obstruction or arrest of the vitality of the higher self-consciousness, so that there comes to be little or no union of it with the various determinations of the sensible self-consciousness, and thus little or no religious life. We may give to this condition, in its most extreme form, the name of *Godlessness* or, better, *God-forgetfulness* (*Gottvergessenheit*)" (§11.2). As Schleiermacher sees it, then, persons may relate to the world as if it – including, but not limited to, their place in it – were absolute or ultimate, and thus forget that the world is absolutely dependent, whether they mean to or not; as a result, they invariably relate to finite oppositions as if they, too, were absolute.

Schleiermacher then claims that persons not only *may* stifle their sense of absolute dependence, but that all persons in fact *do* stifle that sense. This is the case, he argues, for two reasons (cf. §67.2). First, because humans develop as they do, the sensible consciousness emerges before the God-consciousness; when the latter finally materializes, therefore, it is no match for the sensible consciousness, which persons have already become accustomed to treating as if it were absolute. By itself, this would already be sufficient to ensure the God-forgetfulness of all humans. Matters are worsened, however, by the fact that we are social animals, as the forgetfulness of each exacerbates the forgetfulness of all. Schleiermacher thus claims that God-forgetfulness is a universal human condition, because (a) the later emergence of the God-consciousness ensures its subordination to the sensible consciousness, and (b) one is socialized into a community of the forgetful, such that one's self-consciousness is inescapably infused with a God-forgetting "we"-consciousness. Schleiermacher argues that we are universally God-forgetful, therefore, and that this has exactly the consequence we have been led to expect: because we fail to integrate freedom and dependence into our God-consciousness, we experience them as contradicting one another, and our lives are thus marked by dissonance. We thereby reap what we have sown, for if the finite world is treated as if it were absolute, then the oppositions by which that world is constituted will likewise be treated as absolute, and we will experience the world as frozen into intractable contradictions.

On Schleiermacher's account, then, God-consciousness is a necessary as well as a sufficient condition of integrating freedom and dependence, for without it, one cannot integrate them. Unfortunately, once the God-consciousness has been subordinated to the sensible consciousness, one can do nothing to reorient oneself, for the apparent reason that any such reordering would itself necessarily be brought within one's worldly horizon; Schleiermacher thus claims, in this connection, that "if the disposition to the God-consciousness is obscured and vitiated, then man, just because his God-consciousness, though the best thing in him, is thus polluted and untrustworthy, must be wholly incapable not only of developing, but even of consciously aspiring to, such inner states as would harmonize with the proper aim and object of that disposition" (§70.1). One can reintegrate one's freedom and dependence only if one's God-consciousness and sensible-consciousness have been reordered, yet one cannot bring about this reordering for oneself: "Under these conditions", Schleiermacher writes, "no satisfaction (*Befriedigung*) of the impulse towards the God-consciousness will be possible; and so, if such a satisfaction is to be attained, a redemption is necessary, since this condition is nothing but a kind of imprisonment or constraint of the feeling of absolute dependence" (§11.2).

THE REDEEMER OF HUMANITY

This brings us to the heart of Schleiermacher's theology, namely, humanity's redemption in Christ. We should now be well positioned to understand the best-known feature of Schleiermacher's Christology, namely the centrality he accords to Jesus' perfect God-consciousness, as this is precisely what must be restored in us if we are to be redeemed. Schleiermacher thus contends that "the capacity of the God-consciousness to give the impulse to all of life's experiences and to determine them" is the ideal that humanity was meant to instantiate, and that this ideal was perfectly realized in Jesus, inasmuch as he himself "was the ideal (i.e. the ideal became completely historical in him), and each historical moment of his experience at the same time bore within it the ideal" (§93 Thesis; §93.2). Schleiermacher's fundamental Christological claim, then, is that Jesus, unlike all others, had a perfectly potent God-consciousness, and that every moment of his life was perfectly harmonized with this consciousness.

We need to say more about what such harmonization actually looked like. First, though, an objection: in light of Schleiermacher's earlier claims, one might reasonably wonder how anyone's God-consciousness, including that of Jesus, could harmonize each of their experiences, as we have already been told that normal human development, along with the God-forgetfulness of our communities, renders this impossible. Schleiermacher's response to this objection is twofold. He argues, first, that the perfection of Jesus' God-consciousness must have been due to a miraculous act of God, as he grants that such a consciousness could not possibly have arisen in the natural course of human history and development (§93.3; cf. §88.4). Schleiermacher hastens to add, however, that this supernatural act need not be thought to disrupt the hanging-together of nature, and thus the consciousness of absolute dependence, as the act that produces this God-consciousness is one and the same as the act by which the world is created and preserved. Schleiermacher claims, accordingly, that "both events go back to one undivided eternal decree and form, even in a higher sense, only one and the same natural system," and, indeed, that "the first stage of creation," namely the act to which creation owes its very existence, "is ordained by God only in view of the second," namely the act of re-creating humanity in Jesus (§94.3; §89.3). The importance of this point will become clearer in a moment.

The second component of Schleiermacher's response is his argument that, again unlike everyone else, Jesus' development was such that his God-consciousness was at every moment sufficiently powerful to determine his sensible consciousness – though not, for that reason, *all*-powerful. He claims, accordingly, that Jesus

> ... developed in the same way as all others, so that from birth on his powers gradually unfolded, and, from the zero point onward, were developed to completeness in the order natural to the human race. This applies also to his God-consciousness ... which in him, too, had to develop gradually in human fashion into a really manifest consciousness, and antecedently was only present as a germ, although in a certain sense always present as an active power. (§93.3)

Jesus was not born with an absolutely powerful God-consciousness, therefore, but with a sufficiently powerful one – sufficiently powerful, that is, to outpace the development of his sensible consciousness. Hence, whereas human development and corporate sinfulness ensure that everyone else's sensuous consciousness dominates their God-consciousness, Schleiermacher argues that Jesus' God-consciousness was supernaturally implanted by God, in consequence of which his development and participation in society were unable to curb the power of that consciousness.

Schleiermacher thus claims that Jesus' God-consciousness was sufficiently powerful to determine every moment of sensible consciousness; from this, he draws the striking conclusion that Jesus incarnates the pure activity in which God eternally subsists. The argument here is straightforward enough: if (a) the Whence of absolute dependence is pure activity, and (b) Jesus' perfect receptivity to this Whence governs his reception of and activity toward the world, then (c) the latter receptivity and activity are pure activity vis-à-vis the world, as they are conditioned not by the world but only by an absolute receptivity toward God, from which it follows (d) that Jesus' receptivity and activity reproduce, within the world, God's own activity.[4] This explains Schleiermacher's assertion that Jesus is the only creature "in which there is an existence of God in the proper sense, so far, that is, as we posit the God-consciousness in his self-consciousness as continually and exclusively determining every moment," or again, that "every moment of his existence, so far as it can be isolated, presents just such a new incarnation and incarnatedness of God, because always and everywhere all that is human in him springs from the divine" (§94.2; §96.3). It likewise explains what Schleiermacher has in mind when he claims that "to ascribe to Christ an absolutely powerful God-consciousness, and to attribute to him an existence of God in him, are exactly the same thing," as his perfectly receptive God-consciousness ensures that every moment of Jesus' life reproduces, as his own, the pure activity in which God subsists.

The fact that Jesus incarnates this activity demonstrates, moreover, that the One upon whom we depend absolutely is not just any pure activity, but the pure activity of *love*; to be absolutely dependent, therefore, is to depend wholly on God's love, and to let that love govern one's reception of and activity toward the world. That love is the pure activity to which Jesus is perfectly receptive, and which his life therefore

---

[4]   I lack the space to tackle Schleiermacher's doctrine of the Trinity, unfortunately, but the basic points are roughly as follows: (a) God is pure activity; (b) this pure activity is redeeming love; (c) this redeeming love is enacted in Jesus and the Spirit; and (d) God has eternally been in-the-act of begetting Jesus and pouring out the Spirit. Schleiermacher's doctrine seems to imply (e) that God would not be triune apart from redeeming humanity, but this does not entail that God is only contingently triune, for, on Schleiermacher's necessitarian metaphysics, (f) God cannot be otherwise than God is, such that God is necessarily triune.

reproduces as his own pure activity vis-à-vis the world, becomes clear in Jesus' most apparently passive moments, most notably in his suffering. Schleiermacher thus remarks that

> ... we find one passive condition posited as necessary, almost as constant, in Christ, so that in a sense all his actions depend upon it – namely, sympathy with the condition of men; yet at the same time in everything which proceeded from this we shall most distinctly recognize the impulse of the reconciling being of God in Christ ... Now this 'divine' is the divine love in Christ which, once and for all or in every moment – whichever expression be chosen – gave direction to his feelings for the spiritual conditions of men. (§97.3)

Here, then, Jesus' passivity is precisely a reproduction of God's activity, and thus shows us that the activity is reconciling love. Nowhere is this clearer than in Jesus' crucifixion, for "in his suffering unto death, occasioned by his steadfastness, there is manifested to us an absolutely self-denying love; and in this there is represented to us with perfect vividness the way in which God was in him to reconcile the world to himself" (§104.4). Hence, if Jesus perfectly reproduces the pure activity in which God subsists, then it turns out that God subsists in the singular activity of reconciling love. In light of Jesus, therefore, we can see why "love alone is made the equivalent of the being or essence of God" (§167.1).

THE REDEMPTION OF HUMANITY

On this account, therefore, to be absolutely dependent is to depend absolutely on God's reconciling love; this reconciling love has become incarnate in Christ; and one is redeemed from one's God-forgetfulness through being included in this love. To understand how Schleiermacher accounts for such inclusion, we have to consider, first, how Christ's God-consciousness could be communicated to others in order thereby to become their own. Jesus accomplishes this, Schleiermacher argues, by drawing us into the activity of his life – he acts not only on every circumstance of his own life, but also on other persons, in such a way that his activity becomes theirs. Schleiermacher thus asserts that "the activity by which he assumes us into fellowship with him is a creative production in us of the will to assume him into ourselves, or rather – since it is only receptiveness for his activity as involved in the impartation – only our assent to the influence of his activity" (§100.2). More specifically, Schleiermacher argues that "whatever in human nature is assumed into vital fellowship with Christ is assumed into the fellowship of an activity solely determined by the power of the God-consciousness, which God-consciousness is adequate to every new experience and extracts from it all it has to yield," and, therefore, "that each assumption of this sort is simply a continuation of the same creative act which first manifested itself in time by the formation of Christ's person" (§101.4). On this account, then, Jesus is perfectly receptive to God's pure act and perfectly reproduces it as his own action; in redeeming us, Christ makes us receptive to his receptivity so that it becomes ours. Schleiermacher argues, accordingly, that "in him the passivity of his human nature was nothing but a lively susceptibility to an absolutely powerful consciousness of God, accompanied by a desire to be thus seized and determined, which became changed through the creative act into a spontaneous activity constituting a personality. In the same way our desire is heightened in conversion by the self-communication of Christ till it becomes a spontaneous activity of the self that constitutes a coherent new life" (§108.6). For Schleiermacher, then, Jesus is perfectly receptive to God's reconciling love and perfectly reproduces it as his own, and in redeeming us, Jesus makes us receptive to his receptivity so that we, too, can receive and reproduce God's love.

There is, then, a sort of transitive property at work here, which Schleiermacher understands as (and, in turn, uses to explain) the work of Christ's Spirit. To explain how this works, Schleiermacher takes as his model Christ's disciples, as he sees in them exactly the transformation he is trying to explain, namely one where they were initially merely receptive to Christ, but were eventually transformed so that Christ's receptivity (and activity) became their own. Schleiermacher claims, accordingly, that the disciples first had to become susceptible to Christ's activity: "in spending time together with Christ," he writes, "the disciples' receptivity developed, and by perceiving what he held before them, a foundation was laid for their future effectiveness for the kingdom of God." During their time with Christ, then, the disciples watched what Jesus said and did, and from this they began to learn what it meant to follow him. Through such training, the disciples grew in their susceptibility to Christ's influence, but his receptivity had not yet become their own, for they had not yet internalized this influence. A crucial step in their development occurred, therefore, when Jesus recognized them as competent to assess others' receptivity, since, Schleiermacher notes, "the right binding and loosing of sin is essentially just an expression of a fully cultivated receptivity for what pertains to the kingdom of God"

(§122.1).[5] Jesus' recognition of the disciples' authority to bind and loose thus meant that they had learned what it meant to follow him, which meant, in turn, that Jesus' influence on them was no longer merely external (§122.3). This recognition also meant that the disciples were now in position to confer this same recognition upon others, such that Jesus' influence was now fully transitive: the disciples had internalized Jesus' influence through becoming receptive to him, and once they had become sufficiently receptive, he recognized them as competent recognizers of such receptivity; once others had become sufficiently receptive, they too would be recognized as such, and so on.

From this, Schleiermacher extrapolates a more general model according to which a "multifarious community of God-consciousness" is carried on: first, those whose God-consciousness has been attuned to Christ express that attunement through their gestures, words, actions, and recognition-laden responses *to* such expressions; if others recognize this person's expressions as properly receptive of Christ's influence, they may imitate them in similar circumstances until they have become reliably disposed to do so, at which point these expressions become part of their own attunement; still others may then recognize the latter's expressions as attuned to Christ, imitate those expressions, become reliably disposed to repeat them, and so on. In this way, the Spirit of Christ's own receptivity is carried forward through a chain of intersubjective recognition, and persons' lives are thereby reordered to God. Those who have been sufficiently formed by, and who thus contribute to, the community founded by Jesus, are therefore new persons, for, as Schleiermacher writes, "the pervasive activity of Christ cannot establish itself in an individual without becoming person-forming in him too, for now all his activities are differently determined through the working of Christ in him, and even all impressions are differently received – which means that the personal self-consciousness too becomes altogether different" (§100.2).

The community founded by Jesus is the means, therefore, by which his God-consciousness is communicated to others; their reception of his God-consciousness would obviously liberate them from their God-forgetfulness, which is why Schleiermacher terms this the *redemptive* activity of Jesus (§100 Thesis). This is the basis, in turn, of Jesus' *reconciliatory* activity, as having a renewed God-consciousness enables

---

[5] Note well that Schleiermacher is here alluding to the so-called Johannine Pentecost (cf. John 20:22–23), especially the connection there made between the sending of the Spirit and the binding and loosing of sins, rather than to the binding-and-loosing passages in the Synoptic Gospels; cf. §122.1 (565n2).

one to reintegrate relative freedom and dependence, and so restores one to harmony with the world. That is to say, one is *redeemed* when Jesus' God-consciousness becomes one's own, just as one is *reconciled* when his 'unclouded blessedness' becomes so (§101 Thesis). Such reconciliation is brought about, as Schleiermacher has led us to expect, in our relationship to nature as well as in our community with others. Schleiermacher thus argues that, for Jesus,

> ... the hindrances to his activity never determined any moment of his life until the perception of them had been taken up into his inmost self-consciousness, which was so completely one with his powerful God-consciousness that they could appear in it only as belonging to the temporal form of the perfect effectiveness of his being ... It was still less possible that hindrances arising out of his own natural or social life could be taken up in this innermost consciousness as hindrances; they could be no more than indications of the direction set for his activity. (§101.2)

Because every moment of his life was determined by a perfect receptivity toward God's reconciling love, Jesus could be reconciled even to circumstances that seem opposed to this love, for reconciling love is precisely that which relativizes and overcomes such opposition. God-forgetfulness treats worldly oppositions as absolute and so experiences them as contradictions; God-consciousness, by contrast, is conscious of the ultimacy of reconciling love, and so treats these same oppositions as that which is to be united in that which is truly absolute. Once one's God-consciousness has been restored, accordingly, one likewise participates in Jesus' reconciliation to his circumstances: Schleiermacher thus claims that

> ... the redeemed man, too, since he has been assumed into the vital fellowship of Christ, is never filled with the consciousness of any evil, for it cannot touch or hinder the life which he shares with Christ. All hindrances to life, natural and social, come to him even in this region only as indications. They are not taken away, as if he were to be, or could be, without pain and free from suffering, for Christ also knew pain and suffered in the same way. Only the pains and sufferings do not mean simple misery, for they do not as such penetrate into the inmost life ... The assumption into vital fellowship with Christ, therefore, dissolves the connection between sin and evil. (§101.2)

Jesus' redemptive work thus plays a key role in his reconciling work, since, by restoring persons' God-consciousness and, so, their receptivity to God's reconciling love, he enables them to experience worldly oppositions as overcome – or to-be-overcome – by that love. Those who are redeemed can therefore integrate all of their circumstances, and they themselves, into their God-consciousness, because they trust that these circumstances are one and all absolutely dependent on a wise, loving God.

From Schleiermacher's vantage point, accordingly, the seeming antithesis between one's freedom and that upon which one is dependent – manifest in natural as well as social antagonisms – is due to "God-forgetfulness," for the relativity of such antitheses, along with their possible coincidence, can be recognized only when they are set in relation to one on whom both are absolutely dependent, and for whom both coincide. To overcome these antitheses, therefore, reconciliation is necessary, which is what Schleiermacher claims has been accomplished in Christ and mediated through his Spirit: Christ is perfectly God-conscious, Schleiermacher argues, and is thus able to bring every moment of his sensible consciousness, including his relative freedom and dependence, into unity with that God-consciousness; by founding a community and conveying his Spirit to others, Jesus enables them to share in that God-consciousness and, so, to bring their lives into absolute dependence upon God. On Schleiermacher's account, then, all that is depends absolutely on God, and one's ability to live in such dependence is itself absolutely dependent on God.

SCHLEIERMACHER AS REFORMED THEOLOGIAN

With that, we return to the claim with which we began. Alexander Schweizer claimed, recall, that what distinguishes Reformed theology is its emphasis on the absolute primacy of God and, in consequence, on creatures' absolute dependence on God. If this characterization is even roughly accurate, then it should be apparent that Schleiermacher's theology should indeed be counted as Reformed, as he elaborates an account according to which all that is depends absolutely on the God who became incarnate in Christ, just as God-forgetful humans depend absolutely on God's redeeming grace.

This means, in turn, that Schleiermacher's theology may provide helpful, distinctively Reformed resources for those who would carry on this theological tradition today. I will end by mentioning just one. Because (a) Schleiermacher portrays nature as hanging together as a single, organic whole, and (b) he sees this hanging-together as an expression of its absolute dependence upon God, it follows (c) that, on his account, one need not choose between a theological and a natural-scientific understanding of nature. Schleiermacher once suggested that theology must establish an "eternal covenant" between science and Christian faith, a covenant in which these disciplines would neither hinder nor exclude one another, and his understanding of nature's dependence on God provides us with a way of seeing what such a covenant might look like. For contemporary Reformed theologians who are interested in integrating faith with a naturalistic worldview, therefore, it may be good news that Schleiermacher belongs to their tradition.

Further reading

Dole, Andrew. *Schleiermacher on Religion and the Natural Order*. Oxford: Oxford University Press, 2010.

Gerrish, Brian A. *Continuing the Reformation: Essays on Modern Religious Thought*. Chicago: University of Chicago Press, 1993.

Hector, Kevin W. *The Theological Project of Modernism: Faith and the Conditions of Mineness*. Oxford: Oxford University Press, 2015.

Lamm, Julia A. *The Living God: Schleiermacher's Appropriation of Spinoza*. University Park: Pennsylvania University Press, 1996.

Redeker, Martin. *Schleiermacher: Life and Thought*. Philadelphia: Fortress, 1973.

12 Karl Barth

MICHAEL BEINTKER

TRANSLATED BY MICHAEL BRÄUTIGAM

Many regard Karl Barth as the Church Father of the twentieth century. He stimulated and influenced theological debate during this period unlike any other Reformed dogmatician. As the leading figure in the 'dialectical theology' movement of the 1920s, Barth spearheaded the century's most distinctive and influential undertaking in Protestant theology. One of the guiding authors of the Barmen Declaration (1934), he also played a preeminent role in ecclesial conflicts with National Socialism. From his office as teacher of the Protestant church, his revision of essential tenets of Reformation theology called forth a remarkable echo in Roman Catholic theology and in the ecumenical movement. Barth's work was characterised by an exceptional literary productivity, unrivalled by any other twentieth-century theologian in its form, scope and density.

BIOGRAPHICAL SKETCH

Karl Barth was born in Basel, Switzerland on 10 May 1886, the first child of theologian Fritz Barth and his wife Anna Barth-Sartorius. He grew up in Bern, where his father served as Professor of Church History and New Testament from 1889 onwards. From 1904 to 1908, he studied theology in Bern, Berlin, Tübingen and Marburg. In Berlin he was particularly impressed by Adolf von Harnack, while in Marburg it was Wilhelm Herrmann who became his most influential teacher.

The young Barth considered himself to be a staunch adherent of liberal theology. This was clearly evident in 1908–1909, when he worked in Marburg as an editorial assistant to Martin Rade for *Christliche Welt*, the leading journal of the ecclesially and culturally open German liberal Protestantism. Thereafter, Barth served as an assistant preacher in Geneva from 1909 to 1911, following which he became pastor to the farming and working-class community of Safenwil (Aargau). He laboured there for ten years as a minister while becoming involved in social issues. In 1913, he married Nelly Barth-Hoffmann, with whom he had five children.

Barth's time in parish ministry caused him to rethink his theological position, and it became increasingly evident to him that the time was ripe for a foundational reorientation. The historical circumstances, particularly the outbreak and progression of the First World War with its spiritual and cultural upheavals, further provoked his search for theological alternatives. The theological concepts of the nineteenth and early twentieth centuries, chiefly developed by Friedrich Schleiermacher and the school of Albrecht Ritschl, turned out to be increasingly problematic for Barth. His encounters with Hermann Kutter and Christoph Blumhardt, who were affiliated with religious socialism, together with close exchanges with his friend Eduard Thurneysen, reinforced his uneasiness with the theology of neo-Protestantism and its lopsided focus on human religious experience.

Against this backdrop, Barth decided to engage in the exegesis of Paul's Epistle to the Romans in the summer of 1916. This was primarily meant to be a personal endeavour, and initially Barth did not consider publishing his work. Nevertheless, a theological commentary grew out of his analysis of Paul's text (*Epistle to the Romans* [*Der Römerbrief*]) that inspired and stimulated the rise of German-speaking theology after the First World War more than any other work. Through the book's two very different versions (the first edition in 1919 and the second in 1922) – the real impact was made by the second edition – Barth gradually worked towards establishing a new foundation for theology, one rooted in the biblically testified address of God.

The conventional practice accepted since Schleiermacher, namely, to predicate theology on a general concept of religion, had to be overcome. Consequently, Barth sought to express the sovereignty of the living God, who meets us as our superior in judgement and grace. This sovereignty was not religiously fixed, nor was it constrained by idealist conceptualities or ethics. Rather, Barth's strongly pointed dialectical forms of expression intended to provide space for the event of God's self-revelation while safeguarding the non-availability of divine speech and action. At this point there emerged the basic conviction that would characterise Barth's theology as a whole – that human knowledge of God is effected by *God*, resting exclusively on the divine initiative and taking place in the self-revelation of God.

The second edition of *Romans* and Barth's other works from 1921 to 1922 show him at the apex of 'dialectical theology'. This development had been reinforced and shaped by Franz Overbeck's theological critique, by neo-Kantianism through the interpretation of his brother Heinrich Barth and (at least conceptually) by Søren Kierkegaard's dialectic of paradox. His lifelong friendship with Eduard Thurneysen, encounters with Friedrich Gogarten and Emil Brunner and exchanges with Rudolf Bultmann all proved fruitful in his further development. From 1922 until the group's breakup in 1933, the common discussion forum was the journal *Zwischen den Zeiten* ('Between the Times'), which was generally considered the periodical that best represented this new direction in theology.

Barth returned to the academic world in 1922, having been called to an honorary professorship in Göttingen that had been established with the help of an American foundation. In 1925, he was called to a chair in dogmatics and New Testament theology in Münster, and in 1930 he assumed a chair in systematic theology in Bonn. Charlotte von Kirschbaum entered his life in 1925, and their intimate working relationship would last several decades. During the dramatic years 1933–1934, the high point of his work in Germany, he exerted a distinct theological influence on the ecclesial opposition to National Socialism and the formation of the Confessing Church. To this end, he produced the draft edition of the 1934 Barmen Theological Declaration. The National Socialist regime did not tolerate him for long: towards the end of 1934 he was suspended for his refusal to take the compulsory oath to Hitler. In March 1935 he was banned from speaking in public and in June 1935 he was forced to retire, which was tantamount to an occupational ban. At this point he accepted a call to the University of Basel, where he would teach until his retirement in 1962 – except for two semesters during which he served as visiting professor in Bonn in 1946–1947. While in Basel, both before and during the war, he time and again raised his voice to critique both developments in Germany and Switzerland's course of neutrality (*Eine Schweizer Stimme*, 'A Swiss Voice').

After the Second World War Barth became a strong proponent of international reconciliation and agreement. He admonished those who had quickly drawn new frontlines in the Cold War. Furthermore, he took an active role in the newly established ecumenical movement. During his activities of teaching and researching in Basel, he focused mainly on his *magnum opus*, the *Church Dogmatics* (*CD*), of which the first part-volume appeared in 1932, later growing to thirteen extensive volumes with the publication of *Church Dogmatics* IV/4 in 1967.[1] One year later, on 10 December 1968, Barth died in the city of his birth, Basel.

CENTRAL QUESTIONS AND THEOLOGICAL DECISIONS

Barth's work began with the assumption that modern theology was in a complex state of exhaustion. He had grown up theologically in a context where the questions of liberal neo-Protestantism set an agenda with which he had more or less identified. Through his time in the parish, he came to the conclusion that his teachers' theology was not helpful for the tasks of a Christian church; such theology rather stood in its way.

Barth was irritated by the exclusive nature of the historicist approach ('Historicism') which relativised everything else, and by the corresponding distance from the original transmission of the Bible. He also considered proclamation's lopsided orientation towards the religious needs of the audience, together with the related aspirations for resonance and success, to be highly problematic. The same applied to the neo-Protestant reduction of the view of God to a dull, tedious and tentative concept of love. In Barth's view, the church and theology were curiously helpless in the face of real human questions and afflictions. He intended to counter both the limitation of scope to the religious human being and the isolation of religious content from the profane by moving decisively to a theology of 'reality'.

This move was supported by an about-turn in perspective: theology, Barth explained in a 1933 speech delivered in Denmark, 'will not seek to illumine heaven with a floodlight based on earth, but it will try to see and to understand earth in the light of heaven'.[2] According to Barth, the cardinal error of modern theology since the Enlightenment lay in its widespread attempt to connect with reality by correlating human questions with theological answers which were easily available. In so doing, the true theological content of those questions was no longer recognised, having been replaced by abstract constructs which led away

---

[1] Karl Barth, *Church Dogmatics*, 4 vols. in 13 parts, edited by G. W. Bromiley and T. F. Torrance (Edinburgh: T&T Clark, 1956–1975), the translation of Karl Barth, *Die Kirchliche Dogmatik* (Munich: Chr. Kaiser, 1932 and Zürich: EVZ, 1938–1965). References hereafter are given in the form *CD* followed by volume and page number, with the German page number in brackets.

[2] Karl Barth, 'Das erste Gebot als theologisches Axiom' [1933], in *Vorträge und kleinere Arbeiten 1930–1933*, edited by Michael Beintker, Michael Hüttenhoff and Peter Zocher (Barth Gesamtausgabe; Zürich: Theologischer Verlag, 2013), 234.

from the particularity of the truth of God revealed in Jesus Christ. Yet for Barth, connection with reality can be discovered only if theological thinking follows *God's movement towards humanity*, at the same time conceiving of its recipients as existing in a space already touched and supported by this movement.

This change of perspective, with its corresponding way of thinking about God, belongs to the most distinct foundational convictions of Barth's theology. The exegetical differences between the 1919 and 1922 editions of *Romans* attest this new approach. Both texts serve as hermeneutical programmes for a reading of Scripture that allows the biblical text to serve as a seismograph of the modern person's situation before God: 'What was once of grave importance, is so still [...]. If we rightly understand ourselves, our problems are the problems of Paul; and if we are enlightened by the brightness of his answers, those answers must be ours.'[3]

If one wants to understand and trace God's movement towards the human being, one must know God. However, there is no way to God that begins with the human being, who is always sinful and self-centred. By starting with the human being one will only arrive at false gods and idols. Everything depends on whether God turns towards the human being and reveals himself: 'God is known only by God.'[4] God is known in that he reveals himself to the human being in Jesus Christ, making himself knowable by the presence of the Holy Spirit who awakens faith.

In this way, the concept of revelation developed for Barth into a fundamental theological category. In Jesus Christ we are dealing authentically with God himself. The doctrine of the Trinity describes God's self-revelation in the modes of being of Father, Son and Holy Spirit. As such, it involves the cognitive consideration of the authenticity of God's turning towards the human being, which leads Barth to set out the doctrine not in the doctrine of God – as in the traditional order of presentation – but in the very Prolegomena of the *Church Dogmatics*.[5] Barth firmly rejected any attempts that sought access to the reality of God other than by way of the knowledge prescribed by God. This determined most notably his critique of 'natural theology', as well as his firm conviction that religion – by which he first and foremost understood religion

---

[3] Karl Barth, *Epistle to the Romans* [Preface to *Romans* I], translated by Edwyn C. Hoskyns (London: Oxford University Press, 1933 [1968]), 3 [*Der Römerbrief* (Erste Fassung) (1919), edited by Hermann Schmidt (Barth Gesamtausgabe; Zürich: Theologischer Verlag, 1985), 3].

[4] *CD* II/1, 179, see also 44 and 199 [200, also 47 and 200].

[5] See *CD* I/1, 295–489 [311–514].

in its Christian (!) form – is sublated by God's self-revelation.[6] According to Barth, the essence of natural theology consisted in the fact that in describing reality theologically, it relied on the analyses and diagnoses of non-theological description. It therefore discussed theological issues while ignoring the actual relation of the person to God that had always existed. It thus cultivated the assumption that there was 'a union of man with God existing outside God's revelation in Jesus Christ'.[7]

The dominating element of the exegesis of the second edition of *Romans* was a marked awareness of the distance between God and the human being: 'To us God is the Stranger, the Other, whom we finally encounter along the whole frontier of our knowledge.'[8] Any speech about God which ignores the insurmountable distance between God and the world, and which does not surrender to the crisis of everything human in the face of the One who judges and pardons us, will fall short by replacing the God of the biblical witness with religious ideals.

The label 'dialectical theology' was coined in 1922, presumably as an echo of Barth's second edition of *Romans* and his lecture on 'The Word of God as the Task of Theology'.[9] In the latter work, Barth distinguished between the dogmatic, the critical and the dialectical ways of theology, arguing that there was an intriguing tension between the mandate to speak about God and our human inability to comply with this mandate: 'As theologians, we ought to speak of God. But we are humans and as such cannot speak of God. We ought to do both, to know the "ought" and the "not able to", and precisely in this way give God the glory.'[10] Barth thus intended to correct a theological phrase that indiscriminately identified human speech about God with authentic divine truth. In the course of the 1920s, he further developed this notion and modified it significantly. Clearly, if theology and the church had to talk explicitly about God and God's action in the world, then it was necessary to develop coherent propositions of theological doctrine. This is provided for in the concept of *analogia fidei*. Whilst Barth was firmly

---

[6] Cf. particularly *CD* I/2, 280–361 [304–397].

[7] *CD* II/1, 168 [189].

[8] Barth, *Romans*, 318 [*Der Römerbrief* (Zweite Fassung) (1922), edited by Cees van der Kooi and Katja Tolstaja (Barth Gesamtausgabe; Zürich: Theologischer Verlag, 2010), 435].

[9] Karl Barth, 'The Word of God as the Task of Theology', in *The Word of God and Theology*, translated by Amy Marga (London: T&T Clark, 2011), 171–198 ['Das Wort Gottes als Aufgabe der Theologie' [1922], in *Vorträge und kleinere Arbeiten 1922–1925*, edited by Holger Finze (Barth Gesamtausgabe; Zürich: Theologischer Verlag, 1990), 144–175].

[10] Barth, 'The Word of God as the Task of Theology', 177 (original italics omitted) [151].

committed to the categorical distinction between the reality of the triune God and the reality of the human being and of the created world, he developed a theologically satisfying solution for the problem of human speech about God by means of analogy: human words and concepts adequately express the mystery of God when they *correspond* to him – that is, when they relate analogically to him.

Even more importantly, and similarly originating in the second edition of *Romans*, was the dialectic of God's salvific action itself: 'Grace is the KRISIS from death to life. [...] For this reason, the Gospel of Christ is a shattering disturbance, an assault which brings everything into question.'[11] The contradiction that arises through the negation of the human being and the fact that God seeks fellowship with the individual precisely in this negation must be endured. The 'No' that judges sin, and which must not be reduced at any price, is at the same time known as a salvific 'Yes'. The 'Yes' manifests itself in the 'No' and the 'No' in the 'Yes': '*This* "No" is precisely a "Yes". *This* judgement is grace. *This* condemnation is forgiveness. *This* death is life. *This* hell is heaven. *This* terrible God is the loving Father who draws the lost Son into his arms.'[12]

Still, Barth did not stop there. The dialectic of judgment and grace, which originated during his work on *Romans*, already anticipated a rearrangement of the relationship between Law and Gospel and a reformulation of the doctrine of election as the 'sum of the Gospel'.[13] For if the 'Yes' and 'No' of God's *Krisis* are considered to be not two words, but *one* word in two related movements, then the Gospel will come before the Law, to the extent that God's 'Yes' emerges out of the shadow of negation as the supporting foundation of the divine 'No'. Already in 1924 Barth was able to say that Gospel and Law 'are summarised in the higher unity of the Word of God'.[14] When Jesus Christ is described in the first Barmen thesis of 1934 as 'the one Word of God', this is the completion of a development rooted in the discovery of the transforming character of God's grace as expressed in the motif of *Krisis* in the second edition of *Romans*.

---

[11] Barth, *Romans*, 225 [310–311].

[12] Karl Barth, 'Not und Verheißung der christlichen Verkündigung' [1922], in *Vorträge und kleinere Arbeiten 1922–1925*, 86–87.

[13] *CD* II/2, 3 [*KD* II/2, 1].

[14] Karl Barth, *The Göttingen Dogmatics: Instruction in the Christian Religion*, vol. 1, translated by Geoffrey W. Bromiley (Grand Rapids, MI: Eerdmans, 1991), 194 [*Unterricht in der christlichen Religion*, vol. 1, *Prolegomena* (1924), edited by Hannelotte Reiffen (Barth Gesamtausgabe; Zürich: Theologischer Verlag, 1985), 240].

The dialectic of God's salvific action also influences the doctrine of election in *CD* II/2, which Barth reinterpreted in a breath-taking way during the Second World War. At this point, the Christological concentration of Barth's thinking reached its first climax prior to the doctrine of reconciliation in *CD* IV. Everything that can be said about God, the world and the human being, as well as everything that happens between them, is conceived from and towards Jesus Christ. The Reformed concept of double predestination thereby takes a surprising turn. In Jesus Christ, God says 'No' to our sin and executes the judgement of condemnation on him. In Jesus Christ, God says 'Yes' to us as pardoned sinners and those whom he has elected. In Jesus Christ the sinner receives the unreserved approval of the divine 'Yes', as the 'No' that was aimed to strike us has instead been suffered by Christ on the cross. Jesus Christ is exposed to the dialectic of the electing 'Yes' and the condemning 'No' in our place. In light of the victory of the 'Yes' in the death of Christ, '[t]he No pronounced in the cross of Jesus Christ can and should be heard and accepted only as the necessary and in the true sense redemptive form of His Yes'.[15]

The Christ-event is the point at which all the lines between God and the human being converge. The central theme of the sovereignty of God and the divinity of God was 'the anthropologically' discussed even more profoundly in the doctrine of reconciliation (*CD* IV/1–4), published between 1950 and 1967. God demonstrates his divinity precisely in the manifestation of his *humanity* in Jesus Christ, and, by humbling himself, elevates the human being to become his free partner. In Jesus Christ we experience who the true God really is, and in Jesus Christ we experience who the true human being really is. In his person, Jesus Christ embodies God's covenant with humanity – he is the Mediator, Reconciler and Revealer who represents God to humanity and humanity to God.

Barth's movement towards both a Christological concentration and a more comprehensive approach to theological thinking offered a deliberate alternative to the anthropological turn characteristic of modern philosophy and theology. Barth considered the human subject who thematises and explains religious experience and who, in the extreme case, interprets all theological assertions unilaterally as expressions of religious concern as an abstraction which missed what was essential. Behind such a tendency Barth identified the intellectual legacy of Descartes, grounding the certainty of God paradigmatically in the

---

[15] *CD* IV/1, 350 [*KD* IV/1, 387].

knowing subject's self-certainty. In Barth's view, this made the validity of truth fatally dependent on human epistemic abilities.

Barth's study of Anselm in 1931, *Fides quaerens intellectum*,[16] offers a significant alternative to this form of subject-oriented theology. According to the method of Anselm of Canterbury's 'Proslogion', the validity of God's truth is detached from human capacities of knowledge and reasoning. In contrast to Cartesianism and the related transcendental philosophy, which had considerably impressed and influenced him in the early 1920s, Barth came to ground theological thinking in the self-responsible and self-verifying divine truth.

The formula *fides quaerens intellectum* ('faith seeking understanding') indicates that the faith which has obtained assurance seeks rational clarity concerning its content. While the validity of the content cannot be called into question, the content desires to be known in detail and to be grasped, as diligently as possible, by a rationality strengthened and assured by faith. This comprises the task of theology. The truth which is at stake in the thought of the subject does not need to be constituted by the thinking process. Such a task would hopelessly overburden the capacities of the theologian. Rather, the inscrutable prerequisite of all being, and also of all human knowledge, is God's truth, not a construct of the human mind. God himself vouches for the truth of his existence, and theology follows by thinking after it. The statements of theology are certainly located on the noetic level of human knowing, which must be clearly distinguished from the ontic level. Thus they remain – despite a clear focus on God's truth – provisional, corrigible, susceptible to error and open to revision. Nevertheless, statements on the noetic level of knowing can succeed if they exist in a relationship of correspondence to their ontological preconditions.

As a result of the encounter with Anselm, Barth's thinking gained its characteristic confidence, namely that faith is presented with an object of knowledge that defines truth and that any reflection *upon it* will lead to a gain in knowledge. Neither God nor his Word that seeks us deceives. The engaged desire for theological knowledge, which made the *Church Dogmatics* possible in the first place, has its origin here.

---

[16] Karl Barth, *Anselm: Fides Quaerens Intellectum: Anselm's Proof of the Existence of God in the Context of His Theological Scheme*, translated by Ian W. Robertson (London: SCM, 1960) [*Fides quaerens intellectum. Anselms Beweis der Existenz Gottes im Zusammenhang seines theologischen Programms* [1931], 3rd ed., edited by Eberhard Jüngel and Ingolf U. Dalferth (Barth Gesamtausgabe; Zürich: Theologischer Verlag, 2002).

THEOLOGICAL DEVELOPMENT

Barth's thinking was never 'finished'. Rather, it is better described as a movement of thought in constant development, permanently seeking to arrive at better solutions. In his final Basel lectures he compared the task of theology to the tireless '*circling* [of] a high mountain which, although it is one and the same mountain, exists and manifests itself in very different shapes'.[17] This clearly reflects his own theological path. According to Barth, theological work, 'every day, in fact every hour, is to begin anew at the *beginning*',[18] and thus must not simply proceed from 'results that are already achieved, or conclusions that are already arrived at'.[19] This idea is characteristic of Barth and not only recurs repeatedly in his work, but is also evidenced in his biographical course.

There are, of course, important leitmotifs and constants. Barth's central intention, namely to emphasise *God's* authentic reality and truth, as well as to protect human knowledge of God from the danger of becoming obscured, corrupted or instrumentalised, was already evident *before* the period of *Epistle to the Romans*. Later, however, it came expressly to the fore and continued to remain determinative of his work. The same can be said with regard to the strong sense of responsibility and absolute seriousness that characterised Barth's theological work throughout his life. The decision to base his theology upon the address of the Word of God to which the Bible testifies, as stipulated in his first exposition of *Epistle to the Romans*, remained the clear orientation of his thinking. For Barth, such self-disclosure was the way in which God had chosen to reveal himself to humanity.

The early period of Barth's work, lasting until 1915, could be described as a moderately liberal phase in his theology. Barth's texts from the decade prior to the First World War, made available in his collected works in German, reveal him to be a relatively independent exponent of liberal theology. His work demonstrated creative impatience and constantly revealed his attention to genuinely important problems.

In 1916 Barth began his work on *Epistle to the Romans*. Its first edition already reveals his movement towards a new theological position. Revision of the commentary in the years 1920–1922 led to a second edition of the work. The later Göttingen years and the first years in

---

[17] Karl Barth, *Evangelical Theology: An Introduction*, translated by Grover Foley (Grand Rapids, MI: Eerdmans, 1963), 34 [*Einführung in die evangelische Theologie*, 6th ed. (Zürich: Theologischer Verlag, 2006), 39].

[18] Ibid. [169].

[19] Ibid. [169].

Münster (1923–1927) epitomise his transition to 'dogmatic' theology. The theology based on Barth's experience in ministry, which was first merely intended as a 'corrective' to dominant trends, developed within the realm of the university into a technical and ordered presentation of Christian doctrine. It was there that Barth focused on the often undervalued ways of posing problems in the classical tradition of theology, discovering the achievements of Reformed theology, particularly those of John Calvin. During this learning process (1924–1926: 'Instruction in the Christian Religion', 1927: 'Christian Dogmatics in Outline'), the basic commitments underlying Barth's dogmatics were formed. These included the Trinitarian exploration of the theological concept of revelation; the differentiation of the threefold form of the Word of God as revelation, Scripture and proclamation; the insights into the constitutive status of Christology; and the constructive differentiation of the three dimensions of divine action as creation, reconciliation and redemption. From this point onwards the Reformed character of his dogmatic thinking played a thematic role.

The questions provoked by responses to his 'Christian Dogmatics in Outline' stimulated Barth's process of clarification in the years 1928–1931, during which time the positions of the *Church Dogmatics* began to crystallise. A new step towards epistemological clarity was then reached with *Fides quaerens intellectum* (1931). As his work moved into the phase of the *Church Dogmatics* (1932–1967), the intervals at which new insights led to distinct changes lengthened. One should not underestimate the way in which theological knowledge was put to the test in the conflict with National Socialism. Barth's work on the doctrine of election of *Church Dogmatics* II/2, which he took up in 1939, triggered the next innovative move in Barth's dogmatic theology: the breakthrough to Christonomy. This led in the years 1953–1967 to a revision of the traditional doctrine of reconciliation within the horizon of Christonomy.

Today, Barth scholarship typically distinguishes the following periods:

a. pre-1915: phase characterised by liberal theology
b. 1916–1919: phase of the first edition of *Epistle to the Romans*
c. 1920–1923: phase of the second edition of *Epistle to the Romans* and the high point of 'dialectical theology'
d. 1924–1939: first phase of dogmatic theology from 'Instruction in the Christian Religion' to the first volumes of the *Church Dogmatics*
e. 1939–1968: second phase of dogmatic theology, from the revision of the doctrine of election to the consequent Christonomic soteriology.

The transitions between these phases prohibit schematic definitions. Nevertheless, one can observe decisive turning points, such as that between the liberal phase and the phases of the two *Romans* commentaries (ca. 1915/1916). There is also the caesura between the second *Epistle to the Romans* and his development of a dogmatic theology (ca. 1923/1924).

THE *CHURCH DOGMATICS*

Barth's *Church Dogmatics* is the most important and comprehensive theological work of the twentieth century. It grew page by page from the lectures Barth gave in Bonn and, from 1935, in Basel. Every single chapter was tested in the context of academic teaching and was rigorously revised prior to publication. The structure was predetermined from the very beginning[20]: prolegomena (*CD* I/1–2), the doctrine of God (*CD* II/1–2), the doctrine of creation (*CD* III/1–4), the doctrine of reconciliation (*CD* IV/1–4) and the doctrine of redemption (*CD* V). Though never written, the content of the latter can to an extent be deduced from the earlier volumes, particularly from the doctrine of reconciliation.

From the moment he decided to refrain from developing further his 'Christian Dogmatics in Outline',[21] the title of which reflects its preliminary status, and instead to begin anew, Barth's entire academic life revolved around the development of his dogmatics. The first volume of the Prolegomena, *CD* I/1, was published in 1932. In 1967, *CD* IV/4 appeared, treating the doctrine of baptism. In promoting credobaptism and thus rejecting paedobaptism, this volume generated the kind of significant theological debate that Barth's writings had often initiated over the years.

The first and last publication dates of the *Church Dogmatics*, 1932 and 1967, are separated by thirty-five years. This period not only covers the lifespan of a whole generation, and more than half of an academic life, but it also represents the most dramatic period in European history in the twentieth century. The rise of National Socialism and ensuing conflicts with its regime, wartime and the pre- and post-war periods, the Cold War and the polarisation of societal systems: all of these have to be taken into account when a reader delves into any one of the thirteen part-volumes of the near 9,000 pages of the *Church Dogmatics*.

---

[20] *CD* I/1, xvi–xvii [*KD* I/1, XII.]

[21] Karl Barth, *Die christliche Dogmatik im Entwurf,* Erster Band: Die Lehre vom Worte Gottes. Prolegomena zur christlichen Dogmatik (1927), edited by Gerhard Sauter (Barth Gesamtausgabe; Zürich: Theologischer Verlag, 1982).

Even given the momentous context of the work, references to current affairs within it usually remain concealed. Barth never operated superficially, and believed that dogmatics should not attempt to serve as commentary on current affairs. The author's attention was entirely focused on the deeply specific subject-related development of any given topic. This he introduced to the reader by examining it down to the last detail, in continuous conversation with the Bible and the tradition, while also including contemporary theological viewpoints. In this way, theology was to benefit the church as it faced the challenges of current events, and to support it in articulating appropriately the vitality of the free grace of God in the midst of these difficulties. One should not allow oneself to be deceived by Barth's taking up anew several classical themes: there is almost no sentence in the *Church Dogmatics* that could have been written in any century other than the twentieth.

Barth described the task of dogmatics right at the outset: 'As a theological discipline dogmatics is the scientific self-examination of the Christian Church with respect to the content of its distinctive talk about God.'[22] By characterising dogmatics as scientific self-examination performed as a 'function of the Church',[23] Barth pointed to the self-critical, ecclesial nature of the work and thus followed, in formal terms, Schleiermacher's functional understanding of theology. In contrast to Schleiermacher, however, for Barth the task of theology was not so much concerned with the activity of leading the church or the attempt to clarify the truthfulness of religious experience. In his view, it was concerned with the truthfulness of speaking about God in the church: 'Does Christian utterance derive from Him? Does it lead to Him? Is it conformable to Him?'[24] Biblical theology deals with the first question, practical theology with the second and systematic theology with the third.

Barth compares theology with a touch-stone with reference to which one examines critically what is being said in the church. The tasks of the different theological disciplines arise from the particular angle of the questions concerning the truth of Christian speech. Among these, dogmatics is supposed to determine whether the spoken utterances of the church conform with the truth. In addition, however, Barth incorporated ethics into dogmatics, concluding every major part of *Church Dogmatics* with an extensive ethical treatise. He makes the

---

[22] *CD* I/1, 3 (emphasised in original) [*KD* I/1, 1].
[23] Ibid.
[24] *CD* I/1, 4 [*KD* I/1, 2f].

case that one ought to rethink critically the church's ethical stances with reference to their conformity to the truth of God revealed in Jesus Christ, and so point to courses of action that are a living expression of the Christian witness.

The most important change across the *Church Dogmatics* occurs in the understanding of the person of Jesus Christ, which grows ever deeper and more concrete. This has relevance for the interpretation of the reality of God, and the reality of human beings and their relations to one another, as well as for the reality of the Christian community. The confession of Jesus Christ as the one Word of God, as the Barmen Declaration's first thesis states, becomes the focal point that forms and determines all other theological assertions. The Christonomic 'systematics' of the *Church Dogmatics* is adumbrated in paragraph 15 of *Church Dogmatics* I/2 (1938).[25] It manifests itself in the revision of the doctrine of election in *Church Dogmatics* II/2 (1942), which is set out by Barth as the 'sum of the Gospel',[26] for God elects the human being in Jesus Christ to participate in his glory, determining himself for the rejection directed to the sinful human being. This being the case, there emerges the soteriological trajectory of God's creative action in which creation and salvation are closely connected. Their unity is shown in that creation is conceived as the external basis of the covenant of grace, while the covenant of grace is conceived as the internal basis of creation, as is described in *Church Dogmatics* III/1 (1945). From this there emerges an approach to theological anthropology that begins with knowledge of the Christological *vere homo* (true human person) in *Church Dogmatics* III/2 (1948). The Christocentric reformulation of dogmatic topics reaches its climax in the doctrine of reconciliation of *Church Dogmatics* IV (1953–1959). The doctrine of reconciliation predicates its assertions on the promise embodied in Jesus Christ, namely 'God with us'[27]: the subject matter, origin and content of Christian proclamation is 'the free act of the faithfulness of God in which He takes the lost cause of man, who has denied Him as Creator and in so doing ruined himself as creature, and makes it His own in Jesus Christ'.[28]

The elaborate architectural design of Barth's doctrine of reconciliation is unrivalled in recent theological history. With conceptual power and coherence, it interleaves the various levels of statement concerning Christology, hamartiology, justification, ecclesiology, pneumatology

---

[25] See *CD* I/2, 122–202 ('The Mystery of Revelation') [134–221].

[26] *CD* II/2, 3 [1].

[27] See *CD* IV/1, 3–21 [1–22].

[28] *CD* IV/1, 3 (emphasis in original) [1].

and ethics, relating each intensively to the work and significance of Jesus Christ. The innovations associated with this endeavour, particularly in the areas of Christology, hamartiology and the doctrine of justification, are considerable and have not yet received the attention they deserve. In terms of impact, Barth's doctrine of reconciliation still has an important future ahead of it.

Barth's *Church Dogmatics* captures readers, ushering them into a broad movement of thinking. Even if one reads only a little, one will soon discover that the author was an expert in the use of language who cultivated a pleasing style of writing in sharp contrast to the often dry, cumbersome and off-putting presentations of other dogmatic works. Barth's *Church Dogmatics* is exceptional in its breadth, for Barth illumines and deliberates on topics from many angles, and the main text time and again interrupted by excursions in small print which explore relevant exegetical and theological-historical material.

CHURCH DOGMATICS AS REFORMED DOGMATICS

Whilst Barth clearly underlined the 'confessional attitude' of his dogmatics,[29] he was not a confessionalist. Reformed theology ought to emphasise the Gospel as the concern of the one, whole church of Jesus Christ. Confessional determination is a relative entity, that is, it is relative to the whole of the 'one, holy, catholic and apostolic Church'. However, the church always exists concretely in the form of a particular church. From this follows the ecumenical dimension of theological reflection, and thus its commitment towards the whole of Christianity. A confessionally oriented dogmatics cannot be exclusively committed to the intellectual tasks of its corresponding denomination. The *Protestant* dogmatics is not only a dogmatics for the Protestant Church; rather, 'it has to defend and represent with a view to the *whole* Church ... the *one thing* which is necessary'.[30]

Reformed theology thus does not focus unilaterally on nurturing a Reformed identity, a Reformed profile or Reformed interests, for in that case it would inevitably deteriorate into a sectarian business. It always thinks and judges for the 'one, holy, catholic and apostolic church'. This clearly expresses Calvin's view of the church and the essence of the Reformation.

[29] *CD* I/2, 822 [919].
[30] Ibid., 826 [923].

The Protestant church finds concrete expression in its Lutheran, Reformed and Anglican forms. It is worth remarking on the conciliatory tone with which Barth portrays the differences between the three Protestant denominations. What separated the Reformed churches from the other two denominations was not an issue of heresy, such as was the case in respect of the Roman Catholic Church, the Eastern Orthodox Church or neo-Protestantism, the last of which Barth regularly characterised in this context as a degenerate form of Protestant Christianity.[31] Rather, it was separated by 'specific errors, specific theological notions, badly, misleadingly, erroneously and arbitrarily construed, of a type which may easily arise within the Reformed Confession itself without necessitating disruption'.[32] The contrast between conflicting doctrinal views does not consist in an antithesis between church and anti-church, or even non-church, but in an 'antithesis between various *theological schools or movements within the same Church* and its basically agreed confession'.[33] Any assertion of these tensions implies that they will finally be overcome.[34] It almost sounds like an overture to the Leuenberg Concord of 1973 when Barth, as early as 1938, defines the goal of the task of Protestant dogmatics as the 'overcoming of tensions' and the 'working out of a common interpretation of the confession'.[35]

This ecumenical openness has to be taken into account in light of how lucidly and concisely Barth outlined the Reformed perspective which oriented his theology. *Church Dogmatics* is a set of texts that illustrate the *Reformed* view of the Gospel as an insight of the Protestant Church and thus as a concern of the *one whole* church of Jesus Christ:

> For us, therefore, Church dogmatics is necessarily Reformed dogmatics. By this we mean the dogmatics of the particular Church which was purified and reconstituted by the work of Calvin and the confession which sealed his testimony. We mean the dogmatics of the Church which hears the Word of God in this determination imposed upon it.[36]

It is recognised to be the 'best' dogmatics, [37] for the errors of the other Protestant denominations are taken so seriously 'that in view of them

---

[31] See *CD* I/2, 831 and 829 [929 and 927].
[32] Ibid., 831–832 [929].
[33] Ibid., 832 (emphasis in original) [930].
[34] Ibid., 835 [933].
[35] Ibid., 835 [933].
[36] Ibid., 831 [928f].
[37] Ibid., 831 [929].

we hold fast to the testimony of the purer doctrine and therefore the special form of the Reformed Church and theology'.[38] Nevertheless, this is not to be understood in confessionalistic terms, but as being aimed at the goal of Reformed dogmatics, namely to work in a particular way towards the overcoming of doctrinal differences within the Protestant church. In respect of Roman Catholic dogmatics, Barth writes of a 'real dogmatic intolerance', albeit with a clear ecumenical intention.[39] Reviewing the Barmen Declaration and the conflict with National Socialism within and outside the church, both of which were not insignificantly influenced by his views, Barth could even allude to the self-understanding which Calvin and earlier Calvinists had occasionally expressed, namely 'that as the Reformed Church we are the real, true and genuine Lutherans'.[40] With this in mind, 'a certain "Calvinisation"'[41] of other Protestant denominations may be expected, as they may be expected to address inner-Protestant differences as differences of a theological school rather than as differences that could separate denominations.

As a prominent Reformed teacher of the Christian church, Barth promoted new formulations of central insights from the theology of the Reformation. These included a further development of Christology, a redefinition of the relation between Law and Gospel and a reconnection of the concepts of justification and justice. His new definition of the doctrine of election attracted much attention and impacted widely on the Protestant Church, though awareness of the way it informed his overall work and related theological problems was not always present. Barth's interpretation of the Reformational doctrine of justification, drawing on Calvin's understanding of justification and sanctification, gave fresh impetus to the ecumenical debate. And more even than that, the renewal and reconstruction of the traditional Protestant body of teaching rendered Barth's *Church Dogmatics* both a productive challenge to other Christian churches and an impressive example of the ecumenical character of Reformed theology.

Further reading

Von Balthasar, Hans Urs. *The Theology of Karl Barth. Exposition and Interpretation.* San Francisco: Ignatius Press, 1992.

---

[38] Ibid., 832 [930].
[39] Ibid., 827 [924].
[40] Ibid., 839 [938].
[41] Ibid., 838 [938].

Burnett, Richard E. (ed.). *Westminster Handbook to Karl Barth*. Louisville, KY: Westminster John Knox, 2013.

Busch, Eberhard. *Karl Barth: His Life from Letters and Autobiographical Texts*, 2nd ed. Translated by John Bowden. Philadelphia: Fortress, 1976.

The Great Passion. An Introduction to Karl Barth's Theology. Translated by Darrell L. Guder and Judith J. Guder. Grand Rapids, MI: Eerdmans, 2004.

Hart, Trevor A. *Regarding Karl Barth. Toward a Reading of His Theology*. Carlisle: Paternoster, 1999.

Hunsinger, George. *How to Read Karl Barth. The Shape of his Theology*. New York: Oxford University Press, 1991.

Mangina, Joseph L. *Karl Barth. Theologian of Christian Witness*. Aldershot, UK: Ashgate, 2004.

McCormack, Bruce L. *Karl Barth's Critically Realistic Dialectical Theology*. Oxford: Clarendon Press, 1995.

Morgan, Densil. *The SPCK Introduction to Karl Barth*. London: SPCK, 2010.

Torrance, Thomas F. *Karl Barth. Biblical and Evangelical Theologian*. Edinburgh: T&T Clark, 1990.

Webster, John. *Karl Barth*. London: T&T Clark, 2000.

(ed.). *Cambridge Companion to Karl Barth*. Cambridge: Cambridge University Press, 2000.

Part III

Theological contexts

13 Reformed theology and puritanism

SUSAN HARDMAN MOORE

'Theology ... is of all the arts the most supreme, most noble, the masterplan ... a living to God ... as well as a speaking of God.' So wrote William Ames (1576–1633), an English Reformed theologian with influence in the Old World and the New.[1] Ames's definition of theology as not only 'speaking of God' but also 'living to God' pinned intellect and devotion together in a way characteristic of the puritan ethos. The puritan movement sprang up in England during the reign of Elizabeth I, in the mid-sixteenth century. It became a significant factor in some key events of the strife-torn seventeenth century, both in the British Isles and – through migration – in North America. From the beginning, the theological bearings of puritanism were strongly Reformed. This chapter explores the genesis and development of the movement, and the diversity of doctrinal positions within it, and offers some suggestions about its theological significance for the Reformed tradition.

PURITANISM: DEFINITION AND CONTEXT

What was puritanism? In recent scholarship, the meaning of 'puritan', let alone its '-ism', has been highly contentious. Defining the term has become a self-perpetuating industry, with every study obliged to start with a stab at it (this chapter no exception).[2] Admittedly, theologians have not found this such a pressing issue: for a good while, theological discussion focused on 'Calvin versus the Calvinists' – whether later

---

[1] W. Ames, *Medulla Theologiæ* (London, 1629), 3.
[2] Collinson, 'Antipuritanism', in *The Cambridge Companion to Puritanism*, edited by J. Coffey and C. H. Lim (Cambridge: Cambridge University Press, 2008), 19–33; Lake, 'Defining Puritanism – again?', in *Puritanism: Transatlantic Perspectives on a Seventeenth-Century Anglo-American Faith*, edited by F. J. Bremer (Boston: Massachusetts Historical Society, 1993), 3–29; J. Morgan, *Godly Learning: Puritan Attitudes towards Reason, Learning and Education, 1560–1640* (Cambridge: Cambridge University Press, 1986), 9–22.

puritans betrayed Calvin's insights – but now the parameters of debate have shifted, to explore the rich variety of opinions aired in Reformed circles.[3] Historians, however, still puzzle endlessly over what 'puritan' meant in its original setting. Like 'papist', puritan was a term of abuse minted in the heat of controversy and resented by those on the receiving end. Most puritans preferred to call themselves 'the godly'. So, given this polemical context, who were the puritans? Once, historians were content to define puritan in a way that would have been familiar to their Elizabethan critics: as defiant nonconformists or, if more radical, as 'separatists' who abandoned the Church of England to join illegal clandestine congregations. Today, historians are acutely aware of the pitfalls of seeing puritanism through the lens of stereotypes put out by the movement's opponents. The picture that has emerged bucks the binary divide between 'puritan' and 'Anglican' found in older studies. It is clear how interwoven with the establishment many so-called puritans were, and also how their convictions took fluid shape in practice, depending on circumstance. This makes it extremely difficult to nail down a general definition: 'the coherence of our concept of puritanism is dependent upon our knowing as little about particular puritans as possible'.[4] Many historians jettison the monolithic label 'puritanism' and instead sketch out the puritan worldview in the subtle shades of individual case histories. An outcome of this approach is that puritanism is defined less by attitudes to questions of liturgy or ecclesiology or even (in the early decades of the movement) to key points in Reformed theology. Instead, puritans are seen as part of a religious spectrum – 'the hotter sort of protestants'[5] – in an England still working out a long process of Reformation.

England's path to Protestantism had been full of twists and turns. To understand puritanism and its affinity with Reformed theology, a sense of the context is important. The puritan movement originated from a drive by keen Protestants to carry forward aspects of reformation neglected, in their view, by the Elizabethan Settlement of 1559. In the mid-1530s Henry VIII broke with Rome but never embraced Protestant

---

3   R. A. Muller, 'Diversity in the Reformed Tradition: A Historiographical Introduction', in *Drawne into Controversie: Reformed Theological Diversity and Debates within Seventeenth-Century British Puritanism*, edited by M. A. G. Haykin and M. Jones (Göttingen: Vandenhoeck & Ruprecht, 2011), 11–30.

4   Collinson, 'Antipuritanism', 24.

5   Collinson, *The Elizabethan Puritan Movement* (London: Jonathan Cape, 1967), 27, quoting Wiburn, *A checke or reproofe of M. Howlet's untimely shreeching* (London, 1581), f. 15v; Wiburn was quoting the Jesuit Robert Parsons, *A Brief Discours* (1580), f. 39v.

doctrine. During the reign of Henry's son Edward VI (1547–1553), the English church adopted Protestantism, only to have the authority of Rome restored by Mary I (1553–1558). Elizabeth I (1558–1603) cast off Rome once again. With her imprimatur, the Thirty-Nine Articles of 1563 endorsed Protestant doctrine, including 'predestination to life' (Article XVII). Elizabeth's actions, with the benefit of hindsight, took England firmly into the Protestant camp. Nonetheless, at the time, the prospects for Protestantism looked rather fragile. As a result, Elizabeth and her government wanted no diversity of religious practice. At this point in English history (and for long after – except for a bold experiment under Oliver Cromwell) the idea of religious toleration was alien. The bedrock of Elizabeth's religious settlement was the Act of Uniformity (1559), which specified that every minister must use the Book of Common Prayer, with all its set prayers and ceremonies; in addition, lay people could be fined twelve pence on every occasion they missed worship on Sundays or holy days. The Act was to be enforced by archbishops, bishops and their officers, and by civil Justices of the Peace. Elizabeth, famously, did not want to 'make windows into men's souls', but by insisting on outward uniformity she hoped to create religious and political stability. Under her, established religion trod a narrow line: too Protestant for those with Roman Catholic sympathies, but not nearly Reformed enough for zealous Protestants – some of whom had tasted religion in Zürich and Geneva while in exile under Mary I, and now wanted more of the same at home. As a result, both Roman Catholics and Protestants pressed the boundaries of Elizabeth's religious settlement, vying for the souls of the nation.

Setting the rise of the puritan movement in this context – and leaving aside consideration of its affinity with Reformed theology for a moment – it is clear how decisions about whether to conform to ceremonies prescribed by the Act of Uniformity could create thorny questions of conscience. Around 1565, controversy boiled up over the requirement for clergy to wear the alb, cope and surplice – liturgical garments that committed Protestants regarded as remnants of 'popery'. It was at this point that the word 'puritan' seems to have been coined by the movement's opponents: 'we know to wear in the church holy vestments, and to be appareled priestlike seemeth so absurd to the Puritans of our country, to the zealous gospellers of Geneva'.[6]

---

[6] Thomas Stapleton, *A Fortresse of the Faith* (Antwerp, 1565), f. 134v. Stapleton (1535–1598), a Roman Catholic exile in the Low Countries, wanted to persuade the English back to Rome.

From this first appearance in the 1560s until its influence waned post-1660 (in England at least), puritanism evolved through different phases, shaped by pretty seismic shifts in the political context. In tandem, its relation with Reformed theology shifted and changed.

A 'CALVINIST CONSENSUS', 1560–1625

From Elizabethan times until around the Synod of Dort (1618–1619), a 'Calvinist consensus' existed in the Church of England; or so revisionist historians have argued since the 1980s, abandoning the old distinction between 'Anglican' and 'puritan'. It would perhaps be more accurate to term this a 'Reformed' consensus, not simply 'Calvinist', since its theology reflected the diversity of the European Reformed tradition. But the key point is this: for more than half a century, Reformed theology stood at the heart, not the edge, of the Church of England.

The centrality of Reformed theology can be illustrated by a controversy of the 1590s, in which the Archbishop of Canterbury saw off a challenge to Reformed orthodoxy. Archbishop John Whitgift (ca. 1530–1604) – no friend to puritan nonconformists but a correspondent and financial supporter of Theodore Beza and the church in Geneva – opposed the views of Peter Baro (1534–1599), a French Huguenot who had become Lady Margaret Professor of Divinity at the University of Cambridge. At that time, Reformed thought on predestination was well represented at Cambridge, not least by William Perkins (1558–1602), fellow and tutor at Christ's, who was making an international impact with his book *Armilla Aurea* (1590), published in English as *A Golden Chain* (1591). Against the prevailing views of Perkins and of his colleague William Whitaker (1547/1548–1595), Regius Professor of Divinity, Baro questioned the Reformed understanding of predestination. He used a scholastic distinction between the antecedent and consequent will of God, to argue that God might want the salvation of all (antecedent will) but in the context of human free will (consequent will) achieves the best outcome: mercy for those who turn to God, justice for those who do not. This Cambridge controversy erupted a decade before the storm in the Dutch Reformed Church over the ideas of Jacobus Arminius (1560–1609).[7] When the dispute came to the attention of Archbishop Whitgift, he resisted Baro. Reform-minded English Protestants had long

---

[7] Lake, *Moderate Puritans and the Elizabethan Church* (Cambridge: Cambridge University Press, 1982), 218–242; N. Tyacke, *Anti-Calvinists: The Rise of English Arminianism, c. 1590–1640* (Oxford: Clarendon Press, 1987), 29–33.

argued that the glancing reference to predestination in the Thirty-Nine Articles was not enough. Whitgift sent out the Lambeth Articles (1595) to clarify doctrine in a Reformed direction: 'God from eternity has predestined some men to life, and reprobated some to death.' This move offended Queen Elizabeth, who – probably more alarmed by doctrine being spelt out in detail than by the specifics – rapped her archbishop's knuckles and stripped the articles of any official status.[8] In spite of her intervention, Baro still found himself at odds with a religious establishment that favoured Reformed theology, and was soon ejected from his post as a Cambridge professor.

The controversy surrounding Baro shows how Reformed theology – at least as abstract doctrine – occupied the mainstream. However, the practicalities of Reformed church order and liturgy were always another matter. Successive archbishops, backed by Elizabeth I and her successor James I, resisted puritan campaigns to replace bishops and priests with presbyters. Calls for radical reform of the Book of Common Prayer – to its critics, 'an unperfect book, culled ... out of that popish dunghill the Mass book' – fell on deaf ears.[9] The mismatch between the establishment's broad acceptance of Reformed theology but sharp rejection of Reformed practice shaped the evolution of the puritan movement. After efforts to bring national reform peaked and faltered in the 1570s, the movement threw all its energies into bringing reformation at a local level. By 1603, when King James came to the throne, puritanism was strong in London and in pockets across England: East Anglia, Yorkshire, Lancashire and Cheshire, Devon and Dorset, Kent and Sussex. The movement was marked out by a keen appetite for 'voluntary religion', above and beyond what was required by law.

Reformed theology animated puritan religious culture, through preaching and in print. From the start, the puritan movement took to sermons with gusto, promoting the 'art of hearing' not only on Sundays but also on weekdays and special fast days. Sermons usually lasted at least an hour. Where a concentration of parish churches would allow it, lay enthusiasts 'gadded' from sermon to sermon: once, in London, the wood-turner Nehemiah Wallington (1598–1658) heard nineteen in a week.[10] Church officials often turned a blind eye to ministers'

---

[8] Lambeth Articles (1595): Schaff, *Creeds of Christendom* (New York: Harper & Brothers, 1877), III, 523–524. The Irish Articles of 1615 adopted this Reformed emphasis.

[9] [J. Field and T. Wilcox,] *An Admonition to the Parliament* (London, 1572), in *Puritan Manifestoes*, edited by W. H. Frere and C. E. Douglas (London: SPCK, 1954), 21.

[10] A. Hunt, *The Art of Hearing: English Preachers and Their Audiences, 1590–1640* (Cambridge: Cambridge University Press, 2010), 204–205, 188–189.

nonconformity because their able preaching stopped a drift back to Roman Catholicism. If the authorities decided to insist a minister must conform or face suspension, a puritan preacher might suppress his scruples about 'ungodly' vestments or ceremonies, at least for a time – a pragmatic compromise for the greater good of keeping access to his pulpit. Some scholars have argued that preachers steered around the Reformed doctrine of predestination, because it was hard to square with promoting moral responsibility; others have argued that it was often preached, but in a harsh divisive way. Recently, Arnold Hunt and Leif Dixon have shown how preachers tackled predestination in a confident and pastoral manner, as a 'comfortable doctrine' that encouraged assurance by building justification on the foundation of election.[11] From the 1590s 'godly reading' became increasingly important to puritan religious culture. Books poured from the presses: Bibles, Bible-reading aids, sermons and devotional handbooks, guides to holy living.[12] The puritan mindset put godliness next to (not cleanliness) but literacy. Reading Scripture and 'other sound and godly authors' was highly commended. New readers could cut their teeth on simple outlines of Reformed theology such as William Perkins' *Six Principles*.[13] As more people became literate, print and pulpit complemented one another as channels for truth: 'the Writings of Divines are nothing else but a preaching the Gospel to the eye, as the voice preacheth it to the ear'.[14]

All this required well-educated clergy. A Reformed agenda dictated the shape of 'godly learning'. During the reign of Queen Elizabeth, Reformed ideas took hold at Oxford and Cambridge, especially at puritan hothouses such as Emmanuel College, Cambridge. As in other academies across Europe – Geneva, Heidelberg, Leiden, Franeker, Saumur – the curriculum was rewritten to give it a Reformed stamp.[15] The priority was to equip ministers of the Word to interpret Scripture and communicate its meaning. Learning biblical languages was central,

[11] Hunt, *Art of Hearing*, 343–389; L. Dixon, *Practical Predestinarians in England, c.1590–1640* (Farnham, UK: Ashgate, 2014), 253–302.

[12] I. Green, *Print and Protestantism in Early Modern England* (Oxford: Oxford University Press, 2000).

[13] A. Cambers, *Godly Reading: Print, Manuscript and Puritanism in England, 1580–1720* (Cambridge: Cambridge University Press, 2011), 55; William Perkins, *The Foundation of Christian Religion, gathered into Six Principles*, a catechism first published in 1590 and frequently reprinted.

[14] Richard Baxter's *Christian Directory* (1673), cited by Hunt, *Art of Hearing*, 393.

[15] Morgan, *Godly Learning*, 226–271; R. A. Muller, 'Calling, Character, Piety, and Learning: Paradigms for Theological Education', in *After Calvin: Studies in the Development of a Theological Tradition* (Oxford: Oxford University Press, 2003), 105–121.

as was skill in rhetoric, and the ability to use logic to steer rhetoric. At Cambridge, influential academics such as Perkins adopted the method of the French Reformed thinker, Peter Ramus (Pierre de la Ramée, 1515–1572).[16] Ramism set out ideas with a stripped-down logic, arranged in a series of binary possibilities that moved from the general to the particular. It also stressed the need to combine head and heart, analysis and application, 'speaking of God' and 'living to God'. Ramist exposition spread to puritan circles beyond the universities, in numerous tracts and printed sermons, and through handbooks such as Dudley Fenner's *The Arts of Logic and Rhetoric* (1584), which gave worked examples of applying Ramist method to exegesis and Christian instruction. The ethos of puritanism promoted a commitment to the discipline of godly learning, at university and long after. For a time, 'prophesyings' (preaching exercises modelled on Reformed practice in Zürich and elsewhere in Europe) acted as a means of continuing education, but Elizabeth I thought they were subversive, a cover for Presbyterianism. She suppressed the practice in 1577.[17] Later, in James I's reign, 'household seminaries' became common: experienced clergy opened their doors to take in and mentor new graduates.[18] Reformed theology was always fundamental. A popular guide to the qualities of good minister insisted preachers should know the confessions 'of particular Churches now reformed', the Heidelberg Catechism, and other catechisms of 'the most famously learned and soundest Divines, such as are the *Institutions* of Calvin and Ursinus his Catechisme'.[19]

The pervasiveness of Reformed theology in the puritan movement never made it monochromatic. As in the wider European tradition, plenty of debate happened within the bounds of what counted as 'orthodoxy'. One key example is in differences over the details of predestination. Although all agreed that God's decree of election and reprobation took place in eternity, precisely when – in terms of logical priority rather than crude chronology – did it translate into salvation history? Some ('supralapsarians') thought this took place *before* the Fall: this made unfallen humanity the object of the decree, and so placed the Fall within God's decree. Others ('infralapsarians'), keen to avoid making God seem the

---

[16] See Chapter 14 by Dolf te Velde's, 'Reformed Theology and Scholasticism', in this volume.

[17] Collinson, *Elizabethan Puritan Movement*, 168–207. The Archbishop of Canterbury, Edmund Grindal (1519–1583), resisted the Queen's order and was removed from office.

[18] T. Webster, *Godly Clergy in Early Stuart England* (Cambridge: Cambridge University Press, 1997), 23–35.

[19] Richard Bernard, *The Faithful Shepherd* (London, 1621), 62.

author of sin, located God's decree *after* the Fall, and so for fallen humanity. Both strands of opinion co-existed in Reformed tradition and both were represented, for example, in arguments at the Synod of Dort.[20] In England, William Perkins put the supralapsarian position in the 1590s; later, John Preston (1587–1628), a puritan who in 1621 became chaplain to King James's son Charles, made a case for the infralapsarian view.[21]

Another example of diversity was over the extent of Christ's atonement. Did Christ die for the elect only, or for all? On one hand, limiting the salvific effect of Christ's death to the elect (particularism) meant Christ's saving work was always effective, but made preaching seem redundant. On the other hand, the belief that Christ died for all (universalism) ratified the need for preaching the Gospel but raised the awkward question of why Christ's death had no effect for so many. Perkins was a powerful spokesperson for limited atonement. Preston, with others such as the Irish archbishop James Ussher (1581–1656) and John Davenant (ca. 1572–1641), bishop of Salisbury, argued instead for 'hypothetical universalism': Christ truly died for all, but his death had no effect on those who did not recognize his saving work; their attitude meant Christ's blood was 'shed in vain'.[22] To avoid the charge that this made salvation conditional on faith, advocates of hypothetical universalism kept predestination in the picture: Christ's death for all showed God's loving-kindness, but would not bring faith in all; rather, it was God's secret electing grace that created faith in some but left others in sin. Jonathan Moore has argued that this view represents a 'softening' of Reformed theology, but Richard Muller prefers to see a streak of hypothetical universalism in Reformed circles from the start, always a 'dissident, subordinate stream of the tradition'.[23]

A further area for debate, increasingly fractious, concerned the role of moral discipline in the Christian life. William Ames defined theology as not only 'speaking of God', but 'living to God'. A stress on discipline – what Theodore Bozeman calls 'the precisianist strain'[24] – was for many

---

[20] J. V. Fesko, 'Lapsarian Diversity at the Synod of Dort', in *Drawne into Controversie*, 99–123.

[21] J. D. Moore, *English Hypothetical Universalism: John Preston and the Softening of Reformed Theology* (Grand Rapids, MI: Eerdmans, 2007), 36–38, 81–83; R. A. Muller, *Christ and the Decree* (Grand Rapids, MI: Baker Academic, 2008), 164–171.

[22] Preston, cited by Moore, *English Hypothetical Universalism*, 109.

[23] Moore, *English Hypothetical Universalism*; Muller, 'Diversity in the Reformed Tradition', in *Drawne into Controversie*, 25.

[24] T. D. Bozeman, *The Precisianist Strain: Disciplinary Religion and the Antinomian Backlash in Puritanism to 1638* (Chapel Hill: University of North Carolina Press, 2004).

in the puritan movement a crucial aspect of interpreting conversion, assurance, and the Christian life. But not everyone agreed. The roots of controversy lay in different understandings of the role of the Law, and also of the nature of the new covenant of grace. The broad hinterland of Protestant thinking about the relation of Law and Gospel is important here. Lutherans saw an antithesis between Law and Gospel, but with Gospel ultimately overwhelming and negating Law. The Reformed saw the same antithesis in relation to justification but also saw the Gospel as fulfilling and transforming Law in relation to sanctification (which, together with justification, was the fruit of union with Christ for the elect). In the power of the Spirit, the Law had a purpose within the covenant of grace – to foster holiness. This understanding brought the covenant at Sinai within the covenant of grace: although the ceremonial functions of Mosaic law had been abrogated in Christ, its moral dimensions still applied to Christians, as a spur to sanctification. Calvin spelt this out as the 'principal use' of the Law.[25] In consequence, as Reformed covenant theology evolved towards the end of the sixteenth century, it allowed for the covenant of grace to be simultaneously unconditional and conditional. The covenant was fundamentally unconditional, a unilateral act of grace, underwritten by election; yet it was also conditional, because God set requirements for his covenant people, including faith and obedience. How should unconditional and conditional be weighed up in relation to each other? At one extreme, God's unconditional love could be said to determine everything (raising the prospect of 'antinomianism' – of which more in a moment); at the other, the essential need to meet God's covenant conditions could be stressed (raising suspicions of legalism). Most in the puritan mainstream took up points on a spectrum between these extremes. Richard Sibbes (ca. 1577–1635), a popular London preacher, tended to emphasise the unconditional character of God's covenant. For him, the best image for the covenant was marriage, a contract full of affection, and assurance of salvation came by looking for the workings of God's grace in interior religious experience – immediate, mystical, personal. In contrast, William Perkins tended to focus on covenant conditions, arguing that the elect must live by the commandments. For him, the best image for the covenant was a legal contract, with requirements; assurance

---

[25] John Calvin, *Institutes of the Christian Religion*, edited by John T. McNeill and translated by Ford Lewis Battles. Library of Christian Classics. 2 vols. (Philadelphia: Westminster, 1960), II.vii.12–13.

could best be found by self-examination, looking for God's grace at work in small steps of Christian faith and duty.[26]

Such debates within the puritan movement need to be mapped onto the diversity of European Reformed theology, but should also be seen in relation to threats to true religion in England, or, at least, to what 'the godly' perceived (rightly or wrongly) as threats. Fears of a Roman Catholic comeback were ever-present. England had returned to Rome once, under Mary Tudor, and this might happen again. The threat level increased after Spanish forces overwhelmed Protestants in the German Palatinate in 1620, and after Charles I's marriage to a French Roman Catholic, Henrietta Maria, in 1625. First cousin to the threat from Roman Catholicism was Arminianism. One writer saw Arminianism, with its teaching on free will and universal grace, as 'a mere stirrup to help men into the saddle of Popery'.[27] Arminian ideas made headway at the universities of Oxford and Cambridge early in the seventeenth century, and were only temporarily halted by the anti-Arminian rulings of the Synod of Dort. The effect of Dort in England was minimal: King James endorsed Dort's decrees informally, but denied them any official status.[28] Another threat emerged: antinomianism. The word 'antinomian' (from anti-νόμος, against law) was, like 'puritan', coined in the heat of debate and is just as slippery to define. An early antinomian, the minister John Eaton (ca. 1574–1641), argued from around 1615 that the Law had no meaning for a Christian because God looked at the elect, justified from eternity in Christ, and saw no sin – which, to critics of antinomianism at least, made obedience to God's Law seem completely irrelevant. Some have seen antinomianism as a reaction to legalism in the puritan movement, undercutting the stress on moral discipline and 'covenant conditions'.[29] Others, in contrast, play down 'puritan legalism' and suggest antinomianism was a reaction to the rise of Arminianism: a radical rejection of any role for human free will in

---

[26] J. von Rohr, *The Covenant of Grace in Puritan Thought* (Eugene, OR: Wipf & Stock, 1986), 53–85; C. Cohen, *God's Caress: the Psychology of Puritan Religious Experience* (Oxford: Oxford University Press, 1986), 47–74; J. Beeke, 'The Assurance Debate: Key Questions', in *Drawne into Controversie*, 263–283; R. N. Frost, 'Richard Sibbes' Theology of Grace and the Division of English Reformed Theology' (PhD thesis, King's College London, 1996), 175–178.

[27] J. P., *Christ's Confessions and Complaint Concerning his Kingdom and Servants* (London, 1629), 42, 48.

[28] Tyacke, *Anti-Calvinists*, 29–86, 105.

[29] Bozeman, *Precisianist Strain*; David Como, *Blown by the Spirit: Puritanism and the Emergence of an Antinomian Underground in Pre-Civil-War England* (Redwood City: Stanford University Press, 2004).

justification.[30] In the heat of polemics, puritans always drew clear lines between themselves and antinomians, but recent scholarship places antinomianism closer to the heart of puritan debate about the covenant of grace, or at least 'suspended between puritanism and something wholly distinct'.[31] Whatever the case, 'antinomian' would soon become a deadly word for the 'orthodox' godly, conjuring up visions of moral and spiritual anarchy.

The heyday of Reformed consensus in England was over by the close of the 1620s. First came the challenge of the Arminians, then pressure from antinomians and a wide range of radical groups including the anti-Trinitarian Socinians. Puritan engagement with Reformed theology shifted to match these challenges, and in the process Reformed theology became a stronger badge of identity.

THE CHALLENGE OF ARMINIANISM, 1625–1640

Events moved into a new phase after 1625, when Charles I came to the throne. He promoted William Laud (1573–1645) rapidly through the ranks of bishops and made him Archbishop of Canterbury in 1633. Laud can be depicted as a good bureaucrat, an enforcer of conformity, with a love of liturgical ceremony.[32] However, there are strong arguments for seeing religious policy under Charles I and Laud as 'anti-puritan' – even 'anti-Calvinist', doctrinally Arminian. Nicholas Tyacke has documented the case for Laud's efforts to mute and marginalise Reformed talk of predestination. In 1626 Charles I issued a royal proclamation to establish 'the peace and quiet of the Church of England'. Although this was expressed in neutral language, Tyacke argues it was used to suppress debate about predestination at the universities, in the pulpit, and in print. Two years later, Charles instructed universities not to discuss 'those curious points in which the present differences lie' and, Tyacke argues, the king abandoned the neutrality of the 1626 proclamation, by insisting that disputes should be 'shut up in God's promises, as they be generally set forth to us in the Scriptures' – in other words, endorsing

---

[30] R. J. McKelvey, ' "That Error and Pillar of Antinomianism": Eternal Justification', in *Drawne into Controversie*, 223–262; W. Gamble, ' "If Christ fulfilled the Law, we are not bound": the Westminster Assembly against English Antinomian Soteriology, 1643–1647' (PhD thesis, University of Edinburgh, 2014).

[31] T. Cooper, *Fear and Polemic in Seventeenth-Century England: Richard Baxter and Antinomianism* (Farnham, UK: Ashgate, 2001); Como, *Blown by the Spirit*, 438.

[32] K. Sharpe, *The Personal Rule of Charles I* (New Haven, CT and London: Yale University Press, 1992), 275–402.

Arminian universal (general) grace. For Tyacke, the direction of travel is illustrated by a new entry in a standard Latin-English dictionary. In an edition of 1633, dedicated to Laud, the word 'prædestinatiani' appears, defined as 'a kind of heretics that held fatal predestination of every particular matter, person or action, and that all things came to pass and fell out necessarily, especially touching the salvation and damnation of particular men'.[33] In addition, the 1630s saw episcopal campaigns for strict conformity to the Book of Common Prayer, and the introduction of new liturgical practices which to puritans seemed Roman Catholic (such as placing communion tables against the east wall of the chancel, bowing at the name of Jesus). Preachers were put under pressure to comply, or resign. As in the days of Mary Tudor, when many Protestants fled abroad to escape persecution, the godly looked for a way out. Some went to the Netherlands. More – between 13,000 and 20,000 – crossed the Atlantic in search of a 'New England'. Godly families sent their sons to the fledgling Reformed bastion of Harvard, founded in 1636, instead of to the 'corrupted' fountains of learning at Oxford and Cambridge.[34] It has been suggested that Laud was 'the greatest calamity ever visited upon the English Church', because of the divisive character of religious policy in the 1630s.[35] All in all, in this decade, puritanism wore its Reformed identity more defiantly and distinctively than before.

CONFLICT, REFORM, FRAGMENTATION AND 'ORTHODOXY', 1640–1660

In 1640 came another sea-change. Charles I had abandoned ruling with a Parliament in 1629, not least because of incessant cries from puritan Members of Parliament about the threat of 'Papists' and Arminians. But after a Scottish rebellion over religious policy north of the border, he was forced to recall Parliament to raise funds. Before long, Parliament's agenda placed it on a collision course with the King. Laud was arrested and imprisoned, and executed in 1645. Civil War broke out in 1642–1646, and again in 1648–1649 and 1649–1651. John Morrill famously described the English Civil War as 'the last of the Wars of Religion': this has been much debated, but the squeeze on Reformed sensitivities, in theology and

---

[33] Tyacke, *Anti-Calvinists*, 48–50, 183.
[34] S. Hardman Moore, *Pilgrims: New World Settlers and the Call of Home* (New Haven, CT and London: Yale University Press, 2007), 16–34.
[35] Collinson, *The Religion of Protestants: The Church in English Society 1559–1625* (Oxford: Oxford University Press, 1984), 90.

practice, was undoubtedly a factor.[36] A shared commitment to Reformed theology, as well as political resistance to the king, drew the English Parliamentarians to the Presbyterian Scots, and they fought as allies in the First Civil War. By the *Solemn League and Covenant* of 1643 they bound themselves to work for 'the preservation of the reformed religion in the Church of Scotland' and for 'the reformation of religion in the kingdoms of England and Ireland ... according to the Word of God, and the example of the best reformed Churches'.[37]

The documents of the Westminster Assembly, arguably, provide the most formal legacy of puritan engagement with Reformed theology. The Assembly, convened in 1643 as a committee to advise Parliament on religious reform, carried forward the agenda of the *Solemn League and Covenant* with the aid of the formidable Scottish Reformed theologians Samuel Rutherford (ca. 1600–1661) and Robert Baillie (1602–1662). The Assembly, with Parliament's approval, set out the blueprint for a Reformed church: *The Directory of Public Worship* and *Form of Church-Government* in 1645, the *Shorter* and *Longer Catechism* in 1647, and the *Confession of Faith* in 1648. The Assembly's minutes open the door on the discussions – in the Jerusalem Chamber at Westminster Abbey – that hammered these out.[38] Fault-lines in puritanism became apparent over church order, with battles between Presbyterians and Congregationalists. But the Assembly was of a common mind in wanting to create a theological framework that would bring England into line with 'the best reformed churches', and would also see off rising pressure from antinomianism. In the 1630s, when the main threat had been the Arminians, antinomian ideas had spread behind closed doors and in manuscripts passed from hand to hand. In the 1640s, the extent of antinomian sentiment became apparent after censorship collapsed with the advent of Civil War. Suddenly, antinomians had access to pulpits and printing presses. Soldiers in the parliamentary army lapped up the message. Many of the Assembly's early theological debates were galvanised by the need to resist antinomianism.[39] Certainly, by the end of the 1640s the Assembly had set out a pattern for a national Reformed church. But implementing it

---

[36] J. Morrill, 'The Religious Context of the English Civil War', *Transactions of the Royal Historical Society*, Fifth Series 34 (1984), 155–178; C. W. A. Prior and G. Burgess (eds.), *England's Wars of Religion Revisited* (Farnham, UK: Ashgate, 2011).

[37] www.constitution.org/eng/conpuro58.htm (accessed 1 March 2015).

[38] C. Van Dixhoorn (ed.), *The Minutes and Papers of the Westminster Assembly 1643–1652*, 5 vols. (Oxford: Oxford University Press, 2012).

[39] Gamble, ' "If Christ fulfilled the Law, we are not bound" '.

proved impossible. Across the country, religious opinion was becoming increasingly diverse and fragmented.[40]

What came of the puritan vision for 'godly reformation'? After Charles I was tried and executed for treason in 1649, the English republic took shape under Oliver Cromwell (1599–1658), who took the title Lord Protector in 1653. Cromwell's power base came from the New Model Army, radical in religion. He quickly established freedom of conscience in matters of faith. Toleration extended to Roman Catholics, to Jews (expelled from England in 1290, permitted to return from 1656), and to all manner of 'radical' religious groups: Baptists, Diggers, Levellers, Muggletonians, Quakers, Ranters, Seekers, Socinians and more. The religious milieu of the 1650s was a world away from the national Reformed church envisioned by the Westminster Assembly. Many historians take a dim view of puritan achievements under Cromwell: defeat snatched from the jaws of victory. Yet Bernard Capp, from fine-grained research into local activity, judges that 'Over the decade, many Reformers took advantage of the most favourable circumstances they would ever enjoy … And if they fell far short of impossibly ambitious goals, they advanced further than any before them.[41]

A mark of success in the 1650s was the energetic and effective use of Reformed theology to contain radicalism. The 'orthodox' – those who aligned themselves with the Westminster Confession – had to compete in a lively market of religious possibilities. John Owen (1616–1683), one of the most significant Reformed theologians in late seventeenth-century England, strongly supported Cromwell's policy of toleration. Owen managed to combine this with a passion for defending Reformed doctrine. From the 1650s onwards he was a hugely productive writer, known for his polemical dissection of theological error, for his promotion of congregational polity and the right to be nonconformist, and for major works of exegesis and theology – notably his multi-volume commentary on Hebrews (1668–1684) and a series of five books on the Holy Spirit (1674–1693). Many in the puritan movement could not share Owen's enthusiasm for freedom of conscience, because toleration gave no power to enforce 'truth'. In the climate of the 1650s, the case had to be made solely by persuasion. Advocates of mainstream Reformed theology gained privileged access to pulpits, after Cromwell adapted the national parish system to fund a network of public preachers, vetted to

---

[40] J. Morrill, 'The Church in England, 1642–9', in *Reactions to the English Civil War, 1642–1649*, edited by J. Morrill (London: Macmillan, 1982), 89–114.

[41] B. Capp, *England's Culture Wars: Puritan Reformation and Its Enemies in the Interregnum, 1649–1660* (Oxford: Oxford University Press, 2012), 263.

meet a basic standard of orthodoxy. Print was an unmonitored medium, open to all shades of opinion – this catalysed some substantial tomes of Reformed theology, penned in the heat of campaigns to uphold 'truth'. Attacks on the doctrine of the Trinity had increased from the 1640s, drawing on the ideas of the Italian thinker Faustus Socinus (1539–1604). The need to refute Socinian ideas underlies the Trinitarian stress of theologians such as Owen, and of his equally distinguished sparring partner, Richard Baxter (1615–1691).[42] On the whole – in no small part due to robust use of Reformed theology as a safeguard – the bark of religious radicals proved worse than their bite.

AFTER 1660: THE PURITAN LEGACY?

Beyond 1660, the situation for the puritan movement changed again. After Cromwell's death in 1658, pressure grew for the restoration of the monarchy. Once Charles II came to the throne in 1660 and restored episcopacy to the English church, the impetus of puritanism dissolved into nonconformist communities marked by 'the experience of defeat'.[43] In the longer term, Protestant nonconformity, rooted almost entirely in the Reformed tradition until the time of John Wesley (1703–1791), played a striking role in British politics, culture and society down to the twentieth century. Reformed theology also continued to play a part in the Church of England: the 'conforming Reformed' continued to resist Arminianism and made a comeback in eighteenth-century evangelicalism.[44]

This chapter has looked at the evolution of the puritan movement in England, and its relation to Reformed theology from around 1560 to 1660. From the start, puritanism was strongly orientated towards Reformed theology – although modern arguments for a Reformed consensus in the Elizabethan and Jacobean church mean that this was not such a distinctive hallmark as was once thought. Over time, puritan identity became more closely bound up with asserting Reformed theology, especially in response to challenges posed by Arminians and antinomians. In this regard, the Westminster Confession is perhaps the

[42] C. H. Lim, *Mystery Unveiled: the Crisis of the Trinity in Early Modern England* (Oxford: Oxford University Press, 2012); K. Kapic, *Communion with God: the Divine and the Human in the Theology of John Owen* (Grand Rapids, MI: Baker Academic, 2007); S. J. G. Burton, *The Hallowing of Logic: the Trinitarian Method of Richard Baxter's Methodus Theologiae* (Leiden and Boston: Brill, 2012).

[43] From Christopher Hill's title, *The Experience of Defeat: Milton and Some Contemporaries* (London: Faber, 1984).

[44] S. Hampton, *Anti-Arminians: The Anglican Reformed Tradition from Charles II to George I* (Oxford: Oxford University Press, 2008), 267–268, 270.

most formal legacy of English puritan commitment to Reformed theology. Ironically, the Westminster Confession made its mark not in the birthplace of puritanism, England, but in the wider world: in Scotland, New England and around the globe through migrants and missionaries in the Presbyterian tradition.

What theological significance does puritanism have for the Reformed tradition? Too often, seventeenth-century puritans have been hijacked to win debates that are not of their making: for example, the wrangles over 'Calvin versus the Calvinists', which reflect neo-orthodox preoccupations. In recent research, there has been a move away from this. Theologians and historians are learning to unwrap the past and see it in its own terms, understanding the polemical contexts that shaped debate and looking deeper into the content and the method of its theology. A compelling aspect of puritan religious culture is its determination to make Reformed theology connective, linking systematic questions with practical concerns. It is dangerous to try and pin down 'the puritan style', but William Ames's definition of theology must come close: 'a living to God' as well as 'a speaking of God'.

Further reading

Bozeman, T. D. *The Precisianist Strain: Disciplinary Religion and the Antinomian Backlash in Puritanism to 1638*. Chapel Hill: University of North Carolina Press, 2004.

Cambers, A. *Godly Reading: Print, Manuscript and Puritanism in England, 1580–1720*. Cambridge: Cambridge University Press, 2011.

Coffey, J. and P. C. H. Lim (eds.). *The Cambridge Companion to Puritanism*. Cambridge: Cambridge University Press, 2008.

Como, D. *Blown by the Spirit: Puritanism and the Emergence of an Antinomian Underground in Pre-Civil-War England*. Stanford, CA: Stanford University Press, 2004.

Durston, C. and J. Eales. *The Culture of English Puritanism, 1560–1700*. Basingstoke, UK: Macmillan, 1996.

Haykin, M. A. G. and M. Jones (eds.). *Drawn into Controversie: Reformed Theological Diversity and Debates within Seventeenth-Century British Puritanism*. Göttingen: Vandenhoeck & Ruprecht, 2011.

Hunt, A. *The Art of Hearing: English Preachers and Their Audiences, 1590–1640*. Cambridge: Cambridge University Press, 2010.

Kapic, K. and M. Jones (eds.). *The Ashgate Research Companion to John Owen's Theology*. Farnham, UK: Ashgate, 2012.

Lim, P. C. H. *Mystery Unveiled: The Crisis of the Trinity in Early Modern England*. Oxford: Oxford University Press, 2012.

14 Reformed theology and scholasticism

DOLF TE VELDE

'Reformed scholasticism' refers to a form of theology that is historically situated in the period from ca. 1560 to 1750. It is embedded in the confessional and institutional identity of churches emerging in the Reformed strand of Protestantism, while its texts are written in the distinctive genre of scholasticism. The term 'scholasticism' denotes 'a method applied in theology and philosophy characterised by the use (for both instruction and research) of a constantly recurrent system of concepts, distinctions, definitions, propositional analysis, techniques of reasoning and disputation'.[1] The basic pattern of scholastic discourse begins with a 'question' (*quaestio*), which clearly presents the issue under discussion. This is followed by arguments for and against certain positions in respect of the question, and finally by a solution by means of definitions and distinctions that respond to the various positions.[2] This scholastic method is particularly suitable for instruction, inquiry and discussion at an academic level, and developed in diverse ways within different ecclesiastical contexts: Lutheran, Roman Catholic (with its foremost subtypes of Thomist, Scotist and Jesuit scholasticism) and Reformed. While it is worth noting the structural similarities and vivid interaction between scholastic writers across confessional boundaries,[3] this chapter focuses on the scholasticism typical of the era of 'Reformed orthodoxy' in which the confessional identity of the Reformed churches was being shaped, codified and institutionalised.[4]

---

[1] L. M. de Rijk, *Middeleeuwse wijsbegeerte: Traditie en vernieuwing*, 2nd ed. (Assen: Van Gorcum, 1988), 111 (my translation).

[2] Cf. Richard A. Muller, *After Calvin: Studies in the Development of a Theological Tradition*, Oxford Studies in Historical Theology (Oxford: Oxford University Press, 2003), 27.

[3] Cf. Carl R. Trueman and R. Scott Clark, eds., *Protestant Scholasticism: Essays in Reassessment* (Carlisle: Paternoster, 1999; reprint Eugene [OR]: Wipf and Stock, 2007).

[4] Muller, *After Calvin*, 33–36.

THE EMERGENCE OF REFORMED SCHOLASTICISM

It is somewhat inaccurate to speak of the 'introduction' or 're-introduction' of scholastic method after the Reformation. There can indeed be found critical and negative statements on 'the scholastics' in the works of Martin Luther, John Calvin and other leading Reformers. On closer scrutiny, however, the notion of pitting 'Calvin against the Calvinists' fails to account for continuities in method and doctrine.[5] Scholastic approaches to theology have never been absent from Reformation movements, whether Lutheran or Reformed. This is not surprising, as most of the preachers and teachers who participated in the development of Protestant churches had received formal training in philosophy and theology that was based on some variety of late medieval scholasticism.[6]

From the 1540s onwards, the deployment of scholastic approaches in Reformed theology was stimulated by three factors of practical necessity: confession, polemics and education.

First, alongside the Augsburg Confession authored by Philip Melanchthon, several groups of churches in Switzerland, Germany, France, the Netherlands and the British Isles formulated their own doctrinal standards. Though different in genre from the properly academic forms of scholastic discourse, the array of confessional documents that was produced between the 1550s and the 1570s display a comprehensive and systematic grasp of the main points of the Christian faith, expounded both positively and polemically. Moreover, the intentionally concise and popular presentations of doctrine in the confessions presuppose, and sometimes reflect, the more elaborate and argumentative understanding developed in the schools.

The formation of confessional identities was, second, accompanied by the need for a polemical defence of doctrine. During the sixteenth century, Reformed theologians consistently felt obliged to explain and justify their positions over against the Roman Catholic Church. In Switzerland the refutation of Anabaptist claims also played an important role in theological polemics. Despite the common ground

---

[5]   Willem J. van Asselt and others, *Introduction to Reformed Scholasticism*, Reformed Historical-Theological Studies (Grand Rapids: Reformation Heritage Books, 2011), 17–20.

[6]   On the organization of education in the medieval universities, see Van Asselt and others, *Introduction*, 59–61. On the various ways (*viae*) of scholastic theology in the sixteenth century, see Heiko A. Oberman, *Werden und Wertung der Reformation: Vom Wegestreit zum Glaubenskampf*, Spätscholastik und Reformation vol. 2, 3rd ed. (Tübingen: Mohr Siebeck, 1989), 28–55.

acknowledged by first- and second-generation Reformers such as Luther, Philip Melanchthon, Martin Bucer, Calvin and Heinrich Bullinger, tensions between 'Lutheran' and 'Reformed' or 'Calvinist' theology gradually developed into serious disagreement over issues surrounding the sacraments, Christology and predestination. These doctrinal debates required ability in logical reasoning, conceptual analysis of Scripture and profound knowledge of the patristic and medieval traditions to which the various parties appealed. In short, the defence and elaboration of the key points of Reformed faith demanded a more detailed, argumentative theology than that exhibited in the first-order activity of biblical exegesis and preaching.

Finally, the rapid rise of scholastic forms of Reformed theology was stimulated by the need to train new generations of ministers of the Word. The first and second generations of Reformers had found their way by rediscovering biblical truths, but it was soon realised that the transmission of the Reformed faith would require a methodical system of instruction. For this purpose, new institutions of higher education were founded all over Europe, beginning with the Genevan Academy in 1559 and the almost simultaneous 'Calvinist' reconstruction of the University of Heidelberg during the years 1558–1561. These were soon followed by the foundation of Leiden University in 1575 and of similar academies in Herborn, Franeker, Steinfurt and Saumur. These schools provide the natural and proper context for 'scholastic' theology with a Reformed signature.[7]

REFORMED SCHOLASTICISM IN ITS SUBSEQUENT PHASES

The history of Reformed scholastic theology comprises almost two centuries, from the second half of the sixteenth century to the first half of the eighteenth century. It is customary to divide this long era into

---

[7] On Geneva, see Karin Maag, *Seminary or University? The Genevan Academy and Reformed Higher Education (1560–1620)*, St. Andrews Studies in Reformation History (Aldershot: Scolar Press, 1995). On Heidelberg, see Christoph Strohm, Joseph S. Freedman, and Herman J. Selderhuis, eds., *Späthumanismus und reformierte Konfession: Theologie, Jurisprudenz und Philosophie in Heidelberg an der Wende zum 17. Jahrhundert*, Spätmittelalter und Reformation, new series, vol. 31 (Tübingen: Mohr Siebeck, 2006). On Herborn, see Gerhard Menk, *Die Hohe Schule Herborn in ihrer Frühzeit (1584–1660): Ein Beitrag zum Hochschulwesen des deutschen Kalvinismus im Zeitalter der Gegenreformation*, Veröffentlichungen der Historischen Kommission für Nassau vol. 30 (Wiesbaden: Selbstverlag der Historischen Kommission für Nassau, 1981).

three distinct phases: Early Orthodoxy (1560–1620), High Orthodoxy (1620–1700) and Late Orthodoxy (1700–1790). While such periodization remains somewhat arbitrary, it is justified by important shifts in form, content and context.[8]

In the decades following the deaths of important Reformers such as Calvin and Melanchthon, dozens of their direct or indirect pupils engaged in the elaboration and solidification of the Reformed faith. On the one hand, these efforts show commitment to typically Reformed doctrines, including the principal and authoritative role of Scripture, as well as profiled endorsement of doctrines concerning the Trinity, Christology, justification and predestination. On the other hand, this early phase evidences a wide variety of approaches, as well as occasional uncertainty regarding the more technical and argumentative foundational patterns of doctrine. In the newly founded academies, professors and students soon attained a considerable degree of professionalisation in mastering the subtleties of logic, and created a coherent set of terms and concepts applicable to theology, developing more or less 'systematic' forms for presenting the whole of Christian doctrine. Starting with a rather eclectic use of components from medieval scholastic traditions, Reformed theologians managed to create, within the space of some thirty or forty years, a consistent but flexible form of discourse in academic theology.

From the history of this period of Early Orthodoxy, it is clear that scholastic developments involved tension and debate. Reformed theologians of this era were keen on detecting doctrinal differences and committed to maintaining what they considered to be the necessary standards of sound teaching in the church. Within these parameters, differences of orientation and understanding, which clearly existed within and between Reformed churches from various territories, were discussed in vivid exchanges of arguments. Such conflict could result in official ecclesiastical decisions that either reconciled opposing positions at a higher level or else affirmed one position to the exclusion of others. The latter occurred in the decisions of the Synod of Dordrecht (1618–1619), in which the Remonstrants or Arminians were condemned while an orthodox position with respect to issues of predestination, grace, free will and regeneration was codified in the Canons of Dort.

---

[8] Cf. Van Asselt and others, *Introduction*, 103–104 with Richard A. Muller, *Post-Reformation Reformed Dogmatics: The Rise and Development of Reformed Orthodoxy, ca. 1520 to ca. 1725*, 4 vols. (Grand Rapids: Baker Academic, 2003), vol. I, 30–32 and 60–84.

With the proceedings of this synod, in which church leaders and celebrated theologians from many parts of Europe (including various German territories, Switzerland and England) participated, the first phase of Reformed scholasticism came to a close.

During the era of High Orthodoxy, Reformed scholastic theology functioned as a well-established academic practice. Through the efforts of the preceding generation of theologians, scholastics of the later seventeenth century could build on a balanced and elaborate tradition of Reformed thought. The universities and other academic institutions that had been established around the turn of the seventeenth century constituted a formidable network of scholarly co-operation and exchange, extending from the eastern territories of Poland (Danzig) and Hungary to the western countries of England and Scotland. After the first waves of migration to the New World this network spread to the newly founded colleges of Harvard and Yale. The most important positions in the early dissemination and development of Reformed scholastic theology, until around 1620, were the Genevan Academy and the University of Heidelberg. During the later seventeenth century, the Netherlands took the lead with the establishment of theological faculties at the universities of Leiden, Franeker, Groningen, Utrecht and Harderwijk.[9]

During the decades following 1620, the polemical frontiers of Reformed theology were in a constant state of change. Controversies with the Roman Catholic Church over central issues such as the authority of Scripture, justification by faith alone, grace and predestination continued to elicit extensive treatises. Reformed authors especially targeted opponents from the Jesuit order, who took more extreme 'Romanist' positions than those assumed by Dominican, Franciscan and Augustinian theologians during the era of the Council of Trent. By comparison, debates with Lutheran theologians seem to fade once the confessional identities were mutually defined and the political demarcation of religious territories put an end to the relatively indeterminate situation that prevailed in the third quarter of the sixteenth century. Polemical issues against both Roman Catholics and Lutherans were reduced to the level of excurses or 'commonplaces' in the exposition of Reformed doctrine.

---

[9] The survey of theological education in the Netherlands provided by Christiaan Sepp, *Het godgeleerd onderwijs in Nederland gedurende de 16ᵉ en 17ᵉ eeuw*, 2 vols. (Leiden: De Breuk and Smits, 1873–1874) remains unsurpassed.

In their ongoing activity in this period, Reformed theologians had to face new challenges in the form of debates with 'Arminians' and 'Socinians', two groups of opponents often linked because of common tendencies in their teachings. The rejection of Remonstrant views on grace, regeneration and predestination in the Canons of Dort did not mean the end of controversy in respect of these issues; rather, the newly defined confessional position had to be defended and developed by the next generations of theologians. Scholarship of the last fifty years has devoted considerable attention to the debates surrounding the distinctive views on grace emanating from the Academy of Saumur.[10] These internal Reformed debates show that the matter was not yet closed, even if the margins for deviation from the standards set at Dort were small. The prominent Swiss theologians Francis Turretin and Johann Heinrich Heidegger had a strong hand in the formulation of the *Helvetic Consensus* of 1675, in which the views of Amyraut and his followers were gently but clearly rejected.

The Socinians, often lumped together with the Arminians, posed a considerable threat to Reformed doctrine. Following the mid-sixteenth-century Italian radicals Fausto and Lellio Socinus, the Socinians combined the contention that knowledge of God is possible only through revelation with the attribution of a critical role to human reason in religious matters. In terms of doctrine this position resulted in the denial of the Trinity and of the divine nature of Jesus Christ. Given these heresies, the Socinians faced fierce opposition from Reformed scholastics.[11]

While the Socinians can be considered pre-Enlightenment rationalists, Reformed scholastics were also involved in debates with early Enlightenment thinkers such as René Descartes and Baruch Spinoza. The Netherlands played a central role in facilitating the early confrontation between Reformed orthodoxy and revolutionary alternatives, given the relatively high levels of religious tolerance and press freedom in the Dutch Republic. Leading theologians such as Gisbertus Voetius detected fundamental 'errors' in the rational methodology and metaphysics of

---

[10] Brian G. Armstrong, *Calvin and the Amyraut Heresy: Protestant Scholasticism in Seventeenth-Century France* (Madison: University of Wisconsin Press, 1969); Albert Gootjes, *Claude Pajon (1626–1685) and the Academy of Saumur: The First Controversy Over Grace*, Series in Church History vol. 64 (Leiden: Brill, 2013).

[11] For various aspects of Socinianism, see Martin Mulsow and Jan Rohls, eds., *Socinianism and Arminianism: Antitrinitarians, Calvinists and Cultural Exchange in Seventeenth-Century Europe*, Brill's Studies in Intellectual History vol. 134 (Leiden: Brill, 2005).

Descartes that would not only change philosophical discourse but also overturn the foundations of what they saw as true Christian religion. Reformed scholastics fiercely rejected the propagation of methodical doubt, the foundation of knowledge of God on the 'idea of God' formed by clear and distinct perception, the reduction of all substance to the categories of 'thought' and 'extension' and the extreme nominalism crystallised in Descartes' contention that God can deceive us. At the same time, Descartes won several disciples among philosophers, professors of medicine and even theologians.[12]

The partial acceptance of Cartesian views changed the outlook of Reformed orthodox theology to some extent, but the more radical rationalism of Baruch Spinoza elicited a near unanimous rejection from the Reformed. Spinoza's argument that in the final analysis there is only one substance, which is God, ran counter to the basic Reformed conviction that there is an irreducible ontological distinction between God the Creator and the world created by him. As it was precisely this distinction that safeguarded the contingency of the created world for the Reformed, Spinoza's monistic view was thought to destroy created freedom and to impose fatal necessity on human reality.[13]

After the death of leading orthodox theologians such as Voetius and Turretin, Reformed theology gradually moved in the eighteenth century into the phase of Late Orthodoxy. The following generations of theology professors were more inclined to dismiss the 'Aristotelian' philosophy that had gone hand in hand with Reformed theology in the preceding decades and to adapt their 'system' of doctrine to newer ways of thinking. Illustrative of these developments is the shift that took place between Francis Turretin and his son Jean-Alphonse Turretin on the issue of 'natural theology'. Francis argues against the Socinian view that there is a natural theology, divided into innate and acquired knowledge of God. For him, the human mind is no *tabula rasa* (blank slate): although discursive knowledge is acquired during one's lifetime, there are common apprehensive concepts (*notiones communes*) that

[12] Theo Verbeek, *Descartes and the Dutch: Early Reactions to Cartesian Philosophy 1637–1650* (Carbondale: Southern Illinois University Press, 1992); Aza Goudriaan, *Philosophische Gotteserkenntnis bei Suarez und Descartes im Zusammenhang mit der niederländischen reformierten Theologie und Philosophie des 17. Jahrhunderts* (PhD thesis, Rijksuniversiteit Leiden, 1999); J. Martin Bac, *Perfect Will Theology: Divine Agency in Reformed Scholasticism as against Suárez, Episcopius, Descartes, and Spinoza*, Studies in Church History vol. 42 (Leiden: Brill, 2010).
[13] Cf. Bac, *Perfect Will Theology*, 259–305.

reside in the mind from birth. Still, the function of natural theology is very limited: objectively speaking God reveals himself sufficiently to all people, but subjectively and factually the knowledge derived from natural revelation is not sufficient for salvation. However, with Jean-Alphonse, the importance of natural theology increases enormously. In an attempt to counter rationalist attacks on the Christian religion, he gives Christian faith a rational foundation by way of an expansive natural theology. In his view, faith and reason can never be at odds. From this assumption he infers that knowledge of God can be attained by human reason in principle. However, because this way is difficult and humanity lives in a state of corruption, it is convenient for God to provide an easier way, namely, revelation. The universal existence of religions shows the inability of the human race to attain true knowledge of God. With Jean-Alphonse, the proportions between natural and revealed theology are thus reversed: the earlier Reformed orthodox tradition had held that a few things about God are known to all people but that revelation was needed to give fuller understanding; with the younger Turretin, natural theology comprehends all but a few mysterious doctrines.[14]

During the eighteenth century, Reformed theologians variously allied with an array of contemporary philosophical views, such as Cartesianism (Bernard Pictet), Leibnizian thinking, Wolffianism and other branches of Enlightenment thought. At the same time, orthodox theology that followed seventeenth-century models became less prominent in leading theological academies. Franeker University, for example, saw the more or less traditionally Reformed theologian Herman Witsius operating next to biblical scholar Campegius Vitringa and Enlightenment thinker Herman Alexander Roëll. At Leiden University, Bernardinus de Moor held his chair as the last remaining professor holding a Voetian perspective. The ecclesiastical and theological climate had changed in favour of more 'moderate' and 'Enlightened' versions of the Reformed faith, and the 'Aristotelian' philosophy that had accompanied scholastic Reformed theology for almost two centuries was widely abandoned.[15]

---

[14] See Dolf te Velde, *The Doctrine of God in Reformed Orthodoxy, Karl Barth, and the Utrecht School: A Study in Method and Content*, Studies in Reformed Theology vol. 25 (Leiden: Brill, 2013), 71–73.

[15] For the 'after-history' of Reformed scholasticism, see Muller, *Post-Reformation Reformed Dogmatics*, vol. 1, 81–84.

REFORMED SCHOLASTICISM AS A METHOD OF TEACHING

Contrary to the popular understanding that permeates early twentieth-century literature, scholastic theology is not a fixed system of doctrinal truths; it is first of all a method of doing theology. The emergence of Reformed scholasticism during the second half of the sixteenth century is a fascinating phenomenon in part because this era displayed a lively, even feverish search for the right method. Rather than merely copying the scholastic 'Aristotelian' approach inherited from the medieval past, Reformed theologians and philosophers were involved in a vibrant exchange of ideas concerning the appropriate manner of construing the arts and sciences as 'bodies of knowledge'.

From a contemporary perspective there is often a stark contrast drawn between scholasticism and humanism, with the result that the apparently dynamic and modern outlook of the humanists is regularly favoured, with the scholastics often portrayed as outdated relics of abstract and sterile reasoning. As Erika Rummel has pointed out (following the ground-breaking studies by Paul Oskar Kristeller), the seemingly opposed movements labelled 'humanism' and 'scholasticism' drew on the same resources and faced the same methodological and substantial questions, giving them much common ground. The debate between humanism and scholasticism was largely a propaganda campaign with both sides seeking to gain influence in the constantly developing system of higher education.[16]

A famous antagonist in this 'war on education', especially in connection with Reformed theology, was Peter Ramus (Pierre de la Ramée, 1515–1572). Ramism has been praised as a method aiming at practical piety and a purification of theological language, pursuing biblical simplicity without the scholastic intricacies that marked the Aristotelianism of, for example, Calvin's successor Theodore Beza. Ramus' approach is characterised by: first, a humanist demand to return to an 'authentic' reading of Aristotle's works; second, an emphasis on a clear and simple presentation of the disciplines to be taught; third, a 'universal method' divided into 'invention' and 'judgement' in which the Aristotelian instruments of 'categories' and 'syllogism' are replaced by 'commonplaces' (*topoi* or *loci communes*) and an ongoing sequence of 'definition'

---

[16] Erika Rummel, *The Humanist-Scholastic Debate in the Renaissance and Reformation*, Harvard Historical Studies vol. 120 (Cambridge [MA]: Harvard University Press, 1995).

and 'division'. Recent scholarship acknowledges that Ramist philosophy was widely applied as a method of teaching in many Reformed academies. Ramist patterns were also used by several authors to structure their exposition of Christian doctrine. At the same time, theologians and philosophers have pointed to the lack of precision in logical analysis and the omission of metaphysics that characterised Ramus' philosophy. In sum, Ramism played an important role in the organisation of Reformed higher education and in the structural outlook of Reformed dogmatics. It cannot be maintained, however, that it constituted a full-fledged alternative to more 'Aristotelian' variants of Reformed thought.[17]

In the formation of the Reformed scholastic landscape, the influence of Philip Melanchthon can hardly be overestimated. After an initial phase of anti-scholastic sentiment, Melanchthon assumed the task of supporting the Reformation with a remarkably successful program of educational reforms. A humanist scholar of unique stature, he managed to incorporate in his 'school philosophy' the basic elements of both scholastic philosophy and humanist studies.[18] Some prominent Reformed theologians were also skilled logicians, for example, Zacharias Ursinus, Bartholomaeus Keckermann and Amandus Polanus. They participated in the debates of their time concerning methodology, defending Aristotle against Ramus and other innovators, and publishing their own reflections on logical analysis.[19]

Besides the methodological efforts made by these theologians, the contribution of Reformed philosophers is also important. Here the institutional aspect of Reformed scholasticism comes into play, particularly given the arrangement of the faculties. In general, institutions of higher education in the Reformed territories combined the original medieval model of the university with additions and new emphases from the humanist movement. Before entering one of the 'higher' faculties of theology, law or medicine, students were required to spend a number of years in the arts or philosophy faculty. Here they were trained in Greek and Latin, in logic and rhetoric, in mathematics and physics, in ethics and politics, and in some cases also in metaphysics.[20] From the

---

[17] See Te Velde, *Doctrine of God*, 77–85 and the literature mentioned there.

[18] Cf. Karin Maag, ed., *Melanchthon in Europe: His Work and Influence Beyond Wittenberg*, Texts and Studies in Reformation and Post-Reformation Thought (Grand Rapids: Baker; Carlisle: Paternoster, 1999).

[19] Cf. the contributions by Donald Sinnema and Kees Meerhoff in Strohm and others, eds., *Späthumanismus und reformierte Konfession*, 127–152, 169–205. See also Muller, *After Calvin*, 122–136.

[20] On the reserved attitude towards the introduction of public lectures in metaphysics, see Paul A.G. Dibon, *L'enseignement philosophique dans les universités*

establishment of Reformed academies and 'high schools' onward, there was some struggle over the merely preparatory status of this philosophical curriculum: while those in the theological faculty often attempted to keep their 'arts' colleagues in a subordinate position, those in the philosophy faculty strove for a more independent position and were in the long run successful. Important philosophers outside the theological faculty subsequently helped to elaborate the logical and metaphysical implications of the Reformed faith. They also contributed to the gradual change of Reformed philosophy from a dominantly 'Aristotelian' type to an early modern style. Here one might mention Clemens Timpler at Steinfurt, Rudolph Goclenius at Marburg and Franco Burgersdijk at Leiden.[21]

Scholastic method could serve different interests and so present opposing doctrinal positions. Jacobus Arminius, for example, was just as much a scholastic theologian as his opponent Franciscus Gomarus. Arminius was more *en vogue* in assimilating concepts from a new direction in Roman Catholic theology, and in doing so he endorsed certain logical and metaphysical presuppositions over others. The debate between Arminius and Gomarus was not, however, a conflict between 'scholastic' and 'biblical' thought: it was, on the technical level, a contest of the adequacy and consistency of one set of notions and distinctions against another set. The great advantage of the scholastic training most Reformed theologians had received was the provision of a common 'toolkit' of conceptual language and argumentative skills, thus enabling a high degree of mutual understanding even when people strongly disagreed.

DOCTRINAL IMPLICATIONS

In addition to the methodological aspects of scholasticism, more needs to be said about its substantial doctrinal components. Recent studies differ concerning the preference of scholastic Reformed thinkers for one or more particular 'schools' of thought. Richard Muller has emphasized the profoundly eclectic character of Reformed scholasticism. Driven by the quest for truth, and guided by the Scripture principle of the Reformation, Reformed scholastics could accept any element from any strand of the

Néerlandais a l'époque pré-cartésienne (PhD thesis, Rijksuniversiteit Leiden, 1954), 64–71, 148–154, and 214–219.

[21] See Trueman and Clark, eds., *Protestant Scholasticism*, and Günther Frank and Herman J. Selderhuis, eds., *Philosophie der Reformierten*, Melanchthon-Schriften der Stadt Bretten vol. 12 (Stuttgart-Bad Cannstatt: frommann-holzboog, 2012).

philosophical tradition that they deemed to be in accordance with biblical truth.[22] In contrast to this characterisation, a group of scholars in
the Netherlands headed by Antonie Vos has argued for a fundamentally
Scotist orientation in scholastic Reformed theology. In their analysis,
they point to the difference between the terminology employed in scholastic texts and the conceptual structures that govern this terminology.
Often the conceptual language is derived from Thomas Aquinas' *Summa
Theologiae*, but on closer analysis the elaboration and application of the
concepts seems rather to follow the path of Scotus. On this view, the
central element taken from Scotus is his elaborate concept of the divine
will, together with his crucial understanding of the ideas of necessity
and (synchronic) contingency.[23]

To understand the discrepancy between a Thomistic outlook and
a Scotist view, it is helpful to consider the culture of 'authorities' (*auc-
toritates*) in early modernity. University teaching took place through
lectures held on prescribed authoritative texts. In the philosophical disciplines these normally consisted of the Aristotelian *corpus*, while in
Roman Catholic theology the medieval textbook of Peter Lombard's
Sentences was not replaced by Aquinas' *Summa* until the first half
of the sixteenth century.[24] In Protestant theological teaching the pre-
scription of standard texts was less strict. Nevertheless, a discussion
did arise in the theological faculty at Heidelberg when a proposal was
made in 1588 to replace Melanchthon's *Loci communes* by Calvin's
Institutes as the basic source for lectures in systematic theology. The
faculty declined the proposal and continued to use Melanchthon as the
authority.[25] While standard texts did provide a common framework of
reference, they did not always represent the actual content of teaching. In commenting on the text, professors and lecturers would expand
and modify the argument, potentially arriving at positions that differed
from or even contradicted the original statements. In the latter case,
the technique of 'reverend interpretation' was used to reconcile one's

---

[22] Muller, *Post-Reformation Reformed Dogmatics*, vol. 4, 391–397, with explicit discussion of the Scotistic interpretation by Antonie Vos and others.
[23] Cf. the contributions by Vos, 'Scholasticism and Reformation', and Beck,
'Gisbertus Voetius', in Willem J. van Asselt and Eef Dekker, eds., *Reformation
and Scholasticism: An Ecumenical Enterprise*, Texts and Studies in Reformation
and Post-Reformation Thought (Grand Rapids: Baker Academic, 2001), 99–119 and
205–226.
[24] De Rijk, *Middeleeuwse wijsbegeerte*, 115–124.
[25] Strohm and others, eds., *Späthumanismus und reformierte Konfession*, 250–251.

own position with the authoritative source. This tradition and its interpretive techniques may well account for the fact that while Aquinas appears to be the leading scholastic spokesperson for Reformed thinkers, the actual distinctions, structures and implications are more consistent with Scotus.

In nineteenth- and twentieth-century research, the theology of the Reformed scholastics was often understood as a unified system construed on the basis of a 'central dogma'. The idea of a 'system', however, is foreign to scholastic methodology. While Reformed scholastics did assume an inner coherence to the doctrine taught in Scripture and did attempt to elucidate this coherence in their theology, their presentation of doctrine hardly ever takes the shape of an 'axiomatic system' derived from one or more basic principles. The method of 'commonplaces' applied by most professors of systematic theology originated in the practice of biblical exegesis. The running exposition of Scripture was often interrupted to discuss a doctrinal, ethical, or practical issue emerging from the passage under study. In the transitional phase from the Reformation to scholasticism such 'commonplaces' functioned as an excursus, but they were soon assembled in a more or less coherent topical sequence. An important model was the *Loci communes* of Melanchthon, which displayed a historical sequence derived from the apostle Paul's letter to the Romans and was largely followed by, among others, Calvin in his *Institutes*.[26] Broadly speaking, a similar sequence of topics is followed by most Reformed scholastic handbooks: starting with a preliminary chapter on 'theology', the doctrine of Scripture is expounded as theology's 'cognitive foundation', followed by the doctrine of God and of the Trinity as the 'essential foundation'; next, the divine decrees and works of creation, providence and salvation are discussed; then the various elements of Christology and soteriology, including the church and the sacraments as means of grace, receive separate attention; finally the closing chapters often deal with the task of government in the present age, the final judgement of Christ and eternal life. While the fundamental notions are deployed in the first set of loci, each topic contains its own discourse, concepts and arguments. The fact that the doctrinal topics are interconnected does not imply that they are considered from a single point of view.

---

[26] See Richard A. Muller, '*Ordo Docendi*: Melanchthon and the Organization of Calvin's *Institutes*, 1536–1543', in Maag, ed., *Melanchthon in Europe*, 123–140.

CONTINUING RELEVANCE

The disappearance of Reformed scholastic theology from the academic scene in the course of the Enlightenment suggests that it lost its intellectual plausibility because of changes in the cultural and philosophical climate. Surprisingly, however, the last four or five decades have witnessed a strong revival of analytical philosophy, mainly in the English-speaking world. Philosophers such as Alvin Plantinga, William Alston and Vincent Brümmer have developed philosophical approaches in which important issues, notions and arguments from medieval and early modern scholastic thought are recast in a post-Enlightenment form. The historical verdict that scholastic philosophy and theology are outdated has turned out not to be as inescapable as it once seemed.

The abiding significance of Reformed scholasticism for contemporary Reformed theology can be summarised in four points.

First, in continuity with the Reformation of the sixteenth century, Reformed scholasticism endorses the Scripture principle: God's self-revelation in Scripture is seen as the principal source and ultimate norm of Christian doctrine. This principle functions in practice when the various parts of doctrine are expounded with constant reference to biblical texts. Rather than reducing Scripture to a mere store of 'proof texts', Reformed scholasticism fosters a constructive relationship between exegetical and dogmatic theology.

Second, in a wider sense, Reformed theology in its scholastic shape stands out as part of the classical tradition of Christian thought. Continuing the program of 'faith seeking understanding' (*fides quaerens intellectum*), and consciously building on patristic and medieval material, it attempts to clarify the contents of faith and spell out the implications of the great history of redemption.

Third, Reformed scholastic theology has apologetic potential. By elucidating the presuppositions of the Christian faith, scholasticism accounts for its plausibility and coherence while at the same time presenting a challenge to alternative worldviews and conceptions. In this connection, the historical context of Reformed scholasticism at the dawn of modernity is particularly exciting. Reformed theologians of the seventeenth and eighteenth centuries sensed the fundamental changes that were 'in the air' and responded by articulating what they considered the basics of a biblical and Christian worldview.

Fourth, a specific contribution of scholastic Reformed theology lies in its elaboration of an ontology based on the irreducible distinction between God the Creator and human creatures. With the help of this ontology, which rests on the notion of the divine will and is further developed in a careful balancing of necessity and contingency, Reformed scholastics described the interplay between God and humanity in a way that maintains both God's sovereignty as well as human freedom and responsibility. They thus paved a way forward between the emerging sense of human autonomy and the threat of fatalist determinism.

In sum, Reformed theology today would do well to explore its scholastic tradition, and to appropriate and develop the treasures it has in store.

Further reading

Asselt, Willem J. van and Eef Dekker (eds.). *Reformation and Scholasticism: An Ecumenical Enterprise.* Texts and Studies in Reformation and Post-Reformation Thought. Grand Rapids, MI: Baker Academic, 2001.

Asselt, Willem J. van, T. Theo J. Pleizier, Pieter L. Rouwendal and Maarten Wisse. *Introduction to Reformed Scholasticism.* Reformed Historical-Theological Studies. Grand Rapids, MI: Reformation Heritage Books, 2011.

Maag, Karin. *Seminary or University? The Genevan Academy and Reformed Higher Education (1560–1620).* St. Andrews Studies in Reformation History. Aldershot, UK: Scholar Press, 1995.

Muller, Richard A. *After Calvin: Studies in the Development of a Theological Tradition.* Oxford Studies in Historical Theology. Oxford: Oxford University Press, 2003.

Post-Reformation Reformed Dogmatics: The Rise and Development of Reformed Orthodoxy, ca. 1520 to ca. 1725. 4 vols. Grand Rapids, MI: Baker Academic, 2003.

Rummel, Erika. *The Humanist-Scholastic Debate in the Renaissance and Reformation.* Harvard Historical Studies 120. Cambridge, MA: Harvard University Press, 1995.

Trueman, Carl R. and R. Scott Clark (eds.). *Protestant Scholasticism: Essays in Reassessment.* Carlisle, UK: Paternoster, 1999

15 Reformed theology in continental Europe
EBERHARD BUSCH

CHARACTERISTICS OF REFORMED LIFE IN EUROPE

John a Lasco, a humanist nobleman from Poland, student of Erasmus, and later Reformed superintendent in East Frisia, stated that the churches in his region were characterised by a 'harmonious diversity' (concors varietas).[1] This is an apt description for the community of Reformed churches in continental Europe from the seventeenth to the twenty-first century. Sometimes the diversity is so rich that the harmony is difficult to see, or indeed is called into question by the church's own members. While a scholar may lament that the Reformed tradition lacks international solidarity,[2] it is essential to understand the factors behind such a state of affairs, which reveal neither a love of struggle nor a lack of desire for the full unity of the churches.

We begin by setting out two points. First, Reformed Christianity is convinced that the church is, above all, the 'assembled congregation'.[3] It is 'the gathering of those connected to an external society, perceptible by the heard Word, by the use of the sacrament and by church order'.[4] In Reformed thought, a synod or assembly, the delegates of which are called from different congregations, is also a worshipful gathering. Moreover, Reformed Christians see *faith* as the point of unity with Christians throughout the world, though an emphasis on local origin contributes to the diversity of regional churches. The 'Reformed' designation means something particular in each region, with respective

---

[1] Joannis a Lasco, *Opera tam edita quam inedita duobus voluminibus comprehensa*, edited by Abraham Kuyper (Amsterdam: 1866), vol. II, 584, in a letter of 1544 to Konrad Pellikan.

[2] D. G. Hart, *Calvinism. A History* (New Haven, CT and London: Yale University Press, 2013), 300.

[3] See Otto Weber, *Versammelte Gemeinde:Beiträge zum Gespräch die Kirche und Gottesdienst* (Neukirchen, Austria: Buchhandlung des Erziehungsvereins, 1949), 33.

[4] *Leiden Synopsis* (1625), in *Die Dogmatik der evangelisch-reformierten Kirche*, edited by Heinrich Heppe and Ernst Bizer (Neukirchen: Neukirchener Verlag, 1958), 527.

confessions speaking to local priorities even as they are acknowledged by churches elsewhere.

Second, Reformed Christians are committed to verbally sustaining the integrity and continuity of their belief, identifying themselves as existing in a 'state of confession' (*status confessionis*). They make their confessions of faith under the proviso that they may be corrected in light of the teaching of Scripture, whether or not this is explicitly stated.[5] Congregations are invited to assess confessional texts against this criterion continually, which can result in their supplementation or even abolition and replacement. This is why Reformed churches hold a greater range of confessions than other Christian churches, and the work of reformulation carries on today. The verb 'to confess' and the substantive 'the confession' are thus closely linked in Reformed understanding. There is always the risk that a confession is spoken to accommodate alien priorities, instead of truly confessing over and against the most acute problems of the time. To the latter goal belongs the seventeenth-century principle that 'the Reformed church is always in need of reforming' (*ecclesia Reformata semper reformanda*) – that is, the Reformed church is always listening to the biblical message anew.

THE REFORMED CHURCHES IN CONTINENTAL EUROPE

Switzerland is the country of origin for the Reformed churches. Their fundamental doctrinal thesis emerged from the 1528 Disputation of Bern, led by Berchthold Haller, as part of the broader Reformation in Grisons: 'The holy, Christian Church, whose only Head is Christ, is born of the Word of God, abides in the same, and does not listen to the voice of a stranger.'[6] This statement was taken up again in the Düsseldorf Theses in May 1933, the first confession of the church under the Nazi regime in Germany.[7]

There were two different Swiss sources of Reformation from the beginning: Zürich, bearing the imprint of Huldrych Zwingli and Heinrich Bullinger, and Geneva, where John Calvin worked with Theodor

---

[5] See, for example, *The Bern Synod* (1532), in *Reformed Confessions of the 16th and 17th Centuries in English Translation: Vol. I. 1523–1552*, edited by James T. Dennison, Jr. (Grand Rapids, MI: Reformation Heritage Books, 2008), 230.

[6] *The Ten Theses of Berne* (1528), thesis 1, in *Reformed Confessions of the Sixteenth Century*, edited by Arthur Cochrane (Louisville, KY: Westminster John Knox, 2003), 49.

[7] *The Düsseldorf Theses* (1933), in *The Church's Confession under Hitler* by Arthur C. Cochrane (Pittsburgh: Pickwick, 1976), 229.

Beza. Zürich's influence extended primarily to eastern countries: in Austria, for example, the Reformed Church is still referred to as 'HB' (*Helvetisches Bekenntnis*, after the Second Helvetic Confession which Bullinger wrote). Geneva's legacy, meanwhile, primarily spread west, becoming known as 'Calvinism', though German-speaking Reformed Christians do not use this name for themselves. The Reformers in Bern resisted Calvin because of his view that the church decides its own order. Indeed, the 1559 French Confession of Faith, largely written by Calvin in Geneva, explicitly includes material on church order,[8] even as it begins with belief in the one and only God, proceeding to an extended section on Holy Scripture as 'the sure rule of our faith'.[9]

Calvin wanted to overcome the divergent streams of the Reformation in Germany and Switzerland. He thus attempted to resolve the disagreement between Martin Luther and Bullinger on the doctrine of the eucharist. The Reformers in Zürich understood the 'Lord's supper' as an act commemorating Christ's passion, while the Lutherans saw it as an act of Christ's *presentation* in the elements of bread and wine. After a lengthy exchange of views, Calvin and Bullinger came to an agreement, set forth in the Zürich Consensus (*Consensus Tigurinus*) of 1549. In this document, the decisive seventh article comes close to the wording of the Augsburg Confession. It begins by affirming that 'The ends of the sacraments are that they may be marks and badges of Christian profession and of our community,' and continues with the declaration that 'the end which is first among the others is that through them God may testify, represent, and seal his grace to us'. The sacraments, in their close association with the divine Word, thus fortify faith: 'It is also a great benefit that what God has pronounced with his mouth, is confirmed and ratified as if by seals.'[10] Although this represented an agreement between Zürich and Geneva, it did not bring about Lutheran assent.

The year 1675 brought a new attempt at agreement through the Helvetic Consensus Formula, essentially drawn up by Johann Heinrich Heidegger in Zürich.[11] He adapted the theses of the federal theology of Johannes Cocceius, namely that an original covenant of nature between

---

[8] *French Confession of Faith* (1559), articles XXIX–XXXIII, in Cochrane (ed.), *Reformed Confessions of the Sixteenth Century*, 154–156.

[9] Ibid., article IV, 145.

[10] *Zürich Agreement* (1549), article VII, in *Creeds & Confessions of Faith in the Christian Tradition*, vol. II, edited by Jaroslav Pelikan and Valerie Hotchkiss, (New Haven, CT and London: Yale University Press, 2003), 807–808.

[11] *Helvetic Consensus Formula* (1675), translated by Martin I. Klauber, in *Trinity Journal* 11 (1990): 103–123.

God and sinless humanity was replaced after the Fall by a covenant of grace which develops in the Old and New Testaments. The rest of the Consensus text speaks against new doctrines, such as the challenge to the divine inspiration of the Bible at the level of consonants and vowels (Louis Cappel); the reduction of Christ's redemption to an act of passive obedience (Johann Piscator); the contestation of original sin (Josué de la Place); and the moderation of the doctrine of divine election (Moses Amyraut). In a sense, the Consensus was more an expression of concern than a confession, a tone which perhaps led to its lack of publication and the ensuing dissociation of Swiss theologians. Since that time the Swiss churches have not been satisfied by any confession, with the exception of confessional remarks in church order statements. At the end of the nineteenth century some declared that the Second Helvetic Confession was the last Reformed confession, though that idea was soon refuted by the many new confessions of twentieth-century Reformed churches around the world.

In *France* in 1598, King Henry IV enacted the Edict of Nantes. Until then, Protestants in France had been oppressed for their faith, often facing prison or execution. The St. Bartholomew's Day Massacre in August 1572 brought about the murder of countless Protestants, on which occasion Pope Gregory XIII joyfully commissioned a *Te deum laudamus* ('God, we praise thee'). In contrast, the toleration of Protestants effected by the Edict of Nantes gave Protestants a time of relative peace in which they could build their own churches and academies. Among these projects was the important school in Saumur, where in the seventeenth century the Scot John Cameron and his successor Moses Amyraut taught, both posing questions to the doctrine of predestination as stated at the Synod of Dort.

This period of stability came to an end when the Roman Catholic majority blamed Protestants for the statement characterising the pope as 'the anti-Christ' in the Theses of Gap (1603). The Roman Catholic polemic disregarded the larger context of the confession which, by emphasising that justification was achieved by Christ's obedience in the Passion *alone*, resisted the challenge to the term 'alone' they understood the pope to present. After the assassination of Henry IV, the climate became even more threatening for Protestants. Subsequent French rulers strived to remove the Reformed confession entirely, while authorities repeatedly tolerated acts of violence against the Protestant minority.

In 1685, the 'Sun King' Louis XIV repealed the Edict of Nantes by the Edict of Fontainebleau and Reformed Christians were no longer formally 'tolerated'. 'Temples', as their church buildings were known, were destroyed. Preachers had to leave the country, while their congregations had to remain. Roman Catholic education was prescribed for children, with the sentence of becoming a galley slave looming in cases of non-observance. While some conformed to this law, the Protestant church did not disappear. Protestant Christians remained active in the Cévennes, for instance, gathering secretly for worship in woods or quarries, taking along a folding pulpit which became their symbol for this 'church in the desert'. Some wanted to fight the prohibition with violence, but that would have been in vain. Though it was strongly forbidden, more than 200,000 Protestants fled from France to the Netherlands, Switzerland and Germany.

After 1750 the situation improved slightly for Protestants, but the French Revolution in 1793 brought a new suppression of their churches under which many disappeared. Napoleon changed these circumstances with the 'Organic Articles', which contained regulations for members of 'other' religions (including Jews, Lutherans and Reformed Christians), granting them official recognition. The Reformed Church accepted this, although such recognition bound it to the state and so effectively ended its synodal leadership. Preachers were no longer employed directly by congregations but by a semi-political consistory, their salaries paid by the state. In the nineteenth century, the dissolution of this system led to a sharp separation between the state and religion. Among Reformed Protestants there emerged a division between a majority party linked with the revival movement and a minority group espousing religious liberalism.

This division diminished when 'dialectical theology' came to prominence in the twentieth century. One sign of this change was the publication of the Theses of Pomeyrol during the German occupation of France in 1941. The theses took their example from the 1934 Barmen Declaration but had a more overt political stance. After the first anti-Semitic legislation, they provided a basis for resistance against the Nazi regime, making claims about the limits of obedience vis-à-vis the government and emphasising respect for human rights, advocating 'a solemn protest against any law which excludes the Jews from human communities'.[12]

The Reformed Church in Alsace-Lorraine originated during the time of Calvin's residence in 1538–1541, a period when he was in exile from

---

[12] *Theses of Pomeyrol* (1941), article VII, at www.protestants.org/index.php?id=2574 (accessed 1 March 2015).

Geneva. Calvin lived in the house of the Reformer Martin Bucer, giving biblical lectures in the Jean Sturm school and preaching to a small congregation of French refugees at the Church of St. Nicolas. This memory is kept alive today as the church is maintained – uniquely among the Protestant churches of France – as a statutory body under public law in accordance with a special item of regional legislation. However, even it has since been united to a larger Lutheran church, just as the Reformed and Lutheran churches came together in the United Protestant Church of France in 2012.

The Netherlands once formed a unified state with Belgium, in which Reformed Christians were also cruelly oppressed for their Protestant faith. Under the rule of King Philip II of Spain and his executor Alba, countless members of the Protestant church were burned or hanged. These included Guy de Brès, who composed the Belgic Confession (1561), a text which bears a close resemblance to the French Confession of the Huguenots (1559). As with the Scots Confession (1560), the words of this text convey a situation of murderous suppression, with redemption understood as the deliverance of 'the righteous and the elect' from enemies who have 'most cruelly persecuted, oppressed, and tormented them in this world'. Comfort is offered to those 'now condemned by many judges and magistrates as heretical and impious', for one day their cause will 'be known to be the cause of the Son of God'. Drawing on the language of Revelation, it is promised that all tears will be wiped from the eyes of the faithful, who will 'possess such a glory as never entered into the heart of man to conceive'.[13]

In this way, those who confessed the Protestant faith understood themselves to be a 'church under the cross', and their representatives met abroad in 1571 in Emden, the 'shelter of God's congregation', where they created a church order for the oppressed Reformed Church in the Netherlands.[14] It was a radical statement, contrasting with a model of power from above by granting a real voice to particular parishes, the church built 'from below'. This does not imply that the church is reducible to purely individual congregations, for according to Holy Scripture they are connected by the spiritual consensus of faith. Yet this consensus does not overwhelm local parishes, but rather facilitates the active cooperation of all their members. An explicitly democratic church order

---

[13] *Belgic Confession of Faith* (1561), article XXXVII, in Cochrane (ed.), *Reformed Confessions of the Sixteenth Century*, 218–219.

[14] *Acts of the Synod of Emden* (1571), in *Die Akten der Synode der Niederländischen Kirchen zu Emden vom 4.-13. Oktober 1571*, edited by J. F. G. Goeters (ed.), (Neukirchen: Neukirchener Verlag, 1971).

was thus formulated, which in its institutionalised distrust of human hierarchy in the church also bore witness against the authoritarian state power which was trying to suffocate the Protestant movement in the Netherlands. The first principle was freely formulated according to the French Confession: 'no church shall claim any authority or dominion over any other'.[15] These words are preserved today in the order of the German Reformed Church.

The Belgic Confession was revised at the Synod of Dort in 1618–1619 and acknowledged – together with the Heidelberg Catechism – as a Reformed confession. The Synod's decisions about the doctrine of predestination were disputed among theologians, leading to a split between an orthodox Reformed majority and a liberal Arminian minority. The Hervormde Church was rooted in the orthodox tradition, but in the nineteenth century it was thought to have become overly liberal, a charge which led to the formation of the Gereformeerde Church. This latter church became famous through the work of Abraham Kuyper, the conservative pastor who fought first against the liberals, and then against the socialists. He founded a newspaper, a political 'anti-revolutionary' party, and the Free University of Amsterdam, becoming Prime Minister in 1901. Through his influence in Germany and Switzerland the Reformed Youth movement (*Jungreformierte*) came into being.

Reformed Christians in *Germany* have been a minority since the seventeenth century. They originated partly through refugees from the west and partly through the proximity of Reformed churches in neighbouring countries. Today's Reformed churches in Germany include several churches with unique historical profiles: some congregations of Huguenot origin (Lueneburg, Celle, Altona), some in Bavaria or on the Lower Weser, and some in Hesse and in the Plesse. There is also the congregation in Lingen, where a university was founded in 1697, one legacy of which is the Reformed Chair at the University of Göttingen. There are also many Reformed congregations along the Dutch–German border, especially in East Frisia, where Dutch was the church's language until the nineteenth century. The influence of Zwingli's theology was initially evident in this region, as is evident in the Confession of the Preachers, which begins: 'God the Lord knows, loves, and blesses his own from eternity.'[16] Afterwards the religious landscape was influenced by the humanist John a Lasco, who was able – temporarily – to prevent

---

[15] *French Confession of Faith* (1559), article XXX, in Cochrane (ed.), *Reformed Confessions of the Sixteenth Century*, 155.

[16] *East Friesian Preachers' Confession* (1528), in Dennison Jr. (ed.), *Reformed Confessions of the 16th and 17th Centuries*, vol. 1, 45.

the separation of Lutheran and Reformed churches. Then Menso Alting began organising the Reformed communities in the spirit of Calvin.

Some of the Reformed churches formulated their own confessions, such as the Confession and Catechism of Hesse-Kassel (1607). These documents reveal the desire to connect Lutheranism in the spirit of Melanchthon with the confession of the Huguenots who lived in the region of Karlshafen. They accept the Augsburg Confession and make reference to Luther, but they are Reformed in that they call for a celebration of the eucharist with bread, support the prohibition of images in accordance with the Decalogue and oppose the doctrine of the ubiquity of the human nature of Christ. Noticeably, the articles of the Bentheim confession (1613) show little interest in the doctrine of divine election, which five years later became so important at Dort. Another notable element of these articles is their reference to the name of God as 'Jehova', in an attempt to show the unity of both Testaments. In 1614 the Confession of Sigismund was promulgated in the context of the conversion of Brandenburg's rulers to the Reformed faith. In this statement, divine election by grace is seen to be a great consolation, because God elects by sheer grace and not because of the faith of the recipient, which – in Lutheran teaching – God alone knows in advance. However, this teaching did not satisfy the theologians at Dort four years later, because the question of divine rejection was omitted.

Huguenot refugees settled above all in Halle. Though there were only ninety of them, they were given the Gothic cathedral in the middle of the city. The German and French Reformed communities formed a respectable minority in the town, running their own school and seniors' home, with services in both German and French. G. F. Handel grew up near the cathedral, where in his younger years he served as organist and developed his love of the Old Testament. Naturally the Elector expected that the settlement of the Huguenots would contribute to economic progress.

The Margrave of Brandenburg-Bayreuth had a similar interest, which led him to permit Huguenots into Bayreuth and Erlangen in 1886–1887. It took until the nineteenth century for them to gain admission to Nürnberg. The oldest Reformed parishes in Bavaria, Herbishofen and Grönenbach in Allgäu, grew through the work of Swiss immigrants and use the Swiss hymnbook to this day. These Bavarian churches are currently united with the Evangelical Reformed Church in Germany. The Evangelical Church in Lippe-Detmold – a region which is mostly Reformed, but has a Lutheran district – is independent. The Reformed congregations in Rhineland and Westphalia belong to united regional churches, and were active members in the Confessing Church (Paul Schneider was killed in a concentration camp). Another unique church is the Dutch Reformed church in Wuppertal, where in the nineteenth century Hermann Kohlbrügge advanced a strongly Lutheran theology. His son-in-law, Eduard Böhl, was Professor of Reformed Theology in Vienna. In his *Dogmatics* (1887), in which he works mostly with Scripture, he declared that the theology of his time must repent and convert.

Reformed Christians in *Italy* are named Waldensians, because they are rooted in the pre-Reformed lay movement founded by the trader Petrus Valdes at the end of the twelfth century. From the beginning their members were excluded from the Roman Catholic Church and pursued as heretics by the Inquisition, causing them to withdraw to mountain valleys in the French-Italian Alps. In the sixteenth century they joined the Reformation, demonstrating their orthodoxy by presenting the French Confession to the Duke of Savoy in 1560. Waldensians hold an abbreviated form of this confession today. They were often a hard-pressed community on account of false accusations concerning witchcraft and devil-worship. In the winter of 1655, they were forcibly relocated, and the following spring six thousand were killed. Many thousands fled to south-west Germany and to Hesse. Finally Charles Albert I, King of Sardinia-Piemont, granted them freedom of faith, and freedom to choose career and own property. In 1861 the church was recognised by state law as a tolerated religious group. In 1975 the Waldensians united with the Italian Methodists as the Waldensian Evangelical Church (*Chiesa Evangelica Valdese*).

The Reformed movement also left its mark in *Hungary*, which was known as Greater Hungary until the convention of Trianon (1920), in which it lost two-thirds of its land to its neighbours following the First World War. From the sixteenth century onwards, Reformed theologians from Hungary frequently came to western Europe to learn different languages, hear the latest theologians and bring theological books home. As a result, some of the best theological libraries in the world exist there, providing means for the maintenance of the Reformed tradition in the region. Moreover, since the seventeenth century their relationship with the smaller Lutheran church has been friendly, with a policy of mutual co-operation agreed in the Treaty of Nagygeresd (1833).

At the Synod of Debrecen (1567), Reformed Christianity in Hungary received its spiritual form through subscription to the Second Helvetic Confession as well as to the Heidelberg Catechism. Although these confessions have been abolished in Switzerland, they remain alive in

Hungarian churches today. Because of these commitments, the congregations remained steadfast in the dark times that followed. Two leading lights in the seventeenth-century church were the dukes Gábor Bethlen and György Rákóczi. Under Turkish rule Reformed congregations were tolerated but for the long period during which the country was dependent on Austria and the control of the Habsburg government, they endured strong military suppression as alleged adherents of a 'revolutionary religion'. In the eighteenth century the oppression continued by peaceful means, as Roman Catholic clergy made efforts to eliminate Protestantism. Relief came only in 1790–1791, when the Parliament revoked the anti-Reformed decrees. Though there remained yet further distress to come, Reformed Christians worked energetically in literature, research, and education.

Admiral Horthy governed Hungary from 1919–1945, and during this time the country actively sought to protect the West from 'the Bolshevist danger'. This goal – combined with the hope of a restored Greater Hungary – drove the country to collaborate with Nazi Germany. This alliance meant that under Adolf Eichmann's management one million Jews from Greater Hungary were deported to concentration camps to be killed. Church leaders could not resist the winds of the time, although in a 1934 church law it was stated that the Hungarian Reformed Church stands on the basis of Holy Scripture and recognises Jesus Christ as its only head, commitments which were seen to be in continuity with the Second Helvetic Confession and the Heidelberg Catechism. In accordance with this, several Reformed Christians supported the oppressed, such as Bishop Albert Bereczky, who worked with the Swiss consul to save Hungarian Jews. Towards the end of the Second World War, he greeted the incoming Soviet army as the liberators of the survivors of concentration camps and as supporters towards a new beginning for the work of the church. The end of the oppressive communist regime which followed allowed for new relations to be forged between Hungarian churches and western countries.

In *Poland* the Reformed Church is a small minority, though it was larger in former times. In 1645 King Vladislav IV invited an equal number of Roman Catholic, Lutheran and Reformed theologians, as well as some Unitarians, to a synod in Thorn for a 'charitable colloquium' (*colloquium charitativum*). This move prevented the Thirty Years War from directly affecting Poland, although the desire of the irenic Lutheran Georg Calixt for a working arrangement (*modus vivendi*) between the groups was opposed by the strict Lutheran Abraham Calov.

In the *Czech Republic* today, Reformed Christians belong to the United Evangelical Church of the Bohemian Brothers. They are led by synods and presbyteries, with the Second Helvetic Confession belonging to their statements of faith. Of first importance, however, are the 1421 Four Articles of Prague. These articles ruled the pre-Reformed Hussite movement, with their claim to freedom of the sermon and the cup (the latter symbolised the eucharist for all participants and became the symbol of the movement), as well as to freedom from the secular governance of the church and from unjust worldly rule. In 1609 the Protestant Council of States in *Bohemia* wrested a letter from Emperor Rudolf II which recognised the Protestant confession, namely, the Lutherans. But by the end of the sixteenth century the Reformed movement – not covered in the Bohemian Confession – had grown significantly. Bohemia never arrived at a true unification of the different Protestant confessions.

COMMON TOPICS

Reformed theology and church life have taken on manifold forms over the past four centuries and across the different regions of continental Europe. Common characteristics are nevertheless discernible among them, even if some were controversial in their respective contexts. Five particular topics can be highlighted.

First, it is a mark of the Reformed churches that *Holy Scripture* is valued as the fundamental and directing power. The Old and New Testaments and their constitutive books are seen in such close unity that the idea of a 'canon within the canon' is alien to Reformed thinking: if you have such a canon then the Bible recommends that you read on! This emphasis is clear in the older confessions, which often include references to biblical texts in the margin. This demonstrates that these confessions understood themselves as commentaries on the biblical text, highlighting certain messages which have to be rightly received in the present. At the same time, readers are invited to test for themselves the statements of the confession. In church services, expositional sermons on particular biblical texts are often preferred to more thematic and less text-based sermons. Ministers regularly preach through biblical books in their entirety. The model for this practice was Zwingli's preaching. Indeed, the beginning of the Reformation in Zürich can be dated to New Year 1519, when Zwingli started this practice with Matthew 1:1. This change meant that every sermon had to submit to Holy Scripture rather than to ecclesial doctrine, a practice which Calvin followed. Behind this commitment lies the belief that the changing natural seasons should not frame Christian life and thought, but rather the movement of Israel out of Egypt and towards its eschatological end. Under the Nazi regime, when the Old Testament was denigrated by German theologians as 'Jewish', and contrasted with the 'Christian' New Testament, creative Reformed Christians began working towards a new understanding of the First Testament. In Switzerland Karl Barth understood the Old Testament as the book of hope and the New Testament as the book of memory, giving them an inseparable connection.[17] In the Netherlands Arnold van Ruler called the Old Testament the essential Bible and the New Testament its explanatory lexicon.[18] Heiko Miskotte wanted to let the Old Testament 'speak for itself' in all its detail, interpreting it as 'Christian instruction' because of the belief that the Old Testament offers a surplus of meaning rather than a deficit, a surplus elaborated in the New Testament.[19]

Second, in Reformed theology the biblical idea of *covenant* has seminal importance. In 1534 Heinrich Bullinger published his booklet *A Brief Exposition of the One and Eternal Testament or Covenant of God*, drawing this topic to the attention of Reformed circles. In the seventeenth century, 'federal' theology arose, pioneered in the Netherlands by Johannes Coccius. In the wake of Philip Melanchthon the idea of a 'natural covenant' grew, a covenant entered into by God and humanity on the grounds of a law that could be apprehended in nature. After the Fall this was replaced by a covenant of grace which is unilaterally founded by God and evolves subsequently. In the eighteenth century this idea led to the emergence of modern historical thinking. Already in the seventeenth century the relationship between the eternal covenant with Abraham (Gen. 17:17) and the promised and eternal 'new' covenant (Jer. 31:31–34) was under discussion: Is the covenant that is written on the heart instigated with Israel or, as seems to be the case in the Book of Hebrews, with the church of the New Testament? Is the 'eternal covenant' described in the Old Testament confirmed, fulfilled or replaced by the new covenant mentioned in Luke 22:20? These have remained significant questions among Reformed theologians.

Third, the relationship between *Gospel* and *Law* has a unique interpretation in Reformed thought. There is agreement with Lutherans on the belief that salvation is not merited by human works. While this is

---

[17] Karl Barth, *Church Dogmatics*, vol. I/2 (Edinburgh: T&T Clark, 1956), 101–103.

[18] Arnold van Ruler, *The Christian Church and the Old Testament*, translated by Geoffrey W. Bromiley (Grand Rapids, MI: Eerdmans, 1971).

[19] Kornelis Miskotte, *When the Gods Are Silent*, translated by John W. Doberstein (New York: Harper & Row, 1967).

important for Reformed theologians, their emphasis is on the action of *God* as the One who justifies humanity. In the opinion of Alexander Schweizer, the Lutheran tradition is geared towards arguing against a seemingly Jewish notion of works, while the Reformed confessions tend to oppose 'pagan' notions.[20] As a result, Reformed thought stresses the *connection* of the Gospel with the Law. Calvin taught that after Israel's liberation from the yoke of Pharaoh, God does not place a new yoke upon the people but calls them to 'free obedience'.[21] This should not be termed the 'third use of the Law', because it is not a reference to human use but has a unique character given to it by the God of Israel. It is 'incorporated in the covenant to grace',[22] for 'As the law exacts obedience from man, the gospel directs man in affording that obedience'.[23] In the twentieth century the consequences of this idea were disputed. Emil Brunner taught that the rule of Christ extends only to the congregation of believers, whereas the rest of the world is controlled by the divine 'orders of creation'.[24] In opposition to this, Karl Barth stressed that the political realm is not separate from Christ's government and that the church should therefore be vigilant in calling the government to perform its duty in caring for justice and peace.[25]

Fourth, the question of *predestination* has occupied Reformed theologians from the beginning, especially in Geneva. Calvin dealt with it in his dispute with the humanists, stressing that it is the duty of God, and God alone, to save humanity. Along with Luther, he taught that Christians should keep to the revelation of God's grace in Christ and therefore hope for all people, instead of looking into an abyss of despair.[26] But once the fire had been started, it could not be contained. In the seventeenth century the Dutch Arminians taught that the salvation

---

[20] Alexander Schweizer, *Die christliche Glaubenslehre nach protestantischen Grundsätzen*, vol. 1 (Leipzig: S. Hirzel, 1862), 8.
[21] John Calvin, *Institutes of the Christian Religion*, edited by John T. McNeill and translated by Ford Lewis Battles. Library of Christian Classics, 2 vols. (Philadelphia: Westminster, 1960), II.viii.15.
[22] Hermann Ravensperger, *Wegweiser* (Groeningen, 1615), quoted in *Reformed Dogmatics Set Out and Illustrated from the Sources*, 2nd ed., edited by Heinrich Heppe and Ernst Bizer and translated by G. T. Thomson (London: Allen & Unwin, 1950), 401.
[23] Johann Heinrich Heidegger, *Corpus theologiae* (Zürich 1700), in *Reformed Dogmatics Set Out*, 569.
[24] Karl Barth – Emil Brunner, *Briefwechsel 1916–1966*, edited by Eberhard Busch (Barth Gesamtausgabe; Zürich: Theologischer Verlag, 2000), 468–469.
[25] Karl Barth, 'The Christian Community and the Civil Community', in *Against the Stream: Shorter Post-war Writings 1946–52*, edited and translated by R. G. Smith (London: SCM Press, 1954), §8.
[26] Calvin, *Institutes*, III.xxiv.5.

or damnation of human beings lay decisively in their own hands and that God only knows beforehand how they will decide. The Synod of Dort (1618–1619) was called in response to this, drawing delegates from many countries. It stated that from the beginning weal and woe are dependent solely on the decision of God in free grace. God's election of those who are to be saved includes the gift of faith. The leader of the synod, John Bogerman, dismissed the Arminians who were present from the proceedings, as the theologians at Dort concluded in favour of the sovereignty of God in opposition to the rise of the 'modernists'.[27] The dark side of this picture, however, is that Christ saves only those whom God has elected in Christ. Against this, Karl Barth argued that according to the Scriptures Christ is *the* elected one, the very same one who is rejected by God the Father at the cross. In this way he saves precisely those who are lost. To this outcome both Israel and the churches bear witness, each in their own way, for the sake of all humanity.[28]

Fifth, another particularity of the Reformed tradition is its appreciation of *church order*. For Wilhelm Niesel, 'According to Reformed doctrine the order of the church also has the character of a confession … The church testifies as with its confession so with its order that Jesus Christ is its Lord.'[29] The statement's theological roots extend back to the beginning of the Reformation, where it was testified that the church is in the service of Jesus Christ, who as *one* person is prophet, priest and king. The three corresponding offices are not to be united in the church community, for congregational 'members' are not to be confused with the 'head' of the body. As Heidegger explained in 1696, the pastors and teachers of theology exercise the office of prophet; the elders, or presbyters, hold the office of leader in the service of Christ; and the deacons, following Acts 6, carry out the economic duties, especially care for the poor.[30] At the same time, these three offices do not relegate other members of the congregation to passivity. If Christ is the head of the body, then the appropriate fundamental church order is that of brothers and sisters who work with and for one another. Every member in the church has a voice. In the words of the constitution of the

---

27 Cf. Frederik W. Grosheide (ed.), *Christelijke Encyclopedie*, vol. 1 (Kampen, the Netherlands: Kok, 1956), 687–688.

28 Karl Barth, *Church Dogmatics*, vol. II/2 (Edinburgh: T&T Clark, 1957), 94 and 195.

29 Wihelm Niesel, 'Vorwort', in *Bekenntnisschriften und Kirchenordnungen der nach Gottes Wort reformierten Kirche*, edited by Wilhelm Niesel (Zürich: Theologische Buchhandlung, 1985), v.

30 Johann Heinrich Heidegger, *Medulla theologiae christianae* (Zürich 1700), in *Reformed Dogmatics Set Out*, 681.

German Evangelical Reformed Church: 'as an association of sisters and brothers the Evangelical Reformed Church witnesses to Jesus Christ as the head of the church'.[31]

Finally, the broader *political* aspect of the Christian faith has received significant attention in Reformed thought. At the end of the *Institutes* Calvin urges that God has to be heard 'before all and above all', such that when worldly lords 'command anything against him, let it go unesteemed'.[32] With reference to Ezekiel 3:17, Calvin speaks of the church's office as a 'sentinel' for the common welfare. The 1532 Bern Synod states that a preacher should not be a 'dumb dog', because 'the truth bites and always has its sharpness',[33] which is to say that political government has always to remain open to hearing the divine Word. For his part, Zwingli was open to the idea that a tyrant must be deposed by God, while the Belgic Confession declares that resistance against tyranny is framed by hope of God's own vengeance.[34] However, Zwingli and Calvin thought that revolt against a tyrant should not be attempted by unqualified people. Their concern was that such an extreme act must be an act of justice, carried out by those who are called also to ensure that old injustice is not superseded by new injustice. By contrast, Theodore Beza shows a tendency towards democratising the right of resistance against tyranny: 'Everybody can resist those who claim a tyrannical rule over their subjects in breach of their official duty.'[35]

In 1940 Emil Brunner criticised the second thesis of the 1934 Barmen Declaration, namely that there are no areas in which we belong to lords other than Christ. Brunner declared that we have no right to name Christ 'the Lord of the state, too.... His area of government is the parish', while the state is an order of creation.[36] Brunner certainly saw that Barth distinguished between church and state, but he retained doubts since Barth put pressure on churches outside of Germany to call their governments to military resistance against Nazi state aggression.

[31] *Verfassung der [deutschen] Evangelisch-reformierten Kirche*, 3, at www.reformiert .de/tl_files/reformiert.de/Bilder/artikelbilder/pdf/Anlage_1_Verfassung.pdf (Accessed 1 March 2015).
[32] Calvin, *Institutes*, IV.xx.32.
[33] *The Bern Synod* (1532), in *Reformed Confessions of the 16th and 17th Centuries in English Translation*, vol. 1, edited by James T. Dennison, Jr. (Grand Rapids, MI: Reformation Heritage, 2008), 262.
[34] *The Belgic Confession* (1561), article 37, in *Reformed Confessions of the Sixteenth Century*, edited by Arthur Cochrane (Louisville, KY: Westminster John Knox, 2003), 219.
[35] Theodore Beza, *De iure magistratum*, edited by K. Sturm (Neukirchen-Vluyn: Neukirchener Verlag des Erziehungsvereins, 1965), 35.
[36] Barth – Brunner, *Briefwechsel 1916–1966*, 468.

Brunner thus named Barth the 'founder of a sect' who showed 'fanaticism imperilling the churches'.[37] He derived this criticism from the second thesis of Barmen, which claims that the state must be ruled by another law than that of the church. This second thesis does indeed claim that Christians cannot confess Christ as the Lord and live a worldly life in accordance with the laws of another lord, for 'as Jesus Christ is God's assurance of the forgiveness of all our sins, so in the same way and with the same seriousness he is also God's mighty claim on our whole life. Through him befalls us a joyful deliverance from the godless fetters of this world for a free, grateful service to his creatures.'[38] Thus Christians should do nothing alien to God's claim upon the whole of human life; but it is a matter of freedom when they do take action in worldly life – so long as it is done in an orderly manner and in cooperation with others for the benefit of all creatures – because they belong to God.

THE FUTURE OF THE REFORMED CHURCHES IN EUROPE

It remains characteristic of the Reformed confessional family today that sermon and theological instruction are closely united. This is true, at least, in churches which hold Calvin's understanding that both are bound together as the central task of ministers of the Word of God (*verbi divini*) in the congregation – distinct from leadership or diaconal tasks. The 'prophetic office' of preaching and the tasks of theological instruction and leading worship are closely related, but are not to be confused.

As a concluding question, what are the challenges facing Reformed churches and theology in continental Europe today? Which duties and responsibilities are foremost in the present situation? To answer these questions we must remember the characteristic Reformed formula, namely that 'the Reformed church is always in need of reforming'. In other words, churches and their confessions have to be reformed again and again. Christians therefore regularly have to decide whether their first task is to listen anew to the Word of God testified in Scripture or to adapt to the present situation. Timeliness is a legitimate aim, but only when it comes out of listening, speaking and acting in obedience to the will of God in the midst of new situations. Otherwise, in a phrase of Hermann Diem, a 'church without Christianity' can arise.

---

[37] Ibid., 463–464.
[38] *Barmen Theological Declaration* (1934), thesis 2, in *Creeds & Confessions of Faith*, vol. II, edited by Jaroslav Pelikan and Valerie Hotchkiss (New Haven, CT: Yale University Press, 2003), 507.

A significant ecumenical endeavour has been underway for Reformed churches in Europe since the Leuenberg Concord of 1973; today, this is known as the Community of Protestant Churches in Europe (CPCE). This association models the aforementioned 'harmonious diversity' of John a Lasco. In this way, the Reformed churches contribute to the larger aim of reuniting Protestant churches in Europe, and possibly beyond. An important step towards this goal is that there is mutual acceptance of ministerial orders and sacramental practices. Differences between the churches are not passed over in their gatherings, but are subjected to serious discussion. However, this takes place in the understanding that such differences must no longer separate Protestants. In the 'Agreement of the Reformation Churches in Europe', their connection is explained as a 'church fellowship' which is determined to 'strive for the fullest possible cooperation in witness and service to the world'.[39]

Correspondingly, today's Reformed churches in Europe attach great importance to the public and political responsibilities of their congregations and members. They know they are obliged to act on their belief in the one Lord of humanity, raising their voices against violations of the humanity of men and women. In 1941 this was shown in the Theses of Pomeyrol, in which members of the French Reformed Church confronted the injustices perpetrated by the occupying German forces. They made their claims with reference to Jesus Christ, the deliverer and king, declaring in his name that the church 'protests solemnly against all legislation which excludes Jews out of the human society'. The statement calls for 'resistance as spiritual necessity against all totalitarian and idolatrous influence'.[40] Another example is the text published by the Moderamen, leaders of the German Reformed covenant, at the height of the Cold War in 1982, entitled 'The Commitment to Jesus Christ and the Responsibility of the Church for Peace'. It argues against the deployment of arms capable of mass extermination, stating 'an unconditional "No!", a No without any Yes, which is spoken in the confession of faith in God the creator, the redeemer and the liberator'.[41]

The reference in the Leuenberg Concord to 'cooperation in witness and service to the world' points to the missionary task. This picks up

---

[39] *Leuenberg Concord* (1973), article 29, at www.leuenberg.net/sites/default/files/media/PDF/publications/konkordie-en.pdf (accessed 1 March 2015).

[40] *Theses of Pomeyrol* (1941), at www.protestants.org/index.php?id=2574 (accessed 1 March 2015).

[41] *Das Bekenntnis zu Jesus Christus und die Friedensverantwortung der Kirche. Eine Erklärung des Moderamens des Reformierten Bundes* (1982), at www.reformiert-info.de/side.php?news_id=230&part_id=0&part3_id=0&navi=1 (accessed 1 March 2015).

the pronouncement of Reformed churches in the Netherlands, who taught that the worship service is a time of refreshment in the midst of the mission of the whole congregation to serve all people as witnesses of Jesus Christ. In this understanding the Sunday service ends not with a so-called blessing of dismissal, but with a blessing of *commission* as servants of God. This is an important understanding today as Reformed churches lose members, especially in western Europe. In the past, European societies sent missionaries to foreign countries. Today, missionaries from the rest of the world are necessary and welcome partners to Reformed churches in Europe.

European church leaders need not therefore limit themselves to managing decline, attempting, for example, to keep people in the church through reinterpreting sacramental celebrations as life-long 'liminal rites'. Rather, in the present situation they have to follow through on what Karl Barth wrote in 1959:

> The community of Jesus Christ is for the world, i.e., for each and every [human being] ... Even within the world to which it belongs, it does not exist ecstatically or eccentrically with reference to itself, but wholly with reference to it, to the world around. It saves and maintains its own life as it interposes and gives itself for all other human creatures.[42]

This interprets what Jesus said to his disciples, and says again to his disciples today: 'You are the salt of the earth' and 'You are the light of the world' (Matt. 5:13 and 14).

Further reading

Cochrane, Arthur C. (ed.). *Reformed Confessions of the Sixteenth century*. Louisville, KY: Westminster John Knox, 2003.

Hart, Darryl G. *Calvinism. A History*. New Haven, CT and London: Yale University Press, 2013.

Lindberg, Carter. *The European Reformations*, 2nd ed. Oxford: Wiley-Blackwell, 2009.

---

[42] Karl Barth, *Church Dogmatics*, vol. IV/3.2 (Edinburgh: T&T Clark, 1962), 762.

16 Reformed theology in the British Isles
DAVID A. S. FERGUSSON

This chapter explores some developments within Reformed theology in the British Isles from 1700 to 2000. The field is defined by the work of theologians from churches which are formally aligned with the Reformed tradition: these include principally the Presbyterian and Congregational churches of England, Wales, Ireland and Scotland, many of which belong today to the World Communion of Reformed Churches.[1] By restricting the discussion in this way, no attempt will be made to consider the significant influence of Reformed theology in the evangelical wing of the Anglican churches or within Methodist and Baptist circles.[2]

What will emerge are common patterns of engagement with distinctive themes and problems: the legacy of Reformed orthodoxy and debates around election and the scope of Christ's atonement; Arian and Unitarian developments, particularly amongst English Presbyterians; the influence of Enlightenment philosophy; the challenges of biblical criticism; and the impact of German theology from the mid-nineteenth century onwards. Each of these challenges was received and met in ways that reflect the different ecclesiological and socio-political conditions that obtained across the British Isles. The established and national Church of Scotland was Reformed and Presbyterian, and dominated the Divinity Faculties of the ancient universities. In England, by contrast, the Reformed tradition was represented in the dissenting academies and in ways that reflected the greater religious and theological diversity of English nonconformism. The religious culture of Wales was

---

[1] 'The World Communion of Reformed Churches is committed to embody a Reformed identity as articulated in the Ecumenical Creeds of the early church, in the historic confessions of the Reformation, and as continued in the life and witness of the Reformed community.' Article II of the Constitution of the WCRC, at http://wcrc.ch/wp-content/uploads/2015/04/WCRC-ConstitutionAndBylaws.pdf (accessed 1 March 2015).

[2] The exception is Welsh Calvinistic Methodism, which is largely synonymous with the Presbyterian Church of Wales.

somewhat different, with strong revivalist strains ensuring that scholastic debates amongst Calvinist theologians continued much later than elsewhere. And in Northern Ireland, the reception of biblical criticism, evolutionary theory and German theology was more cautious and generally at a slower pace than in Scotland where the socio-political status of the church appeared more secure. So despite many shared features and much interaction, the Reformed tradition developed in different ways across the United Kingdom. One feature that almost all Reformed theologians shared, however, was a strong commitment to the office of preaching. This ensured that the vocation of the theologian was closely related to the demands of the pulpit.

THE CONFESSIONAL LEGACY

Much doctrinal output wrestled with the legacy of standards such as the Westminster Confession (1647) and the Savoy Declaration (1658). Despite their ecclesiological differences, both reflected the prevailing Reformed orthodoxy of the seventeenth century. Yet, by the beginning of the eighteenth century, signs of stress in the reception of these confessional standards were already evident. Most of these were generated by the doctrine of election and related notions such as a limited or particular atonement. Familiar concerns can be detected around the justice of God, the free offer of the Gospel to all and the unconditional love of Christ. These issues were later intensified by the experience of working in mission fields outside the Christian West and the arrival of higher criticism in the British Isles.

Anxieties were also registered about the formal status of confessional standards and the role of the state in enforcing them. This was particularly apparent in the first subscription controversy in Ireland in the 1720s, when a group of Presbyterians insisted upon freedom of individual conscience with reference to the interpretation of Scripture, refusing in principle the subordinate norms of confessional standards enforceable by ecclesiastical or civil authorities.[3] On occasion, this position could be presented as a return to the original ideals of the Reformation and the principle of *sola scriptura*, although it also reflects the New Light tendencies of the early Enlightenment. At the same time, the more evangelical Secession churches in the eighteenth century would also find themselves at odds with traditional Reformed notions

---

[3] See, for example, *Scripture Politics: Ulster Presbyterians and Irish Radicalism in the Late Eighteenth Century*, by I. R. McBride (Oxford: Clarendon Press, 1998), 41–61.

of the state as the enforcer of true religion, despite seeking in other respects to maintain the purity of Reformed doctrine.

In Scotland, the 'Marrow controversy' followed the circulation and promotion of the ideas expounded in *The Marrow of Modern Divinity*, an anonymous mid-seventeenth-century compilation in dialogue form of extracts from the leading Reformers.[4] Thomas Boston, minister at Simprin, came across the *Marrow* while visiting a parishioner and found its teachings to be a light sent from God. The Marrow offers a more evangelical brand of Reformed theology which paved the way after the covenanting era for the transition from a cerebral and legalistic version of Westminster confessionalism as the state-sanctioned religion, to the experiential and individualistic forms of evangelical revivalism that would flourish later in the eighteenth century. Yet the teachings of the Marrow aroused controversy and opposition within the courts of the church, particularly its claims about an evangelical repentance succeeding faith, expressions which suggested an unlimited atonement, and its emphasis on assurance as intrinsic to faith. Its remarks about the role of Law in the Christian life raised familiar hackles against antinomianism. From a distance of three centuries, the actual dogmatic differences between the 'Marrow men' and their opponents such as James Hadow, Principal of St Mary's College in St Andrews, seem paper thin. Yet the teaching of Boston and the Erskine brothers, Ebenezer and Ralph, led to their being formally rebuked by the General Assembly in 1721, an outcome which even at the time seemed unduly harsh. Some of them were later to leave the established church in the First Secession of 1733, a new polity being established which insisted upon the greater spiritual independence of the church from the state. Yet the Marrow theology did not represent a real break with the theology of the Westminster Confession. It is better interpreted as offering a more evangelical reading of the classical Reformed tradition in the face of overbearing legalist tendencies that were in the ascendancy in Scotland after the Act of Settlement (1690) and the Treaty of Union (1707).

Similar concerns were articulated around the same time by Congregationalists in England. Although never as monolithically committed to Westminster orthodoxy as their Scottish Presbyterian counterparts, the Congregationalists included strong defenders of hyper-Calvinism. The Savoy Declaration (1658) modifies or expands

---

[4] The standard work on the Marrow controversy is *The Marrow Controversy 1718–28*, by David C. Lachman (Edinburgh: Rutherford House, 1988). See Stephen G. Myers, *Scottish Federalism and Covenantalism in Transition* (Eugene, OR: Pickwick, 2015).

the Westminster Confession on key points, including a reference to the spread of the Gospel 'in divers times, and by sundry parts', thus suggesting an unrestricted offer to all nations and kinds of people.[5] There is nothing here explicitly to contradict the Westminster Confession, but an emphasis on the unrestricted scope of the Gospel would later lead to a muting of the doctrines of election and particular or limited atonement.

In 1737, Matthias Maurice published a tract *A Modern Question Modestly Answer'd*, in which he argued for a universal preaching of the Gospel together with the duty of all to respond. 'The everlasting gospel is to be preached as God gives opportunity to all people, be they who they will.'[6] His rebuttal of some key tenets of hyper-Calvinism appears to have won the day in England, and it became the position of those such as Philip Doddridge who advocated world mission. One cannot proclaim to the unconverted a doctrine of election which tells them that they might be included in the number of those determined for eternal salvation; such conditionality, as Maurice insisted, was alien to Christ and the teaching of Scripture. As Alan Sell notes, this became 'more than a matter of homiletic pragmatism; it entailed a moral protest against the kind of God scholastic Calvinism was deemed to portray'.[7]

Yet those who continued to adhere to the classical Reformed tradition were not lacking in possible responses. In Wales, five-point Calvinism continued to flourish, with intense debates concerning the nature and extent of the atonement being conducted well into the nineteenth century. The view of John Elias that Christ's sufferings were in exact equivalence to the punishment due to the elect was eventually overcome by a more moderate Calvinist consensus combining notions of sufficiency and efficiency in the 1823 Confession of Faith.[8] The focus increasingly fell upon the doctrine of the atoning work of Christ, rather than election per se. Lesis Edwards, the most significant mid-century

---

[5] *Savoy Declaration* (1658), article 20.3, at www.reformed.org/master/index.html?mainframe=/documents/Savoy_Declaration/ (accessed 1 March 2015).

[6] Matthias Maurice, *A Modern Question Modestly Answer'd* (London: James Buckland, 1737), 21.

[7] Alan P. F. Sell, 'From Worms to Sunbeams: The Dilution of Calvinism in English Congregationalism', in *Enlightenment, Ecumenism, Evangel: Theological Themes and Thinkers 1550–2000* (Milton Keynes, UK: Paternoster, 2005), 151.

[8] See D. Densil Morgan, 'Calvinism in Wales: c1590–1909', *Welsh Journal of Religious History*, 4 (2009), 22–36, and 'Theology Amongst the Welsh Calvinistic Methodists, c.1811–1914', in *The History of Welsh Calvinistic Methodism, III: Growth and Consolidation*, edited by John Gwynfor Jones (Cardiff: Presbyterian Church of Wales, 2013), 70–89.

theologian in Wales, wrote an influential study in 1860 *Athrawiaeth yr Iawn* (The Doctrine of the Atonement) which offered a more irenic yet still recognisably Calvinist account of the personal work of Christ.[9] In Scotland, Ralph Wardlaw, a descendant of Ebenezer Erskine, published *The Extent of the Atonement* (1830), in which he invoked the old medieval formula that the death of Christ was sufficient for the salvation of all, but efficient only for some. This justified the universal offer of the Gospel while making sense of the admixture of responses. But in the interests of propagating the Gospel and reassuring the faithful, the emphasis tended to be placed on the universal love of God rather than a primal decree which separated elect from reprobate.[10] With Greville Ewing, Wardlaw founded a Congregational academy in Glasgow in 1811. A courageous supporter of abolitionism, he exercised an influence on David Livingstone.

During the first half of the nineteenth century, church growth outside the Establishment, particularly in England and Wales, created a strong nonconformist culture which was evident until the early twentieth century.[11] With its stress upon adult literacy, the attention to lengthy sermons, the encouragement of wide reading, discussion of ideas and a commitment to poetry and hymnody, this generated a political progressivism, often allied to the Whig party, in which nonconformists lent support to abolitionism, universal suffrage, temperance and access to university education and later to welfare reforms. Ironically, the political effects of this movement were most evident in the new liberalism which flourished at the beginning of the twentieth century just at a time when nonconformist churches were displaying early signs of their decline.

Within the Scottish Kirk, similar debates surrounding the doctrine of the atonement were conducted against the backdrop of a renascent Calvinist evangelicalism after 1800. The most notable case was that of John McLeod Campbell, who was deposed from his ministerial charge in Rhu by the General Assembly of 1831. He was formally charged with preaching the doctrine of a universal pardon and maintaining that assurance was of the essence of faith. Ministering thereafter to an independent congregation in Glasgow, McLeod Campbell spent the rest of his career in ecclesiastical isolation. Yet his celebrated work *The Nature of the Atonement* (1856) was to prove a landmark study. Here McLeod

---

[9] See Morgan, 'Calvinism in Wales', 76–79.

[10] See Sell, 'From Worms to Sunbeams', 154.

[11] R. Tudor Jones writes of a 'Nonconformist civilization' in the period 1850–1914. See *Congregationalism in Wales* (Cardiff: University of Wales Press, 2004).

Campbell attacks two themes of the classical Reformed tradition – the limitation of the atonement and the idea of penal substitution. In their place, he offers a more relational approach by which Christ's identification with sinners culminated in an act of vicarious repentance on which our reconciliation with God rests. Despite some of the underdeveloped and quixotic features of this account, it can be read as retrieving themes from the Greek Fathers and also Luther, who is quoted more frequently than Calvin. Later theologians would regard it as one of the finest works of the Scottish Reformed tradition. A doctrine of universal atonement became more characteristic of Scottish theology and preaching, especially in the work of James Denney, H. R. Mackintosh and Donald Baillie.[12] On the occasion of the award of the DD degree to McLeod Campbell in 1868, John Caird remarked that in the long run the heretic had converted the church. Forming a triumvirate with Thomas Erskine of Linlathen and Edward Irving, he is generally viewed as adumbrating significant shifts in Scottish theology during the Victorian period.

In the wake of several theological changes, confessional subscription was heavily modified in late Victorian Scotland. While retaining the Westminster Confession as the sole subordinate standard of faith, the Presbyterian churches claimed that it could be consistently upheld alongside a stress on the universal scope of the Gospel, its free offer to all, the possible salvation of those who lived beyond the reach of Christian preaching, a symbolic reading of the six days of creation in Genesis 1, and opposition to compulsory measures in religion. In retrospect, this appears to be an uneasy compromise between rival parties which generated a degree of confusion. More than a century later, the Church of Scotland still awaits a confessional resolution of these matters.

ENGAGEMENT WITH ENLIGHTENMENT PHILOSOPHY

After 1700, Reformed scholars throughout the British Isles were extensively involved in developments in philosophy. Institutional factors were again at work in this process. After the establishment of chairs of philosophy in the Scottish universities, the subject increasingly functioned as a discrete discipline alongside theology. The appearance of dissenting academies to provide higher education for nonconformists, who were excluded from Oxbridge, also ensured that Reformed scholars in

---

[12] See James Denney, *The Christian Doctrine of Reconciliation* (London: Hodder and Stoughton, 1917), H. R. Mackintosh, *The Christian Experience of Forgiveness* (London: Nisbet, 1927), and Donald M. Baillie, *God Was In Christ* (London: Faber and Faber, 1948).

England, Wales and Ireland were receptive to new philosophical ideas from the time of the early Enlightenment. Much of the interaction was with English deist thought, resulting in some theological drift. The moderates in Scotland were suspected of harbouring deist leanings. Professor John Simson of Glasgow was twice tried for heresy on account of suspicions that his teachings inter alia inclined towards Arianism.[13]

In English nonconformism, greater theological latitude proved possible owing to the diversity of institutions, congregational autonomy and an intellectual climate that was more receptive to the ideals of toleration. Many had studied in Glasgow under Simson, Hutcheson and Leechman, scholars who seemed sympathetic to new methods and willing to adopt heterodox conclusions. As a result, we see a movement towards Arianism (in its modern forms) and Unitarianism, partly owing to philosophical influences but also through close engagement with Scripture. This was particularly marked in Presbyterian rather than Congregational churches in the latter part of the eighteenth century. Doubts around traditional formulations of the Trinity and of the person and work of Christ marked out a pathway from Arian subordination-ism through Socinianism to Unitarianism. The outstanding example of this theological journey is Joseph Priestley, a product of the dissenting academy at Daventry. In *An History of the Corruptions of Christianity* (1782), Priestley argues that the doctrine of the Trinity is a sheer contradiction that was softened only by appeals to mystery. His two-volume *Institutes of Natural and Revealed Religion* (1772–1774) became the standard textbook of Unitarian beliefs. For Priestley, Christ is a human being only, albeit one of supreme religious significance. Through a study of Scripture and church tradition, he argues that later doctrines of the incarnation and Trinity are corruptions of an original Christology which understood Jesus as a human person set apart by the providence of God. One estimate suggests that of the 250 Presbyterian chapels in England in 1812, more than one half espoused Unitarianism by 1824.[14]

Many of the Presbyterian ministers of Ulster had trained in Glasgow or on the continent. Francis Hutcheson, the leading philosopher of the early Scottish Enlightenment, had studied initially at the dissenting academy at Killyleagh in County Down and been licensed as a minister by the Presbytery of Armagh. As a result of the close ties between

---

[13] See the discussion in *The Divinity Professors in the University of Glasgow* by H. M. B. Reid (Glasgow: Maclehose, Jackson and Company, 1923), 204–240.

[14] Olive M. Griffiths, *Religion and Learning: A Study in English Presbyterian Thought from 1662 to the Foundations of the Unitarian Movement* (Cambridge: Cambridge University Press, 1935), 150.

Scottish and Irish Presbyterians, the latter tended to mirror the disputes that divided the Church of Scotland, particularly with respect to the status of the civil authorities.[15] The aforementioned first subscription controversy in the 1720s was generated by a minority of ministers who resisted the imposition of creedal tests in principle, unlike the second subscription controversy which involved those overtly sympathetic to Arian claims. Yet recent scholarship has suggested that even at the time of the first controversy there were already signs of the incursion of early Enlightenment views into Irish Presbyterianism, particularly through the work of those such as John Abernethy of Antrim who had established the Belfast Society in 1705. Here parallels with latitudinarianism in England and moderatism in Scotland have been drawn.[16] By the mid-nineteenth century, many of the more liberal and Unitarian trends that could be discerned in England at an earlier period were apparent amongst Irish Presbyterians.

In Scotland, the moderate clergy were at the forefront of debates on epistemology, ethics, history, literature and sociology. The cast of Enlightenment literati included figures such as Frances Hutcheson, Thomas Reid, William Robertson, Adam Ferguson, Hugh Blair and George Campbell, all of whom were ministers of the Kirk. Much effort was expended in responding to the scepticism of their friend David Hume, the doyen of the Scottish Enlightenment, whether through the so-called common-sense philosophy of Reid or the defence of miracles by Campbell.

In the present context, the most pressing question is whether there was anything distinctively Reformed in this range of intellectual activity. In some respects, it appears quite remote from the theological concerns that were evident around the time of the Marrow controversy: little attention is devoted to the doctrines of predestination or the work of Christ. A more positive view of human nature was suggested by Hutcheson's moral sense theory and Reid's account of our intellectual and practical powers than seems warranted by a Calvinist rendition of total depravity. The confidence in the power of reason to provide knowledge about the world, human nature and our social obligations appears to be far removed from the focus on Scripture and revelation that characterised Reformed orthodoxy. A much higher value is now attached to

---

[15] David Hempton and Myrtle Hill, *Evangelical Protestantism in Ulster Society 1740–1890* (London: Routledge, 1992).

[16] For example, A. W. Godfrey Brown, 'A Theological Interpretation of the First Subscription Controversy (1719–1728)', in *Challenge and Conflict: Essays in Irish Presbyterian History and Doctrine*, edited by J. L. M. Haire (Antrim, UK: W&G Baird, 1981), 28–45.

religious toleration, partly as a reaction to the violence of the covenanting era and partly in Scotland through a recognition of the benefits brought by union with England.

Nevertheless, writers such as Alexander Broadie have pointed to ways in which some standard Reformed tenets appear to be present in the sermons of Blair and the philosophical output of Reid.[17] These include a stress on the limits of human knowledge, a sense of an overarching divine providence, and trust in a practical wisdom that is sufficient for the business of life. While these may be shorn of their links to election and the work of Christ, they represent a form of Reformed theism that remains in contact with the earlier theological tradition and is encapsulated in Wolterstorff's account of 'living wisely in the darkness'.[18] God has constituted us in such a way that we are given just sufficient light for our earthly existence. But we cannot speculate beyond this or aspire to the intellectual pretensions of earlier rationalist philosophies.

THE RECEPTION OF GERMAN PHILOSOPHY, THEOLOGY AND BIBLICAL CRITICISM

One of the richest periods in the history of theology, the nineteenth century witnessed a resurgence of interest in the classical Reformed tradition. Reacting against the Moderate hegemony of the Enlightenment period, evangelical theologians in Scotland displayed a renewed adherence to the Westminster Confession and the doctrinal claims of Calvinist theology. After the Disruption of 1843, the theology of the Free Church of Scotland was characterised by a commitment to biblical authority and to traditional Reformed teaching. A leading example is William Cunningham's posthumous *Historical Theology* (1862), which offers a formidable defence of Calvinist theology through the study of church history. Setting Pelagianism, Arminianism and Socianism as stages on a slippery slope, Cunningham maintains that only Calvinist teaching can preserve the scriptural witness to human sin, divine sovereignty and the means of redemption. This is asserted as a recovery of the standard tenets of Reformed faith from the degeneracy of the Moderate era.[19] It is also worth recalling in this context that through the efforts

---

[17] Alexander Broadie, *The Scottish Enlightenment* (Edinburgh: Birlinn, 2001), 113–150.

[18] Nicholas Wolterstorff, 'God and Darkness in Reid', in *Thomas Reid: Context, Influence, Significance*, edited by Joseph Houston (Edinburgh: Dunedin Academic Press, 2004), 77–102.

[19] William Cunningham, *Historical Theology*, vol. II, 2nd ed., (Edinburgh: T&T Clark, 1864), 506–507. Cunningham's work may be seen as continuing the doctrinal

of the Calvin Translation Society a stream of publications appeared in Edinburgh which disseminated the writings of Calvin to a wider public constituency.

Yet by the second half of the nineteenth century, the influence of newer trends can be detected. The reception of idealist philosophy in England and Scotland was delayed, but after the publication of James Hutchison Stirling's *The Secret of Hegel* (1865), its influence became marked, as too did that of Kant, whose critical philosophy provided the backdrop to idealism. Many Reformed theologians from Britain studied in German universities from about the 1860s: Marburg, Göttingen, Berlin and Tübingen became popular student destinations. The linguistic facility acquired by a younger generation of theologians enabled English translations of Schleiermacher, Ritschl, Harnack, Herrmann, Buber, Barth, Brunner, Bultmann and Bonhoeffer. Much of this was facilitated by the emergence of a major theological publishing house in Edinburgh – T&T Clark, founded in 1821.

Idealism was more influential in philosophical than theological circles, although some of the key figures came from Reformed backgrounds, for example, Edward Caird in Scotland and Henry Jones in Wales. Within theology, John Caird, brother of Edward, provided the most striking example of the appropriation of idealist philosophy into Christian doctrine. Caird held the Chair of Divinity in Glasgow and later became University Principal. His work included an exposition of the philosophy of Spinoza (1888), whose work he interpreted and sought to correct along the lines of Hegelian idealism. A similar strategy can be found in the writings of James Martineau, the leading Unitarian philosopher who taught at Manchester New College, who had also produced a study of Spinoza (1882) in which the Spinozist handling of substance is criticised. Martineau's own commitments to an ethical theism had been shaped by the German idealists and American transcendentalism. While his work may seem remote from the Protestant theology of his Huguenot ancestors, it can be understood only by reference to the tradition from which it emerged. For both Martineau and Caird, the link between ethics and theism, the stress on social reform, and the devotion to preaching are conditioned by their Reformed heritage even as they move some distance from its earlier doctrinal basis.

commitments of those eighteenth-century evangelical theologians in Scotland who continued to embrace the terms of Reformed orthodoxy. Several of them, including John Erskine, had close links with Jonathan Edwards.

Another significant figure, influenced if not captured by idealism, was A. M. Fairbairn, whose career began in Scotland in the Evangelical Union but who later migrated to English Congregationalism, eventually becoming in 1886 the first Principal of Mansfield College in Oxford. In many respects, Fairbairn provides a benchmark for the liberalising of Reformed theology in late Victorian Britain. He welcomed evolution and higher criticism, while also advocating the comparative study of religion. Viewing the sovereign power of God as overstated in Calvinism, he preferred instead to emphasise the divine fatherhood. Fairbairn's Christology is shaped by an account of Jesus' realisation of a life of sonship before God. This is the ideal for the human race which God wills to impart to each person.[20]

Idealism may not have captured the hearts and minds of many Reformed theologians, perhaps because it continued to be viewed as pantheist and reductive of the doctrines of the person and work of Christ. But other German trends were more widely adopted by British Reformed theologians. These included the liberal theology of Ritschl, the higher criticism of Wellhausen, and the kenotic Christologies of Gess and Thomasius. Ritschl's commitment was to historical study and to a Jesus whose significance resided in his instantiation of the Kingdom of God, a community to be understood primarily in ethical and religious terms. Not only did this accentuate the importance of historical work, but it also tended towards a deprecation of natural theology and speculative metaphysics. A. E. Garvie, who was later to become Principal of New College and then Hackney College in London, produced an impressive study of Ritschlianism which revealed his immersion in the German theology of his day.[21] Here Ritschl's theology is commended for opposing speculative rationalism in its articulation of central Christian doctrines and for its positive stress on the Bible and Jesus. Discerning a divergence in the later Ritschlian school, he notes the emphasis on more historical and practical work in Harnack, while commending writers such as Kaftan and Herrmann for their return to evangelical themes including sin, atonement, the divinity of Christ and the work of the Spirit. Garvie himself might fairly be reckoned a 'liberal evangelical' throughout his career, and he advances Ritschl's approach as a remedy to the 'undue dependence on ecclesiastical authority' which he finds in Great Britain.[22]

---

[20] A. M. Fairbairn, *Christ in Modern Theology* (London: Hodder and Stoughton, 1868).

[21] A. E. Garvie, *The Ritschlian Theology* (Edinburgh: T&T Clark, 1899).

[22] Garvie, *The Ritschlian Theology*, 395.

The late nineteenth century also witnessed the flourishing of higher criticism in British theology. Although it arrived relatively late from the continent, biblical criticism proved capable of arousing widespread controversy. In Scotland, William Robertson Smith was removed from his post in the Free Church College at Aberdeen in 1881 for opinions expressed in an article on the Bible in the ninth edition of the *Encyclopædia Britannica*. Although his conclusions would now be quite commonplace, the manner in which he propagated his opinions was adjudged irresponsible. A nationwide controversy ensued. Robertson Smith maintained that his teaching was consistent with a strong account of biblical authority – here he appealed to the Lutheran notion that the authority of Scripture resided in its witness to divine revelation in history rather than in any inherent property of inerrancy – but the Free Church of Scotland found this to be insufficient. Smith was later appointed to the Chair of Arabic in Cambridge. Subsequent heresy trials continued in Scotland, although both George Adam Smith, an Aberdeen Old Testament scholar, and Marcus Dods, an Edinburgh New Testament critic, prevailed against their opponents in the courts of the church.

In English nonconformism, a similar process of engagement took place, albeit without the high profile controversies that beset Scotland.[23] Samuel Davidson resigned his position at Lancashire Independent College in Manchester in 1857 after he had raised doubts about the Mosaic authorship of the Pentateuch and the nature of prophetic inspiration. Yet his case was the exception rather than the rule. After 1880, the English Free Churches came quite quickly to accept biblical criticism. Earlier fears of naturalism and doctrinal reductionism were largely banished by a theologically conservative group of scholars demonstrating that historical criticism could be constructively allied to orthodox belief. This approach of 'believing criticism' had gradually won the day in the Free Church of Scotland and so it did also in England around the same time. Alongside their Anglican and Methodist colleagues, the contribution of scholars from Reformed backgrounds to biblical scholarship is evident in two respects. First, several of the leading figures to emerge in the twentieth century were from Presbyterian and Congregational backgrounds – C. H. Dodd, T. W. Manson, W. D. Davies and George Caird all achieved international prominence in the field. And second, some of the most successful attempts to disseminate the findings of biblical scholarship in the wider church were undertaken by those

---

[23] See Willis B. Glover, *Evangelical Nonconformists and Higher Criticism in the Nineteenth Century* (London: Independent Press, 1954).

with Reformed roots. These include William Robertson Nicoll, editor of *the Expositor's Bible, The Expository* (established in 1884) and *The British Weekly* (established in 1886), and James Hastings, who edited the *Dictionary of the Bible* (1898–1902), *The Expository Times* (from 1889) and the renowned thirteen-volume *Encyclopædia of Religion and Ethics* (1908–1921).

In the Presbyterian Church of Ireland, suspicion of biblical criticism continued well into the twentieth century. The rigorous inerrantism of the Free Church of Scotland in its earlier years was maintained until the late nineteenth century in Belfast. A key figure here was Robert Watts, who viewed the work of his more liberal colleagues in Edinburgh with some suspicion, preferring instead the greater orthodoxy of the Hodges and Warfield in Princeton. The influence of Watts and others coupled with the different denominational and political situation in Northern Ireland prevented historical criticism from gaining a foothold until the arrival of a younger generation of biblical scholars such as Thomas Walker. Despite being investigated for heresy in the 1920s both Ernest Davey, a church historian, and James Haire, a theologian, were exonerated, thus suggesting that a cautious adoption of historical criticism could be maintained.

While biblical criticism was being hotly debated, theologians were generally making their peace with Darwinism through advocating theories of theistic evolution which left most of their theological convictions undisturbed. This was certainly true in Scotland in the work of Robert Flint and Robert Rainy, Principal of New College, whose inaugural lecture in 1874 pointed cautiously though decisively towards an accommodation with Darwinism. Like his Anglican counterparts, he was able to offer a qualified welcome to the new evolutionary science. The exception was in Belfast, where John Tyndall's explosive address to the British Association for the Advancement of Science in the same year was widely perceived as an explicit attack on theology. It produced a succession of ripostes from Presbyterian theologians, especially Watts who thundered against the new science as interpreted by Tyndall as redolent of a dangerously immoral Epicureanism. This was a system which had 'wrought the ruin of the communities and individuals who have acted out its principles in the past; and if the people of Belfast substitute it for the holy religion of the Son of God, and practise its degrading dogmas, the moral destiny of the metropolis of Ulster may easily be forecast'.[24] One consequence of this was that Presbyterian theology in

---

[24] Quoted by David N. Livingstone, 'Science, Region and Religion: The Reception of Darwinism in Princeton, Belfast and Edinburgh', in *Disseminating Darwinism: The*

Belfast tended to view evolutionary theory as inherently naturalist and anti-theistic in its loss of teleological notions.[25] As David N. Livingstone has shown, 'the theory of evolution was absorbed in Edinburgh, repudiated in Belfast, and tolerated in Princeton'.[26]

Kenotic Christology, another German import, flourished on Reformed as well as Anglican soil in the writings of A. B. Bruce, H. R. Mackintosh and P. T. Forsyth.[27] Kenoticism enabled theologians to combine a commitment to the historical Jesus as discerned by Gospel criticism with the classical Christology of Chalcedon, while also resonating with the notion of the suffering of God which was so prevalent in Anglican theology from *Lux Mundi* (1889) onwards. The Jesus of the Gospels could not perform miracles in his home town. He confessed his ignorance of the precise conditions of the end times, and he struggled to submit to the will of God in the days of his passion, all of which confirmed his human finitude. To make sense of these creaturely aspects of Christ while yet affirming his divinity, kenotic theologians, following Philippians 2: 5–11, appealed to the notion of the Son of God divesting or emptying himself of his divinity.

In one the most nuanced defences of divine kenosis, P. T. Forsyth, Principal of Hackney College in London, argued that we should not view this as a psychological theory of *how* God became human – this is a hopeless pursuit which is beyond our capacity. Nor should we regard the Son of God as simply abandoning his divinity. We would do much better to think in terms of a contraction or change in the mode in which divinity is expressed. (H. R. Mackintosh spoke similarly of a 'transposition' of powers.) Under the conditions of a human life, divinity is dynamically manifested so as to enable development, growth of self-consciousness and the fulfilment of Christ's divine identity in his resurrection and ascension. Forsyth's kenotic Christology is determined by his conviction that the fundamental characteristic of God is 'holy love' which must be 'intensified within the conditions of the saving

Role of Place, Race, Religion, and Gender, edited by R. L. Numbers and J. Stenhouse (Cambridge: Cambridge University Press, 1999), 14.

[25] For further discussion, see Andrew R. Holmes, 'Presbyterians and Science in the North of Ireland before 1874', *British Journal for the History of Science* 41.4 (2008): 541–565.

[26] Livingstone, 'Science, Region and Religion', 16.

[27] A. B. Bruce, *The Humiliation of Christ* (Edinburgh: T&T Clark, 1876), H. R. Mackintosh, *The Doctrine of the Person of Jesus Christ* (Edinburgh: T&T Clark, 1912), P. T. Forsyth, *The Person and Place of Jesus Christ* (London: Independent Press, 1909). See also David Brown, *Divine Humanity: Kenosis Explored and Defended* (London: SCM, 2011).

work'.[28] This requires us to think of a kenotic movement on the part of God rather than an abandonment of divinity. If we cannot explain the psychology of the incarnation, we must at least affirm that the 'divine qualities were kept, but only in the mode that salvation made necessary'.[29] Forsyth's approach tends to eschew kenosis as the metaphysic fulcrum of the incarnation; instead it becomes a category for understanding the person and work of Christ dramatically and historically. And yet, as Colin Gunton later pointed out, Forsyth does not altogether escape the use of metaphysical language in his claims about different modes of being.[30] Here again some of the standard problems of kenoticism begin to emerge. Forsyth would probably argue that 'it is a choice of difficulties'[31] and that without some use of kenotic language we are unable to make sense of the story of Jesus as genuinely human and historical.

Kenotic Christology faced serious criticism from a subsequent generation of theologians. The standard criticisms were registered by Donald Baillie: the kenoticists, he argued, could not do justice to the eternal humanity of Christ which seems to be a feature of the New Testament and the creeds; they created speculative problems about the cosmic functions of the divine Logos during the years of Christ's life on earth; and the standard theories tended to reduce the incarnation to a temporary metamorphosis rather than to present it as the self-revelation of the eternal being of God.[32] Yet Baillie also suggests, appealing to the work of Sergius Bulgakov, that the concept of kenosis as God's self-giving can be viewed as an expression of God's eternal identity within the Trinity and analogously in creation, incarnation, and atonement. Although this is not developed, it is a view that is not so far from that of P. T. Forsyth. As Gunton remarked, 'Forsyth very nearly said that.'[33]

TWENTIETH-CENTURY PERSONALISM

The category of the 'personal' received close philosophical attention in the philosophy of the late nineteenth century and was adopted by several leading theologians. John Oman, a United Presbyterian minister

---

[28] Forsyth, *The Person and Place of Jesus Christ*, 319.
[29] Ibid.
[30] Colin E. Gunton, *Yesterday and Today: A Study of Continuities in Christology* (London: Darton, Longman and Todd, 1983), 169–173.
[31] Forsyth, *The Person and Place of Jesus Christ*, 294.
[32] Donald M. Baillie, *God Was in Christ* (London: Faber & Faber, 1948), 94–98.
[33] Gunton, *Yesterday and Today*, 172.

from Orkney, taught for most of his career at Westminster College, Cambridge. His personalist theology was ethical, evolutionary and liberal in its leanings.[34] For Oman, the nature of personhood requires us to think of the human subject as ethical, religious and social in its dimensions. Divine grace is not coercive but works with the grain of human freedom in a personal relationship that is life-enhancing and ethically fruitful. Our encounter with God is neither deterministic nor mystical but free and personal. On this basis, Oman reworks traditional accounts of sin, redemption and faith. Here Christ appears as the focal and unifying expression of God's grace who is encountered in the claims of others on us.

Oman's personalist theology moves in a universalist direction, especially with its tendency to break down the sharp distinction between general and special revelation. This proved influential on later generations of theologians who trained at Westminster College, especially H. H. Farmer and John Hick. Farmer, a distinguished preacher, who became Norris Hulse Professor in Cambridge, extended the strong sense of Kantian moral encounter while combining this with his explorations in Christian doctrine in *The Word of Reconciliation* (1966). John Hick, one of Farmer's pupils, developed a religious epistemology around the notion of an interpreted encounter with the divine presence, later extending this into a pluralist theology of religions which became a major focus of debate in later years. Hick viewed his departure from Farmer as a return to the more inclusive approach of Oman.[35]

Returning to Edinburgh in 1934 from Union Theological Seminary in New York, John Baillie adjusted his earlier liberal theology which had been established upon a Kantian moral base. In its place, he develops the notion of 'mediated immediacy' in his most original work, *Our Knowledge of God* (1936). Our knowledge of God is neither unmediated nor inferred but is given in immediate encounter through the forms of other people, nature and the story of Christ. Drawing on much of the personalist and anti-Cartesian philosophical writing of the period, Baillie develops a position that is more Christocentric than his earlier epistemology while still open to more general forms of our knowledge of God. Yet, despite his upbringing in the rigorously Calvinist setting of the Free Church manse at Gairloch, his commitment to the Reformed tradition is at most implicit. It may be more evident in his ecclesial

---

[34] John Oman, *Grace and Personality*, rev. ed. (Cambridge: Cambridge University Press, 1919).

[35] For an account of the relation of Oman and Farmer to Hick, see John Hick, *An Autobiography* (Oxford: One World, 2002), 84–87.

commitments and social theology than in his doctrinal allegiances.[36] His devotional classic – *The Diary of Private Prayer* (1936) – became the best-selling work of any Scottish theologian and is translated into many languages.

Donald Baillie, younger brother of John, taught at the University of St Andrews from 1934. His most distinguished work was the afore-mentioned *God Was in Christ* (1948). Here he attempts to explicate the person of Jesus by reference to what he calls the 'paradox of grace'. Following 1 Corinthians 15:10, he claims that we are most free when our lives are captured by the grace of God working in us. The more God is alive in us, the more we become truly ourselves. Arguing that this provides a clue to the person of Christ as human and divine, Baillie claims that the paradox is present in a form that is complete and per-fect in his life: 'Is it not the same *type* of paradox, taken at the absolute degree, ... [that] the life of Christ ... was the life of a man and yet also, in a deeper and prior sense, the very life of God incarnate?'[37] His work has remained one of the more important twentieth-century essays in Christology, although critics continue to ask whether its key formu-lation can escape the charge of adoptionism despite Baillie's avowed intention to present a high Christology.

In surveying the personalist orientation of these theologians, one must ask again to what extent their work is indebted to the classical Reformed tradition. In terms of their ecclesiological commitments and the piety displayed in their writings, there are clear signs of the habits and ethos of the Reformed churches – all were heavily involved in the life of their denominations and in demand as preachers. There is also an attention to Scripture and to the importance of its critical interpretation. Yet in other respects, there is a scarcely concealed antagonism to the tenets of classical Reformed theology. Robert Mackintosh, who made his mark within English Congregationalism, regarded himself as a refu-gee from the outworn creeds and dogmas of Scottish Calvinism.[38] David S. Cairns in Aberdeen lamented his time as a student in Princeton in the 1880s, citing his hatred of Charles Hodge's dogmatism and Principal Patton's defence of double predestination.[39] In his later years, it was said

---

[36] See *Christ, Church and Society: Essays on John Baillie and Donald Baillie*, edited by David Fergusson (Edinburgh: T&T Clark, 1993).

[37] Baillie, *God Was in Christ*, 129.

[38] Cited by Alan P. F. Sell, *Nonconformist Theology in the Twentieth Century* (Milton Keynes: Paternoster, 2006), 8.

[39] Quoted by A. C. Cheyne, *The Transforming of the Kirk: Victorian Scotland's Religious Revolution* (Edinburgh: St Andrews Press, 1983), 75.

that A. E. Garvie could not contemplate a revival of Calvinism without revulsion. The doctrine of predestination was often regarded as sub-Christian, the account of divine grace was perceived as deterministic, the verbal inspiration of Scripture was viewed as impossible in the age of higher criticism, and the standard teaching on other religions was believed to be in need of radical revision. In all these ways, Reformed theology had seemingly departed from its confessional origins. For the most part, it has not returned. This ambivalence towards earlier phases of the tradition may account for the plasticity of much Reformed theology in the British Isles and the tendency in some quarters easily to absorb intellectual influences from the wider theological culture, especially in the nineteenth and early twentieth centuries. Allied to this was a greater freedom of experimentation which can be perceived as both a strength and a weakness. In other ways, however, subsequent developments were soon to reawaken the dormant interest in the historical roots of the Reformed tradition.

THE RECEPTION OF KARL BARTH'S THEOLOGY

Reaction against the spiritual sterility of liberal theology coincided with the arrival of Karl Barth on the British theological scene after 1920. Densil Morgan's fine study has registered the full range of positive and negative reactions.[40] The most formidable of Barth's exponents in the English-speaking world was Thomas F. Torrance, who established a strong base for Barth scholarship at New College in Edinburgh, despite the more ambivalent attitude of his teacher John Baillie. Building on the earlier reception of John McConnachie and H. R. Mackintosh, Torrance produced an important study of the development of Barth's theology,[41] while also presiding with Geoffrey Bromiley over the translation into English of the *Church Dogmatics*, published by T&T Clark. In addition, the *Scottish Journal of Theology*, which he founded with J. K. S. Reid in 1948, became an important forum for sympathetic scholarly engagement with Barth's theology and the wider Reformed tradition. He was also responsible for oversight of the translation of Calvin's *New Testament Commentaries*.

Torrance's own theology developed from the 1950s, with a steady output of essays and books appearing over the next forty years. Never

---

[40] D. Densil Morgan, *Barth Reception in Britain* (London: T&T Clark, 2010).
[41] Thomas F. Torrance, *Karl Barth: An Introduction to His Early Theology, 1910–31* (London: SCM, 1962).

allowing himself to be narrowly typecast as an interpreter of Barth, with whom he had sharply differed over issues in sacramental theology, he pursued his own lines of enquiry in relation to dogmatics, the relationship of theology to science, and the history of theology. Although undertaken from within the Reformed tradition and in close proximity to his understanding of Calvin, his work was fiercely critical of seventeenth-century Reformed orthodoxy, especially the Westminster Confession. More positively, his affinities with the Greek Fathers, especially Athanasius and Cyril, did much to promote Reformed–Orthodox ecumenical conversations.

Within English nonconformism, a significant if neglected contribution to Barth studies can be found. Although P. T. Forsyth, once described as a 'Barthian before Barth', did not live long enough to interact with Barth, his pupils such as Sydney Cave, F. W. Camfield and H. F. Lovell Cocks were well prepared to do so. Allied to their enthusiasm was a reaction within English Congregationalism against the prevailing liberalism, accompanied by clarion calls to return to the theological origins of the dissenting tradition. Including Nathaniel Micklem, Bernard Lord Manning, and J. S. Whale, 'the new Genevans' advocated a return to a more dialectical theology which re-asserted human sinfulness and divine redemption in more traditional categories. In all this, Barth's theology proved seminal.[42]

Morgan's commentary also reveals the impressive Welsh engagement with Barth's early work.[43] The closing sermon in *Komm, Schöpfer Geist!* was translated into Welsh in a weekly Congregationalist newspaper in 1928; this preceded the first English translation of his work. Barth's dialectical theology aroused enthusiastic reaction amongst Welsh preachers, perhaps owing to some of the similarities between the Swiss Reformed churches and nonconformist congregations in Wales, with their strong traditions in Calvinist theology and preaching. The most effective exponent of Barth's theology was John Edward Daniel (1902–1962), whose exposition of Pauline theology was heavily indebted to the *Römerbrief* and the *Christliche Dogmatik*.[44] Although not a prolific writer, Daniel was highly influential, particularly as a critic of

---

[42] F. W. Camfield, *Revelation and the Holy Spirit: An Essay in the Barthian theology* (London: Elliott Stock, 1933); A. W. Whitehouse, *The Authority of Grace: Essays in Response to Karl Barth* (Edinburgh: T&T Clark, 1981); J. S. Whale, *Christian Doctrine* (Cambridge: Cambridge University Press, 1942).

[43] Densil Morgan, *Barth Reception in Britain*, 48–62.

[44] J. E. Daniel, *Dysgeidiaeth yr Apostol Paul* (Abertawe, Wales: Llyfrfa'r Annibynwr, 1933).

liberalism in his church and in his advocacy of a stronger and more dialectical approach. Daniel wrote: 'Karl Barth's service is to have restored
the ancient scandal of the gospel to our self-sufficient world, without
concern for the views of the philosophers or scientists, but mindful only
of the claims of the gospel.[45] Elsewhere in the United Kingdom, the influence of Barth and the Reformed tradition in general was represented in
post-war ecumenical circles by Daniel Jenkins and Lesslie Newbigin, by
Colin Gunton at King's College, London and at the Assembly's College
(Union College from 1978) in Belfast by J. L. M. Haire and his successor
John Thompson. Haire had been a translator of Barth, and Thompson
later produced valuable studies of his work.[46]

CONCLUSION

Reformed theology in the British Isles reveals a striking latitude and
absorption of intellectual shifts from the Enlightenment onwards. Similar
trends, developments, controversies and challenges can be discerned,
these being handled in ways that could also reflect the different ecclesiastical, intellectual and social conditions that obtained in Scotland, England,
Wales and Northern Ireland. In the face of this theological diversity, we
may doubt whether there is a single coherent tradition in clear continuity
with the confessional standards of the early modern period. Nevertheless,
Reformed theology has also displayed a rootedness in the life of the
churches, particularly in the ministry of preaching, in the attention to
Scripture in theological writing, in social and ecumenical commitment,
and in the intermittent influence of the leading Reformed theologians –
Calvin, Schleiermacher and Barth. If not unifying the work of theologians
across the Reformed churches, these constitute recurrent themes which
are likely to prove vital to any renewal in the twenty-first century.[47]

Further reading

Fergusson, David. *Scottish Philosophical Theology 1700–2000*. Exeter: Imprint
    Press, 2007.
Griffiths, Olive M. *Religion and Learning: A Study in English Presbyterian
    Thought from 1662 to the Foundations of the Unitarian Movement*.
    Cambridge: Cambridge University Press, 1935.

[45] Quoted by Densil Morgan, *Barth Reception in Britain*, 195.
[46] For example, John M. Thompson, *Christ in Perspective: Christological Perspectives
    in the Theology of Karl Barth* (Edinburgh: St Andrews Press, 1978).
[47] I am grateful to Alan Sell, Andrew Holmes, Jay Brown and Densil Morgan for advice
    and reading suggestions on key aspects of this chapter.

McBride I. R. *Scripture Politics: Ulster Presbyterians and Irish Radicalism in the Late Eighteenth Century.* Oxford: Clarendon Press, 1998.

Pope, Robert (ed.). *T&T Clark Companion to Nonconformity.* London: T&T Clark, 2013.

Sell, Alan P. F. *Dissenting Thought and the Life of the Churches: Studies in the English Tradition.* San Francisco: Edwin Mellen, 1990.

Torrance, Thomas F. *Scottish Theology: From John Knox to John McLeod Campbell.* Edinburgh: T&T Clark, 1996.

17 Reformed theology in North America

JAMES D. BRATT

Compared to its counterparts in Europe, Reformed theology in America looks narrow at its base and wide in its crown. It was planted on the Atlantic frontier of New England from almost exclusively British sources; but owing to the early onset in America of church disestablishment, high levels of immigration, and persistent regionalism across a vast territory, it developed amid a wide variety of social contexts and ecclesiastical homes. A substantial part of this chapter therefore deals with developments in that New England base in the century and a half after the closure of its puritan age, before broadening into a consideration of the diversity of Reformed theological currents over the past 200 years.

NEW ENGLAND, 1690–1740

New England can be said to have entered the post-puritan era of its history in the 1690s, with the re-chartering of Massachusetts' government, the embarrassment of the Salem witch craze, the outbreak of a twenty-five-year war with France, and the opening of the Brattle Street Church in Boston on a more liberal platform than New England Congregationalism had known heretofore. By the end of the French wars a new, more generic British Protestant identity had started to overlay puritan memory in the region; twenty years later, the commercial prosperity and "reasonable religion" that Brattle Street signified were ascendant in New England affairs. The most notable theological responses to the situation issued from Solomon Stoddard and Cotton Mather, but a dramatically new initiative would emerge in the 1730s from Stoddard's grandson, Jonathan Edwards.

The baseline for all these developments was the Calvinist orthodoxy of the Westminster Catechism as reaffirmed by Massachusetts' Reforming Synod in 1679–1680 and enshrined in Samuel Willard's *Compleat Body of Divinity*, New England's first published systematic theology. The Brattle Street regime at first did not so much quarrel with this theology as seek to support it by the evidence of nature and canons of reason toward the goals of virtue all voiced in Addisonian tones. Most notably, Brattle Street dropped experiential regeneration from the criteria of church membership.

Solomon Stoddard and Cotton Mather

To this, Solomon Stoddard, "pope" of the Connecticut River Valley, responded with a yes and a no. He too aimed for a more inclusive church, and admitted members under the Halfway Covenant not only to baptism for their children but also to the communion table for themselves. But he still held out experiential conversion as the guarantee of salvation. The church was to be broad so as to surround as many as possible with the means of grace to that end, including the Lord's supper as a "converting ordinance." Covenant concepts diminished as the wellspring of the church, replaced by the periodic revivals that Stoddard's preaching precipitated.

Against both Stoddard on the frontier and Brattle Street nearby in Boston, Cotton Mather reasserted experiential conversion as the test of church membership. This accompanied a theology that can be described as simply the Calvinism of Dort. Yet Mather's preaching and unmatched volume of writing orchestrated a broad range of instruments on its behalf: appeals to reason, as warrant for orthodoxy; invocations of nature, intermixing the new science with "wonders"; an Enlightened-sounding promotion of virtue, as religion's sure product; and correspondence with German pietists as to the means of sealing that connection in individual heart and public sphere alike. The effects could be ironic. Among the few positive memories that Benjamin Franklin took along in flight from his Boston upbringing was the imprint of Mather's *Bonifacius: An Essay Upon the Good.*

Jonathan Edwards

It was just this susceptibility of faith to co-optation by forthrightly Arminian proposals in the 1730s that precipitated Jonathan Edwards's project of radical reconstruction. His theology is treated in detail in Chapter 10 in this volume, permitting a brief summary here. Against all intimations that one could attain the kingdom of heaven by natural reason, virtuous living, or churchly habits, Edwards asserted the necessity of a radical spiritual rebirth sparked by "a divine and supernatural light." This work of the Holy Spirit would implant in the convert a new controlling disposition or set of "holy affections" that would henceforth direct her thoughts, yearnings, and behavior. It was the affections that controlled the will – affections for good or evil, of regenerate or unregenerate aspiration. Persons in either category, Edwards reasoned, were free to do as they pleased, but they were not free to choose what – by the measure of eternity – pleased them: the Law of God or the ways of perdition. The latter, as both Scripture and history made inarguably clear, was the universal inclination of humanity; the doctrine of original sin still held true. But once its bonds were broken by new birth, the regenerate person was able and called to achieve "true virtue": not the calculated benevolences of Enlightened self-interest, but the "love of Being in general," that is, of God. This would, and so must, be manifested in "disinterested benevolence" toward all of God's creatures.

Edwards intended his work to rearticulate classic Calvinism in a voice fit for the age, so as to dispel the enlightened delusions of the time. Just as much he was trying to fathom the dynamics of the First Great Awakening, which had burst forth in his pulpit but rebounded to see him ousted therefrom. The result was a theology with distinctive markers: the controlling place he gave the affections and his all-or-nothing polarization between holiness and ungodliness there; his distinction between the natural freedom and the moral bondage of the will; his argument, respecting original sin, that God conceived of all humanity as organically present (not – or not just – legally represented) in Adam; the strong polarity he drew between self-love, however generously cast, and the disinterested benevolence God demands; and the idealist metaphysics that held that the universe and every particular it contains were not just created but were sustained in being every moment by the active mind of God. Finally, Edwards's system was pervaded by an aesthetic sensibility. The believer's new disposition, he averred, would find God's work "sweet," and would "relish" it beyond all measure, as the gravity holding together the cosmos of God's will was love.

Edwards's vision was so broad and bold that it set the agenda of theological discourse around New England for three generations. But time quickly worked changes in the system, especially in its tone and frame: Edwards's idealism, organicism, and aesthetics gave way to atomism, legalism, and moralism. This development was driven in no small part by the demands of the age. Edwards wrote his great treatises on free will and original sin in a frontier stockade amid a new war with France. British success therein sowed the seeds of the American War of Independence, which triggered a spate of constitution-writing on state and national levels; these in turn provoked intense quarrels among rival visions for what the new land ought to be. The theological consequences were marked. Having cast off earthly monarchs, Americans were in no mood for a divine majesty as Edwards (and Calvin) had conceived him. God became a moral governor instead, bound to rational rules and benevolent ends, to human happiness above all. Implementing new frameworks of law, Americans cast law as God's principal product, a law that had to respect the rights and autonomy of individual persons. Finally, like all revolutionaries, Americans could little afford scepticism or mystery in the foundations of state or church. Nor, with all at stake, could they spare any zeal in fighting for their truth. This included Edwards's successors.

THE NEW DIVINITY

The first generation, led by Edwards's students Joseph Bellamy and Samuel Hopkins, and his son Jonathan Edwards, Jr., aimed to build from the master's principles a "consistent Calvinism," remorselessly pursuing the hard questions of theological speculation to their logical conclusions. At the same time they yearned for a return of the revival that had marked their master's day, the moral fruits of which, they insisted, were the only guarantor of the virtue necessary for the survival of the new republic. In other words, their work aimed to be utterly and simultaneously Reformed, rational, and revival-friendly amid revolutionary times. The result was a "New Divinity" that materially changed the New England, indeed, the Reformed tradition.

Three of its tenets provoked the most controversy. First, Bellamy took over from the now proto-Unitarian opposition the definition of God as moral governor, and then entered into the polemical lists on issues of theodicy to make that God benevolent as measured by a rather utilitarian calculus. Second, Edwards Jr. elaborated a moral-government theory of the atonement that owed much to Jacobus Arminius's ally, Hugo Grotius. On this reading Christ's death did not provide legal satisfaction for a fixed number of the elect but created the legal preconditions under which God might effect any forgiveness at all. Third, the sins for which people needed to be forgiven were strictly their own – not Adam's imputed to them, nor a "nature" inherited from him. This eclipsing of the doctrine of original sin was clearest in the work of Samuel Hopkins, but proceeded from an intention opposite of the liberals with whom Hopkins was apparently agreeing. Hopkins wanted to drive home to each and all their own responsibility for their own sin; tracing the operation of those sins into the toils of religion itself, Hopkins insisted that all self-love had to be purged from the motives at work at each step in the salvation process. His most pointed civic application was to insist – from his pulpit in Newport, Rhode Island, capital of the American slave trade – that the ultimate test of disinterested benevolence was love shown toward the very least in human accounting, the enslaved. It was not the first time that the starkest Calvinism had politically radical conclusions.

The New Divinity faced opposition not only from without but within the Reformed camp. Closest to hand were the "Old Calvinists," New Englanders who doubted both Edwards's innovations and the revivals behind them. Moderates in temper and traditionalists all around, this party held fast to the national covenant, which Edwardseans dismissed; to an inclusive church, not one of proven regenerates only; to Christian nurture under the means of grace, which Edwardseans could disparage as the filthiest of rags. Old Calvinists maintained notions of imputation both in Adam's guilt and Christ's justifying work; the inability of the natural as well as moral will; a sinful nature behind sinful acts, with noetic as well as ethical consequences. Above all, they rejected the Edwardseans' polarized psychology, instead positing stages and gradations in one's status, motives, and spiritual evolution. Their most systematic voice was Moses Hemmenway; their foremost leader, Hopkins's Newport rival and later Yale president, Ezra Stiles; and their most lasting voice, Harriet Beecher Stowe in her novel *Oldtown Folks* (1869).

THE NEW HAVEN THEOLOGY

By the early nineteenth century, the Old Calvinists were subsumed in an alliance with the Edwardseans against the now fully fledged Unitarian party in New England. Timothy Dwight, Edwards's grandson and president of Yale in the years 1795–1817, spoke for both sides in promoting revivals and in rehabilitating the means of grace and the social consequences of piety in the venerable New England way. His program was radicalized at the hands of his students: Lyman Beecher, who became the impresario of the Second Great Awakening's moral crusades; Nathaniel William Taylor, central figure at Yale's new Divinity School; and Charles Grandison Finney, who extended the innovations of these two along the trail of the Yankee diaspora across New York State and the upper Midwest. All three claimed to be following the logic of Edwards even as they could reject some of his positive doctrines, and all three came under intense criticism from Calvinists in other regions and denominations.

The "New Haven theology" personified by Taylor was distinguished by its intense moralism and magnification of human ability.

True religion, he said, was simply the performance of one's duty as codified in the Law of God. It being the demand of God, one had the immediate duty to repent and the full natural ability to do so. Total depravity, which Taylor affirmed, did not imply any limiting condition bespeaking original sin. Everyone sins on every possible occasion, he said, but always retained "power to the contrary." Finney, in the wilder West, took this logic to its final conclusion. If the will is naturally free, then – contra Edwards – there can be no controlling disposition behind it; the will is free to choose its own ends. Nor could God establish an obligation without a commensurate natural ability to fulfil it; any "cannot" is simply a "will not." In the *ordo salutis* Finney allowed no differentiation between regeneration and conversion, and premised justification on obedience to Law. As for sanctification, because every act is the result of free choice, there was no reason a regenerate person could not choose the right thing every time – and if no reason, then no excuse for not doing so. Furthermore, since society was nothing but the sum of the individuals in it, there was nothing preventing the arrival of the millennium but Christians slumbering at their evangelistic duty. These were the grounds of the "Oberlin perfectionism" that Finney expounded at the Ohio college of that name. In the more sober industrial order that followed upon the Civil War, his impulse was modulated into the personalistic Keswick school of Holiness theology, but in the antebellum it was an engine of social crusades, including abolitionism.

BEYOND NEW ENGLAND, 1760–1860

Most contemporary Calvinists were discomfited by Finney's initiatives, none more thoroughly than the Presbyterian traditionalists at Princeton Theological Seminary. Founded in 1812, the seminary had fond memories of the piety of the Great Awakening in which seminary founder Archibald Alexander had been converted. But it was devoted as well to the Westminster Standards in which Alexander found ballast for heart religion – and the rigorous system needed to answer the rationalist excesses of the Enlightenment. Yet a moderate, Scots-derived form of the Enlightenment lay in Princeton's marrow, having been imported to the college there by John Witherspoon in the 1760s. Witherspoon purged the idealism that Edwards had installed during his brief presidency and replaced it with Common Sense Realism, a philosophy well suited to mediate between faith and reason in the churches as it did between revolution and order in the politics of the time.

The arrival of Charles Hodge on the seminary faculty in 1822 began a fifty-year career that made of these elements a complete system of considerable national influence, benefiting from Presbyterianism's spread over the entire country rather than just the upper reaches of the North. Hodge trained more future clergy than did any theologian in the New England tradition, and made the seminary's review into one of the nation's leading scholarly journals. In both offices he was an unbending advocate of what he took to be the timeless faith of the church as exemplified by Augustine and Calvin and embodied in the Westminster standards. As instructional text he assigned Francis Turretin's *Institutes of Elenctic Theology*; as theological method he practiced Baconian induction, taking the Bible to be a storehouse of "facts" that the theologian arranged into proper order according to their inherent principles. As he shared Common Sense axioms with his most of his opponents, Hodge's work was heavily expository and apologetic, arguing Princeton's to be the most rational understanding of Scripture, and seventeenth-century Calvinism to be the most cogent response to the intellectual challenges of modernity.

Hodge's targets outside the Reformed camp were Unitarian and Higher Critical treatments of Scripture, which he countered with an adumbration of plenary-inspiration theory that would become the Princetonian's distinctive long-term legacy. Within Reformed circles he took on (actually, tried to excise) Taylor and Finney not just for Arminian but Pelagian errors, and in the process faulted so many axioms of the New Divinity as to raise questions about the sainted Edwards himself. Edwards was substantially sound, the Princetonians concluded, but his speculative idealism and unfortunate articulations on the affections, the will, and the atonement set in motion the chain of errors that culminated in Taylor. As duty and ability formed the linchpin of New Haven's theology, so legal representation served for Princeton, making immediate imputation, both of Adam's guilt and Christ's righteousness, the sore point between them. Consequently Hodge reasserted limited, forensic substitution, not moral government, as the proper theory of the atonement; divine glory, not human happiness, as the measure of God's purpose in history; and propositional dogma, not affectionate conduct, as the test of truth.

For the more severe members of "Old School" Presbyterianism, proper polity was also an article of faith. Theirs was the call for strict subscription and denominational uniformity that the "Old Side" party had voiced during the First Awakening, now reborn against the

New School's Yankee intrusions and para-church organizations in the Second. Old Schoolers took their revenge by excising all New School presbyteries from the denomination at the 1837 General Assembly. Princeton's hesitation about this move was all the more telling next to the zeal that Southern Presbyterians brought to the matter, not to mention the theological innovation they made to (as they said) clarify tradition on the point. This was the doctrine of "the spirituality of the church" devised by James Henley Thornwell, a pastor and professor of theology at Columbia, South Carolina. Thornwell insisted that no functions of Gospel ministry, including education and evangelism, could be permitted outside of formal church controls. At the same time he sharply demarcated civil from ecclesiastical spheres and limited the church's corporate authority to the latter. Thornwell contended as well for Westminster orthodoxy, especially imputation, but the point of the new doctrine was unmistakable. Slavery being deemed entirely a civil institution, the foundations of Southern society were exempt from the church's judgment in the name of protecting the purity of the Gospel from worldly concerns.

This solicitude did not prevent Thornwell from writing the "Address to All the Churches of Jesus Christ throughout the Earth" by which Presbyterians in the new-found Confederacy warranted ecclesiastical separation from their Northern brethren and gave fulsome support to their region's cause. Although Thornwell himself came to think that the South's subsequent military reverses reflected divine punishment upon some abuses of the system, his denomination never doubted that their slave regime had biblical warrant and that Northern abolitionism necessitated all sorts of departures from orthodoxy. Their social outlook, combined with rigorous Westminster confessionalism and Baconian common-sense hermeneutics, made the Presbyterian Church in the United States (PCUS) a strategic leader in the New South that emerged out of Reconstruction, assimilating such change as was necessary within a matrix of tradition and order.

Far more numerous than Presbyterians or Congregationalists, the Baptists represented the populist winners of the competition for souls in antebellum America, but their demurral at formal pastoral training cost them proportionate theological leadership. Most Baptists were Reformed to greater or lesser degree, but all insisted first on a polity of strict local control and church membership determined by experiential conversion. This pattern was tailor-made for the conditions of revival religion and geographical expansion in the century after the First Awakening. Baptist flourishing in America began when ultra-evangelical New

Englanders separated from their Congregational fellowships and began to spread their message along the backcountry frontier, especially in Virginia and the Carolinas. Theologically these Separate Baptists took a soft Calvinist line, insisting on agreement only in "essentials," but mandating exuberant experience and strict discipline of life and fellowship as the definition of true Christianity. They met and gradually intermingled with Particular Baptists who had been evangelized by the more consistently Calvinistic Philadelphia Association founded in 1707; it affirmed the Westminster Standards on most points save for believer baptism and congregational polity. Together, the Baptists' lay leadership and localism made them self-sufficient subcommunities, averse to making claims on the public order in contrast to the practice of magisterial Calvinism.

They *had* to respond, however, to the innovations raised by Edwardsean theology and the revival-and-reform crusades of the Second Awakening. Baptists from New England found it easiest to enter into denomination-like associations to coordinate and advance missionary and educational enterprises. They also were open to a fairly conservative form of Edwards's theology. Both moves triggered resistance among the staunchest Calvinists in Baptist circles – or made staunch Calvinists out of them in the first place. These Particular or Primitive Baptists reasserted divine election and limited ("particular") atonement in soteriology and held to a strict localism in polity against the spectre of a new religious establishment erected by Yankee pride and imperial ambition. The "anti-mission" Baptists' campaigns in press and pulpit against New School tendencies spread a resolute, populist form of Calvinism across the border states and rural South out to the plains of Texas. Modified for broader appeal, it became the folk religion of the post-bellum South.

A NEW ERA

By the 1840s arguments between the Presbyterians, Edwardseans, and Unitarians had become stale, opening the way to new proposals. As it happened, these inaugurated a distinct century of theological reflection, for they followed new methods and assumptions derived no longer from Britain but Germany. Realism gave way to idealism, common sense to intuition, static to developmental, individualistic to communal. The approach fit a radically altered American scene. First, a sectional politics riven by race and ethnicity was resolved by the bloodiest war effort in American history. Second, a dispersed, centrifugal society gave way to an integrated and concentrated order of urban industrialism. Where the old order was least altered – in the South – the old habits of Reformed theology persisted most. The key innovations appeared in the North in three proposals as markedly different from each other as from that which had come before. The first was a moderate-liberal formula derived from New England Congregationalist Horace Bushnell, which became the preferred option of the Protestant "mainline" from the Civil War to the Second World War – and which, tellingly, left most of its Reformed ballast behind. The second, and far less popular, was a high-church Calvinism espoused at the German Reformed Church's Mercersburg Seminary, which flourished early in the period but then went into hibernation for resurrection at a latter day. The third project, the "crisis theology" associated with Reinhold and H. Richard Niebuhr, came to prominence late in the era, resurrecting certain Reformed themes in keen critique of Protestant liberalism's substance while adhering to some of its methods.

Horace Bushnell

Horace Bushnell seemed destined to follow the New Haven track, having absorbed at Yale both revival conversion and the system of Nathaniel William Taylor. But he reacted against both, finding the first to be shallow and the second ineffectual at resolving the controversies that had long snarled New England theological discourse. Bushnell worked out his alternatives in a long pastoral career in Hartford. In place of the revival he recovered a form of covenant theology – in his famous formulation, parents should so attend to the religious nurture of their children that these would never remember a time when they were not Christian. To resolve doctrinal differences, Bushnell proposed an antipropositional, symbolic idea of language that made theology less a science and more like poetry, delving below the empirical desert of fact into the profound and life-giving waters of imagination. God was immediately apprehended by religious intuition, Bushnell contended, and theology was the logical exposition of this consciousness. It would necessarily reflect human experience, in all its shifts and turns.

This opened the way to resolving tired old disputes over the Trinity, atonement, and two natures of Christ: each rival position turned out to be one facet of the whole truth. That opened the way to the unity that was Bushnell's ultimate goal – a unity, be it noted, of New England blood. Here, in their collective character, not their creeds, lay the value of the puritans. It was the present duty to steel that character in the rising generation so that New England could take its rightful place at the helm of the nation. Just that occurred in the Civil War, and in its wake Northern theologians adapted Bushnell's method to build a theological liberalism that served the business, professional, and managerial classes in the heyday of American industrialization. Little of classic Reformed theology survived this transition, save for a robust sense of the Kingdom of God that history had delivered to American hands for realization. This was a public faith aimed at justice and righteousness, but the norms thereof were to be found less in Scripture and tradition than in science, progress, and the character of good people, properly nurtured.

The Mercersburg theology

The Mercersburg Theology also wished to restore unity, but via the church, not the nation, and by recovering, not reducing, the heritage of Christian theology. Its program grew out of Princeton Presbyterianism as refracted through the lens of German mediating theology by John Williamson Nevin. Originally a protégé of Charles Hodge, Nevin was appalled by the theology and practices of Finneyite revivalism, but he moved beyond his master as well after the Presbyterian split of 1837. His breakthrough was to see Old and New Schools as twins under the skin. Both regarded the church as a voluntary association of believers, beginning and ending with individuals. In soteriology, both apprehended a distant Jesus who, whether temporarily snared by artifice (revival) or fixed by reason (Princeton), still remained a fund of merits in an abstract calculus of justification. The result, Nevin concluded, was an American church neither certain of conversion nor evidencing much holiness. The remedy was uniting believers with Christ – more precisely, having them rooted and fed by the church as Christ's continuing presence on earth. For Nevin the incarnation – Christ's personal entrance into history – formed the pivot of Scripture, indeed of all history, and sacraments, not doctrinal assent or revival excursions, provided the key conduit of grace. Other priorities changed too: Christology before divine decree, creation before atonement, Kingdom before millennium.

Provocatively, Nevin claimed the Reformation on his behalf, demonstrating that much of its heritage had been lost to "puritan" reductions. Then he delved behind the Reformation into patristic writers and practices, addressing questions of polity and liturgy as well as doctrine, and above all the issue of church unity. He declared the regnant American "spirit of sect and schism" to be no less than the "anti-Christ" and began pondering going over to Rome. He finally decided to stay with the German Reformed Church as embodying the Reformed catholicity of Calvin with the potential to be the mediator that would bring together Lutheran and Reformed, and then, perhaps, Protestant and Roman Catholic. He had long left behind his native Westminster for the

Heidelberg Catechism as providing a promising confessional basis for reunion. It also offered an antidote to revivalism by steeping the hearts and minds of children in the apostolic faith. Nevin's was, from start to finish, a churchly nurture that went beyond Bushnell's home remedies.

Nevin's themes were submerged by the Civil War that swirled around his southern Pennsylvania home and would reemerge in mainline Protestantism's ecumenical initiatives only in the mid-twentieth century, and in the recent "ancient-future" quest of disgruntled evangelicals' "emerging-church" program. In the meantime the work of Nevin's Mercersburg partner, the Swiss Reformed immigrant Philip Schaff, injected the method and resources of historical theology into the mainline. Schaff came to love his adopted land as the place where the key antinomies identified in his German theological training – freedom vs. order, vitality vs. stability, innovation vs. tradition – might be resolved into a third way full of creative power. During the Civil War he left Mercersburg for the New School Presbyterians' Union Seminary in New York City, and from that capital of the American industrial empire produced some of the lasting monuments of American church-historical scholarship. Particularly Reformed strands he wove into a larger tapestry of an ecumenical church that had evolved dialectically from the first century toward its prospective global unity in the twentieth. Schaff's contribution was to supply to the mainline a sense of tradition and theological ballast to balance the subjective orientation descended from Bushnell.

Neo-orthodoxy

The third school of Germanic inspiration turned its historicist methods toward very different applications. Writing amidst the Great Depression, the Second World War, and the dawning of the Cold War, the American voices of crisis theology rejected the two fundamental axioms of Protestant liberalism: that human consciousness is the ground of theological reflection, and that history offers the revelatory and redemptive functions once identified with Christ. Instead they reaffirmed the Word of God as a transcendent authority above and beyond all human possibilities, judging all human pretensions, yet offering a redemptive hope enacted by God's sovereign grace in the work of Jesus Christ. These strong Augustinian, even Calvinian, themes, had no more influential voice than Reinhold Niebuhr, social ethicist at Schaff's Union Seminary. It was not in secular rationalism, technocratic fixes, or assimilated religion that the world crises of the times could best be fathomed, Niebuhr thundered, but in a restored understanding of sin – original sin, structural sin, the self-interest hidden behind the pious mantle of the churchgoer. Niebuhr's appeal especially touched the rising generation in American academia and government, steeling them to endurance in the cause of free civilization while alerting them to their own compromises and illusions.

His brother H. Richard Niebuhr, situated at Yale Divinity School, devoted his attentions more to the church, beginning in the 1930s with a searing indictment of its cultural captivity, but then building over the next decades a constructive ethics of "responsibility" that more than echoed Reformed mandates to live *"coram deo"* – in gratitude before the face of God. This was not the holiness of God, the Niebuhrs continued; our best efforts fall short, tempt us to pride, and are crimped by the finitude of our knowledge and dedication. Still, human works can be redeemed in time by transcendent providence. Yet the Niebuhrs' dialectical method, their acceptance of standard biblical criticism, and their evident use of theological terms as metaphors, not literal descriptions, of spiritual things led most traditionally minded Reformed people to deem their project to be "neo-liberalism," not "neo-orthodoxy."

Among the evangelicals

By contrast, Dutch Reformed voices brought something of the continental Reformed tradition to the evangelical side of the modern Protestant divide. The Reformed Church in America, planted in seventeenth-century New Netherland, always took a guarded part in pre–Civil War evangelical collaborations, staying on the Old School side of theological debates and serving its ethnic enclave with a more scholastic understanding of the Heidelberg Catechism than Nevin liked. The Christian Reformed Church, which descended out of nineteenth-century Dutch immigration, had in its background a bitter split from the national Reformed Church in the Netherlands and so hewed to the rather static confessionalism that the seceders favoured. This orthodoxy would be codified in America by Louis Berkhof, professor at Calvin Theological Seminary, whose *Systematic Theology* has become a standard English-language text for conservative Reformed students around the world.

A more public theology arose from these circles after the Second World War under the neo-Calvinist influence of Abraham Kuyper, a multitalented Dutch visionary from the late nineteenth century. Kuyper's theology began with a bracingly supralapsarian understanding of predestination, by which God implanted in the elect a new person in Christ before the foundation of the world. With that came the calling to participate in God's ultimate purpose in history: to bring out of the ruins of the present order a purified new creation. The Holy Spirit had a far grander role to play than in conventional evangelical theology, working not just in individual hearts but also among peoples of every age and culture to bring not just "spiritual" things but all of human potential under divine providence into the realization of the Kingdom of God.

Kuyperian theology thus bears pronounced mandates for Christian engagement with culture and politics. Far more than in conventional evangelicalism, it proceeds from the lasting value of creation, but reflects as well the radical collective character of redemption. As believers are new persons in Christ, they will think and work according to different norms and purposes from people of other loyalties. Their core convictions should be adumbrated into a consistent "worldview," said Kuyper, and then applied unapologetically in every domain of human life. As other groups would do so as well, the result would be a frank pluralism, a fair division of public space based in principle. Besides supporting high levels of political and educational endeavour, Kuyper's influence in North America is notable in the flotilla of philosophers his passion for first principles engendered, most notably Cornelius Van Til, Alvin Plantinga, and Nicholas Wolterstorff. Their work exploded the Baconian common-sense approach inherited from nineteenth-century Princeton, replacing it with a presuppositionalist method that by the century's end dominated American evangelical discourse.

The twentieth century's other explicit train of Reformed reflection followed a conservative Presbyterian track laid out by Benjamin Breckinridge Warfield, Hodge's successor at Princeton. Like Hodge, he held the Princeton tradition of Augustine, Calvin, and Westminster to be perfectly fit for the modern world. Warfield's new contribution was to defend the authority and veracity of Scripture against doubts raised by Darwinian science and higher criticism. At the same time he authored an extensive critique of the claims of evangelical perfectionism. His riposte to the right brought him close to equating faith with doctrinal formulations, submerging religious experience, conscience, and nature beneath the text of Scripture. Yet toward the left he was able to reconcile biblical accounts of creation with evolutionary theory in biology by (like Hodge) faulting Darwinism but not other concepts of evolution on the issue of providence and purpose.

Protestant fundamentalism adopted Princeton inerrancy as its method, though its broad appeal drew off two other themes at variance with Reformed tradition. The perfectionist ethics of "holiness" had already been dispatched by Warfield, while dispensational premillennialism, with its wholesale remapping of eschatology, broke with Reformed understandings of continuity in God's purposes and people. The appearance of Princeton theologian J. Gresham Machen's *Christianity and Liberalism* at the height of the 1920s fundamentalist controversy doubtless cemented the association. Learned as Machen's explication was, his thesis that the two terms of its title constituted entirely different religions conformed to the militant polarization of the era. When Machen was ousted from the Northern Presbyterian Church, the Orthodox Presbyterian Church (OPC) he founded took its identity from an unaltered understanding of historic Westminster standards. Fifty years later the drama was replayed among Southern Presbyterians when conservatives, protesting loose theology and political involvement, withdrew from the Presbyterian Church in the United States into the new Presbyterian Church in America (PCA). Their founding statement replicated the title of James Henley Thornwell's 1861 secessionist address, and their conservative politics were never far from view: 1973, the PCA's founding date, came amid America's second Reconstruction on the front of race and civil rights. The PCA has oscillated between the promise of ecclesiastical purity, represented by the tradition of the spirituality of the church, and the lure of growth via a generic evangelical piety. This replicates the concerns of the New Side in respect of the oldest tension in American Presbyterianism, just as the OPC's passion for strict subscription and uniformity does those of the Old Side.

CONCLUSION

Two phenomena in the twenty-first century show the continuing appeal of, and stark polarities in, American Reformed theology. A much publicized "return to Calvin" among some mega-church evangelicals of Baptist and Presbyterian affiliation makes much of Jonathan Edwards and predestinarian soteriology. The appeal is to people left hungry by the evangelical bromides of their upbringing and also, clearly, to young ambitious males who aspire to a heroic spirituality and vehemently reject feminism, the sexual revolution, and everything thereunto pertaining. Divinely ironic it is, then, that a polar opposite reappropriation of Calvinism has come from the pen of Pulitzer Prize winning novelist Marilynne Robinson. Her novels are an unsparing depiction of Reformed saints as sinners saved by grace amid all their continuing stumbling and errors. Her essays add to American letters' noble line of meditations on the hollowness at the center of national life and her assertion of the possibility that John Calvin had the essential things right, not just for believers' eternal salvation but for moderns' life together.

Further reading

Brackney, William H. *A Genetic History of Baptist Thought*. Macon, GA: Mercer University Press, 2004.

Bratt, James D. *Dutch Calvinism in Modern America: A History of a Conservative Subculture*. Grand Rapids, MI: Eerdmans, 1984.

Crisp, Oliver D., and Douglas A. Sweeney (eds.). *After Jonathan Edwards: The Courses of the New England Theology*. Oxford: Oxford University Press, 2012.

Farmer, James Oscar. *A Metaphysical Confederacy: James Henley Thornwell and the Synthesis of Southern Values*. Macon, GA: Mercer University Press, 1986.

Lovin, Robin W. *Reinhold Niebuhr and Christian Realism*. Cambridge: Cambridge University Press, 1995.

Marsden, George. *Jonathan Edwards: A Life*. New Haven, CT: Yale University Press, 2004.

Mullin, Robert Bruce. *The Puritan as Yankee: A Life of Horace Bushnell*. Grand Rapids, MI: Eerdmans, 2002.

Nichols, James Hastings (ed.). *The Mercersburg Theology*. New York: Oxford University Press, 1966.

Noll, Mark A. *The Princeton Theology, 1812–1921: Scripture, Science, and Theological Method from Archibald Alexander to Benjamin Breckinridge Warfield*. Grand Rapids, MI: Baker Academic, 1983.

Wells, David F. (ed.). *Reformed Theology in America: A History of Its Modern Development*. Grand Rapids, MI: Eerdmans, 1985.

18 Reformed theology in Africa

ISABEL APAWO PHIRI

Reformed identity cannot be appreciated without a clear understanding of Reformed history.[1]

Reformed Theology in South Africa is a story of many stories ...
The stories one heard would therefore depend on the people whom
one asked, and could be radically different stories. What constituted
adventures and what misfortunes would depend on the social locations, the traditions and communities, the experiences and perspectives of those telling the story.[2]

While the words of Dirk Smit, a prominent South African Reformed
theologian, in the second of the preceding quotations refer to the particular context of South Africa, they also hold true for the rest of the African
continent. There are many stories of Reformed theology in Africa.

This particular chapter is a story of Reformed theology mainly
in Southern Africa drawing from my experiences as a Malawian
Presbyterian woman who lived in South Africa for seventeen years.
When I started reflecting on this chapter, I had just been made an elder
in the Church of Scotland in Geneva, worshipping every Sunday in the
Auditoire de Calvin. A collection of photos, hand-written letters and
sermons of John Calvin are on display in this historic building – a constant reminder that of the Reformed theological tradition, with its roots
in sixteenth-century Switzerland. Below the bus-stop for the Auditoire
de Calvin is the Reformation Wall with four statues of the fathers of the
Reformation at its centre: Theodore Beza, John Calvin, William Farel and
John Knox – a further constant reminder of my Reformed roots. However,
my experience of being Reformed in Geneva is far removed from that of
the majority of Reformed Christians in Africa who have no sense of this

---

[1] B. F. Fubara-Manuel, 'Reformed Identity in Nigeria Today', *Reformed World*, 58.4
(2008): 229.
[2] Dirk J. Smit, *Essays on Being Reformed: Collected Essays 3* (Stellenbosch, South
Africa: SUN MeDIA, 2009), 217.

connection with the European roots of their Reformed faith. I became a Reformed African Christian by following in the footsteps of my parents and grandparents without any knowledge of John Calvin or his peers and their contribution to shaping Reformed theology. My grandfather was a minister in the Dutch Reformed Nkhoma Mission[3] in Malawi, which has its roots in the Dutch Reformed Church[4] of South Africa. It was in the Blantyre Synod of the Church of Central Africa Presbyterian[5] in Malawi where I learned the catechism and received baptism. While in South Africa, my search for a Reformed identity that was both evangelical and prophetic led me to join the Rondebosch United Church in Cape Town.[6] Similarly, when I was at the University of KwaZulu Natal in Pietermaritzburg, I chose to join the Scottsville Presbyterian congregation of the Uniting Presbyterian Church in Southern Africa.[7] Yet the fact remains that most African theologians respond to issues in Africa primarily from an ecumenical perspective, and not from a confessional perspective.

The central question that the chapter seeks to answer is what does it mean to be Reformed in Africa? I attempt to respond to this question in three sections. The first explores the connection between Reformed theology and the history of missions and conversion in Africa. The second considers the connection between Reformed theology and the history of colonialism and racism. The third explores briefly the relationship between Reformed theology and issues of sexism and homophobia. In

---

[3] The Dutch Reformed Church Mission (Nkhoma Mission) was established in central Malawi in 1889, and represented the third group of Calvinists to arrive in the country.

[4] The Dutch Reformed Church was the first church in Africa in the Calvinist tradition. It was established by the Dutch settlers who landed at Table Bay (present-day Cape Town) in 1652 under the leadership of Jan van Riebeeck.

[5] Church of Scotland missionaries established the Blantyre Mission in southern Malawi in 1876. The Livingstonia Mission, established in 1875 by the Free Church of Scotland, joined together with the Blantyre Mission in 1924 to form the Church of Central Africa Presbyterian (CCAP). The Dutch Reformed Mission joined the denomination in 1926. Currently CCAP has five synods: Blantyre, Livingstonia, Nkhoma, Harare and Zambia.

[6] Rondebosch United Church was founded in 1900 as part of the Congregationalist denomination in South Africa. In 1989, after negotiations for union between the Congregational and Presbyterian denominations in Southern Africa, the congregation was reconstituted as 'Rondebosch United Church' (Congregational & Presbyterian).

[7] This denomination was formed by the union of the Presbyterian Church of Southern Africa (established in 1820 to take care of British soldiers and settlers in the Cape) and the Reformed Presbyterian Church in Southern Africa (a mission church of the Scottish missionaries to the Africans which became independent in 1923) in 1999.

respect of each of the three issues identified, I will attempt to engage a variety of African scholars from the Reformed tradition.

THE REFORMED HISTORY OF MISSIONS
AND CONVERSION IN AFRICA

Being Reformed in Africa means to acknowledge that we have a heritage of missionary enterprise and to continue to nurture missionary connections. In my story in the preceding text, one can identify three strands of missionary enterprise within the Reformed family which brought the Gospel to Africa – the Dutch Reformed, the Scottish Presbyterian and the Scottish-American Congregationalist.[8] Each of the three strands has further sub-divisions, but it suffices here to point out that in each one of them people felt a strong sense of call from the living God to share the Gospel with the people of Africa. The Reformed message is centred on repentance from sin and salvation of people through acceptance of Jesus Christ as Lord and Saviour. To this end, evangelism is key. Historically, the success of the missionary work could be measured by the number of mission stations established, the number of converts gained, and the number of Christian schools, hospitals, agriculture projects and printing media under the control of the churches. At the same time there was an awareness that much of the evangelisation was done (and indeed continues to be done) by local women and men evangelists who shared the Gospel to their own people in the local languages and using indigenous understandings of the living God. This is the freedom of the Word of God; once planted one cannot control the results. It has the freedom to go where it wills to change people's lives.

As argued by Kwame Bediako, a prominent Ghanaian Reformed theologian, the translation of the Bible into local languages aided the process of the assimilation of the Gospel to local religious understanding.[9] In this way, the African people incarnated the Gospel in their own culture and religion so that they could hear God speaking to them directly.[10] Further research is needed to find out how specifically Reformed doctrines and confessions have been translated into local (African) religiosity. Thus while scholars of Reformed theology have often followed Calvin's teaching that Christians 'are liberated

---

[8] Cf. Setri Nyomi, 'The Reformed Tradition in Ghana and Some of Its Challenges', *Trinity Journal of Church and Theology* 3 (1993): 17.

[9] Kwame Bediako, *Christianity in Africa: The Renewal of a Non-Western Religion* (Edinburgh: Edinburgh University Press, 1995).

[10] Bediako, *Christianity in Africa*, 122.

both from cultural traditions and customs and liberated for the following of God's truth and God's call',[11] the majority of African Reformed theological scholars – such as Bediako – use their Christian freedom to engage with African religiosity[12] and cultural practices,[13] and with economic, gender-related,[14] ecological[15] and political[16] injustices.

Furthermore, in searching for African particularity in the expression of Reformed theology in Africa, one needs to reckon with the influence of Pentecostal and charismatic groups. Being Reformed in Africa has in many cases meant integrating Reformed spirituality and worship with African Pentecostal[17] or charismatic spirituality and worship. This is evident in the areas of intensive prayer life, healing services, praise and worship and the casting out of evil forces. While Setri Nyomi described the presence of the charismatic movement within Ghana's Presbyterian churches as a challenge to Reformed identity in Africa,[18] I see it as one dimension of what it means to be Reformed in Africa. My experiences with the Blantyre Synod of the Church of Central Africa Presbyterian in Malawi and the Scottsville congregation of the Uniting Presbyterian Church in Southern Africa have shown me that this integration of charismatic spirituality is not a challenge to the Reformed emphasis on the preaching of the Word as some have feared. Ghana's Presbyterian churches today are confirming that there can be a charismatic spirituality which is particularly African in origin and expression, within a context of growing acceptance of an African worldview which includes belief in the existence of witchcraft and ancestors, both of which are related to the power of Jesus Christ who is not only the Saviour but also

---

[11] Smit, *Essays on Being Reformed*, 134.

[12] Augustine, C. Musopole, 'Towards a Theological Method for Malawi', *Journal of Theology in Southern Africa* 82 (1993), 37–44.

[13] Isabel Apawo Phiri, *Women, Presbyterianism and Patriarchy: Religious Experiences of Chewa Women in Central Malawi* (Blantyre: CLAM, 1997).

[14] See further in the text that follows.

[15] Harvey Sindima, 'Community of Life: Ecological Theology in African Perspective', in *Liberating Life: Contemporary Approaches in Ecological Theology*, edited by Charles Birch et al. (Maryknoll, NY: Orbis Books, 1990), 137–147.

[16] Joseph Andrew Thipa, *Atonement and Human Rights? Implications of the Classic Reformed Doctrine of Atonement for the Building of a Human Rights Culture in Contemporary Malawi*, DTh dissertation in Systematic Theology, Stellenbosch University, 2009; Billy L. Gama, *The Relationship between Church and State: A Theologically Based Investigation into the Social Doctrine of the Church in Malawi*, MTh thesis, University Of Fort Hare, 2006.

[17] See *African Christianity: An African Story*, edited by Ogbu Kalu (Trenton, NJ: Africa World Press, 2007). Kalu has identified a distinctive African Pentecostalism that is growing throughout sub-Saharan Africa.

[18] Nyomi, 'The Reformed Tradition in Ghana', 22–23.

the Deliverer and Protector of Christians. In an interview with staff of the World Communion of Reformed Churches, Seth Agidi, of the Evangelical Presbyterian Church in Ghana (EPCG), acknowledged that another reason Presbyterians in Ghana have been joining Pentecostal congregations is the healing ceremonies offered for people troubled by evil spirits. In response, EPCG now runs its own 'deliverance and healing' centres that double as spiritual retreat centres.[19] By accommodating charismatic worship within Presbyterian churches in Africa, the Reformed churches have managed to avoid an exodus of the youth from the churches.

In contrast, during the colonial period, Reformed Christians who felt that the Reformed churches in Africa were either too Westernised and spiritually inert or too restrictive to the ministry of women founded their own churches – indeed this occurs to some extent even now. Examples of churches dissatisfied with and broke away from 'Western' Reformed Christianity would include: the Zulu Congregational Church (which broke away from the American Board of Mission in 1892); the African Congregational Church (which broke away from the Congregational Church in 1917 under the leadership of Gardiner Mveyana); and the Presbyterian Church of Africa (which broke away from the Free Church of Scotland in 1893 under the leadership of PJ Mzimba). Since the 1970s, a number of churches and ministries have been founded by women, including: Chilobwe Healing Centre in Malawi, founded by Mai Nyajere; Blessed Hope Church, founded by Bishop Yami; and Namatapa Healing Ministries, founded by Mai Chimpondeni.[20]

THE REFORMED HISTORY OF COLONIALISM AND RACISM IN AFRICA

Being Reformed in South Africa means owning the fact that:

> ... along with the rest of Christendom, Calvinism contributed to the legitimation of colonial conquest, and it was subsumed in secularized versions of the kingdom of God thus contributing to the rise of nationalist doctrines of manifest destiny. For example ... it contributed to what has been described as Afrikaner civil religion

---

[19] See http://wcrc.ch/news/ghanaian-presbyterians-open-african-expressions-christian-faith/ (accessed 1 March 2015).

[20] See Isabel Apawo Phiri, 'The Church and Women in Africa', in *Companion to African Religions*, edited by Elias Bongmba (Oxford: Wiley-Blackwell, 2012), 255–268.

in South Africa and in a convoluted manner, to the sanctification of the ideology of apartheid.[21]

There are many South African scholars who would agree with these words of John W. de Gruchy. For example, Dirk Smit elaborates on this by pointing to the work of Abraham Kuyper, a Dutch theologian, as having fuelled apartheid. Smit argues that Kuyper's stress on pluriformity in creation played a vital role: 'In this theology Kuyper argued that "each race had a God given responsibility to maintain its identity". Each "people" was "chosen" for a specific "calling". Each people accordingly also has a natural right to survival and self-determination.'[22] The Dutch Reformed Church (DRC) implemented these teachings in its mission churches by establishing the Dutch Reformed Mission Church (DRMC) for Coloured people, the Reformed Church in Africa (RCA) for South African Indians, and the Dutch Reformed Church in Africa (DRCA) for indigenous black South Africans. In this way the white Dutch Reformed Christians did not have to worship in the same buildings or share holy communion with Reformed Christians who were Coloured, Indian or indigenous black South African.[23]

Such an interpretation of Reformed theology was considered heresy by other Reformed South African theologians of all races and gender. In fact de Gruchy proceeds to argue that the history of white oppression of indigenous people is not limited to the work of white Dutch Christians in South Africa. Examples in North America, Latin America and Asia have shown that racism was practised by all European cultures and by all European Christians, whether Calvinist or not. De Gruchy argues that it is a myth that the Dutch and the French who came to the Cape in the seventeenth century became settlers on the basis of Reformed theology. He sees them as nominal Christians, whose true motivation to settle in the Cape was commercial and not religious. It was at a later stage that the Afrikaners used religion to justify their self-preservation by supporting apartheid in South Africa.[24] And once apartheid was legalised, Christian denominations across South Africa struggled to avoid segregated congregations.

---

[21] John W. de Gruchy, *Liberating Reformed Theology: A South African Contribution to an Ecumenical Debate* (Cape Town: David Philip, 1991), 3–4.

[22] See Smit, *Essays on Being Reformed*, 242.

[23] Smit names S. J. du Toit as the Afrikaner theologian and poet who write the first biblical justification for apartheid: *Essays on Being Reformed*, 2.

[24] De Gruchy, *Liberating Reformed Theology*, 4–6.

As a sign of protest against apartheid, some Reformed churches started working towards uniting different races in their churches. For example, the Congregational Union of South Africa an all-white denomination, was united with the Bantu Congregational Church (ABCFM) in 1967 to form the United Congregational Church of Southern Africa, connecting the work of the two bodies in South Africa, Botswana, Mozambique, Namibia and Zimbabwe. A further merger took place in 1972, when the United Congregational Church in Southern Africa was reconstituted to include the congregations of the South African Association of the Disciples of Christ. Similarly, the Presbyterian Church in Southern Africa and the Reformed Presbyterian Church were joined in the Uniting Presbyterian Church in Southern Africa in 1999.

The preceding examples bear witness to the work of the South African Reformed theologians who have opposed apartheid by drawing from Reformed theology.[25] It is within this historical context that the Belhar Confession,[26] the declaration of the Dutch Reformed Mission Church (DRMC) of 1982–1986 should be understood. The Belhar Confession makes three important statements. First, drawing on the Gospel, it emphasises the centrality of visible unity among Christians of the same confession, who were people separated on the basis of their race under the laws of apartheid and a false interpretation of Scripture. Second, it calls for real reconciliation among the churches of the Reformed confession by means of forgiving each other in respect of the sin of apartheid. In such forgiveness there is acknowledgement of the hatred, mistrust and hurt that has encroached upon the church as the result of the practices of apartheid. Third, it calls for compassionate justice, because the oppression of apartheid meant structural injustices were introduced between the different racial groups in political, social and economic areas. Only white people enjoyed the full benefits in all areas of life. Therefore to address issues of human dignity, there is a call for justice for all.

The Belhar Confession was taken seriously by the ecumenical movement. One consequence was the expulsion of the Dutch Reformed Church in South Africa from the World Alliance of Reformed Churches

---

[25] This group would include theologians such as Russell Botman, Nico Koopman, Elna Mouton, Christina Landman, Douglas Bax, Willie Jonker, John de Gruchy, Beyers Naude, Allan Boesak, David Bosch, Takatso Mofokeng, Maake Masango, Jaap Durand, Steve de Gruchy and Dirk Smit, among others.

[26] The Belhar Confession was first drafted in 1982 and was adopted by the synod of the Dutch Reformed Mission Church in 1986.

in 1983 for supporting the institutionalisation of apartheid. After the declaration of the end of apartheid in South Africa in 1990, the Dutch Reformed Mission Church (DRMC) and the Dutch Reformed Church in Africa (DRCA) decided to implement the Belhar Confession and they united in 1994 to form the Uniting Reformed Church in Southern Africa (URCSA). Membership to URCSA is extended to the DRC mission churches in Namibia and Lesotho. Unfortunately, even though the Dutch Reformed Church (DRC) has also declared apartheid as sin, its churches have remained separate from its mission congregations. In 2015 the general synod of the DRC failed to get the two-thirds majority needed to adopt the Belhar Confession. This means that unification with its three sister churches, which is based on the condition that the DRC adopt the Belhar Confession, continues to be on hold. However, room has been opened for the adoption of the Belhar Confession at synod level and for unification to take place at provincial level. While this is now taking place in the Western Cape Province between the coloured and white churches, it is not occurring in the Northern Province between the white and black churches.[27].

The South African story of Reformed theology has shown that there are many identities within being Reformed. The negative side of the history of apartheid is a wakeup call to the need to be vigilant in the interpretation of Scripture and the preaching of the Word. The Belhar Confession is a positive indication that Reformed theology can also be drawn upon to bring healing to a divided church. The impact of the Belhar Confession is not limited to the context of South Africa. Other Reformed traditions in Africa and in North America have also adopted the Belhar Confession. The presence of Russell Botman in the drafting of the Accra Confession in 2004 provided a tangible link between the two confessions.

REFORMED THEOLOGY, SEXISM AND HOMOPHOBIA IN AFRICA

Being Reformed in Southern Africa means to grapple with issues of sexism and homophobia in the church. Christina Landman has bluntly stated that in the context of South Africa, 'Local Calvinism was as sexist as it was racist.'[28] In an article that Landman wrote in 2009

---

[27] Interview with Prof. Mary-Anne Plaatjies van Huffel on 16 October 2015, Stellenbosch.

[28] Christina Landman, *The Piety of Afrikaans Women: Diaries of Guilt* (Pretoria: University Press, 1992), cover statement.

when celebrating 500 years of John Calvin, she pointed out that in the 300 years of Calvin history in South Africa not much progress has been made in the inclusion of women in church leadership.[29] Very few women have been ordained and there are many Reformed churches which reject female elders on the basis of a conservative reading of Scripture. Landman argues that the focus on individual sin and salvation in Reformed theology encouraged Afrikaner women towards a pietistic faith which emphasised the submission of women to men both at home and in church. She also contends that today's Afrikaner Reformed women prefer to go to conferences which are only for women, where they receive messages that make them comfortable in leading a submissive life that does not question the denial of female leadership in the church.

Landman's findings correspond to the experiences of women in the Church of Central Africa Presbyterian. Here too in the Blantyre and Livingstonia Synods the ordination of women as ministers only started in 2000 but the number of women who have actually been ordained is very small. In the Nkhoma Synod the furthest they have gone is to ordain women as elders, a decision which was reversed in 2013. There is thus evident a paradox between a Reformed theology of freedom which opens the doors for female participation in leadership and the practices of some Reformed churches which make women feel like they do not belong to the church.[30]

The paradox continues on the issue of homosexuality. Many churches in Africa have made statements on homosexuality which have strong biblical underpinnings. On the one hand, in a statement on same-sex marriage that is posted on the internet, the Presbyterian Church of Ghana describes homosexuality as 'not just ... a moral problem but also ... a spiritual problem. Any help for Christians involved to come out of the practice must require a spiritual warfare exercise; and we believe the spiritual authority at the disposal of the Christian Church can deal with this problem as churches in Ghana are helping practitioners of witchcraft come out of their practice.' The statement continues to state that for the church in Ghana, 'One cannot be a

---

[29] Christina Landman, 'Calvinism and South African Women: A Short Historical Overview', in *Studia Historiae Ecclesiasticae* 35.2 (2009): 89–102. See also Elna Mouton, 'Remembering Forward and Hoping Backward: Some Thoughts on Women and the DRC', in *Scriptura* 70.1 (2001): 77–86; Mary-Anne Plaatyies-Van Huffel, 'About the Empowerment of Women in the Church in the Post-Apartheid South Africa-Structural Approach', in *From Our Side: Emerging Perspectives on Development and Ethics*, edited by Steve de Gruchy, Nico Koopman and Syste Strijbos (Amsterdam: Rozenberg, 2008), 87–100.

[30] See further Phiri, 'The Church and Women in Africa'.

Christian and also be gay and vice versa.'[31] On the other hand, the Dutch Reformed Church in South Africa made history on the 8th October 2015 when an overwhelming majority voted in favour of ordaining gay ministers and blessing same-sex unions on the basis that discrimination is against the will of God.[32]

CONCLUSION

In this chapter I have tried to show another side of being Reformed from the perspective of an African woman from Southern Africa. I have avoided generalising my experience to the whole of the African continent by narrowing my focus down to Malawi and South Africa, the countries which have shaped my Reformed identity. However, I have also taken examples from other parts of Africa. I have shown that Reformed theology came to Africa through missionary enterprise. As such it has been faced with a series of challenges, including connecting Reformed theology to African religiosity and confronting and overcoming racism and sexism. The confession of sins, the acceptance of Jesus Christ as Lord and Saviour of one's soul as well as one's lifestyle have been central to Reformed theology in Africa. I have also argued that the Reformed identity should not be content with its evangelical identity but also open up to accommodate the charismatic spirituality which is in line with African spirituality. The Belhar Confession has been used to highlight the importance of Reformed theology in Africa being prophetic in orientation. To conclude, then, I will paraphrase Dirk Smit's vision that the future of Reformed identity in Africa should focus on visible unity and African spirituality, to give hope for a better world here on earth.

Further reading

Bediako, Kwame. *Christianity in Africa: The Renewal of a Non-Western Religion*. Edinburgh: Edinburgh University Press, 1995.

De Gruchy, John W. *Liberating Reformed Theology: A South African Contribution to an Ecumenical Debate*. Cape Town: David Philip, 1991.

Kalu, Ogbu (ed.). *African Christianity: An African Story*. Trenton, NJ: Africa World Press, 2007.

[31] www.facebook.com/notes/presbyterian-church-of-ghana/response-of-christian-churches-in-ghana-to-homosexuality-and-same-sex-marriages/10150255667939879 (accessed 1 November 2015).

[32] oblogdeeoblogda.me/2015/10/08/history-made-as-south-african-church-votes-to-bless-same-sex-marriage-and-ordain-gay-ministers/ (accessed 1 November 2015).

Phiri, Isabel Apawo. *Women, Presbyterianism and Patriarchy: Religious Experiences of Chewa Women in Central Malawi*. Blantyre: CLAM, 1997.

'The Church and Women in Africa'. In *Companion to African Religions*. Edited by Elias Bongmba. Oxford: Wiley-Blackwell, 2012.

Smit, Dirk J. *Essays on Being Reformed: Collected Essays 3*. Stellenbosch: SUN MeDIA, 2009.

19 Reformed theology in Asia and Oceania

SUNG BIHN YIM, YASUHIRO SEKIKAWA,
ALEXANDER CHOW AND GEOFF THOMPSON

KOREA

Sung Bihn Yim

ENCOUNTERS OF CHRISTIANITY WITH KOREAN CULTURE: SHAMANISM, BUDDHISM, CONFUCIANISM AND TAOISM

For several millennia inhabitants of the Korean Peninsula have displayed varieties of religious experience. Combined with longstanding philosophical traditions, these experiences served a preparatory role for Korean acceptance of the Christian faith: when Protestant Christianity was introduced in the late nineteenth century it did not enter a cultural or religious vacuum. As a result, to understand the genealogy of Reformed theology in Korea it is necessary to review religious philosophies such as Shamanism, Buddhism, Taoism and Confucianism. In fact, we can observe a certain degree of 'elective affinity' between these religious thoughts and theological arguments in Korea.[1]

Shamanism is the most fundamental source of religious philosophy in Korean daily life.[2] It has been rooted in Korean society since the beginning, while other forms of religious philosophy were introduced around the third or fourth century CE. Shamanism explains nature as a set of intricately integrated elements associated with spirits. It also emphasises the leading role of priests or prophets known as shamans.[3] Through the practices and teachings of Shamanism, Koreans had an

---

[1] See Sung Bihn Yim, 'The Relevance of H. R. Niebuhr's "Ethics of Response" to Korean Christian Context: A Critical Inquiry into Niebuhr's Ethics from a Non-Western Perspective' (PhD dissertation, Princeton Theological Seminary, 1994).

[2] See Sung Bum Yun, *Kidokkyo-wa Hanguksasang* (Christianity and Korean Thought) (Seoul: The Christian Literature Society of Korea, 1964), 161–162.

[3] See Tong Shik Ryu, 'Hahnkuk Jonggyo-wa Kidokkyo' (Korean Religion and Christianity) (Seoul: The Christian Literature Society of Korea, 1965), 22. Ryu argues

early understanding of concepts such as good and evil spirits, the supernatural powers of prayer, heaven and hell, and the spiritual possession of human bodies.[4]

When Confucianism was adopted as the state religion in 1392, Korean rulers persecuted Buddhists to the extent that the government in 1456 prohibited Buddhist monks from entering the inner walls of cities. Such severe repudiation prevented Buddhist philosophies from having any major influence on the public sphere. We cannot deny, however, the influence that Buddhism had on Christianity in Korea, for it is likely that the attenuated significance Mahayana Buddhists gave to the end times played a role in the explosive acceptance of the Christian proclamation of the Kingdom of God. In fact, during the Chosun Dynasty (1392–1910), anti-Christian Confucians considered Christian teachings regarding heaven and hell to be identical with those of Buddhists, which they had condemned.[5]

Introduced around the fourth century CE, Confucianism is a mode of philosophical thought centred on moral ideology. Its emphasis lies on the enhancement of one's character in order to achieve a more harmonious world. The earlier, traditional Confucian concept of a divine and supreme will of heaven dissipated quickly under the influence of Buddhism and Taoism in China.[6] As a result, what was traditionally interpreted as the divine and supreme will of heaven came to be understood as heavenly reason.[7] In this school of thought, which came to be known as neo-Confucianism, fundamental truth is understood to reside within nature, meaning that morality is learned through close examination of nature's character and essence. The disputes that took place between the schools of Confucianism[8] predisposed the later disputes among conservative Reformed churches in Korea.

As Confucianism gradually declined in the late nineteenth century, 'Suhndoh', a popular form of Taoism mixed with shamanism, Buddhism and even Confucianism attracted attention. Popular Taoism placed

---

that the notion of a shaman interceding between human beings and gods influenced Korean understandings of Jesus.

[4] L. O. Hartmann, *Popular Aspects of Oriental Religions* (New York: Abingdon Press, 1917), 20–44.

[5] David Chung, 'Religious Syncretism in Korean Society' (PhD dissertation, Yale University, 1959), 218.

[6] Wing-Tsit Chan, *A Source Book in Chinese Philosophy* (Princeton, NJ: Princeton University, 1963), 589.

[7] Chan, *A Source Book in Chinese Philosophy*, 588–590.

[8] See Charles Clark, *Religions of Old Korea* (New York: Fleming H. Revell Company, 1932), 116.

emphasis on a regime of training 'aimed to cultivate physical vitality for longevity and immotality'.[9] While some of the trainers retired to hermitages in the mountains to train themselves, others resided in cities where they did regular jobs and occasionally travelled to the mountains for training. It was a small number of Taoists in Pyongyang who received Protestant Christianity as a new religion around the time of the Sino-Japanese War. Their aversion to Japan was so intense that they could not even contemplate converting to Buddhism or Shinto, either of which would have been considered pro-Japanese, while Roman Catholicism, which was considered a French religion, was seen to totally ignore kings and parents. As a result, many people converted to Protestant Christianity, which was viewed as an American religion.[10] This created an affinity between Taoism and Protestant Christianity.[11] A concept of immortality in Taoism was selectively adopted for hymns about Christian eternal life, which reflected the characteristics of Korean Christian spirituality in the late 1890s.[12] Meanwhile, theological convictions about the physical body as a holy temple led early Protestant missionaries and church leaders to emphasise an organic relationship between body and spirit. This is consonant with the Taoist emphasis on the holistic nature of salvation and its claims concerning the longevity of human body and spirit. Based on this affinity, the Korean church argued for the importance of sanitation and cleanliness, prohibiting alcohol, smoking and opium for a healthier and longer life.[13]

THE CONCEPT OF GOD FOR KOREAN PROTESTANTS

The term *Hananim* was employed in the Korean Bible translation of John Ross, a nineteenth-century Scottish Presbyterian missionary in China, who believed that 'the Sahngdi of contemporary Manchurian Taoism, the Shangdi of original Confucianism, and Hanunim (Hananim) of contemporary Korean shamanism-Taoism' were similar to the Christian

[9] Sung-Deuk Oak, *The Making of Korean Christianity: Protestant Encounters with Korean Religions 1876–1915* (Waco, TX: Baylor University Press, 2013), 272.
[10] Oak, *Korean Christianity*, 276–277.
[11] Ibid., 283–304. Sun Ju Kil, regarded as the initiator of the dawn prayer meeting, is the prototype figure of this transformative affinity between Taoism and Protestant Christianity in Korea.
[12] Sung-Deuk Oak, 'Pyongyang Daebuheung Undong-gwa Kil Sun-Ju Yeongseong-ui Dogyojeok Younghyang' [Spiritual Seismic Shifts among the Taoist-Christians in Pyongyang: Kil Sun-Ju's Daoist-Evangelical Spirituality during the Great Revival Movement], *Korean Christianity and History* 25 (2006): 68.
[13] Oak, 'Pyongyang Daebuheung', 68–69.

God.[14] As one of his contemporaries declared, 'the god of Taoism is also the god of creation, the one who was before time, and the god of omnipotence'.[15] Such a concept of God, combined with the distribution of Ross's Korean Bible, significantly influenced the theology of the Korean church in the 1890s.

The attribute of supreme holiness played a significant role in Korean acceptance of Christian testimony to the one and only God.[16] This can be seen through the transformative adoption of the Korean word *Hananim* as a divine title, with *Hana* meaning 'one' and *nim* referring to God as the highest entity.[17] The term resonates with a kind of monotheistic tradition that can be traced back to Taoism, Shamanism and other indigenous religious systems in which one supreme god rules. This strong emphasis on monotheistic belief in *Hananim* together with theological arguments based on 'the North American missionaries' theology of indigenization and fulfilment theory'[18] enabled H. G. Underwood, the first Presbyterian ordained missionary, to accept the term in spite of his initial opposition based on fears of syncretism. Korean Protestants around 1905 accepted this as the official term for the Christian God. Their creative adoption led to a shift in meaning, from the previous 'Heavenly Lord' to 'the One Great Lord',[19] a concept which is at the core of Reformed theology.

LEGACIES OF THE REFORMED CONFESSIONS AND JOHN CALVIN

Reformed theology was first embraced by the Korean Presbyterian Church in the late nineteenth century, and has continually evolved since then. While the role of American Presbyterian missionaries is widely acknowledged, it is worth noting that in 1901 Samuel A. Moffett established the Presbyterian University and Theological Seminary (PUTS; then the Presbyterian Theological Seminary of Korea), which has played a central role in Korean Presbyterian education. In 1907,

---

[14] Oak, *Korean Christianity*, 52–53.

[15] Ibid., 52.

[16] James Gale, *Korea in Transition* (New York: Young People's Missionary Movement of the United States and Canada, 1909), 78.

[17] L. H. Underwood, *Fifteen Years among the Top-Knots* (Boston: American Tract Society, 1908), 103–105. See J. S. Gale, 'Korea's Preparation for the Bible', *The Korea Mission Field* (March 1912): 86.

[18] See Oak, *Korean Christianity*, 83.

[19] Ibid., 68.

'An Independent Presbytery' of the Presbyterian Church of Korea (PCK) adopted a Confession of Faith, the so-called Twelve Creeds. Both this Confession of Faith and the PUTS curriculum were strongly based on the Westminster Confession of Faith (1647), although this was the American version, revised and edited in 1788 and 1903.

Alongside this Confession of Faith, theologians played a major role in mapping the future direction of Korean Presbyterian theology. The most dominant among them was Hyung Nyong Park, who acknowledged that his orthodox theology was more influenced by conservative American Presbyterianism than by European Reformed theology. In a similar vein, Jong Sung Rhee stressed that Korean orthodox tendencies were not derived from seventeenth- and eighteenth-century European orthodoxy. Rather, their character was formed by early American missionaries who had been educated in seminaries such as Princeton, McCormick, Union (Richmond) and New Brunswick. They tended to import to Korea the different theological stances of their alma mater. Although most were under the influence of the so-called Old School representing the theological tradition of Westminster through Charles Hodge and B. B. Warfield, the early missionaries also demonstrated a degree of theological diversity. For example, Moffet himself was partly under the influence of the New School in relation to the revivalist tradition. There were also differences between systematic theology and practical theology. To this extent, there is an argument that early missionaries in Korea were more evangelical and moderate.[20] However, the overall theological tendency included a stress on 'verbal inspiration' and 'literalism' with regards to the Bible, an emphasis on the absolutism of divine justice allied to a stress on the otherness of God, and a strong doctrine of predestination with regards to soteriology.

It is important to observe that the turbulence of Korean history in the first half of the twentieth century tended to reinforce orthodox convictions. This dynamic can be seen in the failure of the March 1st Independence Movement from Japanese rule (1919) as well as the outbreak of the Korean War (1950–1953). Orthodox theologians cast these events against the backdrop of the advent of Jesus Christ, stressing the transcendence of the Kingdom of God. Some critics have argued that such theological emphases were deeply influenced by the American fundamentalism which prevailed in the first decades of the last century. Other critics maintain that Hyong Nyong Park was influenced mostly by G. Machen. Even though Machen managed to distinguish

[20] Ibid., 82.

his own orthodoxy from fundamentalism, his attempt to protect absolutism against relativism made these critiques justifiable. Critics thus evaluated Hyung Nyong Park's theology as a combination of orthodoxy and fundamentalism.[21]

Nevertheless, it is noteworthy that the influence of Reformed theology on the Korean Church was not one-dimensional. Alongside a time-honoured, conventional Calvinism, a so-called open (liberal) Calvinism had a strong impact on the Korean church. In 1986, the Presbyterian Church of Korea adopted its own indigenous Confession of Faith at its 71st General Assembly. The introduction of this Confession showed the PCK's fidelity to its heritage, recognising the Apostles' Creed, the Westminster Confession and Shorter Catechism (1647) and the Twelve Creeds (1907) as bedrocks of its confessional understanding. Moreover, in a further confirmation of historical continuity and ecumenicity, the new Confession of 1997 included for the first time the Nicene-Constantinopolitan Creed (381). According to Jong Sung Rhee, this approach aimed to advance 'biblical evangelical theology' as well as 'holistic theology'. Over time, the tradition of Reformed theology has been expanded by post-colonial second generation theologians such as Hyung Ki Rhee, Yong Gil Maeng and Myung Yong Kim.

The different strands of Reformed theology in Korea are embodied in its denominational affiliations. Four Presbyterian denominations and their seminaries reproduce their respective theological trends ranging from conservative through moderate to liberal. The Kosin Presbyterian Church (KPC) and the General Assembly of the Presbyterian Church in Korea (GAPCK) represent orthodox Reformed theology. The Presbyterian Church in the Republic of Korea (PROK) develops liberal theology, including Minjung theology. The moderate stance of the PCK attempts to be faithful to both Reformed and ecumenical theology.

The diverse theological perspectives within the Korean Presbyterian churches show their different interpretations of the legacy of John Calvin. First and foremost, the concept of the holiness of the church is said to be based upon Calvin's doctrine of predestination. However, this led to theological conflicts in respect of the church's historical relationship to Japanese Shinto worship, fears of which resulted in the schism of the Korean Presbyterian Church. Yet this split did not resolve the conflict of interpretations regarding the

---

[21] Jong Sung Rhee, 'The Impact of Reformed Theology in the Korean Church', in *Korean Presbyterian Journal of Theology* 3 (1987): 64–85.

holiness of the church, God's election and its consequences. According to the KPC, holiness was to be expressed through confessional secessionism cast in terms set by the doctrine of predestination. This undeniably empowered the minority church to resist Japanese Shinto worship, subsequently goading the KPC to safeguard its 'purity' in the immediate aftermath of Liberation. However, such emphasis on the holiness of the church is liable to disregard the universal sinfulness of humanity, selectively applying holiness to certain denominations and individuals. Also, the divisive outcome of confessional secessionism has been disparaged within the wider Korean church.

Calvin's theology has also proved a strong influence on the way in which the Korean church understands the Bible. His legacy informs the view that Scripture discloses the truth of Jesus Christ. The radical interpretation of this Calvinist perspective has fostered a wide array of people who maintain a type of 'biblicism'. The doctrines of verbal inspiration and inerrancy are the buttresses of a 'biblical' framework which contains both conventional Calvinism and Reformed orthodoxy. This stance is similar to the neo-Confucian perspective on the characteristics of sacred texts in east Asia, which has led scholars to argue for an affinity between the conventional perspective on Scripture in Korean Christianity and that of neo-Confucian culture.

The theology of Calvin played an important role in making the Korean church to be Scripture-centred, while giving particular focus on the doctrine of predestination. Moreover, Calvin's theology was the bedrock of a church-centered faith, especially under the Presbyterian form of governance. It is notable that Reformed theology under the strong influence of Calvin produced remarkable church leaders such as Sun Ju Kil, Ik Du Kim and Kyung Chik Han in the field of pastoral theology. And Chi Yil Pang, the last foreign missionary in China after the Communist party took over, was one of the fruits of this work.

However, there is still much to be resolved, as is evident in the churches' multifarious interpretations of the Bible, confused understandings of the relationship between predestination and ecclesiology, alternation between church-oriented faith and hierocracy based on the sovereignty of God, and tensions between Presbyterian and Reformed identities. Today the church-oriented character of Korean faith should reclaim its role as 'mother of the faithful' rather than as hierocracy. The concept of divine sovereignty ought to be freed from the battle for hegemony in the Korean church, and needs instead to serve the Christian faith to be accountable in the public realm.

THE ENCOUNTER BETWEEN MINJUNG
AND REFORMED THEOLOGY

To understand the emergence of Minjung theology, it is necessary to trace larger theological processes at work in Korea. First, there was a certain degree of tension between nationalistic and depoliticised types of faith in early Korean churches. Nationalistic faith was maintained by Korean Christians who were especially concerned with independence from Japan, while the depoliticisation of the church's message and activities was emphasised by most missionaries.[22] W. N. Blair, one of these Presbyterian missionaries, claimed:

> We felt that the Korean Church needed not only to repent of hating the Japanese, but also a clear vision of all sin against God, that many had come into church sincerely believing in Jesus as their Savior and anxious to do God's will ... We felt ... that embittered souls needed to have their thoughts taken away from the national situation to their own personal relation with the Master.[23]

Such attempts at depoliticisation and denationalisation were successful, at least at an institutional level. In 1910, the year Korea was officially annexed by Japanese forces, the Korean Presbyterian Church announced the following resolution:

> The church is dedicated to God, not designed for the discussion of national affairs. Churches and chapels are facilities for church services but not the place to discuss national affairs nor the place where people can assemble to discuss national affairs. Moreover, no persons, after becoming Christians, can discuss national affairs in pastors' quest rooms; these kinds of affairs cannot be discussed elsewhere either.[24]

[22] Prior to 1905, Western missionaries were generally sympathetic to the helpless Koreans and critical of Japan. But after the Taft-Katsura memorandum, which included the United States' secret approval of Japan's colonisation of Korea in return for a promise not to interfere with American colonisation of the Philippines, Western missionaries chose political reality over morality by officially announcing their cooperation with the Japanese colonial government. Yet the church became the largest Korean community to oppose Japanese colonial rule, in spite of the missionaries' apolitical manoeuvering. It is no surprise, therefore, to find that many anti-Japanese activities occurred in this religious community.

[23] L. George Paik, *The History of Protestant Missions in Korea 1832–1910* (Pyongyang, Korea: Union Christian College Press, 1929), 369.

[24] See *Christian Bulletin*, October 3, 1910.

Even after Korea regained sovereignty and the influence of missionaries declined, the depoliticisation of the church did not cease. The military government which assumed power by means of a coup in 1961 initiated an ambitious five-year Economic Development Plan in the following year. Under this plan, the state played a controlling role in most areas of economic activity, from management of financial resources to investment in industries. The government adopted an export-driven strategy and with the favour of the state, several large corporations, called Chaebol, played a major role in this policy. The state even controlled the disputes between management and labour.[25] As a result, the vast majority of people who were the actual agents of production were alienated in the process of rapid industrialisation. Industrial workers were particularly exploited as low-wage labour suppliers. Materialistic thinking has been widespread in Korean society, which has brought a mixture of other-worldly attitudes and more secular material concerns. Under these circumstances, many churches have produced a deformed individualistic and privatised faith.

The Minjung ('the people') movement erupted in the 1970s as a counter-reaction to this economy-oriented ideology. It tried to break the vicious circle that prevented people from leading their lives with human dignity and becoming the subjects of history. In this sense, Minjung theologians' common conception of the term is as follows: Minjung are the people who are alienated and oppressed politically, economically, socially and culturally.[26]

Taking into serious consideration this social context, a group of Christians raised questions about social responsibility of the Korean church. This group, in which Reformed Christians were actively involved, initiated a struggle for justice and human rights against the authoritarian government. When the military government changed the constitution in order to justify the incumbent president's third term, some Christian leaders rose to criticise the totalitarian system and repressive policies of the government. They issued the 'Theological Declaration of Korean Christians, 1973,' which argued for 'being witnesses to truth, always struggling to break any system of deception and manipulation'.[27]

[25] Cf. Hyun Chae Park, *Minjok Kyongje-wa Minjung Undong* (National Economy and Minjung Movement) (Seoul: Changjak-kwa Bipyong, 1988), 190.
[26] However most of them, including Suh, tend to argue that class analysis based on an *economic* perspective is the most valid way to answer emerging questions. They argue that economically oppressed people are also oppressed politically, socially and culturally.
[27] Text in *Mission Trend No.3: Third World Theologies*, edited by Gerald H. Anderson and Thomas F. Stransk (Grand Rapids, MI: Eerdmans, 1976), 227–232.

It is against this historical backdrop that Minjung theology emerged,[28] with the term 'theology of Minjung' appearing in the work of Nam Dong Suh for the first time in April 1975.[29] There were two events which caused Suh to think of Minjung as the theme of his theology. The first event was Suh's encounter with the Minjung poet, Chi Ha Kim. Suh argued that he began to recognise Minjung as a historical agency through Kim. The second cause was his encounter with a body of social literature through which Suh began to appreciate the meaning of being both Korean and Minjung. There were other theologians who argued for Minjung theology alongside Suh, but it was Suh who set Minjung as a core theme. He dreamed of it as the centre of all theologies, arguing for a consensus to this end among scholars in the fields of biblical studies, church history and systematic theology. Above all, the dominant theme for Suh is that 'Minjung is the subject of history'.[30]

After Suh, theologians such as Byung Mu Ahn and Yong Bock Kim developed Minjung theology to challenge the Korean church's mission in response to both the oppressed and their oppressors. Minjung theology thus represents a radical change in the socio-political biography of Korean Christians in the 1970s. One of the notable aspects of this shift in trend is that it was not initiated by a newly imported theology, but by a re-orientation of the Korean church heritage which had been exploited by political ideologies (de-politicisation, national defence and anti-communism) and an economic ideology of hedonistic materialism. For Korean Christianity there has been a noble tradition of concern for an independent nation with an accompanying attention to the ethical improvement of society, especially in regards to human rights and freedom based on the *imago Dei*.

Though the contribution of Minjung theology in the 1970s and 1980s is undeniable, an important theological question arises: Is its exclusive interpretation of the Minjung perspective really accountable to Scripture as well as to Korean culture? Minjung's interpretation of history is based upon a dualistic view of the oppressors against the oppressed. While this is defensible to a certain extent, it has a risky

[28] David Kwang Sun Suh, 'A Biographical Sketch of an Asian Theological Consultation', in *Minjung Theology: People as the Subjects of History*, edited by Commission on the Theological Concerns of the Christian Conference of Asia (Maryknoll, NY: Orbis Books, 1983), 18.

[29] Nam Dong Suh, *Minjung Sinhak-ui Tamgu* (In Search of Minjung Theology) (Seoul: Hangilsa, 1983), 29.

[30] Suh, *Minjung*, 173–174.

tendency to reduce a more complicated and ambiguous reality to a simplistic binary pattern.

THE TASKS OF REFORMED THEOLOGY IN TWENTY-FIRST CENTURY KOREA

First, Reformed theology has to provide a vision for a united community of North and South Korea. Above all, the Reformed churches should lead the reformation of South Korean society as a prototype for a unified Korean community, overcoming the divisions of South and North. It should also challenge the church to educate and sensitise Christians, who make up almost 30 percent of the total population in South Korea, towards a God-centered communal unification *before* teaching the ideology of division between North and South Korea. A God-centred covenant community is based on the highest dignity of all members according to the *imago Dei*, and thus does not favour one particular group such as Christians or South Koreans. This will not be an overly nationalistic community, but one embracing both the global community and regional neighbours such as China and Japan.

Second, Reformed theology has to foster an inclusive social culture. In an era of globalisation, Reformed theology should make a strong effort to accommodate cultural diversity. The Korean church should also overcome socio-cultural differences between North and South Korea. And it should also try to enhance the cultural understanding of migrant workers to facilitate their settlement. Furthermore, the Korean church needs to work together with non-governmental organisations (NGOs) to avoid being isolated from civil society. Working with diverse NGOs, the church should build a healthy and inclusive culture which embraces not only North Koreans but also the global community. A church that bears witness to the sovereignty of God needs to play a leading role in the creation of a peaceful global community.

Third, Reformed theology has to support the building of political and economic institutions. It is crucial that the church take the lead in creating a just social structure to produce peace. The church should take an interest in making and executing a just legal system that protects human dignity, freedom, equality and justice. The church should also take an interest in building a transparent and cooperative ethic in a highly competitive global market system. If we think these matters are not tasks for the church, we are eventually denying God's sovereignty and abandoning our responsibility as God's children.

Further reading

Adams, Daniel J. *Korean Theology in Historical Perspective*. Delhi: ISPCK, 2012.
Chung, Paul S., Veli-Matti Karkkainen and Kin Kyoung-Jae (eds.). *Asian Contextual Theology for the Third Millennium: Theology of Minjung in Fourth-Eye Formation*. Princeton Theological Monograph Series; Eugene, Oregon: Wipf & Stock, 2010.
Kim, Kyung Jae. *Christianity and the Encounter of Asian Religions*. Zoeterme er: Boekencentrum, 1994.
Korea Association of Christian Studies, (ed.). *Wells of Our Theology: Rethinking of Discipline in the Korean Context*. Seoul: Dong Yeon Press, 2013.
Oak, Sung-Deuk. *The Making of Korean Christianity: Protestant Encounters with Korean Religions 1876–1915*. Texas: Baylor University Press, 2013.

JAPAN

Yasuhiro Sekikawa

Reformed theology in Japan was inherited from missionaries sent after the Meiji Restoration in 1868. These missionaries came mainly from the Reformed Church in America and the Presbyterian Church (USA). Japan had previously adopted a policy of self-isolation (*sakoku*) for more than 250 years during the Edo period. This was partly because the Tokugawa shogunate feared the influence of the Christian West and banned any missionary activity in Japan. However, the inner turmoil of the late nineteenth century divided the nation into two groups, the pro-emperor group (*Sonnoujoi*) and the pro-Shogunate (*Sabaku*), and created an unstable political situation which led to a harsh power struggle. As the *Sonnoujoi* group gained victory over the *Sabaku* group, the Tokugawa shogunate finally decided to return power to the emperor and to open the gates to the West. This was the beginning of the Meiji Period, during which Japan embarked on modernisation and Western churches began to send missionaries to Japan to build Christian churches and schools.

Reformed churches such as the Reformed Church in America (RCA), the Presbyterian Church USA (PCUSA), and the German Reformed Church in Pennsylvania sent many missionaries to Japan. In the early period, Reformed theology was taught in small seminaries by missionaries such as J. H. Ballagh and Samuel R. Brown. Japanese Christians were soon well-educated and well-trained in the theological disciplines. However, as in the United States, Reformed theology divided into an Old School Calvinism with a strict adherence to the Westminster Confession and a New School Calvinism which reinterpreted Christian doctrine along more liberal lines. According to recent research, the early missionaries to Japan were more heavily influenced by the liberal rendition of Calvinist theology.

The bulk of Japanese Christian leaders in this period were drawn from the *samurai* (warrior) class, many of whom were politically and economically disposed towards the Meiji Restoration. They valued the potential of Christianity to map out a new era for Japan. One of the most prominent leaders was Uemura Masahisa (1858–1925), who was undoubtedly the foremost representative of the Presbyterian-Reformed tradition. He was born into a family of the *samurai* class which had supported the Tokugawa regime. Owing to the radical changes in Japanese society and the decline of the Tokugawa shogunate, the Uemura family experienced economic and social hardship. He entered the Ballagh *Juku* (a private school run by J. H. Ballagh) at the age of fifteen and later became a student in the school led by Samuel R. Brown. Baptised in 1873, he committed himself to the work of a Christian evangelist and writer. Yet Uemura aspired to a greater degree of spiritual independence from the American missionaries, and this proved a formative influence on his own approach to theology. For example, while maintaining orthodox Reformed traditions, he sought to discern the history of salvation within the context of his own pre-Christian religious background. He came to regard the neo-Confucian *Bushido* (the Way of the Samurai) as a singular gift of God to Japan which could be compared to the Old Testament in its preparatory role. This has often been called the theology of *Kokorozashi* (aspiration), which was considered to be the highest virtue of the Bushido in obeying God. *Kokorozashi* was for him already a form of sanctification by God. In his early writings, some traces of the New School Calvinism can be detected in certain Pelagian elements within his doctrine of the atonement. Yet, in his later work, these traces tend to disappear as does the self-conscious move towards independence from the Reformed missions.

Uemura possessed a remarkable ability to grasp the distinctiveness of the Reformed approach to the person and work of Christ. In his first important theological study, *Shinri Ippan* (A View of Truth, 1884), he insisted on the centrality of Christ's vicarious death in securing the forgiveness of sins. This was the earliest appearance of a strong Reformed theology on native Japanese soil. Uemura's intimate contact with foreign culture and scholarly writing also opened new dimensions in the fields of literature, education and political thought. Besides his pastoral and theological work in the Fijimicho Church, his wider scholarly gifts were evident in other contexts. He assumed responsibility for the publication of several periodicals and did much to introduce Christian concepts of the human person, society, literature and art to an educated Japanese public. This in turn contributed to the promotion of Christian culture in Japan.

Though Uemura maintained a close relationship with the Reformed missionaries, he soon reached the conclusion that Christian missions could succeed only if Japanese Christians assumed responsibility for this work. This was evident in his attitude to the confessions which were accepted by the Nihon Itchi Kyokai, a small board of home missions. Though Nihon Itchi Kyokai accepted four confessions (the Heidelberg Catechism, the Westminster Confession and Shorter Catechism and the standards of Dort) as norms of faith, Uemura was against such confessionalism and insisted on minimising the influence of foreign missions. Shortly before 1890, the Japanese Congregationalists (the Nihon Kumiai Kyokai) and the Reformed-Presbyterians (the Nihon Itchi Kyokai) led by Uemura planned to establish one united church in Japan. But this plan eventually failed and the Nihon Itchi Kyokai changed its name to the Nihon Kirisuto Kyoukai (Japan Christian Church), setting forth a brief confession called the 1890 *Shinko no Kokuhaku* (the Confession of Faith). This brief and concise confession retains a strong theological significance, partly because of its affirmation of the Nicene faith of the ecumenical church and its inclusion of certain formulae from the Reformed tradition.

One of the major figures in the Reformed tradition between the two world wars was Takakura Tokutaro (1885–1934), who is considered the successor of Uemura Masahisa. With a thorough knowledge of German theology from Schleiermacher onwards, he was one of those principally responsible for introducing dialectical theology into Japan. Displaying a clear affinity with P. T. Forsyth and other Scottish theologians of the twentieth century, he emphasised the grace (*oncho*) of God in Jesus Christ and the church as a community of faith living by grace. His major work, *Fukuinteki Kirisutokyou* (Evangelical Christianity), insisted upon the necessity of prevenient grace for the self-centred and sinful self (*Jiga*). Here one can observe a new existential development of Reformed theology based on God's grace with ethics understood as our grateful response.

During the Second World War, Japanese churches came under the control of the military government. In 1941, more than thirty Protestant denominations were forced to unite by the military government under the name of the *Nihon Kirisuto Kyodan* (the United Church of Christ in Japan). Without an agreed confession, the sole standard accepted by all the churches was a brief statement of faith (*Kyogi no Taiyou*). This created tensions within Kyodan after 1945. Some of the denominations such as the Lutheran and the Episcopal churches withdrew soon after the war ended, while the remaining churches sought a clearer theological expression of their identity. In the early 1950s, most of the Reformed-Presbyterian churches which remained in Kyodan proposed the preparation of a distinctive confession. Yet progress was slow, with the result that some of the churches adhering to the Reformed tradition withdrew from Kyodan. Those churches which had formerly belonged to the Nihon Kirisuto Kyoukai took the first step towards forming a new Reformed church in Japan. As a result, the main Reformed churches divided into two different groupings. The first group formed the association of Reformed-Presbyterian churches and United Presbyterian churches (Lengo Chorokai) within Kyodan. A second group withdrew from Kyodan and formed a new church (the new Nihon Kirisuto Kyokai). These churches, including the Nihon Kaikakuha Kyokai (the Reformed Church in Japan) with its strict adherence to the Westminster Confession, maintained a commitment to the traditions of classical Reformed theology.

One of the most respected systematic theologians from the first grouping was Kumano Yoshitaka (1899–1981) who taught theology in Tokyo Union Theological Seminary. His various books on Christian doctrine reveal a strong interest in the doctrine of the church. Drummond remarks that, 'His theology is centred in the sovereign God who is uniquely revealed in Jesus Christ, and his understanding is essentially in the tradition of John Calvin and Karl Barth. For him the church is the primary place where the eternal God is by grace creating the new man. Anthropologically viewed, the existence of the church is created by obedience to the Word of God.'[31] In his *Dogmatics* (*Kyogigaku*), Kumano leans heavily on Barth, though as the heir of Takakura and other theologians of the Japanese church, he displays his own creativity. In doing so, Kumano exemplifies the remarkable intellectual and spiritual maturity of Japanese Reformed traditions. In his *Shumatsuron to Rekisitetsugaku* (Eschatology and Philosophy of History, 1933), Kumano raises the question as to what it means to say that the foundation of faith is historical. Aware of Troeltsch's theological challenge, he articulates the relationship of history to faith in such a way as to overcome some perceived difficulties in Barth's approach.

---

[31] Richard H. Drummond, *A History of Christianity in Japan* (Grand Rapids, MI: Eerdmans, 1971), 298.

Pastors following Kumano's theology formed the Rengo Chorokai (the United Presbyterian Movement in the Kyodan) in the 1960s and the Kaikakuchorokyokai Kyogikai (the Association for Reformed-Presbyterian Churches in the Kyodan) in the 1980s. These two groups have been the most active movements for the promotion of Reformed theology in the United Church of Christ in Japan until the present day.

Further reading

Drummond, Richard H. *A History of Christianity in Japan*. Grand Rapids, MI: Eerdmans, 1971.
Laman, Gordon D. *Pioneers To Partners. The Reformed Church in America and Christian Mission with the Japanese*. Grand Rapids, MI: Eerdmans, 2012.
Michalson, Carl. *Japanese Contributions to Christian Theology*. Philadelphia: Westminster, 1960.

CHINA

Alexander Chow

Reformed Christianity was part of the two earliest Protestant missionary endeavours to Chinese lands. The first dates back to the Dutch colonial rule of the island they called Formosa (1624–1662), now known as Taiwan, when Dutch Reformed missionaries worked amongst aborigines and Han Chinese immigrants.[32] The second attempt was by Robert Morrison, the son of Scottish Presbyterians, who in 1807 would become the first Protestant missionary to mainland China. Morrison produced many Chinese Christian works, such as a catechism in 1811, based on the Westminster Shorter Catechism, and a New Testament in 1812.[33]

As the Opium Wars ensued and treaty ports were forced open in the mid-nineteenth century, waves of missionaries were sent from every major denomination to evangelise China. Many Chinese Christians became discontent with the paternalism of foreign denominations, and a number of Presbyterian and Reformed churches united, establishing the Presbyterian Church of China. After inviting other denominations to join this union, the organisation would be renamed the Church of Christ

---

[32] See *Handbook of Christianity in China*, vol. 1, edited by Nicolas Standaert (Leiden: Brill, 2001), 376–377.
[33] Christopher Daily, *Robert Morrison and the Protestant Plan for China* (Hong Kong: Hong Kong University Press, 2013), 136–139, 148.

in China and held its first general assembly under this name in 1927.[34] However, after the Communist Party won the civil war against the Nationalist Party in 1949, all foreigners were ejected from the mainland and all public forms of religious life would eventually come to an end.[35]

As a result of these events, many Chinese Christians and foreign missionaries fled the mainland to neighbouring regions. The earlier church union was preserved through the Hong Kong Council of the Church of Christ in China, a reorganisation of the former Canton Synod, which today has congregations in Hong Kong and Macau. In Taiwan, the Presbyterian Church has played a significant role in socio-political activism, particularly after the Nationalist Party relocated the capital of the Republic of China to Taipei and began ruling the island under martial law.[36] Fighting this hegemonic state, the Presbyterian Church has resisted the state-mandated use of the Mandarin dialect, has been a proponent of aboriginal rights and has been closely associated with the Taiwan independence movement and the Democratic Progressive Party. Moreover, Taiwanese Presbyterians such as Shoki Coe (Huang Zhanghui),[37] Choan-Seng Song (Song Quansheng) and Huang Po Ho (Huang Bohe) have engaged this socio-political climate through the practice of theological contextualisation – a concept popularised by Coe through the World Council of Churches in the 1970s – emphasising theologies that identify with the Taiwanese people.

In the last few decades, diasporic Chinese have played an important role in bringing Reformed theology back to mainland China. Charles Chao (Zhao Zhonghui), a Chinese Christian who fled to Hong Kong in 1949, helped to establish the Reformation Translation Fellowship (RTF) to produce Chinese translations of Reformed literature. After the end of the Cultural Revolution (1966–1976), one of Chao's sons, Jonathan Chao (Zhao Tianen), began to travel to mainland China and distribute Bibles and translated works produced by the RTF.[38] Others such as Stephen Tong (Tang Chongrong) and Samuel Ling (Lin Cixin), together with a

---

[34] Sumiko Yamamoto, *History of Protestantism in China: The Indigenization of Christianity* (Tokyo: Tōhō Gakkai, 2000), 76–81.

[35] Alexander Chow, 'Protestant Ecumenism and Theology in China since Edinburgh 1910', *Missiology* 42.2 (2014): 170–171.

[36] Murray Rubinstein, 'The Presbyterian Church in the Formation of Taiwan's Democratic Society, 1945–2001', *American Asian Review* 19.4 (2001): 63–95.

[37] The standard form of Romanisation used in scholarly literature is pinyin. In this section of the chapter, personal names will be given in their more well-known forms and followed by pinyin in parentheses when appropriate.

[38] David Aikman, *Jesus in Beijing*, rev. ed. (Washington, DC: Regnery, 2006), 278–280.

growing number of South Korean and Korean American missionaries, were later involved in similar work to propagate Reformed Christianity.

In the mid-1980s, internal government reports began to speak of a 'Christianity fever' (*jidujiao re*) spreading across all sectors of Chinese society, developing mainly in pietistic and so-called 'Pentecostal' forms that emphasised a sectarian otherworldliness. Reformed theology was not as prominent at this time, despite the efforts of Jonathan Chao and others.[39] However, this period also saw the growth of Christianity-based new religious movements like the Shouters (Huhan Pai) and Eastern Lightning (Dongfang Shandian); these groups often looked to Christian communities as sources for new converts. In response, by the 1990s, a growing number of Chinese Christians turned to the Reformed tradition to underscore the importance of theology and reason above that of subjective experiences and emotions. The move tended to focus on Reformed soteriological formulations, leading to debates on predestination – particularly around supralapsarianism and infralapsarianism – and whether supernatural gifts continue to exist today.

Mainland China has since been experiencing a surge of interest in Reformed Christianity. A number of studies have shown that one reason for this growth is a parallel growth in China's 'socialist market economy'. The country's ascent as an economic superpower has resulted in a growing number of Christian entrepreneurs in coastal cities, often described as 'boss Christians' (*laoban jidutu*), giving some credibility to Max Weber's thesis about the close connection between the Christian work ethic and the spirit of capitalism.[40]

There is also a growing number of urban churches being established by 'intellectual elite Christians' (*zhishi jingying jidutu*) who can be connected to the 4 June 1989 Tiananmen Square democracy movement.[41] Owing to the failure of the 1989 movement, many of these young intellectuals became disillusioned in their pursuits and found in

---

[39] There are some churches today which trace their roots back to the early Calvinist missionaries. There are also some church leaders such as Wang Aiming who have attempted to argue the case for Reformed theology in the state-sanctioned church. However, the interest in Reformed theology began to become more widespread only in the 1990s.

[40] Chen Cunfu and Huang Tianhai, 'The Emergence of a New Type of Christians in China Today', *Review of Religious Research* 46.2 (2004): 190–191.

[41] Fredrik Fällman, 'Calvin, Culture and Christ? Developments of Faith among Chinese Intellectuals', in *Christianity in Contemporary China: Socio-Cultural Perspectives*, edited by Francis Khek Gee Lim (London: Routledge, 2013), 152–168; Alexander Chow, 'Calvinist Public Theology in Urban China Today', *International Journal of Public Theology* 8.2 (2014): 158–175.

Reformed Christianity existential resolve and a new approach to transform China. One group of urban intellectual Christians has drawn on covenantal theology to argue for a stronger understanding of constitutionalism. Another group has relied on the Dutch neo-Calvinist understanding of the cultural mandate to emphasise a stronger engagement with both state and society. Both of these groups have thus placed a higher emphasis on Reformed ecclesiology.

Today, there is a growing body of Reformed literature being translated into Chinese. The writings of many Calvinist and New Calvinist thinkers such as John Piper, D. A. Carson and Tim Keller can be found in Christian bookstores throughout China, and a lively discussion about Calvinism can likewise be found online. However, only time will tell if this translation of Reformed theology is merely a phase in the shifting history of Chinese Christianity or if it will become deeply rooted in Chinese soil.

Further reading

Cao Nanlai. *Constructing China's Jerusalem: Christians, Power, and Place in Contemporary Wenzhou*. Stanford, CA: Stanford University Press, 2011.

Chow, Alexander. 'Calvinist Public Theology in Urban China Today'. *International Journal of Public Theology* 8.2 (2014): 158–175.

Fällman, Fredrik. 'Calvin, Culture and Christ? Developments of Faith among Chinese Intellectuals'. In *Christianity in Contemporary China: Socio-Cultural Perspectives*. Edited by Francis Khek Gee Lim. London: Routledge, 2013: 152–168.

Rubinstein, Murray. 'The Presbyterian Church in the Formation of Taiwan's Democratic Society, 1945–2001'. *American Asian Review* 19.4 (2001): 63–95.

Wielander, Gerda. *Christian Values in Communist China*. Abingdon, UK: Routledge, 2013.

AUSTRALIA AND AOTEAROA NEW ZEALAND

Geoff Thompson

A focussed presence of Reformed Christianity and its theology in Australia and Aotearoa New Zealand was originally due to the nineteenth-century migration of Scottish and Irish Presbyterians to both nations. Notwithstanding some evidence of theological debate during the nineteenth century,[42] more energy was invested in establishing

---

[42] Notably in the 'Strong Affair', when prominent Presbyterian minister Charles Strong was criticised for denying orthodox claims for the saving significance of Jesus' life,

visible and organised Presbyterian denominations. The nineteenth century also saw the arrival in both nations of Baptist, Congregationalist, and Calvinistic Methodist churches as well as (at least in Australia) a growing presence of evangelical Anglicans who looked to Calvin alongside Cranmer. Reformed theology was, therefore, mediated to this region via the pre-existing denominational fault-lines of British Christianity and those denominations' allegiances to various Reformed confessions. In the twentieth century, Dutch migration to Australia added to this mix of Reformed traditions.[43]

Three developments from these origins can be highlighted: engagement with sources, unity and confessions and post-Christendom trajectories.

ENGAGEMENT WITH SOURCES

Although there is evidence of some direct engagement with Calvin in the nineteenth century, the emerging Reformed theology in this region was typically due to engagement with the Westminster Confession. The early twentieth century witnessed a brief renaissance of the study and promotion of Calvin in Aotearoa New Zealand, largely driven by the emerging awareness of Barth and Brunner in the 1930s.[44] Despite the lack of any sustained scholarship on Schleiermacher, the liberal Protestantism he provoked also shaped theological discussion in the Presbyterian churches of both nations during the twentieth century. In this new theological climate, Calvin and the Westminster Confession were often invoked to defend biblical authority, substitutionary atonement and justification by faith.

In the 1960s Sydney's Anglican Moore College began to require its students to read Calvin's *Institutes*. The intent was to expose the students to one classic text of Christian theology in its entirety, to demonstrate by Calvin's systematic example that Christianity is an

---

death and resurrection. See C. F. Bale, 'Calvinism in Australia 1788–2009: A Historical Assessment', in *Engaging with Calvin: Aspects of the Reformer's Legacy for Today*, edited by M. D. Thompson (Nottingham: Apollos, 2009), 274–297.

43 For historical details see I. Breward, *A History of the Churches in Australasia* (Oxford: Clarendon, 2001), I. Breward, 'Calvin in Australia and New Zealand', in *Calvin: The Man and the Legacy*, edited by M. Rae, P. Matheson and B. Knowles (Adelaide: ATF Theology, 2014), 235–255, and Bale, 'Calvinism in Australia 1788–2009'.

44 See P. Matheson, 'The Reception of Calvin and Calvinism in New Zealand: A Preliminary Trawl', in Rae et al., *Calvin*, 185–187.

intellectually coherent faith and to learn from Calvin's *theological* engagement with Scripture.[45]

Celebrations of Calvin's quincentenary throughout Australia and Aotearoa New Zealand included academic conferences in Dunedin, Melbourne and three in Sydney. The conferences addressed issues conventionally associated with Calvin as well as those drawing Calvin into conversation with contemporary hermeneutics, modern politics and the natural sciences. Adding to this interest in Calvin, Jonathan Edwards' work has become the focus of renewed interest with the establishment of the Jonathan Edwards Centre at Ridley College, Melbourne.

UNITY AND CONFESSIONS

Despite a shared commitment to the Westminster Confession there were twenty-five Presbyterian and Reformed denominations in Australia alone in 2009.[46] As elsewhere, the Reformed tradition's theological insistence on the church's catholicity and unity has been heavily qualified in practice.

A significant attempt to correct this was the formation of the Uniting Church in Australia (UCA) in 1977 out of the Presbyterian, Methodist and Congregational Churches.[47] Resisting 'ecclesiastical carpentry'[48] as a path to union, the three churches were invited to enter 'union on the basis of a fresh confession of the faith of the church'.[49] The Reformation confessions functioned paradigmatically in two ways. First, whilst written 'to serve the particular needs of the Church of that day' their particularity did 'not invalidate [their] universal significance'.[50] Any new confession would similarly be particular but not parochial. Secondly, they embodied the 'Church's re-enactment or reflection of the witness borne by prophet and apostle in Holy Scripture'.[51] Consequently, the theological centre of the UCA's Basis of Union is a confession of the church's

---

[45] See P. F. Jensen, 'Calvin Among the Students: Shaping Theological Education', in Thompson, *Engaging with Calvin*, 268.

[46] See Bale, 'Calvinism in Australia 1788–2009', 282.

[47] The Presbyterian Church of Australia continues since approximately one-third of the Presbyterian membership declined to enter Union.

[48] J. D. McCaughey, 'The Formation of the Basis of Union', *Proceedings of the Uniting Church Historical Society (Victoria)* 1.1 (1994), 9.

[49] Joint Commission on Church Union, *The Faith of the Church*, in *Theology for Pilgrims: Selected Theological Documents of the Uniting Church in Australia*, edited by R. Bos and G. Thompson (Sydney: Uniting Church Press, 2008), 40.

[50] *The Faith of the Church*, 23.

[51] *The Faith of the Church*, 24.

faith articulated not through the repetition of creedal formulae but, strikingly, through a narrative summary of the New Testament witness to Jesus articulated exclusively in biblical concepts and terminology.[52]

In the 1960s the Presbyterian Church of New Zealand also entered union negotiations with the Churches of Christ, Anglicans, Methodists and Congregationalists of Aotearoa New Zealand. Despite the union not eventuating, the proposed Basis of Union remains a 'statement of faith' for the renamed Presbyterian Church of Aotearoa New Zealand (PCANZ); it stands alongside other ancient and contemporary statements, the most recent of which (2010) bears the Maori title *Kupu Whakapono* (Confession of Faith). The latter declares God's triunity, Jesus' identity and saving significance, and (sharing the widely adopted correction to the Creeds' and Reformers' formulaic marks of the church) a confession of the nexus between ecclesial identity and the call to mission.[53]

POST-CHRISTENDOM TRAJECTORIES

In recent decades the development of Reformed theology in both nations has been significantly influenced by engagements with Karl Barth, Jürgen Moltmann, T. F. Torrance and Colin Gunton. A steady stream of Barth scholarship has emerged. Arguably Moltmann, with his interest in ecumenical, contextual and political theologies, is the Reformed theologian most read in both nations' non-Reformation churches. Students of both Torrance and Gunton have been involved in theological education and research in both countries. These four twentieth-century heirs of the Reformation recast Reformed theology as a conversation partner with both the church catholic and an increasingly post-Christendom culture. In doing so, they brought Reformed theology to bear on issues never, or barely, in dispute during the Reformation itself: the Trinity, pneumatology, eschatology, cosmology and the natural sciences, the mission of the church, and dialogue with the Eastern Orthodox tradition. Likewise, the region's contemporary theologians variously drawing on the Reformed tradition are attending to such issues as theosis, holocaust studies, theological hermeneutics and contemporary missiology.[54]

---

[52] See Paragraph 3 of the Basis of Union (1992 edition) at www.uca.org.au/basisofunion .htm (accessed 1 March 2015).

[53] See the PCANZ's statements of faith at www.presbyterian.org.nz/about-us/statements-of-faith (accessed 1 March 2015).

[54] For example: M. Habets, *Theosis in the Theology of Thomas Torrance* (Farnham, UK: Ashgate, 2009), M. R. Lindsay, *Reading Auschwitz with Barth: The Holocaust*

Acknowledging the radically post-Christendom nature of both Australia and Aotearoa New Zealand is likely to be the key to the future development of Reformed theology in these nations. Repetition of sixteenth-century polemics risks theological isolationism, albeit with a strong sense of identity and faithfulness. On the other hand, if the inheritance of Reformed theology is to engage the region's emerging theological and cultural landscape it will need to address issues of gender, indigenous histories and spiritualities, public theology, an increasingly confident atheism and the realities of multi-religious and multi-cultural societies. It is likely that both trajectories will be pursued for the foreseeable future.

Further reading

Breward, Ian. *A History of the Churches in Australasia*. Oxford: Clarendon, 2001.
Rae, Murray, Peter Matheson and Brett Knowles (eds.). *Calvin: The Man and the Legacy*. Adelaide, South Australia: ATF Press, 2014.
Reformed Theological Review – an Australian-based journal existing to provide 'scholarly exposition, defence and propagation of the Reformed faith'. See http://rtr.org.au/
Uniting Church Studies, vol. 17.1 (2011) – a special issue devoted to Calvin's Quincentenary.

as *Problem and Promise for Barthian Theology* (Eugene, OR: Pickwick, 2014), M. Rae, *History and Hermeneutics* (Edinburgh: T&T Clark, 2006), and J. G. Flett, *The Witness of God: The Trinity, Missio Dei, Karl Barth and the Nature of Christian Community* (Grand Rapids, MI: Eerdmans, 2010).

20 Reformed theology, mission, and ecumenism

DARRELL L. GUDER

Reformed theological engagement with mission is shaped by the ambiguous history of Western Christendom with regard to the Christian mission. That ambiguity did not characterize the early Christian church's sense of its purpose. Traced back to its biblical roots, "mission" defines the church. The calling and gathering of God's particular people to serve God's healing purposes for all of creation results in the "sending" of that people: "As my Father has sent me, so I send you" (John 20:21). Jesus' Easter mandate to the gathered disciples locates the mission of the apostolic movement in God's universal purpose and actions. The Trinitarian sending of the Son leads to the Father and the Son sending the Spirit to empower the Easter community to embark on God's mission with a clearly defined purpose: "You shall be my witnesses in Jerusalem, Judea, Samaria, and to the end of the earth" (Acts 1:8). From Pentecost onward, the apostolic mission is to form communities of believers that are empowered to continue the Gospel witness that brought them into existence. The biblical texts, all addressed to such witnessing communities, function as the Spirit's instrument for their ongoing formation for their mission. Every dimension of the emerging Christian movement was shaped and defined by the fundamentally missionary nature of the church.

The vision of the early Christian mission was universal. The Gospel of God's love for and the healing of the world was intended for all creation; the message was fundamentally translatable into every language and culture, as demonstrated at Pentecost. If "all authority on heaven and earth has been given to [Jesus Christ]" (Matt. 28:16), then Christian witnesses could not cross any boundary into a territory in which Jesus was not already the reigning Lord. With that confident sense of sentness and in spite of resistance and overt oppression, the Christian witness spread and the Christian church grew on all sides of the Mediterranean and began its movement outward to the "ends of the earth." By the time the Roman Empire began to favor the Christian movement in the fourth century, it represented a strong and growing minority in the religiously plural world of classic antiquity. It was, however, a minority with a strong sense of missionary purpose.

The complex process of "Christianization" lasting over several centuries had a major impact on the church's understanding and interpretation of mission. As the Christian church became the officially sanctioned religious institution of late Roman societies, the activity of mission became more and more the expansion of the institutional church and the Christian culture that it fostered. It was these "Christianized" cultures that continued to spread geographically through the first half of the medieval period. The loss of the Christian cultures of northern Africa to militant Islam was compensated for by the territorial spread of Roman Christendom northward and eastward. Byzantine Christendom spread out throughout eastern Europe, with Russian Christianity continuing the process from 1000 CE onward. From approximately 500 CE, the "diffusion" of existing Christendom structures was the ongoing and dominant form of mission in actual practice. The activity of mission was not accompanied by theological reflection on the missionary character of the church from its founding onward.

While the theological discourse of Western Christendom neglected the theme of mission, the biblical focus on the formation of witnessing communities was replaced by Christendom's endeavors to maintain the already Christianized cultures of western, central, and eastern Europe. Thus, Wilbert Shenk's trenchant comment, "The Christendom model of church may be characterized as *church without mission*,"[1] should be altered to read "Christendom's theologies of the church neglect mission." This does not mean that mission was not happening. It was – St. Patrick in Ireland, St. Columba in Scotland, St. Boniface in Germany. But this "mission by cultural diffusion" was not guided by a biblical theology of the missionary church. There is no evidence that the Great Commission at the end of the Gospel of Matthew was ever read and applied to the actual life and work of medieval Christendom. It was generally regarded as relevant to the apostolic and sub-apostolic periods but was now replaced by the formal establishment of the Christian church and the validation of Christianity as the only licit organized religion in the then-known world.

---

[1] Wilbert R. Shenk, *Write the Vision: The Church Renewed* (Valley Forge, PA: Trinity Press International, 1995), 35.

MISSION AND THE REFORMATION

The Reformation of the sixteenth century was a wide-ranging and profound theological course correction. Centered on the doctrine of salvation, it redefined the Gospel in terms of grace alone, faith alone, and Scripture alone. In that process, virtually every major theme of theology was addressed. Western theologies of the person and work of Christ, the authority and interpretation of Scripture (and tradition), the doctrines of providence and election, and the church were debated and reframed. But the theological impact of the Reformation upon ecclesiology did not include a rediscovery of the fundamentally missionary nature of the church. The controversies related to the theology of the church focused rather on the doctrine and practice of the sacraments and of the ordered offices of ministry. The numerous Protestant confessions and catechisms that were formulated from the sixteenth century on did not address mission. The biblical language of mission as sentness was not reclaimed by the various strands of the Reformation. The assumption that Europe was already long since Christian continued to hold sway, even though the interpretation of what that Christian identity meant in actual practice was undergoing massive critical rethinking. The established forms of church–state relationship were critically tested and even reformulated, but they were not fundamentally questioned. Only the so-called Radical Reformation (the Anabaptists and Mennonites) challenged the partnership of church and state, which resulted in their persecution by both Roman Catholics and Protestants.

If there was no overt theological engagement with the theme of mission in the emerging Reformed tradition, basic themes of that tradition can be looked upon retrospectively as the tilling of the soil for what would emerge much later as the reclamation of the centrality of mission for the church's nature and action. Georg Plasger has summarized the Reformed understanding of the church, especially as articulated by Calvin: "the church is elected by God to serve as a tool of God and to make community with Christ possible and real".[2] This emphasis on God's salvific purposes and the church's calling to serve those purposes would gradually reemerge in Reformed theological discourse and find expression in the language of the "mission of God" in the late twentieth century. That emphasis is a variant of the Reformed insistence on the primacy of God's sovereignty which complements the understanding of

---

[2] Georg Plasger, '10. Ecclesiology', in *The Calvin Handbook*, edited by Herman J. Selderhuis (Grand Rapids, MI: Eerdmans, 2009), 323.

the church as "a tool of God." As a result, there is among many Reformed theologians a profound skepticism about regarding the church as an end in itself. From the earliest days of the Swiss Reformation, the claim was reiterated that the Christian church is "born of the Word of God," and that it can only exist as it listens to that voice and refuses to follow any other voice.[3] What it hears is the good news of God's healing love for the world, the witness to which defines the church's purpose. And as it hears that Word, the church undergoes ongoing reformation toward faithfulness to its vocation. So, if the Swiss Reformation did not develop a mission-centered ecclesiology, its unequivocal focus on the ongoing task of evangelization as the responsibility of the church pointed toward the later reemergence of such a "missional" doctrine of the church. Merwyn Johnson has summarized how the Genevan understanding of the task of evangelization was shaped by the central thrust of Reformed Christianity: "According to Calvin's view of grace, God alone saves, and God alone does the work of evangelism. Grace proclaims the redeeming presence and activity of God in our midst. Our relationship with God is alive and valuable for its own sake, because God is alive, active, and gracious."[4]

That certainty of God's redemptive Word present and active in the gathered church found its concrete expression in the practice of missionary "sending" that characterizes the Swiss Reformation from early on. Geneva became known as a major center for the theological formation of pastors who were sent out into the challenging "mission fields" of Europe. Calvin devoted considerable effort not only to their equipping but also to their support and encouragement through his voluminous correspondence with Reformed leaders and communities all across Europe. They were in effect "Reformed missionaries," whose mission was often the reevangelization of congregations shaped by the distortions of inherited Christendom. The outcome was often persecution and martyrdom. When European Protestantism began to send missionaries beyond the boundaries of Christendom to "pagan mission fields," the pattern had long been set in Geneva. Especially noteworthy was the Genevan involvement in one of the earliest ventures in European mission beyond the boundaries of Christendom. In 1556, the Genevan Reformed leaders and their French colleagues formally sponsored a

---

[3]   *The Ten Theses of Berne* (1528), thesis 1, in *Reformed Confessions of the Sixteenth Century*, edited by Arthur Cochrane (Louisville, KY: Westminster John Knox, 2003), 49.

[4]   Merwyn Johnson, 'Calvin's Significance for Evangelism Today', in *Calvin Studies V*, edited by John H. Leith (Davidson, NC: Colloquium on Calvin Studies, 1990), 119.

cross-cultural missionary venture to Brazil, with the intent of planting new churches in a French colony near Rio de Janeiro. The mission failed, but one of its Genevan participants later published an account of the venture in which he described their purpose: "so that the gospel would be preached not only in the whole kingdom but also in the whole world."[5]

THE MODERN MISSIONARY MOVEMENT
AND THE REFORMED TRADITION

While Spanish and Portuguese colonialism fostered Roman Catholic missionary activity beyond the boundaries of Christendom from the late fifteenth century onward, the Protestant movements of northern Europe did not follow suit for at least a century. The broad consensus of both Lutheran and Reformed theologians was that the apostolic mission had ended in the early Christian period. In the early seventeenth century, Dutch theologians began to advocate Christian mission to unevangelized cultures, arguing from the scriptural witness and often in reaction to Roman Catholic mission. Gisbertus Voetius (1589–1676), professor at the University of Utrecht, argued that the goals of mission were the conversion of the heathen, the planting of churches, and supremely the glory of God. Thus, the church in Christendom must become a sending community.[6]

In the eighteenth century, the engagement in foreign mission gained momentum, and it was supported by early expressions of theological reflection on the task and challenge of mission. The waves of revival on both shores of the North Atlantic motivated growing numbers of lay persons to volunteer for mission service under the auspices of the increasingly numerous mission societies, many of them Reformed. Jonathan Edwards (1703–1758) emerged as an especially influential advocate of foreign mission, which he argued was motivated by God's love with the Kingdom of God as the goal. Particularly powerful was a treatise whose title summarized his argument: *A Humble Attempt to Promote Explicit Agreement and Visible Union among God's People in Extraordinary Prayer for the Revival of Religion and Advancement of Christ's Kingdom on Earth, Pursuant to Scripture Promises and Prophecies Concerning the Last Time* (1747).[7] Comparable influence

---

[5] Sidney Rooy, 'Lèry, Jean de', in *Biographical Dictionary of Christian Missions*, edited by Gerald H. Anderson (New York: Simon and Shuster, MacMillan, 1998), 396–397.

[6] J. Verkuyl, *Contemporary Missiology: An Introduction* (Grand Rapids, MI: Eerdmans, 1978), 21.

[7] Verkuyl, *Contemporary Missiology*, 24.

was exercised by the Baptist missionary advocate, William Carey (1761–1834), who was shaped by Calvinism. His pamphlet, *An Enquiry into the Obligations of Christians to Use Means for the Conversion of the Heathens* (1792), asserted the relevance of Matthew's Great Commission for the contemporary church. For Carey, the missionary mandate was a matter of Christians' obedience to their Lord's command, about which there could be no debate.

THEOLOGICAL REFLECTION ON MISSION

The neglect of mission in the theological traditions of the West began to be addressed with the early theological reflection on mission of especially the Dutch Reformed theologians of the sixteenth and seventeenth centuries.[8] The thrust of their various theological approaches to mission was the obligation of Christian communities in the West to proclaim the Gospel in the non-Christian cultures now being encountered as a result of colonial expansion. The arguments built on solid Reformed convictions: serving the glory of God, obedience to Scripture, commitment to Christ's mission. They continued, however, to be shaped by the unquestioned assumption that the partnership between church and state, although often in need of reform, was the divinely ordained context for European Christianity as it was exported around the world. Often the advocacy of mission was linked with the assumption that the secular power of the state, exercised through its colonializing agencies, would create the opportunities for Christian mission abroad.

When Princeton Theological Seminary was established in 1812, the General Assembly of the Presbyterian Church in the United States adopted a design for the Seminary that included the church's intention "to found a nursery for missionaries to the heathen ... in which youth may receive the appropriate training which may lay a foundation for their ultimately becoming eminently qualified for missionary work."[9] In 1830, the church decided to appoint a professor of pastoral theology and missionary instruction. The General Assembly's rationale emphasized that "the spirit of the religion of Jesus Christ is essentially a spirit of Missions," and thus the church should "make all her establishment tributary to [this spirit's] advancement."[10] Myklebust concludes that this was first instance of formal academic treatment of the theme of

---

[8] Verkuyl, *Contemporary Missiology*, 20–22.

[9] Otto Myklebust, *Study of Missions in Theological Education*, 2 vols. (Oslo: Forlaget og Kirke, 1955), 1: 146.

[10] Myklebust, *The Study of Missions*, 1: 147.

mission anywhere, although at approximately the same time, Friedrich Schleiermacher (1768–1834) mentioned the study of mission as one component of his draft of the university theological curriculum. Although he called it "the theory of the essence of mission," it was assigned to Practical Theology, with the comment, "Possibly a theory of mission which for all intents and purposes still does not exist could be added at this point."[11] In this first stage of modern academic attention to mission, absent any broad interest in "the theory" if not "the theology" of mission, the emphasis was primarily practical training for missionary service.

In spite of the enormous expansion of missionary work during the nineteenth century, theological reflection on mission emerged very slowly, The theologian whose work profoundly shaped the "Princeton theology" up into the early twentieth century, Charles Hodge (1797–1878), preached on mission, and sent his sons into the foreign mission field, but never mentioned the subject in his three volume *Systematic Theology* (1872–1873). Early in the twentieth century, the northern stream of the Presbyterian Church in the United States was compelled to address the absence of the theme mission in its confessional standards. In 1903, the church amended the Westminster Confession by adding paragraph XXXV: "Of the Gospel of the Love of God and Missions." True to its Reformed roots, this confessional statement grounded mission in God's grace revealed in Christ, claiming that "in the gospel God declares his love for the world and his desire that all men should be saved; reveals fully and clearly the only way of salvation; promises eternal life to all who truly repent and believe in Christ; invites and commands all to embrace the offered mercy; and by his Spirit accompanying the word pleads with men to accept his gracious invitation."[12] To make that Gospel known, "Christ hath commissioned his Church to go into all the world and to make disciples of all nations."[13] However, the conclusion to which this addition then comes reveals the mindset of the Christendom legacy which reduces the church's missionary mandate to the maintenance of Western institutional Christianity and its expansion through foreign mission to the rest of the world: "All believers are, therefore, under obligation to sustain the ordinances of the Christian religion where they are already established, and to contribute by their

---

[11] Verkuyl, *Contemporary Missiology*, 7.
[12] Presbyterian Church (USA), *Book of Confessions* (Louisville, KY: Office of the General Assembly, 1999), 6.188.
[13] Ibid., 6.190.

prayers, gifts, and personal efforts to the extension of the Kingdom of Christ throughout the whole earth."[14]

The rapid expansion of the Western foreign mission enterprise in the nineteenth century began finally to generate, in the churches and academic institutions of the sending Western cultures, an interest in mission and mission-related studies that went beyond the practical concerns of training for the mission field. The German Lutheran Gustav Warneck (1834–1919) argued that the disciplined study of mission belonged in the university canon, and to substantiate his claim, he published a widely regarded three-volume "Evangelical Doctrine of Mission" (*Evangelische Missionslehre*, 1897–1980). He is generally regarded as the founder of the modern discipline of missiology. With the continuing growth of Western mission into the first third of the twentieth century, its Reformed exponents in the Netherlands, Scotland, Switzerland, France, and North America were engaged both with the planting of churches in the non-Western world, and the development of educational institutions for missionary training both in the West and in the so-called "daughter churches." In the twentieth century, Reformed theology reengaged the theme of mission, rediscovering the biblical claim of the church's essentially missionary nature, and drawing on resources within the tradition that fostered rigorous theological reflection on the church's missionary nature and practice.

THE END OF CHRISTENDOM AND THE GLOBALIZATION OF CHRISTIANITY

The Reformed reengagement of the theme of mission as a theological discipline was motivated and shaped by two major paradigm shifts in the world Christian movement that became both obvious and the subject of intense investigation in the twentieth century. The first of these shifts was the decline of Western Christendom, a complex process that included many interacting factors. Chief among these were (a) the gradual disestablishment of Western institutional churches, represented by the separation of church and state; (b) the secularization of Western thought represented by the Enlightenment and its profound skepticism about fundamental tenets of inherited faith traditions; (c) the displacement of the church from its dominant role in Western cultures that had for centuries defined themselves as "Christian"; and (d) the credibility crisis arising from the wars of the twentieth century, waged among

[14] Ibid., 6.190.

so-called Christian states. In central and eastern Europe, all of these factors coalesced in the concerted repression of Christianity under the aegis of atheistic socialism in the Soviet bloc. Although recognized by many alert interpreters of Western culture, Christendom's decline is complex and difficult to assimilate. The influence of the centuries of the Constantinian project is still very real, and taking leave of it is painful.

The general decline of North Atlantic Christendom was paralleled in a truly paradoxical way by the rapid growth of the Christian movement in the non-Western world, as the churches that resulted from the foreign missionary movement shook off their colonial dependence and became themselves missionary churches, taking up the biblical mandate that defines the apostolic church's nature and purpose. This entailed their challenging the cultural captivities of the Gospel brought by Western missionaries, as the emerging churches of the two-thirds world proclaimed the Gospel using Bibles translated into hundreds of non-Western languages. By the middle of the twentieth century, it became clear that the demography of the global Christian movement had radically shifted. Given the dynamic growth and independence of the churches outside Western Christendom, Christianity's center of gravity moved away from the societies bordering the North Atlantic to the Southern Hemisphere. This shift has had and continues to have an enormous impact on the inherited Christendom traditions of the West. They are challenged to recognize that they do not represent normative Christianity. They are confronted by their long and complicated history of accommodation, compromise, and captivity that has often been the cost of the privileges of political and cultural establishment. The partnership between Western colonialism and Western missionary expansion is now subject to criticism, which is often painful, generally justified, and on occasion oversimplified. In spite of those problems, the fact remains that the Christian movement today is a global, multicultural, multilingual, and multiorganizational reality, and that the most dynamic missionary activity today is emerging not out of the older Christendom churches but from the non-Western churches that resulted from that problematic Western missionary activity.

THE EMERGENCE OF THE ECUMENICAL MOVEMENT AND THE THEOLOGICAL RECLAMATION OF MISSION

In the course of the twentieth century, a growing network of theologians in the various Christian traditions reclaimed mission as the centering and driving theme of the doctrine of the Christian church. It has been a process that has unfolded in diverse ways in these various traditions. The engagement with mission as *a* if not *the* integrative and centering theological discourse has been a particular focus of many Reformed theologians throughout the last century and into the present one. A major theological impulse that contributed to this reclamation was the emergence of the concern for the unity of the church. That concern arose on the non–North Atlantic mission fields around the world. In a series of mission conferences during the nineteenth century, the consensus grew that the Christian mission was profoundly impeded by the divisions of the church exported by the Western missionaries. The Edinburgh Missionary Conference (1910) is commonly described as the event that gave birth to the contemporary Ecumenical Movement. The Reformed movement was deeply engaged in the undertaking: the event took place in the Assembly Hall of the United Free Church of Scotland. Among the participants were numerous missionaries and mission society leaders representing various strands of the worldwide Reformed movement. The focus of the conference was on the strategies, challenges, and methods of mission. The entire undertaking was marked by a spirit of high optimism as the modern missionary movement looked back on the remarkable outcome of its labors during the nineteenth century and moved into the twentieth century committed to the "evangelization of the world in this generation." To be sure, the conference also revealed its rootedness in the Western neglect of mission as a theological concern. There was, in fact, an advance commitment not to address theological and ecclesiological concerns at the conference. But as the energies it marshaled began to bear fruit in the twentieth century, the theological issues of mission and unity, and their essential connection to one another, demanded attention.

Reformed participation was strong from the outset, not least because of the well-known and emphatic commitment of John Calvin to the unity of the church as an article of faith. For Calvin, 'the unity of the church is believed and is therefore assumed, and this, namely, is the task to which the church collectively must conform – in both great and small things. Thus the unity of the body of Christ is not purely formulaic, but demands concreteness.'[15] Throughout the twentieth century, Reformed commitment to concrete ecumenism has been demonstrated in the numerous church unions (such as in Australia, Canada, South India, England, the United States) in which Reformed churches were deeply involved and often the catalysts.

---

[15] Plasger, "Ecclesiology," 327.

The theological reclamation of mission took place in diverse expressions of the growing ecumenical movement. One can see the emerging momentum toward serious theological engagement with the church's mission in the deliberations of the International Missionary Council (1921), the Faith and Order Movement (1920), and the Life and Work Movement (1920). Reformed theologians and missionaries played key roles in all of them. Representative of the Reformed leadership that contributed importantly to the reclamation of mission as definitive of the church truly united in Christ was the work of the Scottish missionary and mission leader, John Alexander Mackay (1889–1983). As President of Princeton Seminary (1936–1959), he was deeply involved in many of the major ecumenical undertakings of the twentieth century, including the consultations that led to the formation of the World Council of Churches in 1948. But his engagement was just as intensive on the theological front. When he became president of Princeton Seminary in 1936, he named himself Professor of Ecumenics, thereby inventing the discipline, and he proceeded to teach in this emerging field in the following decades. In 1964, he published the first major textbook in the field: *Ecumenics: The Science of the Church Universal*. His approach to the church's vocation to be visibly one body enriches and challenges Reformed theology both with regard to the doctrine as well as the practices of the church. He was profoundly concerned about the church's faithfulness to its missionary vocation, which entails addressing the historical compromises of that vocation, especially as the legacy of Western Christendom. It was in support of this call to the church to be faithful to its missionary mandate to be Christ's witness that he made the often cited appeal at the Oxford Life and Work Conference (1937) to "let the church be the church." For this to happen, it is necessary to move beyond the "science of mission" to rigorous engagement with the "theology of mission": "The moment has arrived when the world wide Christian Community must be studied in its essential character as a missionary reality, together with all that is involved when this ecumenical society is true to its nature and fulfills its destiny. This is the task of the Science of Ecumenics."[16]

There are many areas and themes in the Reformed theological conversation in which Mackay has contributions to make, but there is none as important as his insistence that the church's faithfulness to its missionary vocation cannot be separated from its commitment to unity.

[16] John A. Mackay, *Ecumenics: The Science of the Church Universal* (Englewood Cliffs, NJ: Prentice-Hall, 1964), vii.

Unity is not merely a matter of institutional reorganization. It has to do with the basic apostolic instruction that the witnessing community is to lead its public life "worthy of the gospel of Christ" (Phil. 1:27). Both in his scholarship and in his personal conduct, Mackay demonstrated the gracious hospitality, the combination of conviction and modesty, and the unabashed commitment to serving Jesus Christ by making him known, that have characterized Reformed theology at its most faithful.

The most comprehensive reclamation of the theology of mission was, however, carried out by the Reformed theologian Karl Barth (1886–1968). Barth's monumental theological project was pervasively shaped by his conviction that the era of Western Christendom was over and that the rapidly changing context of the Christian movement in the West called for a theological revolution. Crucial for the revolution was a massive reorientation of the church's understanding of its identity and purpose. This reorientation arises out of the Gospel itself: the church must turn its focus away from itself to the world to which it is sent. It is God's love for that world which results in the salvific action of Jesus Christ on the cross and at the empty tomb. For the world to hear and respond to that good news, God gathers a community to serve his healing purposes for the whole creation. The Spirit enables the hearing, the responding, and the submitting to the person and message of Jesus Christ. The church which results from the Spirit's empowering action is centered on the mandate of mission.

This conviction was expressed by Barth as early as 1932, when in his lecture on "Theology and Mission in the Present Situation" to the Brandenburg Mission Society, he stated that "all activity of the church is mission."[17] As then the *Church Dogmatics* unfolds, volume by volume, it becomes clear that God's mission operates as a fundamental claim of the project, constantly addressed from various perspectives.

> What it means to be in the Church, and even what the Church itself truly is, may be seen typically in what is described in the New Testament as the reality of the apostolate.... In and with the grace which comes to it, the Church ... has its essential direction outwards to mission, to the world, because it is not merely based upon the apostolate but is identical with it.... The apostolate consists of this sharing in Jesus' own mission.[18]

---

[17] Karl Barth, 'Die Theologie und die Mission in der Gegenwart', in *Theologische Fragen und Antworten* (Zollikon: Theologischer Verlag Zürich, 1957), 100.

[18] Karl Barth, *Church Dogmatics*, vol. II/2 (Edinburgh: T&T Clark, 1957), 430–432.

The theological structure that defines how this "sharing in Jesus' own mission" happens is laid out in the fourth volume, addressing the doctrine of reconciliation. Classic themes of especially Reformation thought are profoundly appropriated and interpreted under the sign of the missionary nature of the Gospel and the church. The polemical challenge of the project centers on Barth's critique of the classic definitions of Christian identity. He rejects the deeply embedded assumption that the Christian is properly defined as one who enjoys the benefits of the Gospel. Rather, he claims that the Christian is properly understood as the person called and equipped to be a witness as part of the witnessing community. The emphasis on witness as vocation is made all the more emphatic by Barth's insistence that the Gospel of reconciliation not only entails justification and sanctification, but also issues forth in vocation. If vocation does not follow from justification and sanctification, then the understanding of both the Christian person and the Christian community is inward, self-centered, and fundamentally at odds with God's saving purposes.

The reclamation of mission as the driving force of ecclesiology is further explored by Barth's dynamic interpretation of the church in terms of its gathering, upbuilding, and sending. The work of justification results in the gathering of those whom God elects and calls to serve his mission to the world. Sanctification is the work of the Spirit to "upbuild" the community for its calling, that is, to equip the community for its vocation. The vocation entails the sending of the community to live and work in the world as witnesses to the inbreaking reign of God in Christ. The "being of the community" is its mission, its sending: "Its mission is not additional to its being. It is, as it is sent and active in its mission. It builds up itself for the sake of its mission and in relation to it. It does it seriously and actively as it is aware of its mission and in the freedom from itself which this gives."[19]

The "freedom from itself" is to be understood as the Gospel's liberation of the church from the compromises and captivities of the long tradition of Western Christendom. Thus, Barth's reclamation of mission as definitive of the church's purpose and action is at the same time a rejection of any version of the concept of the church as an end in itself. The church is the called, upbuilt, and sent people of God for God's purposes for the world. Barth writes:

> It is with a [commission], and to fulfill this [commission], that the community is sent into the world and exists for it.... The

---

[19] Karl Barth, *Church Dogmatics*, vol. IV/1 (Edinburgh: T&T Clark, 1956), 725.

community is given its [commission] by Jesus Christ.... He calls them together. He calls them to the community. He makes of them His people, His body, and makes them its members. He is also the origin and content of their commonly given [commission].... His person, His work, His revealed name, the prophetic Word by which He proclaims Himself within it, is the matter at issue in its [commission]. To use the simplest and biblical formulation: Ye shall be witnesses unto me (Acts 1:8).[20]

DOING "MISSIONAL" THEOLOGY

It is not an overstatement to claim that, by the end of the twentieth century, the reclamation of mission as definitive of the church's being and action had not only happened but had become a theological concern in virtually all of the major confessional traditions. The enterprise of "missional theology" models ecumenical engagement as it draws a great diversity of theologians into constructive conversation and research. It is a remarkable example of the complementarity of charisms to see Reformed, Roman Catholic, Anabaptist, Lutheran, Wesleyan, Anglican, Pentecostal, and Evangelical missiologists building on each other's work and deepening their shared understandings of the mission of God and its mandate for the church.

Of course, the contemporary discussion is also shaped by a theological pluralism that results in diverse interpretations of the missionary mandate and its appropriate expressions. The Reformed theologies of mission expounded by, for example, Karl Barth, John Mackay, David Bosch, and Lesslie Newbigin are criticized for diverse reasons, chief among which is the concern about Christocentric mission in a religious plural world. These critiques also reflect varying understandings of "salvation," revelation, the reign of God, and thus the Gospel itself.

Representative of the constructive role of Reformed theology in contemporary missional thought is the work of Lesslie Newbigin (1909–1998) and David Bosch (1929–1992). It is notable that their theological projects are profoundly shaped by their own activity as missionaries in India and South Africa, respectively, which merges with their energetic interest in the challenges of Western Christendom and its decline. Bosch's magisterial textbook *Transforming Mission* has demonstrated how a thoroughly Reformed theology of mission works as an integrative

---

[20] Karl Barth, *Church Dogmatics*, vol. IV/3.2 (Edinburgh: T&T Clark, 1962), 795–797.

discipline that relates biblical, historical, and doctrinal scholarship to each other in the service of the formation of churches that know that they are defined by their apostolic vocation. The understanding of mission as the "mission of God" (*missio Dei*) corrects the reduction of the church to "addressing the needs of its members" or to an agency serving society's religious interests. Rather it is God's mission that creates the church as its servant and instrument. The church is "missional" when it is defined by God's saving mission and serves intentionally as its witness and instrument. What Bosch initiated with his comprehensive and cross-disciplinary approach to the theology of mission represents Reformed theology in its most generative mode. It is seeking ongoing reformation guided by the Word of God. It demonstrates what it means to glorify God by submitting to God's mission and becoming a part of its realization.

Although Newbigin never used the concept of the "mission of God," he developed his theology of mission under the theme "the mission of the triune God."[21] Thus, mission is expounded first of all as *"proclaiming* the Kingdom of the Father." That proclamation is understood as holistic witness, which is "mission as faith in action." The public evidence provided by the witnessing community is to demonstrate that God's reign is breaking in and that it brings healing, blessing, and hope. Then, mission is *"sharing* the life of the Son" which is demonstrated by "love in action." This emphasis is developed by Newbigin in other texts as "doing mission in Jesus Christ's way." It is a theological appeal for integrity and congruence in the practice of Christian mission: the message must define the way in which it is communicated. Paul's wording for this emphasis is the frequent injunction: "lead your public life worthy of the gospel of Christ" (Phil. 1:27). *"Bearing* the witness of the Spirit" must necessarily follow. It is "mission as hope in action," empowered by the promised and present Spirit. With this Trinitarian emphasis on God's sovereign grace at work in the world and through his church, a clearly Reformed consensus defines the "essential tenets" of missional theology today. Barth, Bosch, Mackay (and countless others) would readily concur with Newbigin that "the reign of God which the church proclaims is indeed also present in the life of the church, but it is not the church's possession."[22] Rather, as Newbigin expounds elsewhere, the gathered community, the congregation in a particular place, is enabled by God's Spirit to understand itself as "the hermeneutic of the

---

[21] See Lesslie Newbigin, *The Open Secret: an Introduction to the Theology of Mission*, rev. ed. (Grand Rapids, MI: Eerdmans, 1995).

[22] Lesslie Newbigin, *The Open Secret*, 64.

Gospel" and to practice that vocation.[23] That is what it means to live out the vocation of the witness, to be the first fruits, the sign, the instrument of God's inbreaking reign. It is the task of Reformed missional theology to serve the formation of such communities for that vocation.

Further reading

Bauckham, Richard. *The Bible and Mission: Christian Witness in a Post-Modern World*. Grand Rapids, MI: Baker Academic, 2003.

Brownson, James. *Speaking the Truth in Love: New Testament Resources for a Missional Hermeneutic*. Harrisburg: Trinity Press International, 1998.

Flett, John. *The Witness of God: The Trinity, Missio Dei, Karl Barth, and the Nature of Christian Community*. Grand Rapids, MI: Eerdmans, 2010.

Goheen, Michael. *A Light to the Nations: The Missional Church and the Biblical Story*. Grand Rapids, MI: Baker Academic, 2011.

Guder, Darrell L. *The Continuing Conversion of the Church*. Grand Rapids, MI: Eerdmans, 2000.

Kirk, J. Andrew. *What Is Mission?: Theological Explorations*. Minneapolis, MN: Fortress, 2000.

Moltmann, Jürgen. *The Church in the Power of the Spirit: A Contribution to Messianic Ecclesiology*. London: SCM, 1967.

Moynagh, Michael, with Philip Harrold. *Church for Every Context: An Introduction to Theology and Practice*. London: SCM, 2012.

Walls, Andrew F. *The Cross-Cultural Process in Christian History*. Maryknoll, NY: Orbis Books, 2002.

---

[23] Lesslie Newbigin, *The Gospel in a Pluralist Society* (Grand Rapids, MI: Eerdmans, 1989), 222–233.

Index

a Lasco, John, 230, 236, 246
Abernethy of Antrim, John, 255
accommodation, divine, 15, 16, 18, 24, 25, 56, 69, 83, 85, 97
Adam, 47, 53, 54, 71, 81, 154, 155, 271–273, 275
adiaphora, 100
aesthetics, 151, 157, 158, 271
affections, religious, 155, 160, 270, 271, 275
African Congregational Church, 289
Ahn, Byung Mu, 305
Alexander, Archibald, 274
Alston, William, 156, 228
Alting, Menso, 237
Ames, William, 199, 206, 214
Amyraut, Moses, 40, 52–54, 220, 233
Anabaptists [Baptists], 12, 21, 36, 81, 124–126, 136, 212, 216, 248, 276, 277, 283, 315, 321, 324, 332
Anglicanism, 194, 200, 202, 248, 259–261, 315, 317, 332
Anselm of Canterbury, 110, 187
antinomianism, 39, 207–209, 211, 213, 250
Aquinas, Thomas, 117, 226, 227
Arianism, 157, 248, 254, 255
Aristotelianism, 37, 45, 221–226
Aristotle, 133, 223, 224
Arminianism, 39, 40, 50–52, 153, 208–211, 213, 218, 220, 236, 242, 243, 256, 270, 275
Arminius, Jacobus, 39, 50, 53, 202, 225, 272
Armstrong, Brian, 48
assurance, 37, 40, 55, 81, 83, 84, 87, 97, 102, 104, 105, 128, 187, 204, 207, 245, 250, 252
Athanasius of Alexandria, 73, 266

atonement, 3, 35, 36, 40, 71, 74, 77, 206, 248–253, 258, 262, 272, 275, 277–279, 308, 315
extent of, 3, 40, 51–53, 58, 206, 208, 210, 249–253, 263, 275, 277, 319
Augustine, 28, 29, 44, 70, 128, 132, 275, 282
Augustinian, 39, 44, 45, 55, 58, 157–159, 219, 280
authority
civic, 120, 121, 126, 139
of God, 13, 21, 29, 111
of Jesus Christ, 13, 29, 31, 280
of Scripture, 12, 13, 19, 20, 30, 34, 219, 256, 259, 282, 315, 321
of tradition, 20, 21, 38

Baconianism, 275, 276, 282
Baillie, Donald, 253, 262, 264
Baillie, John, 263, 265
Baillie, Robert, 211
Ballagh, J. H., 307, 308
Bantu Congregational Church, 291
baptism, 41, 79–95, 102, 125, 126, 144, 190, 270, 277, 286
of infants, 41, 81, 82, 84, 85, 90, 92, 94, 95, 125, 126, 190, 270
Baptists, *see* Anabaptists
Baro, Peter, 202, 203
Barth, Heinrich, 181
Barth, Karl, 6, 24–26, 31, 33, 49, 54, 56–58, 72, 75–78, 92–94, 97, 98, 100, 102, 105, 108, 109, 112, 113, 179–195, 241–245, 247, 257, 265–267, 310, 315, 317, 330–333
Bavinck, Herman, 24, 25, 34, 111
Baxter, Richard, 213
Bediako, Kwame, 287, 288
Beecher, Lyman, 273